Wren's "Tracts" on  ings

Wren's "Tracts" on Archi... rst scholarly study devoted to the theoretical work of one of the most important architects of early modern Europe. Trained as an astronomer, Wren applied seventeenth-century scientific methods to his investigation of ancient, medieval, and Renaissance architecture. From his analysis of ancient buildings, he posited a new version of the origins and development of the Classical style, thereby becoming one of the first to challenge theoretical principles of architecture that had been upheld since the fifteenth century. Rejecting the idea of beauty as absolute and innate, Wren formulated an empirical definition of it based on visual perception and custom. His understanding of the relativity of beauty led him to reaffirm the eternal validity of the Classical style, but also to recognize the Gothic, disparaged since the Renaissance, as a legitimate style that had evolved within particular cultural circumstances.

This edition of Wren's architectural writings includes, for the first time, accurate, annotated transcriptions of the texts.

Lydia M. Soo is Assistant Professor of Architecture at the College of Architecture and Urban Planning, The University of Michigan, Ann Arbor.

Wren's "Tracts" on Architecture and Other Writings

LYDIA M. SOO

CAMBRIDGE
UNIVERSITY PRESS

CAMBRIDGE UNIVERSITY PRESS
Cambridge, New York, Melbourne, Madrid, Cape Town, Singapore, São Paulo

Cambridge University Press
The Edinburgh Building, Cambridge CB2 8RU, UK

Published in the United States of America by Cambridge University Press, New York

www.cambridge.org
Information on this title: www.cambridge.org/9780521573696

© Lydia M. Soo 1998

This publication is in copyright. Subject to statutory exception
and to the provisions of relevant collective licensing agreements,
no reproduction of any part may take place without the written
permission of Cambridge University Press.

First published 1998
This digitally printed version 2007

A catalogue record for this publication is available from the British Library

Library of Congress Cataloguing in Publication data
Soo, Lydia M.
Wren's "tracts" on architecture and other writings / Lydia M. Soo.
p.   cm.
Includes bibliographical references and index.
ISBN 0-521-57369-6 (hc)
1. Wren, Christopher, Sir, 1632–1723 – Criticism and
interpretation.   2. Architecture, Modern – 17th–18th centuries –
England.   3. Architecture – England.   I. Title.
NA997.W8S66   1997
720'.92 – dc21   97-13148
                                                                           CIP

ISBN 978-0-521-57369-6 hardback
ISBN 978-0-521-04424-0 paperback

This publication is supported by grants from the Graham Foundation for Advanced
Studies in the Fine Arts and the Office of the Vice President for Research and the
College of Architecture and Urban Planning at the University of Michigan.

For my father

Contents

List of Illustrations	*page* ix
Acknowledgments	xiii
Editorial Note	xv
Introduction	1
I. Notes on the Antiquities of London	18
Introduction	18
"Of *London* in ancient Times, and the Boundary of the *Roman* Colony, discern'd by the *Surveyor*, after the great Fire."	22
Excerpt from "Of the taking down of the vast Ruins of the *old* Cathedral, and of the Foundations of the *old* and *new* Structure."	31
II. Notes and Reports on Gothic Churches	34
Introduction	34
Excerpt from "Of the ancient cathedral Churches of St. *Paul;* from the first Age of *Christianity,* to the last great Fire of London, in *1666.*"	39
Report on Old St. Paul's before the Fire (7 May 1666)	48
Report on Old St. Paul's after the Fire (between 5 September 1666 and 26 February 1667)	56
Report on Salisbury Cathedral for Dr. Seth Ward, Bishop (31 August 1668)	61
Report on Westminster Abbey to Francis Atterbury, Dean (1713)	79
III. Letter from Paris	93
Introduction	93
Letter to a Friend from Paris (late September/October 1665)	103
IV. Letter on Building Churches	107
Introduction	107
Letter to a Friend on the Commission for Building Fifty New City Churches (1711)	112

V. Tracts on Architecture   119
Introduction   119
Tracts I through IV (beginning in the mid-1670s)   153
Tract V, "Discourse on Architecture" (beginning in the mid-1670s)   188

Conclusion: Wren's Method of Design   196

Appendix: Comparison of Tracts IV and V   242
List of Abbreviations   247
Notes   249
Selected Bibliography   312
Index   314

Illustrations

1. Title page of *Parentalia: or Memoirs of the Family of the Wrens* (London, 1750) — page 9
2. Map of Wren's finds in the City of London — 24
3. Monument found on Ludgate Hill in 1669, drawn by John Aubrey — 27
4. Pottery lamp found at St. Paul's, from an old drawing — 28
5. Spitalfields urn discovered August 1678, drawn by John Aubrey — 29
6. Old St. Paul's, plan, drawn by Wenceslas Hollar, 1656 — 41
7. Old St. Paul's from the south, drawn by Wenceslas Hollar, 1656 — 42
8. Old St. Paul's from the east, drawn by Wenceslas Hollar, 1656 — 44
9. Old St. Paul's, interior of choir, drawn by Wenceslas Hollar, 1656 — 45
10. Old St. Paul's from the north, drawn by Wenceslas Hollar, 1656 — 46
11. Old St. Paul's from the west, drawn by Wenceslas Hollar, 1656 — 47
12. Old St. Paul's, interior of nave, drawn by Wenceslas Hollar, 1656 — 49
13. Pre-Fire Design for Old St. Paul's, plan, 1666 — 51
14. Pre-Fire Design for Old St. Paul's, section through nave showing Jones's recasing of the exterior, 1666 — 52
15. Pre-Fire Design for Old St. Paul's, longitudinal section, 1666 — 53
16. Old St. Paul's after the Fire toward the southwest, drawn by Thomas Wyck, c. 1672 — 57
17. Salisbury Cathedral from the north, drawn by Wenceslas Hollar, 1673 — 63
18. Salisbury Cathedral, "Part of the Plan and a Perspective View . . . Taken from the North East," drawn by Francis Price, 1753 — 64
19. Salisbury Cathedral, "A Geometrical Plan," drawn by Francis Price, 1753 — 65

Illustrations

20. Salisbury Cathedral, "Part of the Plan, with the Section of the Body of the Church; shewing it's Mechanism, and part of the Vaulting," drawn by Francis Price, 1753 — 66
21. Salisbury Cathedral, "A Section of the Church, with the Tower and Spire: Shewing the Critical Mechanism of the whole Structure," drawn by Francis Price, 1753 — 70
22. Salisbury Cathedral, "A Plan and part of the section of the Tower, shewing the form of the Iron Bandage," drawn by Francis Price, 1753 — 71
23. Salisbury Cathedral, Wren's drawing showing a detail of how to join iron pieces, 1668 — 73
24. Salisbury Cathedral, Wren's drawing of how to repair the roof and wall of the west end and a detail of how to splice timber, 1668 — 75
25. Westminster Abbey, view of west facade, drawn by Wenceslas Hollar, 1655 — 80
26. Westminster Abbey, view of north side, drawn by Wenceslas Hollar, 1654 — 81
27. Westminster Abbey, Wren's diagram showing the section through the aisle, with weight of tower at E, 1713 — 89
28. Westminster Abbey, Wren's design for the central tower and spire, 1722 — 90
29. Westminster Abbey, Wren's design for the north transept, 1719 — 92
30. Map of sites around Paris visited by Wren in 1665–6 — 104
31. London, St. James, Piccadilly, plan, east elevation, and section, 1676–84, drawn by John Clayton, 1848 — 116
32. London, St. James, Piccadilly, transverse and longitudinal sections, 1676–84, drawn by John Clayton, 1848 — 117
33. Structural diagrams in Tract II, 1750. *Fig. 1.* Rule-of-thumb method for determining the thickness of the piers supporting an arch. *Fig. 2.* Wren's method for determining the abutment of an arch by means of centers of gravity — 160
34. Diagrams of structural systems according to Wren's descriptions in Tract II — 164
    A. Fan vault, cf. Fig. 33, *Fig. 5* — 164
    B. Dome on pendentives, including alternative with drum (top), cf. Fig. 33, *Figs. 3, 4* — 164
    C. Structural system used at St. Paul's — 165

	D. Cross vault, including alternative with pointed arch (top), cf. Fig. 33, *Fig. 6*	165
35.	Wren's reconstruction of the Temple of Diana at Ephesus, elevation, with the shrine, 1750	170
36.	Wren's reconstruction of the Temple of Diana at Ephesus, plan, 1750	171
37.	Palladio's reconstruction of the "Temple of Peace" (Basilica of Maxentius and Constantine), plan, 1570	174
38.	Palladio's reconstruction of the "Temple of Peace" (Basilica of Maxentius and Constantine), section and elevation, 1570	175
39.	Palladio's reconstruction of the "Temple of Peace" (Basilica of Maxentius and Constantine), interior order, 1570	177
40.	Plan of the Temple of Mars Ultor in *Parentalia*, 1750	179
41.	Palladio's reconstruction of the Temple of Mars Ultor, plan and elevation, 1570	181
42.	Palladio's reconstruction of the Temple of Mars Ultor, detailed elevation and section, 1570	182
43.	Palladio's reconstruction of the Temple of Mars Ultor, interior order, 1570	183
44.	Wren's reconstruction of the Mausoleum of Halicarnassus, elevation, drawn by Nicholas Hawksmoor, date unknown	186
45.	Wren's reconstruction of Porsenna's Tomb, plan and elevation, drawn by Robert Hooke, 17 October 1677	194
46.	Cambridge, Trinity College Library, exterior from west, 1676–84	204
47.	Cambridge, Trinity College Library, exterior from east, 1676–84	205
48.	Oxford, Christ Church, Tom Tower, 1681–2	219
49.	Greek Cross Design for St. Paul's, plan, 1672	224
50.	Greek Cross Design for St. Paul's, section, 1672	226
51.	Greek Cross Design for St. Paul's, west elevation, 1672	227
52.	Great Model Design for St. Paul's, plan, 1673, engraving from 1726(?)	228
53.	Great Model Design for St. Paul's, view of model, 1673	229
54.	Warrant Design for St. Paul's, plan, 1674–5	230
55.	Warrant Design for St. Paul's, cross-section, 1674–5	232
56.	Warrant Design for St. Paul's, west elevation, 1674–5	233

57. Warrant Design for St. Paul's, longitudinal section, 1674–5 — 234
58. Warrant Design for St. Paul's, south elevation, 1674–5 — 235
59. St. Paul's Cathedral, London, plan, 1675–1710, drawn by Arthur Poley, 1927 — 236
60. St. Paul's Cathedral, London, interior of nave, 1675–1710 — 237
61. St. Paul's Cathedral, London, exterior from southeast, 1675–1710 — 238
62. St. Paul's Cathedral, London, section through choir, 1675–1710, drawn by Arthur Poley, 1927 — 239
63. St. Paul's Cathedral, London, section through crossing, 1675–1710, drawn by Arthur Poley, 1927 — 240

Acknowledgments

This book represents a stage in my continuing investigation of the interrelationships existing among architecture, architectural theory, and cultural history, which for several years has focused on the case of Sir Christopher Wren. As such it owes a special debt to historians of Wren, especially Kerry Downes, J. A. Bennett, and the late John Summerson, all of whose work was critical as a foundation for my study of Wren's architectural theory. This book builds upon much of their research and ideas, and seeks to contribute new material and interpretations as well.

My research on Wren's theory, which began as a dissertation completed at Princeton University, has since its inception benefited from the wisdom and encouragement of several teachers. Special thanks must go to the advisor of my dissertation, David R. Coffin, as well as to Richard J. Betts and Anthony Grafton. Much appreciated assistance has also come from British scholars: Michael Hunter of Birkbeck College, University of London, and Ralph Hyde of Guildhall Library. Thanks are due to the helpful librarians and staff members at several institutions where I have conducted research. In England these included the Royal Society, the British Library, the Royal Institute of British Architects, Guildhall Library, Westminster Abbey, the Codrington Library at All Souls College, Oxford, the Bodleian Library, and Salisbury Cathedral. Three of these institutions kindly gave permission for the transcriptions of manuscript material: the Bodleian Library for MS Tanner 145, fols. 129–130v; the British Architectural Library, RIBA, for the "Discourse on Architecture" in the "Heirloom" copy of *Parentalia*, 1750; and the Dean and Chapter of Salisbury Cathedral for MS 192. Closer to home the library at the University of Illinois at Urbana-Champaign has remained an invaluable and dependable resource, in particular, the Ricker Library of Architecture and Art, as well as the Rare Book Room and Special Collections Library.

The book has also benefited greatly from the evaluations of the anonymous reviewers of the manuscript. In some specific areas it depended upon the expertise of several colleagues, including Michael Rabens (for seventeenth-century French architecture), as well as Christian Zacher and James Girsch (for Latin translations). The graphic material was produced meticulously by two graduate students in architecture, Christopher Moore and Anselmo Canfora. Some of the photographic work was provided by John Edwards. Acknowledgment must also be made of

Acknowledgments

the organized and careful work of my editors at Cambridge University Press during each stage of the publication process.

Generous financial support for the project came from two institutions. The manuscript was prepared with the assistance of a grant from the Graham Foundation for Advanced Studies in the Fine Arts. The book was produced with the help of a publication subvention from the Office of the Vice President for Research and the College of Architecture and Urban Planning at the University of Michigan.

Finally, I extend thanks to my family and friends for their quiet but enduring support, particularly to my father, to whom this book is dedicated.

Editorial Note

All of Wren's writings presented in this work have been transcribed either from the published *Parentalia* (1750) or from original manuscripts in the hand of Wren or his son. Changes and additions have been limited to what is described below.

For texts transcribed from *Parentalia* (1750): The printed "f" has been changed to "s" where appropriate. Obvious typographical errors have been corrected. Original editorial insertions, marginalia, and footnotes have been preserved.

For texts transcribed from manuscripts, the guidelines proposed by Michael Hunter ("How to Edit a Seventeenth-Century Manuscript: Principles and Practice," *The Seventeenth Century* 10, no. 2 [Autumn 1995]: 277–310) have been adopted, specifically: Standard abbreviations have been expanded. First words of sentences have been capitalized throughout. Manuscript insertions have been indicated by angled brackets (< >), and deletions noted. Editorial insertions have been indicated by square brackets ([ ]).

No annotations have been made of textual variations found in later versions, both manuscript and published, of the manuscripts existing in Wren's hand. Annotations have been made indicating significant differences found in the earlier manuscript versions of *Parentalia* in comparison to the texts transcribed from the final publication, as well as Tract V in the hand of Christopher Wren, Jr.

Introduction

The architectural writings of Sir Christopher Wren, although limited in number and extent, have always been of interest to his biographers, beginning with his own son Christopher Jr. He preserved almost all of them in *Parentalia*, a history of the Wren family published in 1750. Since that time, historians have been aware that these writings can provide a glimpse into the mind of Wren – his particular intellectual orientation in relationship to architecture – and hence give greater insight into the nature of his building designs. By revealing his intellectual basis, Wren's writings can be used to gain an understanding of the unique relationship between his training as a scientist and his work as an architect. Furthermore, these writings can provide evidence of an important, but generally unexplored, period in the history of architectural theory, when principles established since the Renaissance were seriously challenged on the basis of seventeenth-century science. For these reasons, and because earlier publications are flawed or not easily accessible, Wren's architectural writings are now presented in a single volume. In addition, they are accompanied by a series of essays that explore their relationship to Renaissance architectural theory, seventeenth-century scientific thought, and Wren's production of architecture.

By writing on architecture, Wren was continuing a long tradition, followed by many architects since the mid-fifteenth century in Italy, of consciously attempting to articulate a theory of architecture. By presenting in written form definitions of architecture and methods of design, supported by philosophical arguments, architects were able not only to explain and justify their own designs but also to disseminate their theories. The enormous impact of these published treatises, as well as some that remained in manuscript, indicates that in architecture the writing of theory could have a significance equal to the making of buildings.

In contrast to the majority of these earlier works, Wren's literary production in architecture does not take the form of a finished treatise. Instead of the precepts of a successful practitioner looking back on a long career, most of his writings suggest the hastily noted cogitations of a recent, but enthusiastic, initiate into architecture. They suggest the ongoing struggle of someone trained in another discipline who is trying to record newly acquired information, to make sense out of the established rules and traditions, and to work out specific problems. Even though Wren had the opportunity to revise many of the texts up to his death, most remain in the form of fragmentary personal notes and raw reports on work-in-progress, retaining an immediacy that suggests either that he never intended them for publication or, if that had been his goal, never had the time and opportunity to rework them. Only the two latest texts of known date, the "Letter to a Friend on the Commission for Building Fifty New City Churches" of 1711 and the "Report on Westminster Abbey" of 1713, read as if they were composed in the leisure of retirement, as the summations of many years of observation and experience.

The texts found in this volume are presented in several groups in order to lend some coherence to their diverse subject matter. They begin with his notes on the antiquities of London, two excerpts from *Parentalia* on archaeological finds in London, written by Christopher Jr. using information from his father. Wren's notes and reports on Gothic churches include another *Parentalia* text by Christopher Jr. on the antiquities his father discovered at St. Paul's, followed by Wren's four reports on Gothic churches – Old St. Paul's before and after the Great Fire, Salisbury Cathedral, and Westminster Abbey. Next there are two letters written by Wren: his "Letter to a Friend from Paris," containing his observations on French architecture and other matters, and his letter on building churches, containing his precepts for church design. The final group contains the five "Tracts" on architecture, Tracts I through IV, printed in *Parentalia*, and Tract V, surviving in manuscript. The first presents a definition of beauty in architecture, followed by a discussion of the origin of the classical orders. This subject is continued in the second tract, which also treats the origin of temples and fora, as well as the structure of arches and vaults. Tract III returns to the subject of the orders. Tract IV presents a history of architecture, beginning with biblical buildings followed by separate sections on four classical monuments. Some of the same material is repeated in the fifth tract, with the addition of a few other biblical and classical examples.

The provenance of Wren's texts and the associated illustrations will be examined at the end of this introduction. The texts themselves will be treated in thematic groups in the ensuing chapters. At present they need to be considered as a totality, embodying a common set of ideas that reflects Wren's intellectual foundation in two traditionally separate, but for him interrelated, spheres: science and architecture. Wren adopted an established body of architectural knowledge, represented by past buildings and accepted theories, which he went on to test and reformulate based on the values and methods of seventeenth-century science, as well as on the new architectural data they generated.

Introduction

Wren's writings are composed of two interrelated subjects. There are the investigations into past and present architecture – ancient, Gothic, and contemporary; and there are the general theoretical statements, on beauty, the origin of classical architecture, and structure. The first provides, in essence, the architectural data upon which Wren formed the second: his particular theory and method of architecture.

Given the topics that are treated, it is evident that Wren was responding to a two-hundred-year-old system of architectural beliefs that was first established by Leon Battista Alberti in his *De re aedificatoria*, written around 1450 and published in 1485. Using the treatise of the ancient Roman Vitruvius, dating from the first century B.C. and "rediscovered" in 1414, as well as the evidence of the antiquities of Rome, Alberti established the theoretical basis for Renaissance architecture, which continued through the seventeenth century: the universal laws of architecture – beauty, utility, and strength – found in nature and providing the rationale for the forms and rules of the Classical style. Furthermore, he described how these principles had been applied in the architecture of antiquity and how they could be applied once more in the building types of his own time.

Subsequent writers, fully embracing Alberti's theoretical principles, went on to demonstrate his theory in use by means of illustrated treatises, with drawings of geometrical methods, ancient buildings of all periods and places, and contemporary designs, often by the author himself. Most prominent of this genre were the publications of Sebastiano Serlio (from 1537) and Andrea Palladio (1570), which were extremely popular outside of Italy where they were used as handbooks of design by the ordinary practitioner. In England up to Wren's time, the architect depended upon these and other foreign publications for his knowledge of the Classical style and its theoretical basis. Apart from Henry Wotton's *Elements of Architecture* of 1624, a summary of Italian theory, the few architectural books that were published in England focused only on the five orders. The most popular were John Shute's *First and Chiefe Groundes of Architecture* (1563), the first English architectural publication, and the English editions of works by the German Hans Blum (1601), and by the Italians Giovanni Paolo Lomazzo (1598) and Giacomo Barozzi da Vignola (1655).[1]

Wren's writings indicate that he had made a close study of the treatises of Vitruvius, Alberti, Serlio, and Palladio, all of which can be found in the inventory of his library.[2] Although he treats many of the same subjects addressed by these and other Renaissance authors, Wren also challenges traditional notions by using new sources and interpretations. His studies of past and present architecture are of a kind unprecedented in the history of theory. In the notes on London antiquities, he was responsible for creating one of the earliest archaeological records of material remains in the area, which he used to speculate on the layout of Roman London, the history of building on the site of St. Paul's, as well as the geographic prehistory of this site and nearby areas. In his reports on Gothic churches, based on accurate surveys of the existing structures and used as preliminaries to repairs, Wren began to characterize the different forms of English medieval architecture, presented a new explanation for the origin of the Gothic, and attempted to analyze its structure. In his observations on contemporary French architecture, written in a letter from Paris, Wren recorded the sixteenth- and seventeenth-century French buildings that influenced his subsequent development, and went further to postulate the existence of a French national style, based on custom and fashion. Wren formulated for the first time, in a letter to a church commissioner, general principles for the siting, planning, and construction of Protestant churches that were derived from his over forty years of experience in the design and construction of the City churches.

Wren's original contribution consists, furthermore, of his radically different viewpoint in addressing the theoretical themes discussed by Vitruvius and Alberti, and accepted by all theorists from the late fifteenth to the mid-seventeenth centuries. Wren postulated a relativistic definition of beauty based on perception and custom that challenged the Renaissance conception of absolute beauty. He established a new hypothesis of the origin of architecture and the Classical orders that broke with the traditional Vitruvian myth. In Tracts IV and V he used reliable literary and material evidence to write the first history of architecture, creating a single chronology of biblical and classical buildings that went far beyond the undifferentiated catalog of classical antiquities found in the treatises of Serlio, Palladio, and others. Finally, taking his cue from mathematical treatises, he introduced new methods based on statics for designing the form and abutment of the arch and various types of vaults, superseding the geometrical constructions employed to determine the size of structural elements and their relative placement during the Renaissance.

The particular nature and content of Wren's architectural writings can be better understood when considered in terms of his training as a natural philosopher and the milieu in which his scientific work took place – the Royal Society. "That miracle of a youth," as Evelyn described him,[3] Wren at a young age had already received recognition for his talents in mathematics and mechanics, subjects that invigorated his otherwise conservative High Church upbringing and humanist education at Westminster School. He went on to conduct significant research in mathematics, astronomy, and experimental philosophy during his tenure as an undergraduate at Wadham College at Oxford, fellow of All Souls, and professor of astronomy at Gresham College in London. In 1660, the year of the Restoration, Wren and a small group of colleagues from Oxford and London founded the Royal Society, the first English scientific institution, chartered by the king. During the next year Wren returned to Oxford as Savilian Professor of Astronomy, but also began to take on architectural work. After only eight years he was granted the most powerful post in his new profession – Surveyor General. As he had completed only three buildings by this time, his appointment probably represented a recognition less of his blossoming talent than of his family's steadfast loyalty to the royalist cause throughout the Civil War and protectorate. Nevertheless, through the rapid succession of designs and completed projects for the City churches, St. Paul's Cathedral, royal palaces, and other public works, Wren soon proved his exceptional abilities and continued as Surveyor General almost to the end of his long life. At no point, however, did his scientific activities cease. He remained an active participant in the Royal Society, serving a term as president, although his scientific contributions became more and more limited as his duties as Surveyor increased.

Wren's second career constituted more of a change in employment than in intellect. His skills in geometry and mechanics were directly applicable to solving technological problems in architecture, and because of them he was offered his first commissions in 1661: to supervise the construction of the fortification at Tangier, which he declined, and to repair Old St. Paul's Cathedral. His scientific training, however, did little to prepare him for solving problems of form and style in architecture. Although as a gentleman he would have been exposed to the subject since childhood, Wren was essentially self-taught as an architect, depending on two sources – buildings and books – many never before of interest to architects.

Wren's first designs testify that early on he must have made a close study of the buildings of Inigo Jones, gaining a direct knowledge of a Palladian mode of classicism that influenced him immediately. Soon, a visit to Paris in 1665/6 exposed him to sixteenth- and early seventeenth-century French architecture that was to influence him for years to come. From the beginning, however, and because he never traveled abroad again, Wren largely had to depend on books to teach himself about architecture, and it appears that they remained crucial resources even after he had attained mastery in the field. His extensive library indicates that he searched out every available source for guidance. These included standard architectural treatises, beginning with Perrault's 1684 edition of Vitruvius, which Wren probably already knew from one of many earlier editions, and the 1512 Paris edition of Alberti.[4] Vitruvius and Alberti together presented the principles of classicism and described their implementation in ancient, as well as, in the case of Alberti, modern buildings. Editions of the illustrated treatises of Serlio (Venice, 1663) and Palladio (Venice, 1601)[5] provided instruction on the orders, antiquities, and contemporary building designs. In addition, there were more up-to-date and detailed books on the orders, including the 1664 English edition by John Evelyn of Fréart de Chambray's *Parallèle* (1650)[6] and Perrault's *Ordonnance* (1683).[7] French treatises devoted to presenting the designs of the author alone, for example, Le Pautre's *Desseins de plusieurs palais* (1652), or in conjunction with recent works by others, for example, du Cerceau's *Les plus excellents bastiments de France* (1708 edition, original edition 1576–9),[8] provided examples of how to design contemporary building types in the Classical style. Finally, Wren owned numerous works on Roman antiquities,[9] the touchstone for all modern artistic production. Of those which discussed and illustrated buildings, the most important was Desgodets's *Edifices* (original edition 1682), containing the most accurate drawings of ancient buildings in Rome up to this time.[10] Any gaps in visual information left by the published texts in Wren's library were filled by a large number of loose prints: "Miscellaneous Collection of Prints, of Palaces, Views, Ruins, &c.," "Collection of Prints of Roman Antiquities," "Collection of Prints and Drawings relating to antient Architecture, 79 in Number," and prints of "Antient and modern Rome."[11]

Wren's education in architecture did not stop with these traditional architectural sources. His writings indicate that he was interested in buildings that existed beyond the boundaries of ancient Rome and the Renaissance, and his library included a wide variety of texts that described and sometimes illustrated them. Wren studied the descriptions of biblical, Egyptian, Babylonian, Etruscan, and Greek buildings contained in the texts of Pliny the Younger and Herodotus, but also any discussed in the Bible and the writings of Josephus. In addition, he examined later interpretations, often supplemented by reconstructions, of these descriptions by scholars, exegetical writers, and travelers to the Levant. Wren's library contained numerous travel books of visitors to the Near and Far East, including Sandys (1670), Spon (1679), Wheler (1682), Grelot (1683), Chardin (1686), Thévenot (1687), de Bruyn (1702), and Maundrell (1703).[12] In addition to these were books of voyages to remote parts of the world.[13] Wren would have known of others, particularly those in the prodigiously large library of his friend and collaborator Robert Hooke.[14]

These books provided him with more up-to-date information on classical antiquities and, in addition, introduced him to primitive dwellings, as well as Islamic and Chinese buildings, making him one of the earliest European architects to notice these forms of architecture.

At the same time, Wren turned his attention to buildings closer to home. His own direct study of local antiquities, such as stone circles, as well as Gothic churches, was supplemented by the descriptions and drawings contained in topographical and antiquarian works. His library included the county histories of Dugdale (1656), Plot (1677, 1686), and Leigh (1700), Dugdale's *St. Paul's* (1658) and *Monasticon Anglicanum* (1693 and 1718 editions), as well as books on Stonehenge by Webb (1655) and Sammes (1676).[15]

Throughout his life Wren sought knowledge of all forms of architecture, and in every instance, when examining literary and material sources, he applied the critical methods of the scientist. This point of view is reflected in his writings, where he adopts a long tradition of architectural ideas but also radically alters it, using the values and methods of the New Science as propounded by the Royal Society. The society in its early program established the means by which existing architectural principles could be reassessed and new kinds of evidence could be gathered. It rejected all received knowledge, particularly that of the ancients, in favor of a Baconian history of nature and the mechanical arts as the basis for formulating hypotheses.[16] By gathering all kinds of facts relating to nature and man for this history, the society pursued investigations of matters not strictly scientific in the modern sense, including architecture.

Architecture fell within the scope of the history of the mechanical arts, or the history of trades, which dealt with nature formed by man. As a result, fellows pursued studies of the types and strengths of building materials, as well as the instruments and techniques of the building trades. As part of its interest in the practical applications of mathematics, there were discussions of architectural structures, such as Wren's roof truss used at the Sheldonian Theater, presented in 1663. Because the trades of foreign lands often utilized materials and techniques unknown in Europe, the society recorded building practices in the New World, Africa, and the Near East. The investigation of the mechanical arts at the society was also truly "historical," in that it included the mechanical arts of earlier times, including the architectural antiquities of Italy, Greece, and the Near East, as well as of Britain. In all of its work the society applied the methods of science: skepticism toward existing knowledge, emphasis on material evidence, accuracy in observation and recording, and the testing of hypotheses by experiment.

The Royal Society's research into the technological, mathematical, and historical aspects of architecture was carried out primarily by Wren and his close circle of friends and collaborators: John Evelyn (1620–1706), Robert Hooke (1635–1703), and John Aubrey (1626–97). Among their contributions to the society's history program can be included Wren's writings on architecture. By applying the values and methods of science to the discipline of architecture, Wren created new data on past and present architecture that contradicted a long tradition of beliefs. Using this data, he created a version of the origin and history of architecture and a definition of beauty, which, while not completely abandoning it, constituted one of the first serious challenges to Renaissance theory.

The eleven texts on architecture by Wren included in this volume have been preserved in a variety of states. Eight of them, with their associated illustrations, owe their survival to the publication of *Parentalia* in 1750. In it the editor, Christopher Jr. (1675–1747), was able to present his father's writings in one of three possible states: (1) as a transcript of original and complete material that once existed in Wren's hand, (2) as a transcript of lost fragmentary material in Wren's hand, or (3) as a text written by Christopher Jr. using information transmitted to him by his father. Of the remaining three texts, two survive as manuscripts written by Wren, and one as a manuscript in the hand of Wren's son. The latter, the so-called Tract V with one drawing, is located in the Royal Institute of British Architects (RIBA) "Heirloom" copy of *Parentalia* once owned by the Wren family, along with a large number of architectural engravings, which may or may not be the work of Wren. Because almost all of the original material in Wren's hand is lost, an inquiry needs to be made into Christopher Jr.'s treatment of his father's documents, as well as the authenticity and reliability of the texts and illustrations that survive.

A few years before Wren's death in 1723, his son began to compile his writings, which were ultimately published in 1750 by Wren's grandson Stephen as *Parentalia, or Memoirs of the Family of Wrens.*[17] *Parentalia* is a history of the Wren family, focusing on the lives of Bishop Matthew Wren (Sir Christopher's uncle), Dean Christopher Wren (his father), and Sir Christopher himself (Fig. 1). Within each of these sections material transcribed from primary sources is interspersed as well as attached in an appendix. It is evident that Christopher Jr. made changes and additions to the original texts, but exactly to what extent cannot be determined because so little of his father's original manuscript material is extant.

Some insight into the level of authenticity and accuracy of this material can be gained from the three manuscript volumes of *Parentalia*

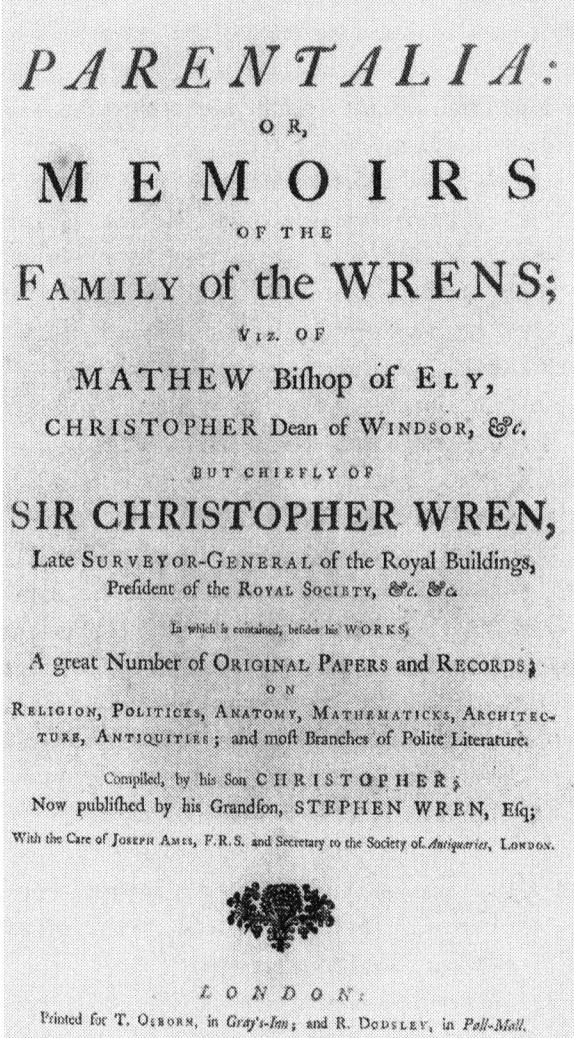

FIGURE 1. Title page of Christopher Wren, Jr., *Parentalia: or Memoirs of the Family of the Wrens* (London, 1750). The Ohio State University Libraries, Rare Book and Manuscripts.

that survive, two in Christopher Jr.'s hand and one in the hand of a scribe. In his study of these manuscripts, J. A. Bennett determined their relative dates.[18] The earliest, British Library MS Additional 25,071, predominantly in Christopher Jr.'s hand and containing unpublished primary material, was begun in 1719, before Wren's death. It is composed of only a small portion of the material found in the final publication and does not include Wren's writings on architecture. In contrast, Royal Society MS 249, begun around 1728, has the full contents of the printed work. For the most part in Christopher Jr.'s hand, it was a working manuscript, altered and added to over a number of years. All Souls MS 313, in the hand of a copyist, was made some time after 1734 as a fair copy of the Royal Society manuscript at that particular time. The versions of Wren's writings on architecture in the later two manuscripts are virtually identical to the final published state, leaving aside orthography and punctuation.

As a whole, based on Bennett's checks for internal consistency, comparisons among the three manuscript volumes, and comparisons with the available original texts and other reprints or copies, the texts published in *Parentalia* as primary material can be accepted as having a high level of accuracy. It is clear that, when he began his work, Christopher Jr. possessed many important manuscripts in Wren's hand. For example, although the British Library manuscript does not contain Tracts I through IV, Christopher Jr. must have collected some of them in their original form by this time, around 1719, as is indicated by several catalogs of his father's writings and drawings then in his possession. One catalog lists "Of Architecture in general," "Observations on the most Magnificent of the Antient Roman Temples, Templum Pacis," "Observations on the Temple of Mars Ultor";[19] another, "*Divers Discourses* of Architecture Ancient and Modern."[20] These items correspond to the collective title for the four tracts in *Parentalia*: "Of ARCHITECTURE; and Observations on *Antique Temples*, &c." and to the published accounts of the temples of Diana at Ephesus, of Peace, and of Mars Ultor, as well as of the Mausoleum of Halicarnassus, all of which are contained in Tract IV under separate headings. The wording of these entries also suggests that they might have included Tract V, which is entitled "Discourse on Architecture." Christopher Jr. also had in his possession "An Historical and Architectonical Account of the old Abbey Church of St. Peter in Westminster."[21]

Despite his lapses in biographical accuracy,[22] Christopher Jr. was personally concerned with preserving his father's memory and attempted to transcribe Wren's writings as accurately as possible, without revisions. In a catalog in the British Library manuscript he wrote, "This is a short Retail of such Tracts and Experiments as at present occurr, what have not been published in the Philosophical Transactions, are here quoted from the Original Drafts."[23] Christopher Jr. apparently felt that posterity would be best served if he simply made an accurate transcription, with no additions, of his father's unpublished writings.

In some cases this was an easy task, because the original writings in Wren's hand were in his son's possession as finished, intact pieces. These include the letter from Paris, the letter on building churches, and the "Report on St. Paul's before the Fire," which is printed in *Parentalia* as "Ex Autographo."[24] Christopher Jr. had no trouble making transcripts of these manuscripts, which unfortunately he then discarded or lost.

In other cases a verbatim copy of his father's original written text was not possible because of its chaotic or damaged state. A typical example is the original 1713 report on Westminster Abbey. "The Original Account of Westminster-Abbey is in my hands," Christopher Jr. wrote, "the MS. is a first sketch, blotted and interlined (as my father's Papers generally are). It bears no Date, or Direction." Nevertheless, "As I was best acquainted with my father's hand, I transcrib'd It as accurately as I could."[25] Although the manuscript is now lost, presumably both the text and the diagram in the printed and manuscript versions of *Parentalia* are copied from that original.

The tracts probably were in a similar state as the report on the abbey. They are printed in *Parentalia* in the appendix to the section on Sir Christopher under the collective heading "Of ARCHITECTURE; and Observations on *Antique Temples*; &c." as being "From some rough Draughts, imperfect."[26] This phrase corresponds to Christopher Jr.'s statement that "It is necessary to be known, that many of my Father's Manuscript Papers were only the First rough Draughts, not perfected, nor intended by him for the Press."[27] The texts of the four tracts themselves certainly confirm this statement. They often do not read sequentially, some subjects ending and reappearing later.[28] Christopher Jr. experienced further difficulties due to the physical condition and incompleteness of these documents. A catalog entry from the British Library volume reads "A discourse on Antient Architecture; and Observations on the Templum Pacis (imperfect viz: the Beginning obliterated by some Accident of Moysture & dust)."[29] Although the account of the Temple of Peace did reach publication in *Parentalia*, the "discourse" mentioned, probably the manuscript of Tract V, was probably too damaged to be printed. The original Tracts I and II apparently also were incomplete. In *Parentalia* both end in mid-thought with the remark "The rest is wanting." Therefore, it is probable that in the published *Parentalia* Christopher Jr. produced as exact a copy as was possible, making additions only in quotations and as marginal and footnotes.

Not only did Christopher Jr. work from the original manuscripts for Tracts I through IV, but during this early phase of the project Wren himself may have had a hand in preserving these writings. In October 1720 he endorsed a manuscript that contained the catalog "Chronologica series Vitae et Actorum Dni Christophori Wren Eq: Aur: Ec, Ec, Ec," which is written in his son's hand and includes the items "De Architectura," "De Templo Pacis," and "De Templo Martis Ultoris."[30] Wren therefore may have overseen his son's work until his death in 1723. This possibility and the correspondence found between the various catalog entries and the final publication lend support to the accuracy of the tracts.

It is evident that for some of his father's notes Christopher Jr. found it absolutely impossible to make a transcript. In the three sections in *Parentalia* dealing with antiquities found in London and on the site of Old St. Paul's,[31] the language indicates that they were not written by Wren himself, but by Christopher Jr. There are passages, however, where Christopher Jr. specifically states the activity or opinion of his father with the phrases "the Surveyor had Occasion to discover," "He concluded," "He was of Opinion," "The Surveyor discover'd," and so forth. These phrases suggest the possibility that Christopher Jr. possessed notes by his father of various findings and interpretations, but that they were probably not substantial enough to be included in the appendix as primary material, along with the Tracts on Architecture. Although he had to embellish them extensively to make the discussion coherent, the passages directly attributed to Wren can be considered a reasonably reliable record of his work and ideas.

Two of the texts presented in this volume are transcribed from existing manuscripts in Wren's hand. Apparently the original manuscript of the "Report on Old St. Paul's after the Fire," now at the Bodleian,[32] was never in Christopher Jr.'s possession, so it was not printed in *Parentalia*. The original report on Salisbury Cathedral, with three diagrams (Figs. 23–4), dated 31 August 1668, exists today in the registry of the Dean and Chapter of the church, after passing through several hands.[33] John Aubrey thought the report had been lost, writing, "'tis a great pity the paines of so great an Artist should be lost," but he later found a copy with Anthony Wood, which he had transcribed without the diagrams into the manuscript of *Natural History of Wiltshire*.[34] During the early eighteenth century the report was reprinted in a history of the church, with minor modifications.[35] Although the report is listed in one of his catalogs of his father's works, Christopher Jr. did not have the original manuscript and took his excerpt in *Parentalia* from this or another reprint.[36] None of the printed versions include the diagrams.

The so-called Tract V, the manuscript entitled "Discourse on Architecture. By Sr C: W:," is in the hand of Christopher Wren Jr. It is interleaved in the "Heirloom" copy of *Parentalia* at the Royal Institute of British Architects, along with other architectural engravings and an elevation drawing of the Mausoleum of Halicarnassus (Fig. 44).

There is evidence that Christopher Jr. copied Tract V from an original manuscript in his father's hand. In the British Library catalogs he lists "Divers Discourses of Architecture Ancient and Modern" and "Discourses on Architecture, and Descriptions of Anctient Temples &:c."[37] This manuscript, however, must have been damaged or incomplete, as Christopher Jr. chose not to include it in his publication.

The authenticity of the text is further supported by the context in which it survived. The discourse did not come to light until 1881, when it became available to Lucy Phillimore along with other original manuscripts and transcriptions interleaved in the "Heirloom" copy of *Parentalia*, owned by Catherine Piggott, the last surviving member of the Wren family. After her death in 1909, it was left to the Royal Institute of British Architects.[38] This copy apparently had been in the family for generations, for the title page bears the signature of Margaret Wren, the daughter of Stephen Wren, who saw the book through to publication after the death of his father, Christopher Jr. Therefore it is likely that the manuscript documents were found among Christopher Jr.'s papers at his death and were subsequently kept with this copy of *Parentalia*, just as another copy, owned by Stephen Wren and now at St. Paul's Cathedral Library, contains several manuscript insertions.[39] Besides these original documents, the RIBA "Heirloom" copy contains 140 engraved illustrations, some of which accompany the sections on architecture, along with the drawing of the Mausoleum of Halicarnassus.

Further support for the authenticity of Tract V is given by what is known of Christopher Jr.'s efforts to ensure accuracy in transcription and by the fact that it appears with other original material. This includes sixteen documents and letters relating to Matthew Wren, Dean Christopher Wren, and Stephen Wren.[40] There are also documents relating to Sir Christopher: letters in his own hand, juvenilia, scientific work, his inaugural speech at Gresham College in 1657 in Christopher Jr.'s hand, and the "Chronologica Series Vitæ et Actorum Domini Christophori Wren" in the hand of a copyist.[41] The material not in Wren's hand corresponds to what is known of his investigations and has been generally accepted as authentic records of his work.

Tract V also appears authentic because it duplicates several passages found in the published Tract IV. Limited but useful comparisons can be made, serving as a check for the reliability of all five tracts as a whole, both printed and manuscript. These also can give an idea of how far Christopher Jr. departed from his father's writings. The texts of Tracts I through IV in the manuscripts at the Royal Society and All Souls are essentially identical to the printed copy, therefore, any changes must have been made earlier.

Two comparisons of passages in Tract IV and V are presented in the Appendix. The first demonstrates that the text on folios 6 and 7 of Tract V, with minor changes, duplicates all of the material that appears in Tract IV, except for the initial discussion of the theater destroyed by Samson. The second comparison is made between Tract IV and a short passage in Christopher Jr.'s hand located on the last page of Tract V, covered over by the sketch of the Mausoleum of Halicarnassus pasted onto the last leaf below the description of Porsenna's tomb. Although this text, describing the Temple of Diana at Ephesus, is probably incomplete, it corresponds in content to the first half of the slightly fuller version printed on pages 360 and 361 of *Parentalia*. Because it is in Christopher Jr.'s hand, one can assume that these passages in Tracts V are closer to the original version than the printed text, and may even be transcriptions. These comparisons suggest that, although Christopher Jr. made very few changes from the original, he did make certain deletions and additions to clarify the text. Another possibility is that he had other versions available in Wren's hand. Based on these limited checks, recognition of the imperfect state of the originals, and knowledge of Christopher Jr.'s efforts for accurate transcriptions, all five tracts can be accepted as authentic until further information is available.

A variety of illustrations are associated with Wren's texts on architecture. They include diagrams, plans, sections, and elevations. Only one set of drawings survives in Wren's hand – the three small diagrams found on the pages of his manuscript report on Salisbury Cathedral (Figs. 23–4). The other illustrations pose more complicated problems relating to authorship.

The entire section on Christopher Wren in *Parentalia* is illustrated by engravings. They include a diagram found within the text of Wren's "Report on Westminster Abbey," depicting a section through the aisle (Fig. 27). Because it coincides completely with the text, it is probably based on an original drawing by Wren. Four engravings accompany the four tracts: in Tract II a group of eight structural diagrams (Fig. 33) and in Tract IV the plan and elevation of the Temple of Diana at Ephesus and the plan of the Temple of Mars Ultor (Figs. 35–6, 40). These and other engravings of buildings in *Parentalia* are generally thought to be from lost drawings in Wren's own hand. It is evident that they were made particularly for this publication, along with the portraits of the three famous members of the Wren family, the diagrams of planetary orbit, and the illustrations of the roof and rafters of the Sheldonian Theater.[42]

The plan and elevation of the Temple of Diana at Ephesus, as well as the plates of the Sheldonian, are signed by the draftsman Henry

Flitcroft (1697–1769) and the engraver Gerard Vandergucht (1696–1776).[43] Identical drawings exist at two other locations: in the Royal Society *Parentalia* manuscript, unsigned, and in the manuscript collection of drawings by Flitcroft at the British Library. Because there are reconstructions among Flitcroft's drawings of the Temple of Fortuna Virilis, the Temple of Vesta at Tivoli, the Pantheon, an Egyptian hall, and a Corinthian hall, the question arises whether the drawings of the Temple of Diana at Ephesus are indeed Wren's, or are Flitcroft's, borrowed for the publication.[44] From what we know of Christopher Jr.'s desire to preserve his father's work, and also from the correspondence of the drawings with the description in the text of Tract IV, it would appear that the drawings are based on lost originals drawn by Wren. The same can be assumed for Flitcroft's drawing of the Sheldonian Theater.[45]

The structural diagrams in Tract II and a plan of the Temple of Mars Ultor in Tract IV are both signed by the engraver J. Mynde, of whom little is known.[46] The same structural diagrams are found in the Royal Society manuscript of *Parentalia* and appear to be redrawn, probably by Christopher Jr., from sketches by Wren. The plan of the Temple of Mars Ultor is not found in any of the manuscript volumes but is a reprint, with modifications, of plate IV in Book IV of Palladio's treatise of 1570 or a later edition (Fig. 41), but certainly earlier than Isaac Ware's 1738 English edition where the plates are reversed. Modifications of Palladio's original plan include the eradication of structures shown behind the temple and the addition of a colonnaded forecourt with curving wings matching those shown by Palladio. Palladio's plan and the revisions are discussed in Wren's text, so it appears that Wren made a lost sketch altering Palladio's plan, which was the basis for the engraving. Another possibility is that someone else altered the Palladio plate based on Wren's written reconstruction. In either case, it is clear from the text that Wren wrote the section on the Temple of Mars Ultor, as well as that on the Temple of Peace (Basilica of Constantine), in reference to the description and illustrations by Palladio (Figs. 37–9, 41–3).

An elevation of the Mausoleum of Halicarnassus is pasted on the last leaf of the "Discourse on Architecture" in the RIBA "Heirloom" copy of *Parentalia* (Fig. 44). In the discussion of the Mausoleum in Tract IV, there are references to drawings that must have existed in 1750: "The Plate of the above is omitted, on account of the Drawing being imperfect," and "[It] contained in all 36 Pillars . . . in the Manner expressed in the Plan."[47] Although the elevation in Tract V and two small sketch plans found in the Royal Society manuscript all coincide with the description in Tract IV, none of them can be attributed to Wren. Kerry Downes has concluded, based on graphic style, that the elevation was drawn by Nicholas Hawksmoor, using Wren's description.[48] Hawksmoor probably drew it out of his own interest in the mausoleum, stimulated by his teacher Wren, which led him to make other reconstructions, now at All Souls.[49] No evidence exists to determine the author of the two diagrammatic plans, whether it be Wren, a member of his circle, or a later reader of the manuscript.

Interleaved within the "Heirloom" copy of the *Parentalia* are a large number of engravings, many depicting buildings. Because they appear with authentic documents, the question arises whether these engravings were intended for publication in 1750, as often has been assumed, particularly in the case of those pertaining to architecture.

Most of the forty-two portraits and four miscellaneous illustrations can be traced to plates in books and loose engravings that date from the mid-seventeenth century to the mid-eighteenth century, that is, before 1750, the date of *Parentalia*'s publication. Most of the eighty-one architectural engravings depict Wren's buildings. The bulk are from a book that postdates the publication of *Parentalia*: *English Architecture, or the Public Buildings of London and Westminster*, published in London by T. Osborne in 1758, which is also the source for the thirty pages of text on Wren's buildings inserted in the RIBA copy.[50] The remaining architectural engravings, from a variety of sources, generally predate *Parentalia*. Some originate from David Loggan's *Cantabrigia Illustrata* (1690), and others from a variety of topographical books or collections.[51] Four are from the group of fifteen engravings, commissioned by Christopher Jr. between 1724 and 1728, of St. Paul's Cathedral.[52] Others were engraved singly.[53]

It is possible that the pre-1750 engravings were collected by Wren and his son because they provided a record of his work, and were subsequently inserted in the RIBA copy. On the whole, however, all of the engravings can certainly be accepted as an instance of grangerizing – the common practice during the seventeenth and eighteenth centuries of inserting illustrations from other sources into a book to enhance the text.[54] Christopher Jr., or his son Stephen, may have collected these engravings with the intent to publish them with the text, or perhaps Margaret did so with the hope of including them in an expanded edition.

The same can be said for those architectural engravings inserted, along with Tract V, after the printed tracts in the "Heirloom" copy. Lucy Phillimore thought that some of these might have been drawn by Wren and intended for publication,[55] but it is clear that they were taken from other books and inserted much later, and as a result have little to do directly with the text.[56] This fact is very important in the case of the plan of the Temple of Solomon, the source of which cannot be determined, but which has been assumed by various historians to be Wren's own reconstruction.[57] Wren's discussions of the temple in Tracts IV and V do not include descriptions of the plan. Until further evidence appears, neither the engraved plan of the temple in the RIBA copy nor any of the other architectural engravings of unknown origin can be accepted as his work.

CHAPTER 1

Notes on the Antiquities of London

INTRODUCTION

In his study of the architecture of the classical past, Wren was forced by circumstances to depend primarily upon written descriptions, both ancient and contemporary. In the case of the Roman and pre-Roman antiquities in London, however, he was able to make his own direct observations of material remains. *Parentalia* preserves two valuable texts that provide the only coherent record of these investigations. The first, entitled "Of *London* in ancient Times, and the Boundary of the *Roman* Colony, discern'd by the *Surveyor*, after the *great Fire*,"[1] describes the various finds Wren made in the City and the conclusions he drew from them about its general history. The second, "Of the taking down of the vast Ruins of the *old Cathedral*, and of the Foundations of the *old* and *new Structure*"[2] records Wren's natural and archaeological discoveries on the site of St. Paul's and Ludgate Hill and, based on them, his speculations on their geological development. A summary of Wren's discoveries, shown in relationship to what is known today of Roman London, is given in the map (see Fig. 2).

Wren's observations on London antiquities were the direct result of the Great Fire that burned from September 2 to 5, 1666, destroying three-quarters of the City of London and leaving Old St. Paul's a ruin. As a member of the rebuilding commission chosen by the king, and later as Surveyor General from 1669, Wren made extensive discoveries of archaeological remains during excavations for rebuilding, particularly while taking test borings and constructing the foundations of the new St. Paul's. Similar work conducted by Wren at other building sites in England also resulted in discoveries.[3]

Although the discussion of London antiquities found in the *Parentalia* was written by Christopher Jr. from information provided by his father, by means of either notes or conversations, there is evidence that Wren had intended to collect his discoveries into a complete account. At the Royal Society on 7 January 1702, "Dr [John] Harwood said that Sir Christopher Wren had given Dr [Robert] Plott an Account of what Observations he had made on digging foundations in London. The Vice President [John Hoskins] was desired to procure a copy of it from Sir

Christopher Wren for the Society."[4] The account had been sent to Robert Plot (1640–96), first Keeper of the Ashmolean Museum and secretary of the Royal Society, probably because he had been working on a natural history of London and Middlesex since 1693. In the same manner as his histories of Oxfordshire and Staffordshire, it would have included a chapter entitled "Of Antiquities." As Plot died in 1696, this purported account by Wren probably dated from before the 1690s. It does not exist at the Royal Society or among Plot's papers.

The possibility of a discourse by Wren is confirmed by the physician John Woodward (1665–1728). On 23 June 1707 he wrote a letter to Wren, later published in 1713 as *An account of some Roman Urns and other Antiquities lately digg'd up near Bishopsgate. With brief reflections upon the antient and present state of London.*[5] In it Woodward implies that Wren had promised him an account of London antiquities:

> As to the Remains of Roman Workmanship, that were discover'd upon Occasion of Rebuilding the City, no Man had greater opportunity of making Remarks upon them than you: nor Sir, has any Man ever done it to better Purpose. And, as you have long promised me an Account of those Observations, so I shall ever insist upon it, and not cease to Challenge it, as a Debt your Generosity has made due to me, 'till you acquit yourself of the Obligation.[6]

Woodward's knowledge of Wren's proposed account was probably the result of their mutual interest in the subject. Woodward owned an extensive scientific museum that held one of the largest collections of antiquities, many, according to Strype, "retrieved upon the occasion of that great digging, . . . and the Removal of Rubbish that was made in all Parts, after the late great Fire."[7]

In the absence of a definitive account by Wren, the information contained in the *Parentalia* texts can be confirmed and supplemented by outside sources related to the Royal Society. These indicate that Wren was only one of many, directly or indirectly tied to the society, who observed, collected, and recorded material remains in London and all over Great Britain. For these men the Royal Society was the milieu in which findings could be reported and preserved. The minutes of meetings record numerous artifacts that were presented and deposited in the repository, which, while it no longer exists, fortunately was inventoried by Grew in 1681.[8] There, Bagford observed, "several other valuable Remains of Roman Antiquities are carefully preserv'd, which may hereafter afford very good Hints to such as shall attempt to write the Antiquities of this famous City."[9]

Wren's discoveries in London were often made in association with Robert Hooke, the Society's Curator of Experiments and secretary, who was acting as a city commissioner for rebuilding. In his *Monumenta Britannica*, John Aubrey noted, in the section on London: "Remarks taken, at the rebuilding of the city of London, from Dr. Christopher Wren, surveyor of his Majesty's Buildings: and surveyor of all the churches in London: and also from Mr. Robert Hooke R.S.S. Surveyor of the City of London."[10] Aubrey's manuscript is sprinkled with the phrase "From Mr Robert Hooke," as well as "From Dr Christopher Wren," "Sir Christopher Wren told me," "Dr. Wren also sayeth," and "Dr Wren makes it out." In other instances he notes: "Query Mr. Hooke" and "Query Dr Christopher Wren."[11] *Monumenta Britannica* was written primarily between 1663 and 1672, with material added until the early 1690s,[12] and it confirms several of the artifacts presented in the *Parentalia* notes. In addition it includes drawings of two of Wren's finds (see Figs. 3, 5).

Wren and Hooke often obtained news of recent finds or even the artifacts themselves from the apothecary John Conyers, an avid collector who occasionally attended society meetings, although he was never elected fellow. According to John Bagford, Conyers "made it his chief Business to make curious Observations, and to collect such Antiquities as were daily found in and about London."[13] Aubrey wrote, "Mr Conyers (Apothecary) at the White Lion in Fleet Street, hath preserved a world of antique curiosities found in digging of the ruins of London, principally Fleet Ditch."[14] One of Conyers's most important finds, a pottery kiln, was made while digging foundations on the northeast side of St. Paul's and is preserved in his manuscript account dated 20 August 1675.[15] It confirms and elaborates upon some of the same discoveries recorded in *Parentalia*.

Secondhand information on the finds of Wren and his associates exists in later publications. They include the additions to Middlesex in the 1695 edition of Camden's *Britannia*, written by Robert Plot and the only published results of his research for a natural history of London and Middlesex. In a letter to Thomas Hearne, dated 1 February 1715 and printed in Hearne's edition of Leland's *Collecteana* (1715),[16] John Bagford (c. 1650–1716) presented a survey of antiquarian finds in London that "hath been discovered within my own Memory" by Conyers and others. Bagford's friend John Strype (1643–1737) began a new edition of John Stow's *A Survey of the Cities of London and Westminster* in 1694, published in 1720. It included an appendix entitled "Of divers Roman and other Antique Curiosities found in London, before and since the great Fire," that had come to him "by diligent Enquiry of my Friends," Wren, Woodward, and Bagford.[17]

Wren's notes on London antiquities were the product of the general interest at the Royal Society in studying the ancient remains of London and all the counties of England, as well as Scotland and Ireland. Although the study of local antiquities in England had had a long tradition since the sixteenth century, the society gave it a new focus. Antiquities were studied because of a belief that they were records of the mechanical arts of the past, and thus relevant for the advancement of knowledge. Literary sources for the ancient arts were rejected in favor of material remains found in the field, observed, recorded, and collected, using scientific standards of accuracy applied to the study of natural phenomena. Thus conclusions were drawn and hypotheses made on the basis of material evidence rather than received knowledge. As a result, long before the founding of the Society of Antiquaries in 1708, the society constituted an early center for archaeological study, its culminating work being John Aubrey's *Monumenta Britannica*.[18] In this context, Wren's notes are significant not only as a small but important record of London antiquities, but also as a characteristic example of the kind of archaeological work that took place at the early Royal Society.

"Of *London* in ancient Times, and the Boundary of the *Roman* Colony, discern'd by the *Surveyor*, after the *great Fire*."

Source
 Original manuscript missing. *Parentalia* (London, 1750), "The Life of Sir Christopher Wren, Knt.," pt. 2, sec. 1, 264–7
Other Manuscript Versions
 RS MS 249, fols. 298v–302
 AS MS 313, fols. 439–48
Date
 Unknown

(page 264)

To have a right Idea of *London* of old, it will be necessary to consider the State of the *Britains*, at the Time the *Romans* made their first Descent on the *Island*; and surely we cannot reasonably think them so barbarous, at least in that Age, (and the Accounts before that, are too fabulous) as is commonly believ'd. Their Manner of Fighting was in Chariots, like the ancient Heroes of *Greece*, in the *Trojan* War, and occasionally on Foot, with such good Order and Discipline, as much embarrass'd the *Roman* Legions, and put a Stop to the Progress of the invincible Cæsar;[1] who could do nothing great, nor conquer any Part, but, says *Tacitus*,[2] only shew'd the Country to the *Romans*; and, according to *Lucan*,[3] was oblig'd shamefully to retreat.

Territa quæsitis ostendit terga Britannis.

The *Britains* went to Sea in Vessels cover'd with Hides, for they wanted Pitch: They traded chiefly with the *Gauls*, and certainly the principal *Emporium*, or Town of Trade to which the *Gallic* Ships resorted, must be *London*; tho' situated far up the Country, yet most commodiously accessible by a noble River, among the thickest Inhabitants; taking its Name (according *(page 265)* to some Derivations from the old *British* Term) of *Ship-hill*; or otherwise, a *Harbour of Ships*.[4]

Here the *Romans* fix'd a civil, or trading Colony, in the Reign of *Claudius*,[5] which greatly increas'd under *Nero*,[6] by the Concourse of Merchants, and Convenience of Commerce, and was inhabited by *Christians* and *Heathens* together.

The Extent of the *Roman* Colony, or *Præfecture*, particularly Northward, the *Surveyor*[7] had Occasion to discover by this Accident. The parochial Church of St. *Mary le Bow*, in *Cheapside*,[8] requir'd to be rebuilt after the *great Fire*: the Building had been mean and low, with one Corner taken out for a Tower, but upon restoring that, the new Church could be render'd square. Upon opening the Ground, a Foundation was discern'd firm enough for the new intended Fabrick, which, (on further Inspection, after digging down sufficiently, and removing what Earth or Rubbish lay in the Way) appear'd to be the Walls, with the Windows also, and the Pavement of a Temple, or Church, of *Roman* Workmanship, intirely bury'd under the Level of the present Street. Hereupon, he determin'd to erect his new Church over the old; and in order to the necessary Regularity and Square of the new Design, restor'd the Corner; but then another Place was to be found for the Steeple: The Church stood about 40 Feet backwards from the high Street, and by purchasing the Ground of one private House not yet rebuilt, he was enabled to bring the Steeple forward so as to range with the Street-houses of *Cheapside*. Here, to his Surprise, he sunk about 18 Feet deep through made-ground, and then imagin'd he was come to the natural Soil, and hard Gravel, but upon full Examination, it appear'd to be a *Roman* Causeway of rough Stone, close and well rammed, with *Roman* Brick and Rubbish at the Bottom, for a Foundation, and all firmly cemented.[9] This *Causeway* was four Feet thick [the Thickness of the *via Appia*, according as Mons. *Montfaucon*[10] measur'd, it was about three *Parisian* Feet, or three Feet two Inches and a half *English*.] Underneath *this Causeway* lay the natural Clay, over which that Part of the City stands, and which descends at least forty Feet lower. He concluded then to lay the Foundation of the Tower upon the very *Roman Causeway*, as most proper to bear what he had design'd, a weighty and lofty Structure.

He was of Opinion for divers Reasons, that this *High-way* ran along the *North* Boundary of the *Colony*. The Breadth then *North* and *South*, was from the *Causeway* now *Cheapside*, to the River *Thames*; the Extent *East* and *West*, from *Tower-hill* to *Ludgate*, and the principal middle Street, or *Prætorian Way*, was *Watling-street*.[11]

The Colony was wall'd next the *Thames*, and had a Gate there called *Dow-gate*, but anciently *Dour-gate*, which signified the *Water-gate*.[12]

On the North Side, beyond the *Causeway*, was a great Fen, or Morass, in those Times; which the *Surveyor* discover'd more particularly when he had Occasion to build a new East-front to the parochial Church of St. *Laurence* near *Guildhall*;[13] for the Foundation of which, after sinking seven Feet, he was obliged to pile twelve Feet deeper; and if there was no Causeway over the Bog, there could be no Reason for a Gate that Way.

At length, about the year 1414, all this moorish Ground was drain'd by the Industry and Charge of *Francerius*,[14] a Lord-mayor,

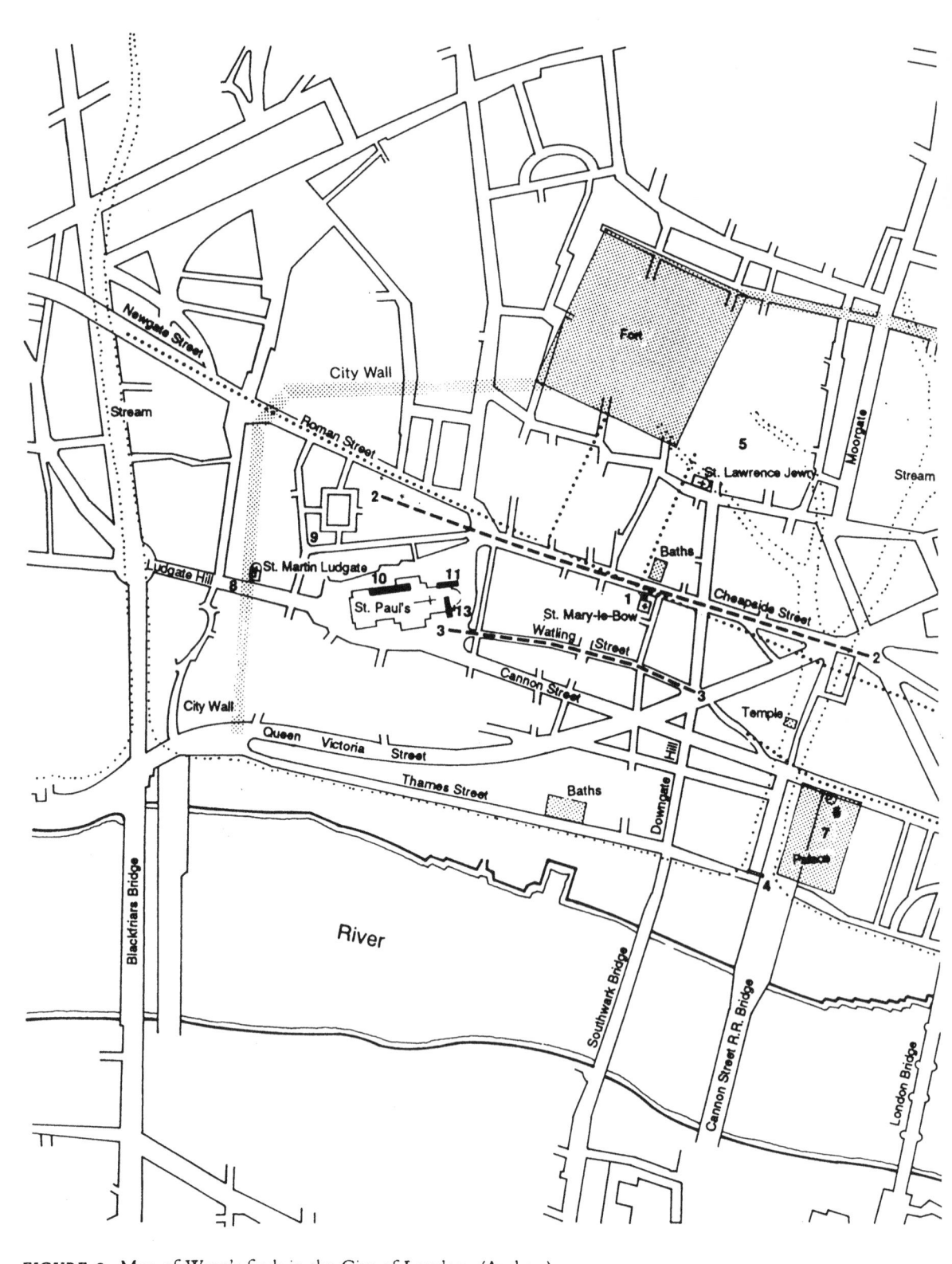

FIGURE 2. Map of Wren's finds in the City of London. (Author.)

12

Key to Map of Wren's Finds in the City of London

■ Wren's Finds

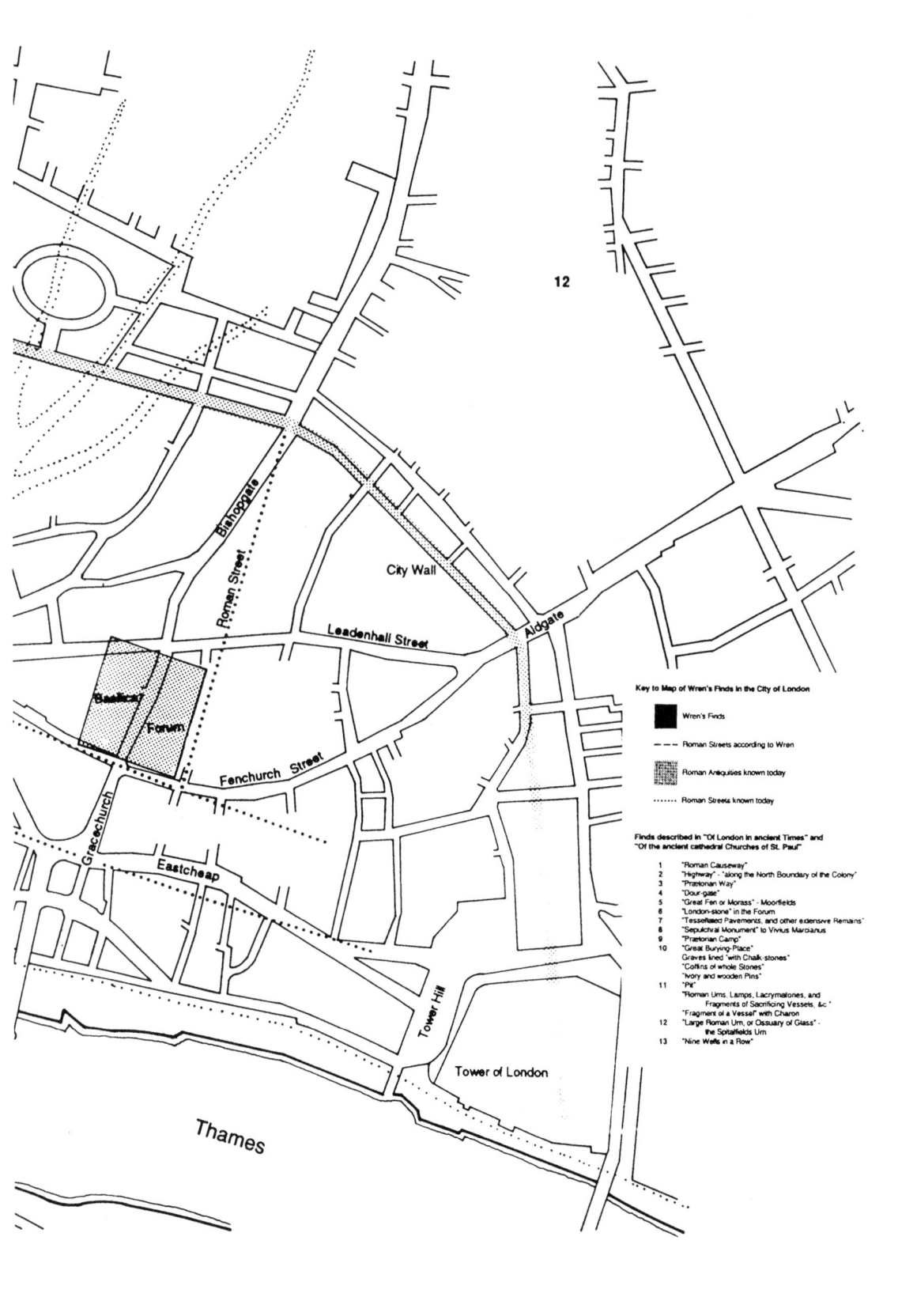

--- Roman Streets according to Wren

▨ Roman Antiquities known today

······ Roman Streets known today

Finds described in "Of London in ancient Times" and
"Of the ancient cathedral Churches of St. Paul"

1	"Roman Causeway"
2	"Highway" - "along the North Boundary of the Colony"
3	"Praetorian Way"
4	"Dour-gate"
5	"Great Fen or Morass" - Moorfields
6	"London-stone" in the Forum
7	"Tesselated Pavements, and other extensive Remains"
8	"Sepulchral Monument" to Vivius Marcianus
9	"Praetorian Camp"
10	"Great Burying-Place"
	Graves lined "with Chalk-stones"
	"Coffins of whole Stones"
	"Ivory and wooden Pins"
11	"Pit"
	"Roman Urns, Lamps, Lacrymatories, and Fragments of Sacrificing Vessels, &c."
	"Fragment of a Vessel" with Charon
12	"Large Roman Urn, or Ossuary of Glass" - the Spitalfields Urn
13	"Nine Wells in a Row"

and still retains the Name of *Moor-fields*, and the Gate, *Moor-gate*. *London-stone*,[15] as generally suppos'd, was a Pillar, in the Manner of the *Milliarium Aureum*, at *Rome*,[16] from whence the Account of their Miles began; but the Surveyor was of Opinion, by Reason of the large Foundation, it was rather some more considerable Monument in the *Forum*; for in the adjoining Ground on the South *(page 266)* Side, (upon digging for Cellars, after the great Fire) were discovered some *tessellated* Pavements,[17] and other extensive Remains of *Roman* Workmanship, and Buildings.*

On the West-side was situated the *Prætorian Camp*, which was also wall'd in to *Ludgate*,[19] in the *Vallum* of which, was dug up near the *Gate*, after the *Fire*, a Stone, with an Inscription, and the Figure of a *Roman* Soldier, which the *Surveyor* presented to the Archbishop of *Canterbury*, who sent it to *Oxford*, and it is reposited among the *Arundellian* Marbles.[20] This is a sepulchral Monument dedicated to the Memory of *Vivius Marcianus*, a Soldier of the second Legion, stil'd *Augusta*, by his Wife *Januaria Matrina*.[21] The Inscription is in this Manner:

FIGURE 3

Camden's Britannia, 2d Edit. by Bp. Gibson, vol. I. p. 375.[22]

D. M.
VIVIO MARC⸱
-ANO M̄L. LEG. II.
AVG. IANVARIA
MAR̄INA CoNIVNX
PIENTISSIMA POSV
-IT ME MOR̄AM.[23]

N.B. The Extract of this Inscription published in the *Marmora Oxoniensia*, Numb. 147. is erroneous.

See Part 2. Sect. 7[24]

The Soldiers used to be buried *in Vallo*, as the Citizens, *extrà Portas in Pomærio*;[25] there[26] 'tis most probable the Extent of the Camp reached to *Ludgate*, to the declining of the Hill, that Way. The *Surveyor* gave but little Credit to the common Story, that a Temple had been here to *Diana*,[27] (which some have believed,

---

*Probably this might in some degree, have imitated the *Milliarium Aureum* at *Constantinople*,[18] which was not in the Form of a Pillar as at *Rome*, but an eminent Building; for under its Roof, (according to *Cedrenus* and *Suidas*) stood the Statues of *Constantine* and *Helena*; *Trajan*; an equestrian Statue of *Hadrian*; a Statue of *Fortune*; and many other Figures and Decorations.

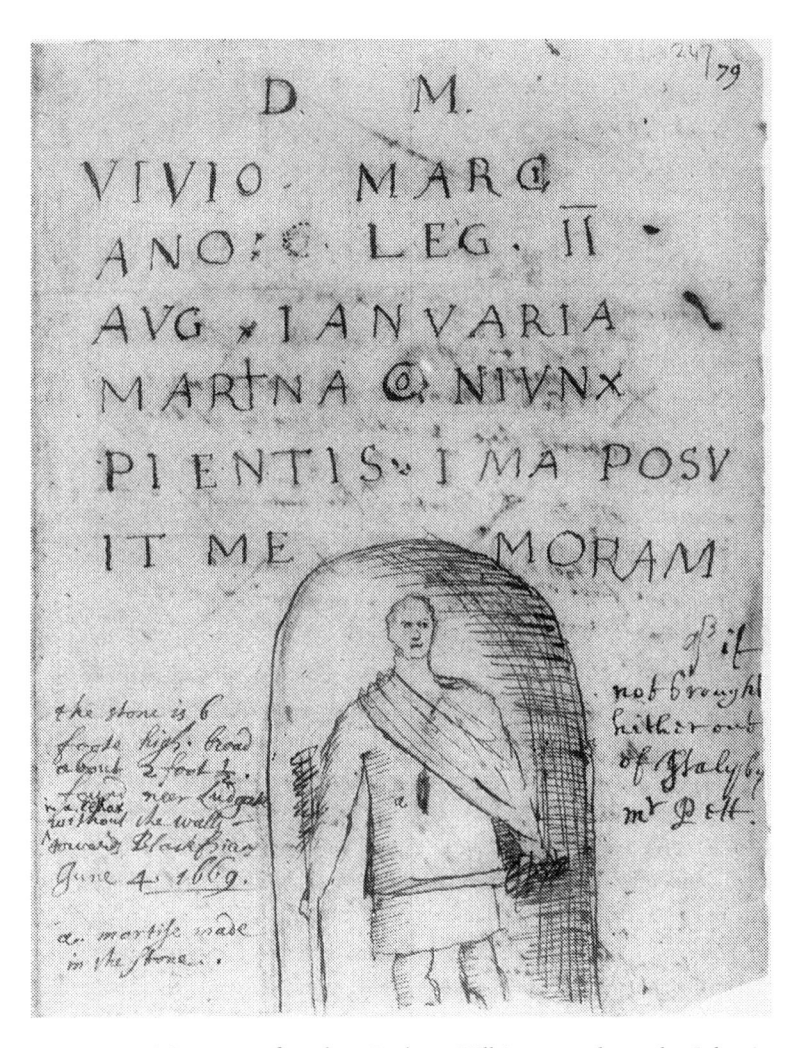

FIGURE 3. Monument found on Ludgate Hill in 1669, drawn by John Aubrey (John Aubrey, *Monumenta Britannica*, Bodleian MS Top. Gen. c. 24, fol. 247). The Bodleian Library, Oxford.

upon the Report of the digging up, formerly, and of later Years, Horns of Stags, Ox-heads, Tusks of Boars, &c.)[28] meeting with no such Indications in all his Searches; but that the North-side of this Ground had been very anciently a great Burying-place, was manifest; for upon the digging the Foundations of the present Fabrick of St. *Paul*'s, he found under the Graves of the latter Ages, in a Row below them, the Burial Places of the *Saxon* Times: the *Saxons*, as it appeared, were accustomed to line their Graves with Chalkstones, though some more eminent were entombed in Coffins of

27

FIGURE 4. Pottery lamp found at St. Paul's, from an old drawing. (*The Victoria History of London*, ed. William Page [London: Constable, 1909], 25, fig. 9). University of Illinois Library at Urbana-Champaign.

whole Stones. Below these were *British* Graves, where were found Ivory and wooden Pins, of a hard Wood seemingly Box, in Abundance, of about 6 Inches long; it seems the Bodies were only wrapped up, and pinned in woollen Shrouds, which being consumed, the Pins remained entire.[29] In the same Row and deeper, were *Roman* Urns intermixed: This was eighteen Feet deep or more, and belonged to the *Colony* when *Romans* and *Britains* lived and died together.[30]

The most remarkable *Roman* Urns, Lamps, Lacrymatories, and Fragments of Sacrificing-vessels, *&c.* were found deep in the Ground, towards the North-east Corner of St. *Paul's* Church, near *Cheapside*; these were generally well wrought, and embossed with various Figures and Devices, of the Colour of the modern red *Portugal* Ware, some brighter like Coral, and of a Hardness equal to *China* Ware, and as well glaz'd.[31] Among divers Pieces **(page 267)** which happened to have been preserved, are, a Fragment of a Vessel, in Shape of a Bason, whereon *Charon* is represented with his Oar in his Hand receiving a naked Ghost;[32] a *Patera*[33] *sacrificalis* with an Inscription PATER. CLO. a remarkable small Urn of a fine hard Earth, and leaden Colour, containing about half a Pint; many Pieces of Urns with the Names of the Potters embossed on the Bottoms, such as, for Instance; ALBUCI. ★ M. VICTORINUS. PATER. † F. MOSSI. M. ‡ OF. NIGRI. AƆ. MAPILII. M. *&c.* a sepulchral earthen Lamp, figured with two Branches of Palms, supposed *Christian*; and two *Lacrymatories* of Glass.

Among the many Antiquities the *Surveyor* had the Fortune to

★ *Manibus.*
† *Fecit.*
‡ *Officina.*

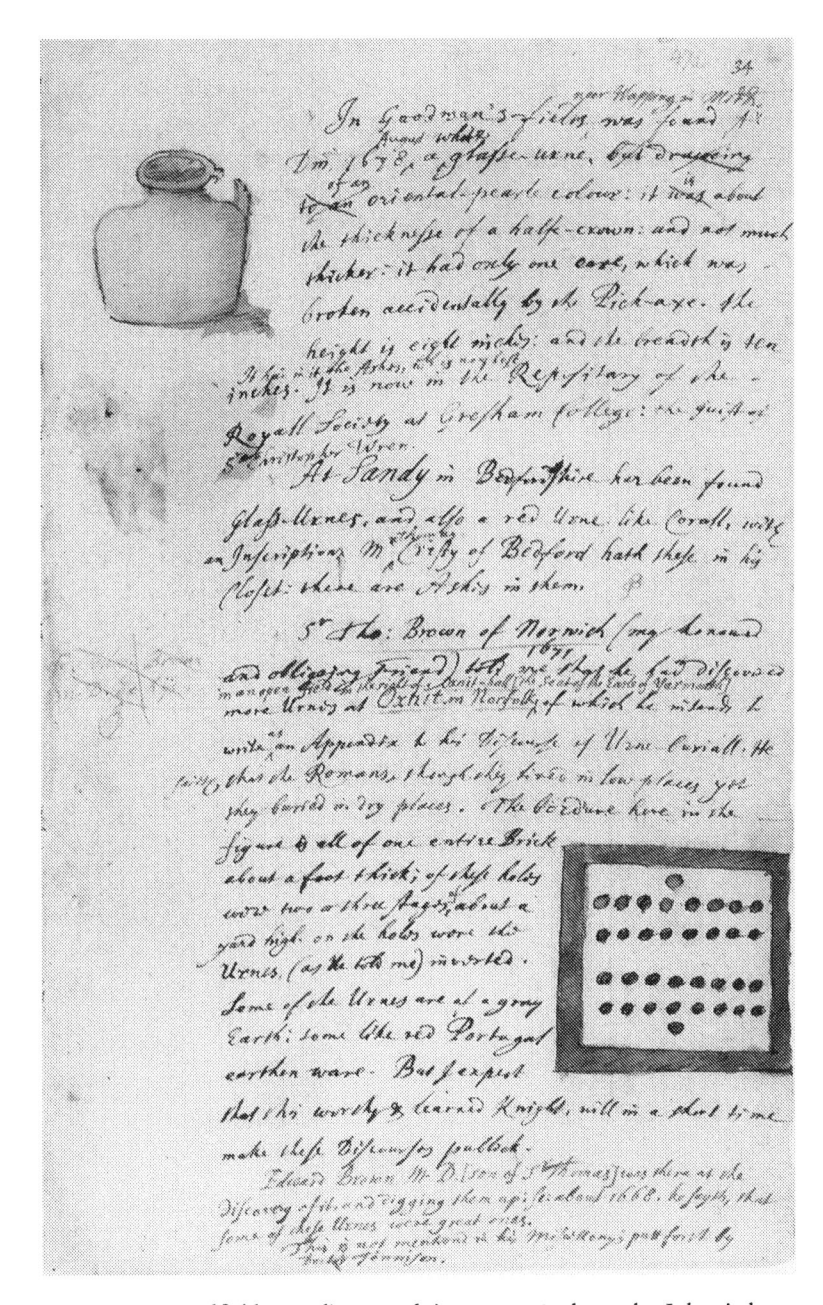

FIGURE 5. Spitalfields urn discovered August 1678, drawn by John Aubrey (John Aubrey, *Monumenta Britannica*, Bodleian MS Top. Gen. c. 24, fol. 47a). The Bodleian Library, Oxford.

FIGURE 5

discover in other Parts of the Town, after the *Fire*, the most curious was a large *Roman* Urn, or Ossuary of *Glass*, with a Handle, containing a Gallon and half, but with a very short Neck, and wide Mouth, of whiter Metal, encompassed Girth-wise, with five parallel Circles. This was found in *Spital-fields*, which he presented to the *Royal-society*, and is preserved in their *Museum*.[34]

Excerpt from "Of the taking down of the vast Ruins of the *old Cathedral*, and of the Foundations of the *old* and *new Structure*."

Source
   Original manuscript missing. *Parentalia* (London, 1750), "The Life of Sir Christopher Wren, Knt.," pt. 2, sec. 5, 285–6.
Other Manuscript Versions
   RS MS 249, fols. 325–7
   AS MS 313, fols. 503–7
Date
   Unknown

(page 285)

It has been observ'd, (SECT. I.)[1] that the Graves of several Ages and Fashions in *strata*, or Layers of Earth one above another, particularly at the North-side of *Paul's*, manifestly shew'd a great Antiquity from the *British* and *Roman* Times, by the Means whereof the Ground had been raised; but upon searching for the natural Ground below these Graves, the *Surveyor* observed that the Foundation of the old Church stood upon a Layer of very close and hard Pot-earth, and concluded that the same Ground which had born so weighty a Building, might reasonably be trusted again. However, he had the Curiosity to search further, and accordingly dug Wells in several Places, and discern'd this hard Pot-earth to be on the North-side of the Church-yard about six Feet thick, and more, but thinner and thinner towards the South, till it was upon the declining of the Hill scarce four Feet: still he searched lower, and found nothing but dry Sand, mix'd sometimes unequally, but loose, so that it would run through the Fingers. He went on till he came to Water and Sand mixed with Periwincles and other Seashells; these were about the Level of Low-water Mark. He continued boreing till he came to hard Beach, and still under that, till he came to the natural hard Clay, which lies under the City, and Country, and *Thames* also far and wide.

By these Shells it was evident the Sea had been where now the Hill is, on which *Paul's* stands.

The *Surveyor* was of Opinion, the whole Country between *Camberwell-hill*, and the Hills of *Essex* might have been a great *Frith* or *Sinus* of the Sea, and much wider near the Mouth of the *Thames*, which made a large Plain of Sand at Low-water, through which the River found its Way; but at Low-water, as oft as it happen'd in Summer-weather, when the Sun dried the Surface of the Sand,

and a strong Wind happen'd at the same Time, before the Flood came on, the Sands would drive with the Wind, and raise Heaps, and in Time large and lofty Sand-hills; for so are the Sand-hills rais'd upon the opposite Coasts of *Flanders* and *Holland*. The Sands upon such a Conjuncture of Sun-shine and Wind, drive in visible Clouds: this might be the Effect of many Ages, before History, and yet without having Recourse to the Flood.

This mighty broad Sand (now good Meadow) was restrain'd by large Banks still remaining, and reducing the River into its Channel; a great Work, of which no History gives Account: the *Britains* were too rude to attempt it; the *Saxons* too much busied with continual Wars; he concluded therefore it was a *Roman* Work;[2] one little Breach in his Time cost 17000 *l.* to restore.[3]

The Sand-hill at *Paul's* in the Time of the *Roman* Colony, was about 12 Feet lower than now it is; and the finer Sand easier driving with the Wind lay uppermost, and the hard Coat of Pot-earth might be thus made; for Pot-earth dissolv'd in Water, and view'd by a Microscope is but impalpable fine Sand, which with the Fire will vitrify; and, of this Earth upon the *(page 286)* Place, were those Urns, sacrificing Vessels, and other Pottery-ware, made, which (as noted before) were found here in great Abundance, more especially towards the North-east of the Ground.[4]

In the Progress of the Works of the Foundations, the *Surveyor* met with one unexpected Difficulty; he began to lay the Foundations from the West-end, and had proceeded successfully through the *Dome* to the East-end, where the Brick-earth Bottom was yet very good; but as he went on to the North-east Corner, which was the last, and where nothing was expected to interrupt, he fell, in prosecuting the Design, upon a Pit, where all the Pot-earth had been robb'd by the Potters of old Time: Here were discovered Quantities of Urns, broken Vessels, and Pottery-ware of divers Sorts and Shapes;[5] how far this Pit extended northward, there was no Occasion to examine; no Ox-sculls, Horns of Stags, and Tusks of Boars were found, to corroborate the Accounts of *Stow, Camden,*[6] and others; nor any Foundations more Eastward. If there was formerly any Temple to *Diana*, he supposed it might have been within the Walls of the *Colony*, and more to the South. It was no little Perplexity to fall into this Pit at last: He wanted but six or seven Feet to compleat the Design, and this fell in the very Angle Northeast; he knew very well, that under the Layer of Pot-earth, there was no other good Ground to be found till he came to the Lowwater Mark of the *Thames*, at least forty Feet lower: his Artificers propos'd to him to pile, which he refus'd; for, tho' Piles may last for ever, when always in Water, (otherwise *London-Bridge*[7] would fall) yet if they are driven through dry Sand, tho' sometimes moist, they will rot: His Endeavours were to build for Eternity. He therefore sunk a Pit of about eighteen Feet square, wharfing up the Sand with Timber, till he came forty Feet lower into Water and Sea-shells, where there was a firm Sea-beach which confirmed what was before asserted, that the Sea had been in Ages past, where now *Paul's* is; he bored through this Beach till he came to the original Clay; being then satisfied, he began from the Beach a square Peer of solid good Masonry; ten Feet square, till he came within fifteen Feet of the present Ground, then he turned a short Arch under Ground to the former Foundation, which was broken off by the untoward Accident of the Pit. Thus this North-east Coin of the Quire stands very firm, and, no doubt, will stand.

CHAPTER 2

Notes and Reports on Gothic Churches

INTRODUCTION

Although Wren observed Gothic churches while in Paris,[1] his understanding of the Gothic style was derived primarily from his direct involvement with the repairs of three prominent English medieval churches – Old St. Paul's, Salisbury Cathedral, and Westminster Abbey. On the basis of surveys conducted as a preliminary to repairs, as well as observations made during excavations, Wren produced several writings that treat specific formal and structural problems relating to each church. For the most part unillustrated, they fortunately can be supplemented by contemporary visual records: Hollar's engravings of 1654–6 and, for Salisbury Cathedral, the measured drawings found in Francis Price's 1753 survey. Most importantly, Wren's notes and reports provide general conclusions on the origin and nature of the Gothic style, echoed in isolated remarks found in Tract II, which formed part of the foundation for his theories of beauty and structure.

There are three documents relating to the history of Old St. Paul's. The first is the section in *Parentalia* entitled "Of the ancient cathedral Churches of St. Paul."[2] Citing Wren's discoveries during excavations for the new cathedral, begun around or after November 1673,[3] Christopher Jr. presents a history of the first structures on the site, from the legendary Early Christian cathedral destroyed under Dioclesian, to its rebuilding under Constantine and its subsequent destruction by the Saxons, to the seventh-century Saxon church, and ending with the existing fabric of Norman (1087) and Gothic (thirteenth century) origin. There are also comments by Wren on the "modern *Gothick*-stile," as well as the style (of the Normans) that preceded it, with related observations on materials and construction methods.

The other documents relating to Old St. Paul's are Wren's two reports on the condition of the medieval fabric, recased by Inigo Jones from 1633 to 1642, before and after the Great Fire of 1666. The reports were written as part of a debate that began, soon after the Restoration of Charles II, over what exactly were the particular problems of the venerable cathedral, and how to remedy them. As early as mid-October 1661, Wren was consulted about repairs for St. Paul's.[4] He was not, however, a member of the Commission for the Repairs of Old St. Paul's, established by Charles II on 18 April 1663.[5] This commission produced two undated reports, the earliest by the architect John Webb, Surveyor General John Denham, and the mason Edward Marshall. Soon after, the architects Hugh May and Roger Pratt became involved and Pratt prepared his own report.[6] Wren's involvement dates from after his return from Paris, by March 1666, when he was invited by Dean William Sancroft to make recommendations to the commission. These are found in his first written proposal, the "Report on Old St. Paul's before the Fire," now lost in manuscript but preserved in *Parentalia* as "Ex Autographo," dated 1 May in the margin. More reliable is 7 May, the date of the cover letter to the report, written by Wren to Dean Sancroft.[7] Another copy of the report, in an unknown hand and with slight differences in wording, is found at the Bodleian Library.[8]

Wren wrote his report in response to Pratt's arguments for piecemeal repairs. He determined that there were two major structural problems that needed attention. Some record of these defects is provided by Hollar's engravings (see Figs. 6–12). First, the outward bending of the walls, due to their inadequate abutment of the heavy roof, could be remedied by recasing the walls with stone and replacing the roof with a new, lighter construction. The second problem concerned the tower. At an earlier period one of the four supports had sunk, so new arches were added between them, which, unfortunately, made the space of the crossing too narrow and blocked the perspective view down the length of the church. According to Wren, the tower should be completely replaced by "a spacious *Dome* or *Rotundo*, with a Cupola, or hemispherical Roof" supported on four new arches and built using the existing tower as a scaffold during construction. Wren's dome idea, inspired by his recent experience in Paris, was recorded in drawings, "with a great deal of paines finished" on 5 August 1666,[9] which are now preserved at All Souls (Figs. 13–15). They show that, in addition to a pointed, double-shelled dome on a high drum in the Classical style, Wren planned to recase the interior of the nave and transept arms with composite pilasters and saucer domes.

Pratt soon responded to Wren in a second paper wherein he denied the existence of the defects described by Wren and criticized his dome proposal as needless and very expensive.[10] On 27 August a meeting was held on site with Wren, John Evelyn, Pratt, May, the bishop, the dean, other important commissioners, and the principal workmen all present. According to Evelyn in his diary, Pratt continued to claim that the old structure and foundation had no faults, even going so far as to explain away the outward tilt of the walls as a perspective effect created deliberately by the original builders. Evelyn sided with Wren against this opinion. After much discussion, the majority approved of Wren's ideas for a cupola and asked to see a design and estimate.[11]

After Old St. Paul's was destroyed in the Great Fire, Wren prepared a second report on the conditions of the ruins sometime after the fire (i.e., 5 September 1666) and before 26 February 1667, the date given at the end of the text with the masons' endorsement. The report in Wren's hand, now preserved at the Bodleian,[12] is primarily concerned with how part of the ruins, which are recorded in Thomas Wyck's sketch of c. 1672 (Fig. 16), might be refurbished to make a usable choir. Referring to his previous report, Wren describes the decay of the building resulting from the defects of the design and material of the first structure, the fire during the reign of Queen Elizabeth I, the subsequent repairs, and finally the Great Fire.

Around this same time Wren was asked to examine Salisbury Cathedral (Fig. 17) by the bishop, Dr. Seth Ward. Wren's original report with three diagrams (Figs. 23–4), written on 31 August 1668, exists today in manuscript in the registry of the dean and chapter of the church.[13] In his report, written after "a few hours inspection," Wren provides the first written survey of the cathedral. After describing the overall fabric, he goes further to discuss specific problems found in the foundation and interior supports as the basis for a more general analysis of structural defects found in all Gothic churches in the side-aisle vaults and in the abutment of the crossing. He presents a detailed description of the tower, concluding from the evidence that the construction of the immense spire was an afterthought that led to several expedients, including iron ties and additional buttressing, to ensure its stability. To solve problems caused by the original design, the addition of the spire, and weathering, Wren goes on to propose eleven remedies for the failures, bending, or cracks found in the tower and spire, the roof, and the buttresses of the church. Other remarks are made on the condition and repair of the chapter house and cloister. A clearer picture of the conditions described by Wren is provided by Hollar's perspective of the cathedral and by the detailed measured drawings made by Francis Price in his survey of 1753 (Figs. 18–22).[14] Many of Wren's observations and conclusions about the cathedral's history have been confirmed by Price and later investigators.[15]

Wren's report on Westminster Abbey was made in 1713 at the request of Dean Francis Atterbury as a record of the repairs made under his tenure as Surveyor of the Abbey, a post he obtained in 1698, replacing Robert Hooke.[16] In the course of chronicling the work of successive rulers at the abbey, based on written records, Wren gives a general history of Gothic architecture, proposing a Saracenic origin and characterizing the

"Modes of Building" from that time on.[17] He believed that the problems detected in the stonework, buttresses, vaults, and roof demonstrated the defects of the style, although his completed and proposed repairs proved that they could be remedied. He gives a drawing showing a partial section of the nave and side aisle (Fig. 27), demonstrating his principle of adding a vertical load (e.g., a steeple or pinnacle) above a column or pier to counteract the horizontal thrust of the arch it supports. He also makes suggestions on how to complete what was left imperfect by the original builders – the west front, the steeple, and the north facade, all recorded by Hollar – so that they agree with the original design (Figs. 25–6). Wren produced drawings for all of these (Figs. 28–9), but only the north transept design was executed.[18]

Wren's notes and reports on Gothic churches are important documents in revealing his particular attitude toward the Gothic style and how he formed it. Generally he gives a negative appraisal of the style, although it is mild in comparison to those of some of his contemporaries. For example, his friend John Evelyn, F.R.S., described the Gothic as "a certain Fantastical and Licentious manner of Building, . . . Congestions of Heavy, Dark, Melancholy and Monkish Piles, without any just Proportion, Use or Beauty,"[19] thus echoing the rhetoric of fifteenth- and sixteenth-century Italian theorists, beginning with Alberti, who upheld the primacy of the Classical as the only good style, the epitome of beauty during antiquity and, now, the present.[20]

At the same time, however, using the data of the churches he surveyed, Wren presents a clear analysis of the characteristic forms, structures, materials, and construction methods of the Gothic style. Based on this analysis, he provides a reasonable hypothesis of its origin and development in response to particular and changing cultural circumstances. Wren was the first to propose that the Gothic style originated in the Levant with the "Saracens" or Arabs and was brought to the West by the returning Crusaders of the eleventh and twelfth centuries. The Saracen pointed arch and masonry construction, created in response to local conditions, was first adopted in the immensely high buildings of the French, who were responsible for adding another feature – the flying buttress. Later on, the style was borrowed by the English.

Furthermore, in Wren's notes and reports there is evidence that he recognized, based on his knowledge of history and of specific monuments, four different periods of the Gothic. The earliest he called "Saxon" and dated to the reign of King Edgar (959–75). From the various churches that he cites, all having this style's main characteristic, the round arch, it is clear that Wren was mistaken in his dating and was referring to eleventh-century Norman examples. He described a second Gothic style that also used round arches, found in monuments dating from the beginning of the reign of William the Conqueror (1066–87). This was followed by the "more modern *Gothick*-stile" from the time of Henry III (1216–72), which employed, as in the choirs of Old St. Paul's and Salisbury, pointed arches. Finally, there was a Gothic style "of later date," as is found in the upper parts of the tower of Salisbury and the chapel of Henry VII at Westminster.

A similar study, conducted with greater rigor, was made by Wren's friend John Aubrey, F.R.S., in *Chronologia Architectonica*, part of his *Monumenta Britannica*.[21] Aubrey began by drawing examples of Gothic ornament, primarily of windows, from about eighty Gothic churches. He then arranged them chronologically, with the help of written records. By using a simple method that made formal comparisons possible, Aubrey was able to characterize the styles of a series of historical periods or reigns.

The way in which Wren, as well as Aubrey, went about studying Gothic architecture clearly reflects the scientific methods practiced at the Royal Society. Despite prejudice against the style held for over two centuries, Wren was able to set aside inherited precepts and to study Gothic monuments directly. Based on this data, he began to draw conclusions, acknowledging, for the first time, that the Gothic style was a product of a particular time and place. Based on this new understanding, Wren was compelled, not to reject the Gothic, but to formulate a theory that acknowledged the existence of this and other culturally specific phenomena.

Excerpt from "Of the ancient cathedral Churches of St. *Paul;* from the first Age of *Christianity,* to the last *great Fire* of London, in *1666.*"

Source
  Original manuscript missing. *Parentalia* (London, 1750), "The Life of Sir Christopher Wren, Knt.," pt. 2, sec. 3, 271–4.
Other Manuscript Versions
  RS MS 249, fols. 308–12
  AS MS 313, fols. 461–71
Date
  Unknown

(page 271)

The *Christian* Faith, without doubt, was very early received in *Britain*; and without having recourse to the *monkish* Tale of *Joseph of Arimathea,*[2] and other *legendary* Fictions; there is authentick Testimony of a *Christian Church* planted here by the *Apostles* themselves, and, in particular, very probably by St. *Paul.*

‡It is very certain *this Apostle,*[4] from his first Imprisonment at *Rome,* to his Return to *Jerusalem,* had spent eight Years in preaching in divers Places, but more especially in the *Western Countries.* We know he design'd for *Spain,* and it is not improbable, but his Earnestness to convert the *Britains* might have carried him to this *Island.*

This Opinion may be strengthened by the Evidence of *Vanutius Fortunatus,*[5] who says the same Thing, speaking of the Travels of St. *Paul,* in his Poem on the Life of St. *Martin.*

Transit & oceanum, vel quà facit insula portum,
Quasque Britannus *habet terras, quasque ultima* Thule.

Every *Christian Church* derived from the *Apostles,* had a Succession of *Bishops* from them too, and the Condition of the *British Church* was so early establish'd, that some maintain there were *Bishops* of the *Britains* at the Council of *Nice,* assembled in 325:[6] and 'tis certain, that twenty-two Years after, *Restitutus* Bishop of *London* was one of the three *British* Bishops present at the Council of *Arles.*[7]

Some *British* Prelates were likewise at the Council of *Ariminum,*

Stillingfleet, see Bp. of Worcester's Origines Britanicae.[1]

‡Rapin's *Hist. of* Eng. Lib. I.[3]

†Du Pin.[8]

assembled in 359, and these were of such Dignity, that they refused the Emperor's† Allowance, thinking it beneath them not to bear their own Expences.

The first Cathedral of this episcopal See of *London*, (built in the Area, where had been the *Roman Prætorian Camp*,[9] the Situation of all the succeeding Fabricks to this Time) was demolished under the great and general Persecution by *Dioclesian*:[10] But although in Pursuance of the Strictness of his Edicts, the *Christian Churches* in all the Provinces of the *Roman* Government were ordered to be pull'd down, yet possibly the *Præfects* might not take the Pains, when they had made them unfit for Use, to tear up the Foundations also. The Time of the Persecution was short, for under *Constantine*,[11] the Church flourish'd again; the Churches in *Rome*, and other Parts of the Empire were soon rebuilt, and most likely ours among the first, after the Pattern of the *Roman Basilica* of St. *Peter*, and St. *Paul*, in the *Vatican*; and, as the *Surveyor* conceiv'd, upon the old Foundations left by the Persecutors; for, the *Christians* were zealous, and in haste to be settled again.

(page 272) The Church thus re-edified under *Constantine*, was afterwards destroy'd by the *Pagan Saxons*; and restor'd again, upon the old Foundations, when they embrac'd *Christianity*, in the seventh Century, by *Mellitus,* Bishop of *London*, under *Ethelbert* King of *Kent*, the first *Saxon* King of the *Christian* Faith.[12]

This Church, together with the whole City was destroy'd by a casual Fire, in the Year 1083.[13] *Mauritius*[14] then Bishop of *London*, obtain'd of the King,[15] the old Stone of a spacious Castle in the Neighborhood, call'd the *Palatine Tower*, demolished by the same Fire; (this *Fort* stood at the Entrance of the *Fleet-river*, as if to defend the little Haven, then capable of Ships)[16] and began the Building, upon the old Foundations, a fourth Time of that *Pile*; which after

FIGURES 6–12

Additions, at several Times, to the East and West, continu'd till the last general Conflagration of the City, in 1666.

The Fabrick thus began by *Mauritius*, had originally, as the *Surveyor* believ'd, a semicircular *Presbyterium* or Chancel, after the usual Mode of the *Primitive Churches*,[17] and came near the Form of a *Cross*, short to the East;[18] as he concluded for this Reason; a *Quire* in after Times was added to give a greater Length Eastward than at first; this Building was apparently of a more modern *Gothick*-stile, not with *Round* (as in the old Church) but *sharp-headed Arches*;[19] to make Way for which, the semicircular *Presbyterium*[20] had been taken down.[21] Upon demolishing the Ruins, after the last *Fire*, and searching the Foundations of this *Quire*, the *Surveyor* discover'd *nine Wells* in a Row; which, no doubt, had anciently belong'd to a Street of Houses, that lay aslope from the High-street, (then *Watling-street*)[22]

FIGURE 2

40

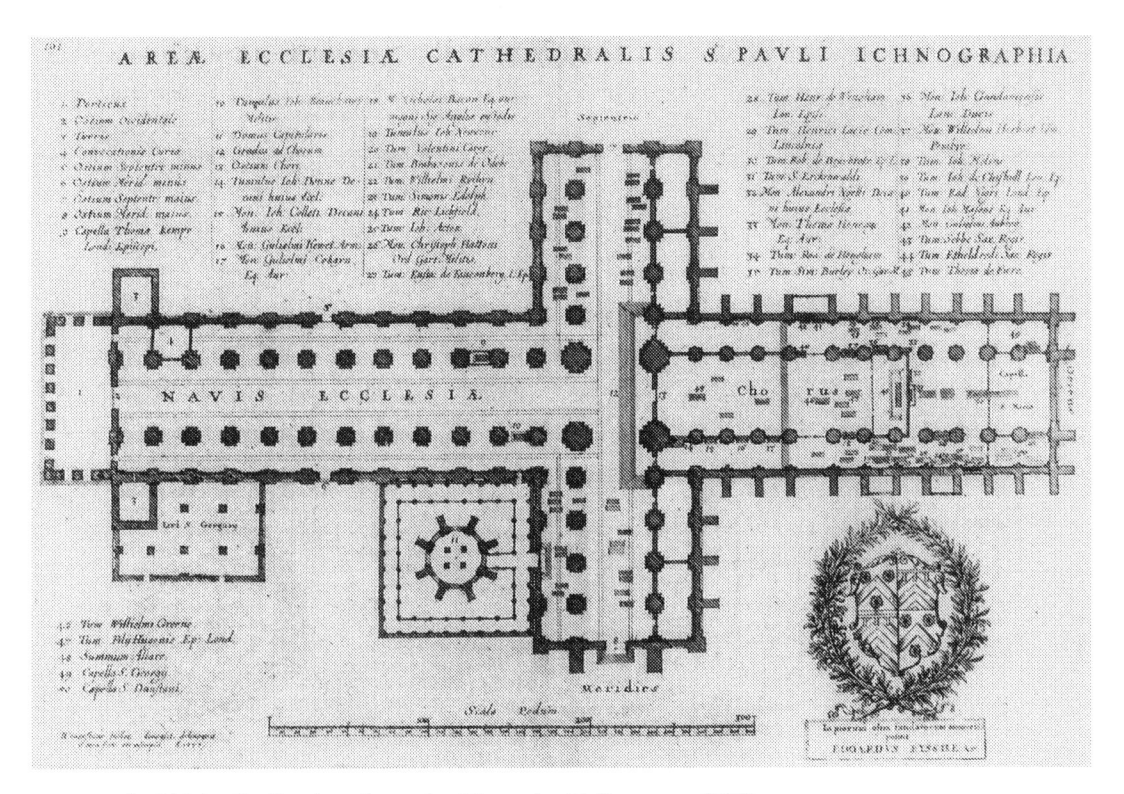

FIGURE 6. Old St. Paul's, plan, drawn by Wenceslas Hollar, 1656 (William Dugdale, *History of St. Paul's Cathedral* [London, 1656], pl. 161). Photo Courtesy of The Newberry Library.

to the *Roman Causeway*, (now *Cheapside*) and this Street,[23] which was taken away to make room for the new *Quire*, came so near the old *Presbyterium*,[24] that the Church could not extend farther that Way at first. He discover'd also, there had been a considerable Addition, and a new Front to the West, but in what Age is not ascertain'd.[25]

The Reason the *Surveyor* was of Opinion, that though several Times the Fabrick had been ruin'd, yet that the Foundations might remain, as originally they were laid, was upon his observing, that they consisted of nothing but *Kentish*-rubble-stone, artfully work'd, and consolidated with exceeding hard Mortar, in the *Roman* Manner, much excelling what he found in the Superstructure; the Outside of which was built chiefly with the Free-stone of the old *Palatine Tower*, and Free-stone suppos'd from the Quarries of *Yorkshire*, and in every Part was apparently less skillfully perform'd, and with worse Mortar.

Tho' there be now no History or Record notifying directly

Dudgale's *St. Paul's*, p. 6.[26]

FIGURE 7. Old St. Paul's from the south, drawn by Wenceslas Hollar, 1656 (William Dugdale, *History of St. Paul's Cathedral* [London, 1656], pl. 162). Photo Courtesy of The Newberry Library.

the first Building of the first[27] new *Quire,* yet 'tis probable it might have been executed by *Richard*[28] who was Bishop of *London* in the first Year of the Reign of King *Richard the First,*[29] and had been Treasurer to King *Henry the Second;*[30] *who is said to have expended a vast Sum of Money on the Buildings of his Church,* &c.

<small>Godwin de Præful. *p.* 237.[31]</small>

<small>Dudgale's *St. Paul's, p.* 12.[32]</small>

But the said *Quire* being, afterwards, not thought beautiful enough, and a Resolution taken for an Improvement, they began with the *Steeple,* which was finish'd in the year 1221, (5 *Hen.* III.)[33] and then going on with the *Quire,* perfected it in 1240, (24 *Hen.* III.)[34] in the Form it continued to the last great Fire, 1666.

Under the *Quire* was a noble Vault, wherein were three Ranks of large and massy Pillars, which being made a Parish-church, was dedicated to St. *Faith.*[35]

Upon the happy *Restoration* of King *Charles* II.[36] it was determin'd to proceed in the Repairs of the old cathedral Church, which had been interrupted by the *great Rebellion*; and Dr. *Wren* was order'd to prepare proper Designs **(page 273)** for that Purpose: his Predecessor Mr. *Inigo Jones*[37] had (pursuant to a Royal-commission in 1631, 7 *Car.* I.)[38] put the *Quire,* of a more modern *Gothick* Stile, as before specified, than the rest of the Fabrick, into very good Repair; he had proceeded to case great Part of the Outside with

Portland-stone; had rebuilt the North and South-fronts; and also the West-front, with the Addition of a very graceful *Portico* of the *Corinthian* Order, built of large *Portland-stone*. The great Tower remained to be new cased Inside and Outside; and the whole Inside from the *Quire* to the West-door to be new cased, and reformed in some Measure.

The Vaulting wanted much to be amended, in order to which it was all well center'd, and upheld with Standards of some hundreds of tall Masts.

In this State was the Fabrick when the great Rebellion began; "but in 1643, all the Materials, &c. assign'd for the Repairs were seized, the Scaffolds pull'd down; and the Body of the Church converted to a Horse-quarter for Soldiers; the beautiful Pillars of *Inigo Jones's Portico* were shamefully hew'd and defaced for support of the Timber-work of Shops, for Seamstresses, and other Trades; for which sordid Uses, that stately *Colonade* was wholly taken up, and defil'd. Upon taking away the inner Scaffolds, which supported the arched Vaults, in order to their late intended Repair, the whole Roof of the South-cross tumbled down; and the rest in several Places of the Church, did often fall; so that the Structure continued a woeful Spectacle of Ruin, till the happy Restoration.

Dudgale's *St. Paul's, p.* 146, &c.[39]

"In 1662, the Dean and Chapter had taken Care to fit up for divine Service, the East-part of the Church beyond the old *Quire*, enlarging it the length of one Arch, into the *Quire*,[40] until the Repairs of the remaining Part of the old Fabrick should be perfected.

"For the expediting of which general Repair, a royal Commission pass'd in 1663. After this, the Time was spent, in taking down Houses and Nusances that had been rais'd by the late Usurpers, at the West-end, and Sides of the Church; in clearing the Rubbish; searching the Decays; repairing the *Portico*; in Provision of Stone, Timber, and all necessary Preparations; until the Beginning of the Year, 1666. By which Time Dr. *Wren* had finish'd and adjusted his Designs for the whole Reparation, and laid the same before the King, and the Commissioners."

Continuation of Dudgale's *St. Paul's, p.* 149.[41]

The first Business Dr. *Wren* had enter'd upon, previous to the forming Designs for the general Repairs, was to take an exact Plan, Orthography, and Section, upon an accurate Survey of the whole Structure, even to Inches;[42] in the Prosecution of which, he was astonish'd to find how negligent the first Builders had been; they seem'd *Normans*, and to have used the *Norman* Foot; but they valu'd not Exactness: some Inter-columns were one Inch and a half too large, others as much, or more, too little. Nor were they true in their Levels. It consisted in great Part of old Materials, which the Founder, *Mauritius* Bishop of *London*, had procur'd of King *William*

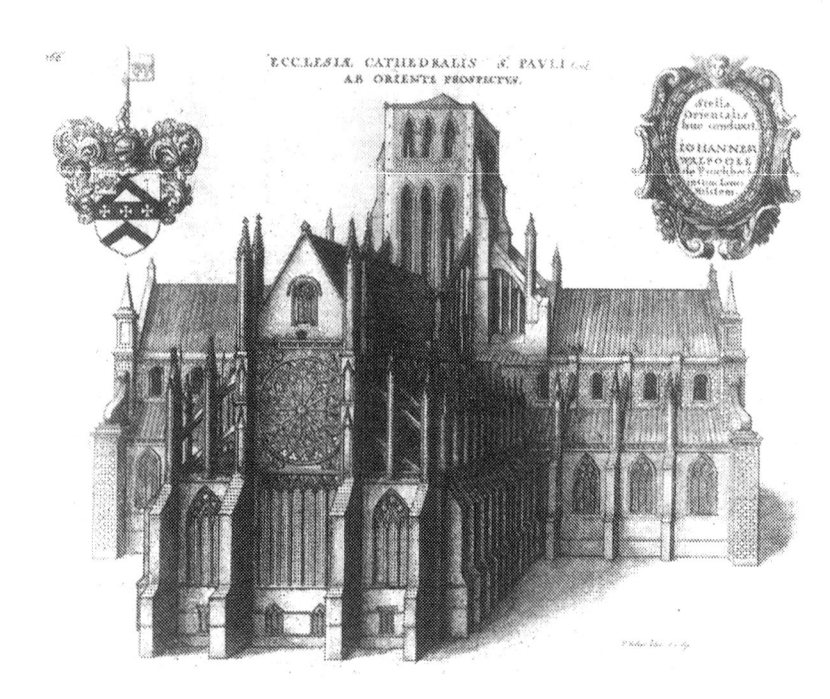

FIGURE 8. Old St. Paul's from the east, drawn by Wenceslas Hollar, 1656 (William Dugdale, *History of St. Paul's Cathedral* [London, 1658], pl. 166). Photo Courtesy of The Newberry Library.

the First, out of the Ruins of the *Palatine Tower*; these were small *Yorkshire* Free-stone, *Kentish*-ashlar, and *Kentish*-rag from *Maidstone*. They made great Pillars without any graceful Manner; and thick Walls without Judgment. They had not as yet fallen into the *Gothick* pointed-arch, as was follow'd in the *Quire* of a later Date, but kept to the circular Arch; so much they retain'd of the *Roman* Manner, but nothing else: Cornices they could not have, for want of larger Stone: in short, it was a vast, but heavy Building.[43] – Adjoining to the South-cross was a Chapter-house of a more elegant *Gothick* Manner, with a Cloyster of two Stories high.[44]

(page 274) The lofty *Spire* which anciently rose from the great middle Stone-tower, the *Surveyor* observed, was not originally intended of Stone, for there were no diagonal Arches to reduce it into an Octogon, 'twas therefore finish'd of Timber cover'd with Lead: this was twice fir'd by Lightning, and the last Time, in 1561, totally consum'd.[45]

Antiquaries differ in their Accounts of its Altitude. By *Stow*'s[46] Measures, the Stone-tower, and Spire, were equally 260 Feet each in height, the whole 520 Feet. Mr. *Camden*'s[47] Dimensions rise to 534 Feet. *Dudgale*[48] (seemingly by good Authority, who took his

FIGURE 9. Old St. Paul's, interior of choir, drawn by Wenceslas Hollar, 1656 (William Dugdale, *History of St. Paul's Cathedral* [London, 1658], pl. 169). Photo Courtesy of The Newberry Library.

Relation from a Brass-table heretofore hung on a Pillar on the north Part of the Quire) makes the Heighth of the Tower 260 Feet, and of the Spire 274 Feet, and yet the whole, *viz.* both of Tower and Spire did not exceed 520 Feet, as is testified by the Table, (whereof there is a MS Copy also in the publick Library in *Cambridge*) which is 14 Feet short of the Height of the two Dimensions

FIGURE 10. Old St. Paul's from the north, drawn by Wenceslas Hollar, 1656 (William Dugdale, *History of St. Paul's Cathedral* [London, 1656], pl. 163). Photo Courtesy of The Newberry Library.

Camden's Britan. 2d Edit. p. 378.[49]

of the Tower and Spire added together; "This, (says the Right Rev. and Learned Editor of *Camden's Britannia*) must indeed have been true, had the Spire risen from the *Summit* of the Battlements: whereas, I suppose, it rose, (as the Spires of most Steeples do) much below them; the Battlements here rising 14 Feet above the Base of the Spire, must occasion the Difference."

All the stone Tower was standing when the *Surveyor* measur'd it before the *Fire*, and, agreeable with the other Accounts, was in Height 260 Feet; the *Basis* of the Spire he found was 40 Feet, therefore according to the usual Proportion of Spires in *Gothick* Fabricks, which was 4 Diameters, or 5 at most, it could rise no higher than 200 Feet, and make the whole Altitude not to exceed 460 Feet to the *Ball* of Copper gilt and *Cross*: upon which after the first Fire by Lightning was added a *Weathercock* representing an *Eagle*, of Copper gilt likewise.

The Proportions of these copper *Ornaments* are thus recorded; the *Ball* was in Circumference 9 Feet one Inch. The Height of the *Cross*, from the *Ball*, 15 Feet 6 Inches, and its Traverse 5 Feet 10 Inches. The *Eagle* from the Bill to the Tail, 4 Feet, the Breadth over the Wings, 3 Feet and a half.

In order to a further View of this ancient cathedral Church, some Particulars relating to the Architecture, the original Defects, and at length ruinous Parts thereof; the Design for the Repairs, and

FIGURE 11. Old St. Paul's from the west, drawn by Wenceslas Hollar, 1656 (William Dugdale, *History of St. Paul's Cathedral* [London, 1656], pl. 164). Photo Courtesy of The Newberry Library.

for erecting a new *Cupola* in the Place of the great Tower; will most properly and distinctly appear from an Extract of the Proposals of Dr. *Wren*, to the Right Honourable the Commissioners for the Reparation, upon an accurate Survey taken in 1666; which, together with the several respective Drawings, were laid before the King and Commissioners, some Months before the *great Fire* of London.[50]

May 1.

Report on Old St. Paul's before the Fire
(7 May 1666)

Source
   Original manuscript missing. *Parentalia* (London, 1750), "The Life of Sir Christopher Wren, Knt.," pt. 2, sec. 3, 274–7. Dated May 1 and given as "Ex Autographo"
Other Manuscript Versions
   RS MS 249 fols. 312v–16.
   AS MS 313, fols. 472–81
   Bodleian, Tanner 145, fols. 110–12, entitled "Proposals"/ "To the right Honourable the Commissioners for the Reparation of St. Paul's Cathedral," in hand of copyist with slight changes in wording (transcript in *WS*, 13:15–17)
Date
   7 May 1666

(page 274)
   Amongst the many Propositions, that may be made to your Lordships,[1] concerning the Repair of St. *Paul's*, some may possibly aim at too great a Magnificence, which neither the Disposition, nor Extent of this Age will probably bring to a Period. Others again may fall so low as to think of piecing up the old Fabrick, here with Stone, there with Brick, and cover all Faults with a Coat of Plaister, leaving it still to Posterity, as a further Object of Charity.

   I suppose your Lordships may think proper to take a middle Way, and to neglect nothing that may conduce to a decent uniform Beauty, or durable Firmness in the Fabrick, or Suitableness to the Expence already laid out on the Outside: especially since it is a Pile both for Ornament and Use. For, all the Occasions either of a Quire, Consistory, Chapter-house, Library, Court of Arches, Preaching-auditory, might have been supplied in less Room, with less Expence, and yet more Beauty; but then it had *(page 275)* wanted of the Grandeur, which exceeds all little Curiosity; this being the Effect of Wit only, the other a Monument of Power, and mighty Zeal in our Ancestors to publick Works in those Times, when the City had neither a fifth Part of the People, nor a tenth Part of the Wealth it now boasts off.

   I shall presume therefore to enumerate as well the Defects of Comeliness as Firmness, that the one may be reconcil'd with the other in the Restitution. And yet I should not propose any Thing of meer Beauty to be added, but where there is a Necessity of

FIGURE 12. Old St. Paul's, interior of nave, drawn by Wenceslas Hollar, 1656 (William Dugdale, *History of St. Paul's Cathedral* [London, 1658], pl. 167). Photo Courtesy of The Newberry Library.

rebuilding, and where it will be near the same Thing to perform it well as ill.

First, it is evident by the Ruin of the Roof, that the Work was both ill design'd, and ill built from the Beginning: ill design'd, because the Architect gave not Butment enough to counterpoise, and resist the Weight of the Roof from spreading the Walls;[2] for, the Eye alone will discover to any Man, that those Pillars as vast as they are, even eleven Foot diameter, are bent outward at least six Inches from their first Position; which being done on both Sides, it necessarily follows, that the whole Roof must first open in large and wide Cracks along by the Walls and Windows, and lastly drop down between the yielding Pillars.

This bending of the Pillars was facilitated by their ill Building; for, they are only cased without, and that with small Stones, not one greater than a Man's Burden; but within is nothing but a Core of small Rubbish-stone, and much Mortar, which easily crushes and yields to the Weight: and this outward Coat of Free-stone is so much torn with Age, and the Neglect of the Roof, that there are few Stones to be found that are not moulder'd, and flaw'd away with the Salt-peter that is in them; an incurable Disease, which perpetually throws off whatever Coat of Plaister is laid on it, and therefore not to be palliated.

From hence I infer, that as the Outside of the Church was new flagg'd with Stone of larger Size than before,[3] so ought the Inside also: And in doing this, it will be as easy to perform it, after a good *Roman* Manner, as to follow the *Gothick* Rudeness of the old Design; and that, without placing the Face of the new Work in any Part many Inches farther out or in, than the Superficies of the old Work; or adding to the Expence that would arise were it perform'd the worse Way.

This also may be safely affirm'd, not only by an Architect, taking his Measures from the Precepts and Examples of the Antients, but by a Geometrician, (this Part being liable to Demonstration) that the Roof is, and ever was, too heavy for its Butment; and therefore any Part of the old Roof new pieced, will still but occasion further Ruin, and the second Ruin will much sooner follow than the first, since 'tis easier to force a Thing already declining. It must therefore be either a timber Roof plaister'd, (which, in such Buildings where a little Soke of Weather is not presently discover'd or remedied, will soon decay) or else, a thinner and lighter Shell of Stone, very geometrically proportion'd to the Strength of the Butment. The Roof may be Brick, if it be plaister'd with *Stucco*, which is a harder Plaister, that will not fall off with the Drip of a few Winters, and which to this Day remains firm in many ancient *Roman* Buildings.

The middle Part is most defective both in Beauty and Firmness, without and within; for, the Tower leans manifestly by the settling of one of the ancient Pillars that supported it. Four new Arches were, therefore, of later Years, incorporated within the old ones, which hath straighten'd and hinder'd both the Room, and the clear thorough View of the Nave, *(page 276)* in that Part, where it had been more graceful to have been rather wider than the rest.

The excessive Length of Buildings is no otherwise commendable, but because it yields a pleasing Perspective by the continu'd optical Diminution of the Columns; and if this be cut off by Columns ranging within their Fellows, the Grace that would be acquir'd by the Length is totally lost.

Besides this Deformity of the Tower itself within, there are

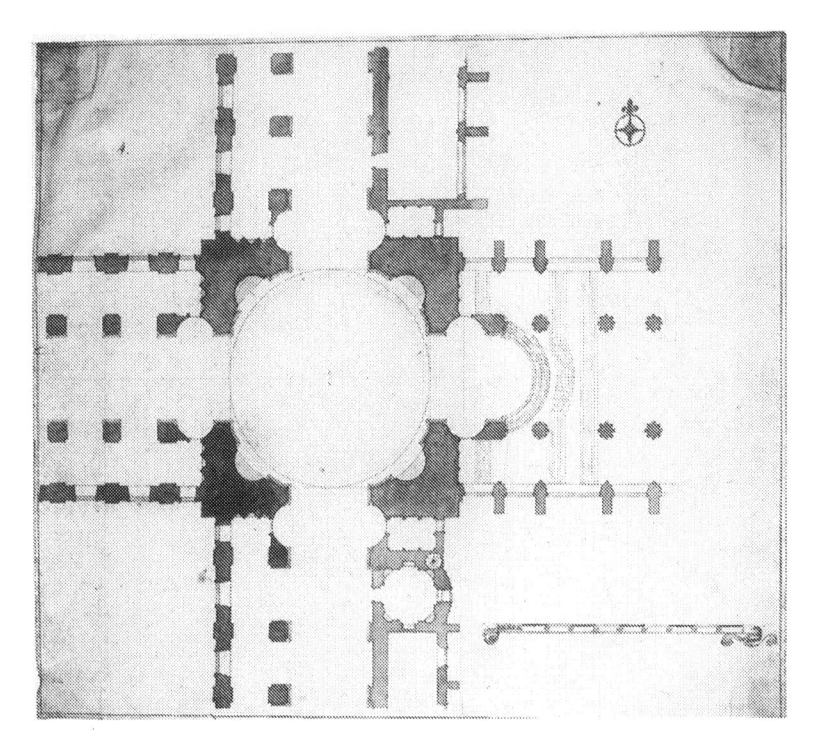

FIGURE 13. Pre-Fire Design for Old St. Paul's, plan, 1666 (AS II. 4. All Souls College, Oxford). The Warden and Fellows of All Souls College, Oxford.

others near it; as, the next Intercolumnation in the *Navis* or Body of the Church, is much less than all the rest. Also the North and South-wings have Aisles only on the West-Side, the others being originally shut up for the Consistory. Lastly, the Intercolumnations or Spaces between the Pillars of the Quire next adjoining to the Tower are very unequal. Again, on the Outside of the Tower, the Buttresses that have been erected one upon the Back of another to secure three Corners on the inclining Sides, (for the fourth wants a Buttress) are so irregular, that upon the whole Matter, it must be concluded, that the Tower from Top to Bottom, and the next adjacent Parts, are such a Heap of Deformities, that no judicious Architect will think it corrigible, by any Expence that can be laid out upon new dressing it, but that it will still remain unworthy the rest of the Work, infirm and tottering; and for these Reasons, as I conjecture, was formerly resolv'd to be taken down.

 I cannot propose a better Remedy, than by cutting off the inner Corners of the Cross, to reduce this middle Part into a spacious *Dome* or *Rotundo*, with a *Cupola*, or hemispherical Roof, and upon the *Cupola*, (for the outward Ornament) a *Lantern* with a spiring

FIGURE 14. Pre-Fire Design for Old St. Paul's, section through nave showing Jones's recasing of the exterior, 1666 (AS II. 6. All Souls College, Oxford). The Warden and Fellows of All Souls College, Oxford.

FIGURE 15. Pre-Fire Design for Old St. Paul's, longitudinal section, 1666 (AS II. 7. All Souls College, Oxford). The Warden and Fellows of All Souls College, Oxford.

Top, to rise proportionably, tho' not to that unnecessary Height of the former Spire of Timber and Lead burnt by Lightning.[4]

By this Means the Deformities of the unequal Intercolumnations will be taken away; the Church, which is much too narrow for the Heighth, render'd spacious in the Middle, which may be a very proper Place for a vast Auditory: the outward Appearance of the Church will seem to swell in the Middle by Degrees, from a large Basis rising into a *Rotundo* bearing a *Cupola*, and then ending in a *Lantern*: and this with incomparable more Grace in the remoter Aspect, than it is possible for the lean Shaft of a Steeple to afford. Nor if it be rightly order'd, will the Expence be much more than that of investing the Tower and Corners yet unfinish'd, with new Stone, and adding the old Steeple anew; the Lead of which will be sufficient for a *Cupola*; and the same Quantity of Ashler makes the Corners outward, that would make them inward as they now are: And the Materials of the old Corners of the Ailes will be filling Stone for the new Work: for I should not persuade the Tower to be pull'd down at first, but the new Work to be built round it, partly because the Expectations of Persons are to be kept up; for, many Unbelievers would bewail the Loss of old *Paul's* Steeple, and despond if they did not see a hopeful Successor rise in its stead; and chiefly because it will save a great Quantity of scaffolding Poles; the Scaffolds which are needful being fix'd from the old to the new Work; and when the *Tholus* or inward Vault is to be laid, the Tower taken down to that Height will rest the Centers of the Vault with great Convenience, and facilitate the planting of Engines for raising the Stones; and after all is finish'd and settl'd, the Tower that is left may be taken clear away from within. All which can only from the Designs be perfectly understood.[5]

(page 277) And for the Encouragement and Satisfaction of Benefactors that comprehend not readily Designs and Draughts on Paper, as well as for the inferior Artificers clearer Intelligence of their Business, it will be requisite that a large and exact Model be made; which will also have this Use, that if the Work should happen to be interrupted, or retarded, Posterity may proceed where the Work was left off, pursuing still the same Design.

And as the *Portico* built by *Inigo Jones*, being an intire and excellent Piece, gave great Reputation to the Work in the first Repairs, and occasion'd fair Contributions; so to begin now with the *Dome* may probably prove the best Advice, being an absolute Piece of itself, and what will most likely be finished in our Time; will make by far the most splendid Appearance; may be of present Use for the Auditory, will make up all the outward Repairs perfect; and become an Ornament to his Majesty's most excellent Reign, to the Church of *England*, and to this great City, which it is pity, in the Opinion of our *Neighbours*, should longer continue the most unadorn'd of her Bigness in the World.

In the mean Time, till a good Quantity of Stone be provided, Things of less Expence, but no less Consequence, ought to be regarded; such as fixing again all Cramps that the Roof hath been spoil'd of; covering all Timber from Weather; taking down the falling Roofs; searching the Vaults beneath, and securing them. And before the Foundations be digg'd for the *Dome*, the Arches on which the Tower stands must be secur'd after a peculiar Manner represented in the Designs.

P.S. I shall crave leave to subjoin, that if there be Use of *Stucco*, I have great Hopes, from some Experience already had, that there are *English* Materials to be brought by Sea at an easy Rate, that will afford as good Plaister as is any where to be found in the World; and that with the Mixture of cheaper Ingredients than Marble-meal, which was the old, and is now the modern Way of *Italy*.

The Proposer also, (considering that high Buildings grow more and more expensive as they rise, by reason of the Time and Labour spent in raising the Materials), takes this Occasion to acquaint your Lordships, that having had the Opportunity of seeing several Structures of greater Expence than this, while they were in raising, conducted by the best Artists, *Italian* and *French*; and having had daily Conference with them, and observing their Engines and Methods,[6] he hath promoted this *geometrical* Part of *Architecture* yet farther, and thinks the raising of Materials may yet be more facilitated, so as to save in lofty Fabricks, a very considerable Part of the Time, and Labourers Hire.

Report on Old St. Paul's after the Fire
(between 5 September 1666 and 26 February 1667)

Source
  Original manuscript in Wren's hand, Bodleian, Tanner 145, fol. 129–130v (transcript in *WS* 13:20–2).
Date
  Between 5 September 1666 and 26 February 1667
Editorial Note
  The first line of fol. 129 and all of fol. 130v are written in an unknown hand.

(fol. 129)
  Not long after the Fire: to be sure, before Feb. 26. 1666.[1]

FIGURE 16

Advise to the Reverend the Deane & Chapter of St. Pauls concerning the ruines of that Cathedrall.

What time & weather had left intire in the old, & art in the new repaired parts of this great pile of Pauls, the late Calamity of fire hath soe weakened & defaced, that it now appeares like some antique ruine of 2000 yeares standing, & to repaire it sufficiently will be like the mending of the Argo navis,[2] scarce any thing will at last be left of the old.

The first decayes of it were great,[3] from severall causes first from the originall building it selfe, for it was not well shaped & designed for the firme bearing of its one vault how massie soever the walls seemed to be (as I formerly shewed in another paper)[4] nor were the materialls good, for it seemed to have been built out of the stone of some other auncient ruines, the walls being of 2 severall sorts of freestone & those small, & the coare within was ragge-stone cast in rough with mortar & putty, which is not a durable way of building unlesse there had been that peculiar sort of banding <with> some thorowe-courses which is necessary in this kind[5] of filling worke, but was omitted in this fabrick. This accusation belonges cheifly to the west, north, & south partes, the Quire was of later & better worke, not inferiour to most Gothick Fabricks of that Age. The Tower though it had the effects of an ill manner of building & small stones & filling worke yet was it more carefully banded & cramped with much Iron. A second reason of the decayes, which[6] appeared before the last fire, was in probability

56

FIGURE 16. Old St. Paul's after the Fire toward the southwest, drawn by Thomas Wyck, c. 1672. Guildhall Library, Corporation of London.

the former fire which consumed the whole roofe in the raine of Queen Elizabeth.[7] The fall of timber then upon the vault was certainly one maine cause of the crackes which appeared in the vault & of the spreading out of the walls above 10 inches in some places from their trew perpendicular as it now appeares more manifestly. This giving out of the walls was endeavored to be corrected by the Artist of the last repaires,[8] who placed his new case of portland stone trewly perpendicular, & if he had proceeded with casing it within, the whole had been tollerably corrected, but now even this new worke is gon away from its perpendicular alsoe, by this second fall of the roofe in the last fire. This is most manifest in the Northwest Isle.

These 2d ruines are they that have put the restauration past remedy the effects of which I shall breifly enumerate.

First the portick is totally deprived of that excellent beauty & streangth, which time alone & weather could have noe more overthrown then the naturall rocks; soe great & good were the materialls

& soe skilfully were they layd after a trew Roman manner. But soe impatient is the portland stone of Fire, that many tunnes of stone are scaled off, & the Columnes flawed quite thorow.

(fol. 129v) Next the Southwest Corner one of the vast pillars of the Body of the church with all that it supported is fallen.

All along the Body of the Church the pillars are more given out then they were before the fire, & more flawed towards the botome by the burning of the goods below, & the timbers fallen from abov[e.][9]

This farther spreading of the pillars within hath alsoe carried out the walles of the Isles & reduced the circular ribs of the vaults of the Isles to be of a forme which to the eye appeares distorted & compressed, especially in the northwest Isle of the body of the church.

The Tower & the parts next about it have suffered the least, for there by reason that the walls lying in forme of a crosse give a firme <& immovable> butment each to other, they stand still in their position & support their vaults, which shewes manifestly that the fall of the Tim[ber] alone could not breake the vaults unlesse <where> the same concussion had force enough to make the walls alsoe give out.

And this is the reason of the great Desolation which appeares in the new Quire, for there the falling vaults in spite of all the <small> buttresses, have[10] broke them short or dislocated the stouter of them, & overthrowing the north wall & pillars & consequently the vaults of the northeast Isle[11] have[12] broken open the vaults of St. Faithes,[13] (though those wer[e] of very great streanth) but irresistable is the force of soe many thousand Tunnes augmented by the highth of the fall.

Having shewn in part the deplorable condition of our patient wee are to consult of the Cure if possibly art may effect it, & heerin wee must imitate the Physician who when he finds a totall decay of Nature bends his skill to a palliation, to give respite for a better settlement of the estate of the patient. The Question is then where bes[t] to begin this kind of practice, that is to make a Quire for present use.

It will worst of all be effected in the new Quire. For there the walls <& pillars> being fallen[14] it will cost a Large summe to restore <them> to their former highth & before this can be effected the very substruction & repaire of St. Faithes will cost soe much, that I shall but fright this age with the computation of that which is to be don in the darke before any thing will appeare for the use desired.

The old Quire seemes to some a convenient place & that which

58

will be most easily effected, because the vault there lookes firme or easily reparable as far as to the place where was once the <old> pulpit. But this designe will not be without very materiall objections. First the place is very short and litle between the stone skreen & the breach, & only capable of a litle quire, not of an auditory: & if the auditory be made without yet <2dly> all the adjacent places are under the ruines of a falling Tower, whi[ch] every day throwes off smaller scales, & in frost will yield such showe[rs] of the outside stones (if noe greater parts come down with tempests) tha[t] the new roofes (yet to be made) will be brouken up, if noe farther mischeifes ensue. 3dly You are to make such a dismall procession through *(fol. 130)* ruines to come thither, that the very passage will be a pennance. 4thly This cannot be effected without considerable expence of making 4 partition walls to the Top to sever this part on every side from the ruines, & covering with Timber & Lead these 4 <short> parts of the Crosse <next the Tower> & covering the Tower alsoe: that is, if you make roome for the auditory as well as the Quire, the Quire it selfe being very litle.

These waies being found inconvenient & expencefull either of taking out a part where the new Quire was, or where the old quire is, with the parts west north & south next the Tower as farr as the vaults stand; it remaines that wee seeke it in the Body of the Church, & this is that which I should humbly advise as the properest & cheapest way of making a sufficient Quire & auditory, after this manner.

I would take the lesser north & south dores for the entrances & leaving 2 Intercolumnations eastward & 3 or 4 westward I would there make partition walls of the fallen stone upon the place, the east part above the dores may be contrived into a Quire the west into the Auditory. I would lay a Timber roofe as lowe as the bottomes of the upper windowes with a flat fretted ceeling, the lead[15] saved out of the burning will more then cover it: of iron & of pavement there is enough for all uses. The roofe lying low will not appear above the walls, & since wee cannot mend this great Ruine wee will not disfigure it, but that it shall still have its full motives[16] to worke if possible upon this or the next ages: & yet within it shall have all convenience & light (by turning the 2d story[17] of Arches into windowes) & a[18] beauty[19] durable to the next <2> centuries[20] of Yeares: & yet prove soe cheape that between 3 & 4000 £ shall effect it all in one summer.

And having with this Ease obtained a present[21] Cathedrall, there will be time to consider of a more durable & noble Fabrick to be made in the place of the Tower & easterne parts of the Church, when the minds of men now contracted to many objects of necessary charge, shall by Gods blessings be more widened after an happy restauration both of the buildings & wealth of the City & nation. In the meane <while> to derive if not a streame yet some litle drills of Charity this way, or at least to preserve that already obtained from being diverted, it may not prove ill advise to seeme to begin somthing of this new fabrick. But I confesse this cannot well be put in execution without taking down all that part of the ruines, which whither it be yet seasonable to doe wee must leave to our superiors.

(fol. 130v)

Dr Wrens Advice, Jan after the fire

A Report touching the Decaies of the Walls, & peers on the North & S. Isles at the W. End of the Cathedral of S. Paul's London.

We find the Walls to be of a sufficient strength to sustain the Weight of the Roof intended to be lay'd thereon. But the 2 Pillars on the Southside next to that, which is fallen down, are so much decayed, and perished by the Fire, that it is necessary to new case them; & so to rebuild the pillar, which is fallen down, which will be a great Strength, & Support to all the whole Isle on the Southside of the Church.

Febr. 26. 1666.[22]

John Davenport
John Young
Josuah Marshall
Richard Rider[23]

Report on Salisbury Cathedral for Dr. Seth Ward, Bishop (31 August 1668)

Source
   Original manuscript in Wren's hand in Salisbury Cathedral
   Library MS 192, fols. 1–10v (transcript in *WS*, 11:21–6)
Other Manuscript Versions
   RS MS 249, fols. 409v–12
   AS MS 313, fols. 558–63
Other Printed Versions
   "An Architectonical Account of the Cathedral Church of
   Salisbury" in Richard Rawlinson, *The History and Antiquities of
   the Cathedral Church of Salisbury, and the Abbey Church of Bath*
   (London, 1723), 1–21. [London: E. Curll, 1719?]
   Partially reprinted in *Parentalia* (London, 1750), "The Life of
   Sir Christopher Wren, Knt.," pt. 2, sec. 8, 304–6
   Partially reprinted in Francis Price, *A Series of particular and
   useful Observations, made with great Diligence and Care, upon that
   Admirable Structure, the Cathedral-Church of Salisbury* (London:
   Ackers, 1753), 16–18
Date
   31 August 1668
Editorial Note
   The lines on fol. 1 are written in two different unknown
   hands. The text centered on fol. 2 is in a third hand; the en-
   suing text referring again to Dodsworth, as well as the dates
   below, match the second hand. The text on fol. 10v is in yet
   a fourth unknown hand.

(fol. 1)
   Sir C. Wren's Report

This was given me by Mr. Dodsworth[1] – some months before I was chosen Clerk of the Works to the Cathedral.

(fol. 2)
   The State of the Cathedral Church
   of St. Mary Sarum represented,
   & the particular Defects enumerated
   by the most ingenious & worthy
   Dr. Christopher Wren
   August 31. *1668*

Since, His Majesties Surveyor Generall

This survey was given to me by Mr. William Dodsworth

T. A.

1834
1668
166²

(fol. 3)
1668.

The Cathedral Church of Salisburie seeming to threaten no inconsiderable decayes, it is desired that the State of it be fully represented, & the particular defects enumerated, that so proper remedies may be applyed to restore it, where age, injuries of weather or the neglect of it in times of trouble, have occasioned weaknesse, & tendency, towards Ruine.

The whole Pile is large & magnificent, and may be justly accounted one of the best patternes of Architecture in that age wherein it was built.[3] The Figure of it is a Crosse upon the intersection of which standes a Tower & Steeple of Stone, as high from the Foundation as the whole length of the Navis or body of ye Church, & it is founded only upon the four pillars & Arches of the intersection: between the Steeple & the East end is an other crossing of the Navis which on the West side only wants its Iles, all other Sides of the maine body & the Crosses are[4] supported on Pillars with Iles annexed and Buttresses with out the Iles, from whence arise bowes or flying Buttresses to the walls of the Navis, which are concealed within the Timber roofe of the Iles. The Roofe is almost as sharpe as an equilaterall Triangle, made of small timber after the aunciert manner without Principall rafters, but the wall plates are double and tied together with couples of above 40 foot long. The whole Church is vaulted with Chaulke, between Arches and Crosse Springers only, after the auncienter manner without Orbes & Tracery, excepting under the Tower, where the Springers divide and represent a wider sort of Tracery: and this appeares to me to have been a later worke & to be done by some other hand, then that of the first Architect[5] whose judgmen[t][6] *(fol. 3v)* I must justly commend for many things, beyond what I find in divers Gothick Fabricks of later date, which though more elaborated with nice and small workes, yet[7] want the naturall beauty which arises from proportion of the first dimensions: For here the breadth to

FIGURES 17–22

62

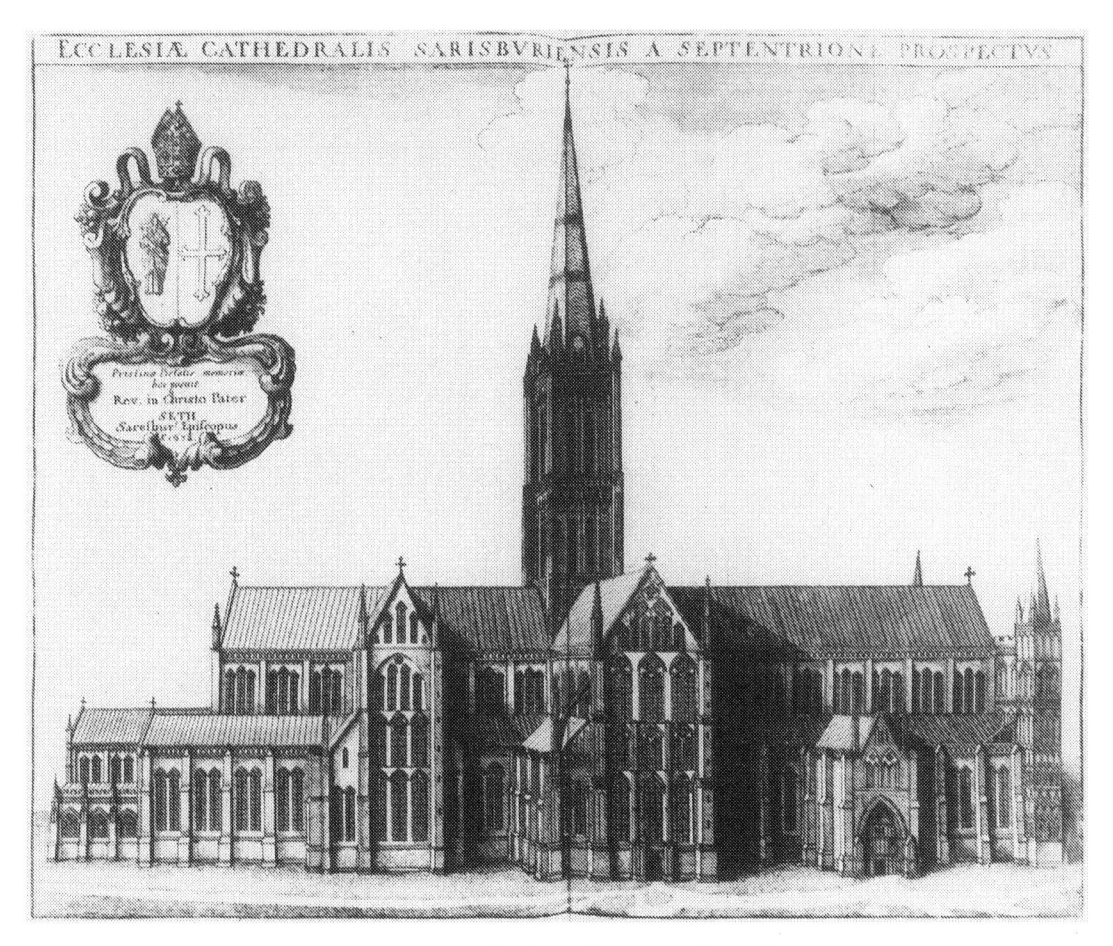

FIGURE 17. Salisbury Cathedral from the north, drawn by Wenceslas Hollar, 1673 (William Dugdale, *Monasticon Anglicanum* [1673], vol. 3, after p. 374). Photo Courtesy of The Newberry Library.

the highth of the Navis, and both to the shape of the Iles beare a good proportion. The pillars and the intercolumnations (or spaces between pillar & pilla[r])[8] are well suited to the highth of the arches, the Mouldings are decently mixed with large planes, without an affectation of filling every corner with ornaments, which (unlesse they are admirably good) glut the eye, as much as in Musick too much division cloyes the eare: The Windowes are not made too great, nor yet the light obstructed with many mullions, & transomes of Tracery-worke which was the ill fashion of the next following Age: our Artist knew better that nothing could adde beauty to light, he trusted in a stately and rich Plainenesse that his marble shafts gave to his worke. I cannot call them Pillars because they are so

FIGURE 18. Salisbury Cathedral, "Part of the Plan and a Perspective View, ... Taken from the North East," drawn by Francis Price, 1753 (Francis Price, *A Series of particular and useful Observations ... upon that Admirable Structure, the Cathedral-Church of Salisbury* [London: Ackers, 1753], pl. 1). University of Illinois Library at Urbana-Champaign, Ricker Library of Architecture and Art.

long <& slender> and generally beare nothing, but are only added for ornament to the outside of the great pillars, & decently fastned with brasse.

Notwithstanding this commendation of our Architect there are some originall errours which I must lay to his charge, the discovery of which will give us light to the cause[s] of the present decayes.

First I must accuse him that building in a low & marshy soyle he did not take sufficient care of the foundation especially under the Pillars that foundation which will beare a [w]all[9] will not beare a pillar for Pillars thrust themselves *(fol. 4)* into the earth and force open the solid Ground if the foundation under them be not broad, and if it be not hard stone, it will be ground & crushed, as things are bruised in a mortar, if the weight be great.

A 2d Fault was the not raising the floor of the Church above

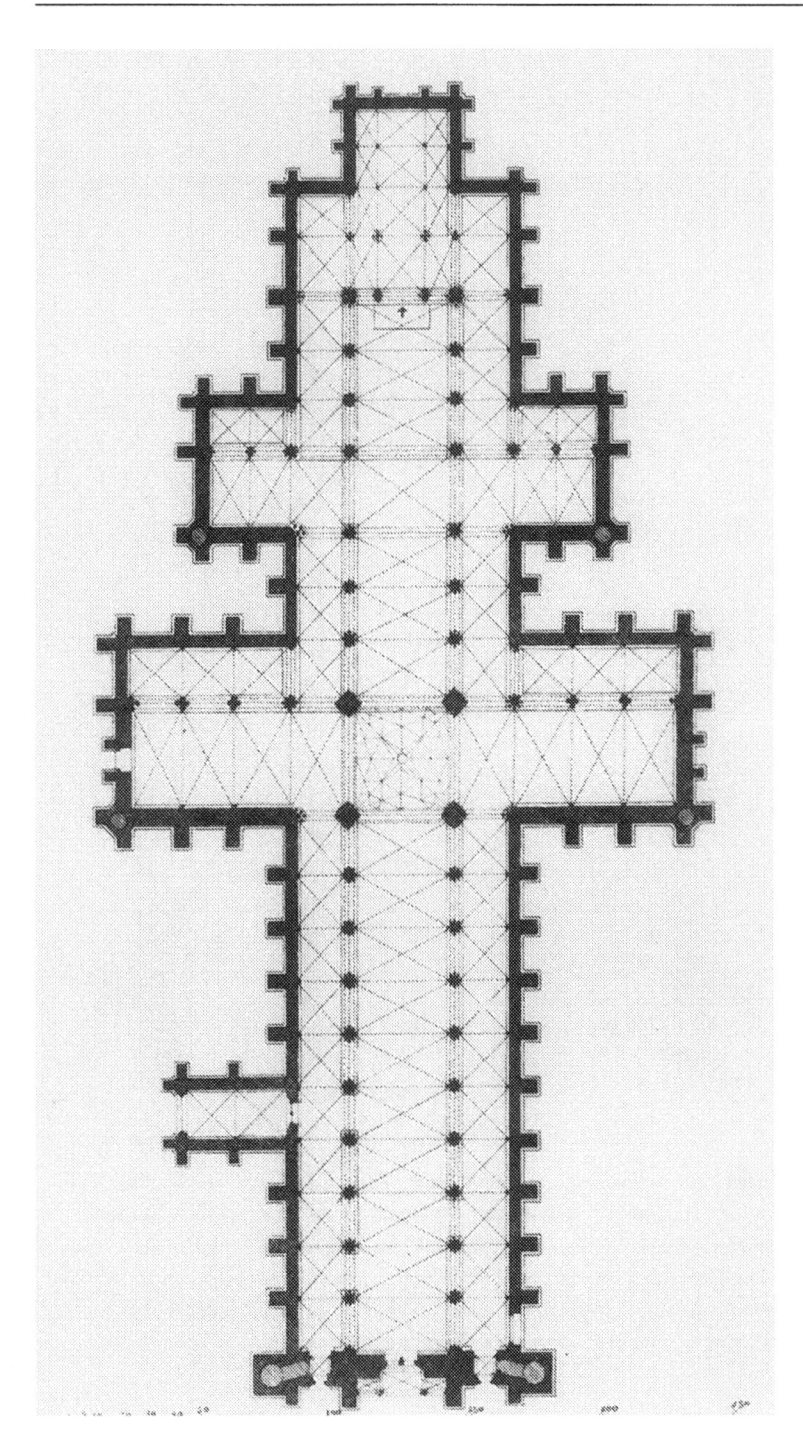

FIGURE 19. Salisbury Cathedral, "A Geometrical Plan," drawn by Francis Price, 1753 (Francis Price, *A Series of particular and useful Observations . . . upon that Admirable Structure, the Cathedral-Church of Salisbury* [London: Ackers, 1753], pl. 2). University of Illinois Library at Urbana-Champaign, Ricker Library of Architecture and Art.

FIGURE 20. Salisbury Cathedral, "Part of the Plan, with the Section of the Body of the Church; shewing it's Mechanism, and part of the Vaulting," drawn by Francis Price, 1753 (Francis Price, *A Series of particular and useful Observations . . . upon that Admirable Structure, the Cathedral-Church of Salisbury* [London: Ackers, 1753], pl. 3). University of Illinois Library at Urbana-Champaign, Ricker Library of Architecture and Art.

the feare of inundations, many sufficient foundations have failed after the Earth hath been too much drenched with unusuall floods besides it is unhandsome to descend into a place.

The Third Fault is in the Poyse of the building: generally the substructions are too slender for the weights above. The Pillars appear small enough and yet they shew much greater then they are, for the Shafts of Marble that encompasse them seem to fill out the Pillar to a proportionable bulke, but indeed they beare little or nothing, & some of those that are pressed breake & splitt; if these ornaments should be taken off, the pillar would then appear extreamely too little for its burthen; but this is no where so enormous as under the Steeple, which being 400 foot in height, is borne by 4 pillars, not much[10] larger then the Pillars of the Iles, & therefore out of feare to overburthen them the Inside of the tower for 40 foot heighth above the Navis is made with[11] a slender hollow worke of Pillars and Arches, nor hath it any buttresses, and the spire it selfe is but 7 inches thick, though the heighth be above 150 foot. This worke of Pillars and arches within the Tower makes me believe that the Architect laid his first floor of Timber 40 foot higher then the Vault beneath (which as I sayd was since added) and without doubt intended a belfery above (as appeares by places left in the walls for Timbers and the fastning[12] of the frames for the bells) and so would have concluded with the Tower only without a Spire. And if this addition of the Spire *(fol. 4v)* were a second thought, the Artist is more excusable for having omitted buttresses to the tower, & his ingenuity commendable for supplying this defect by bracing the walls together with many large bandes of Iron within and without, keyed together with much industry & exactnesse, & besides those that appeare I have[13] reason to beleeve that there are divers other braces concealed within the thicknesse of the walls. And these are so essentiall to the Standing of the worke, that if they were dissolved the Spire would spread open the walls of the tower, nor could it stand one minute. But this way of tying walls together with Iron, instead of making them of that substance and forme, that they shall naturally poyse themselves upon their butment is against the Rules of good Architecture, not only because Iron is corruptible by rust, but because it is fallacious, having unequall veines in the metall some peeces of the same barr being 3 times stronger then others & yet all sound to appearance.[14] I shall not impute to our Artist those errours which were the generall mistakes of builders in that age, yet it will not be amisse to insist a little upon those which seeme to concerne us, & to occasion some of the infirmities[15] in our building.

Almost all the Cathedralls of the Gothick Forme are weak and defective in the poyse of the vault of the Iles;[16] as for the vaults of the Navis they are on both sides equally supported & propped up from spreading by the bowes <or>[17] flying buttresses which rise from the outward walls of the Iles; but for the vaults of the Iles they are indeed supported on the outside by the buttresses, but inwardly they have no other stay but the pillars themselves which (as they are usually proportioned) if they stood alone without the weight above, could not resist the spreading of the Iles one minute; trew indeed the great load above of the walls *(fol. 5)* & Vaults of the Navis should seem so to confirme the Pillars in their perpendicular station, that there should be no need of butment inward, but experience hath shewn the contrary, & there is scarce any Gothick Cathedrall, that I have seen at home or abroad,[18] wherein I have not observed the Pillars to yield, and bend inward from the weight of the Vault of the Ile; but this defect is most conspicuous upon the angular pillars of the Crosse, for there not only the Vault wants butment, but also the angular arches that rest upon that pillar and therefore both conspire to thrust it inward toward the Center of the Crosse and this is very apparent in the fabrick wee treat of. For this reason this forme for Churches hath been rejected, by Moderne Architects abroad, who use the better & Roma[n][19] Forme of Architecture.[20]

Having thus in generall discoursed of the first defects[21] arising from want of trew judgement in the Artist, to enforme us the better of the causes of the present decayes, it will be more to our purpose (because fundamentall errours are incorrigible) to reckon what faults upon a cursory surveigh I have found necessary to be amended, and restored where possible or at least to be palliated and kept from farther[22] declension, and together with the diseases I shall suggest the Cures.

1. The Faults of the Tower and Steeple deserve the first consideration because it cannot ruine alone without drawing with it the roofe and vaults of the Church.

It stands (as I sayd) upon 4 Pillars like a Table upon its 4 leggs. 2 of these towards the west are sunke but not equally that to the South-west is sunke 7 or 8 inches that to the North-west <halfe so much> this hath occasioned the *(fol. 5v)* leaning of the Tower & Spire toward the South west. Where the walls of the Tower where plaine within, wee plumbed it to see the declension of it. The plummett was applyed from the Top of the Tower within (that is from the floor where the Spire begins) to the second floore belowe, (which is somthing above the Ridge of the Church) the distance between these Floors & consequently the length of the

68

plumb-line was 78 foot. By this tryall at such a distance wee found the west wall to leane to the west 3 inches & ½; and the East wall to follow it, to the west 3 inches ¼; but the South wall declined to the South 5 inches & ½; the North seemed to follow it, but wee could not plumbe it being hindered by Timber there. From this experiment of Part wee may conclude how much the Variation from the perpendicular will amount to in the whole; for if 78 foot or (to use a round number) if 80 foot give 5 inches & ½ the whole heighth 400 foot will give 27 inches ½, and so much it declines to the South: againe if 80 foot give 3 inches ½, 400 will give 17 ½, and so much it declines to the west. I cannot say that this tryall will conclude to an inch, but it is sufficient to shew that it declines considerably to the S. W. from the great settlement of that pillar. I could wish that an exact triall were made (by mooving away some timbers within) of plumbing it from the Top to the floor of the Church, & that this tryall were often repeated at some distance of time to see if it continue to decline; for if it stand at a stay there is yet no great fear of danger in my Opinion, considering how well the walls are braced together, but if it proceed in its motion considerably, it will be then high time to seek for *(fol. 6)* remedie: for by reason of the thinnesse of the Spire in proportion to its highth, I dare not be assured it will stand so long as to decline so much more as it hath gone already. Therefore for some yeares it should be often plumbed and a Register kept; if the foundation settle no farther (as possibly it will not) it is undoubtedly secure enough. But if it moove the remedy will be to build up 8 bowes from the walls of the Navis, it is I confesse a chargable[23] but I fear the only cure, for when so great a pyle is once overpoysed, all Bandage of Iron will be but as Pack thread. There is an easier way which I could suggest, if the foundation be what I expect it, but because there is at present no need, & I hope never shall bee I forebeare & proceed to consider some lesser defects of the Steeple, & such as are more managable, & very necessary to be done out of hand.

2. One of the 4 Pinnacles which are built upon the 4 Arches at the Coines where the Spire begins to rise, a little above that part usually called the 8 dores hath been shaken by some storme of Lightning, & also the wall of the Spire which adheres to it, and there is a little passage dore from the inside of the Spire into this Pinnacle, one of the Jambes of which dore is broken and fallen away, and this hath occasioned divers long[24] craks in the wall of the Spire above it, all which happening upon the declining side doe much weaken the Spire, and therefore call for speedy amendment, and first the broken Jamb must be restored because it beares much weight which may be don after this manner. The little dore

FIGURES 21–22

FIGURE 21. Salisbury Cathedral, "A Section of the Church, with the Tower and Spire: Shewing the Critical Mechanism of the whole Structure," drawn by Francis Price, 1753 (Francis Price, *A Series of particular and useful Observations . . . upon that Admirable Structure, the Cathedral-Church of Salisbury* [London: Ackers, 1753], pl. 6). University of Illinois Library at Urbana-Champaign, Ricker Library of Architecture and Art.

FIGURE 22. Salisbury Cathedral, "A Plan and part of the section of the Tower, shewing the form of the Iron Bandage," drawn by Francis Price, 1753 (Francis Price, *A Series of particular and useful Observations . . . upon that Admirable Structure, the Cathedral-Church of Salisbury* [London: Ackers, 1753], pl. 7). University of Illinois Library at Urbana-Champaign, Ricker Library of Architecture and Art.

must be centred up not with Timber but with hard Stone set dry and well wedged up to the dore head with Tiles & Oystershells, that done, the broken Jamb (which was before of too small stones) may be taken away, and a Jamb of new and larger stone, may be fitted in and wedged with shells, & runned *(fol. 6v)* with putty, & when it is well fixed the Centering may be taken away: In like manner all the Cracks & Flawes above the Dore, and in the Pinnacle, & in other places of the Spire must be serv'd. For it signifies but little to point it only, unlesse there be an uniting & knitting[25] again of the parts together, which is done by wedging all close, & experience hath shewn there is nothing properer for this then thin Flints, or which is better the upper Oystershell which is commonly thin and Flatt. I have once caused to be used another thing with good successe. A large Vault which was ready to drop through default of butment, (after the butment was secured) I caused to be wedged up in all the Cracks & joynts with little Cedar pinnes as big as Tyle pinnes, and some lesse & afterwards pointed the Cracks, & runne them with Putty, which done the whole Vault which was loose before sounded like a bell. I chose Cedar because it is hard & incorruptible, nor is it deare for a little will make many pinnes, it may be old Sugar Chests which is a kind of Cypresse in the Barbadoes would doe as well, but whatsoever materiall you use, wedging is the thing which will unite all: and then if the Cracks be pointed & well searched with Putty by a man that will make conscience to doe it diligently, the wall will be rendred as firme as the builder left it. Note the wedges must not be forced but just fixed in.

 3. There are other decayes in the Spire, and the higher you goe the more, some of which are the effects of the sinking & declining of the whole from the foundation, others are the effects of tempests that have shaken it, especially those which are toward the top are of this nature. From both causes many stones chiefly those which be out of their bed are frushed[26] (as the Masons say) that is riven & flawed with downward Cracks in the thicknesse of the Stone, where divers stones neer together are thus bruised, the wall is *(fol. 7)* rendered very weake. And I should advise that heer & there in such places[27] a new stone were put in & well wedged, and run with puttie, having first well wedged the upright joynts, of the Courses above the Stone that is to be taken out: this may be don with very good successe by a skillful setter, who is not rash, & considers well how the courses lie above his worke. The wall of the Spire being Perpin[dicular].[28]

 4. Besides the declining of the Spire from the foundation, it is also bended a little towards the Top from its right line, whether

FIGURE 23. Salisbury Cathedral, Wren's drawing showing a detail of how to join iron pieces, 1668 (Salisbury Cathedral MS 192, fol. 7). By kind permission of the Dean and Chapter of Salisbury.

this proceeds from the sinking below (the point of the Spire being once carried off from its perpendicular) or whither it hath been since bowed by some tempest, or whither some violent tempest might not at once bend the top, and with the same concussion force downe the pillars and foundation on that side (which is reasonable enough to believe because the Steeple being in height 9 times the breadth of its Basis at the foundation, any force above would be multiplied as in a leaver and be 9 times as much upon the Pillars) I say which soever of these were the cause twill be hard to determine; it will be enough to advise the speedy cure, and because the Artist at first hath much trusted to Iron I should advise that this be likewise secured by Iron. The place of bending is about the upper Circle <or below it> there let a Curbe of Iron made of 8 peeces be fixed cleane round on the out side, and joynted at the corners after this manner and in the middle of every side let there be an hole, then let 8 upright barres of 12 or 15 foot long with 3 holes in each barre (viz. at the ends and in the middle) be fixed to the middle of each inside wall, soe that the middle hole of the barrs within may be keyed to the middle hole of the[29] barres without *(fol. 7v)* and likewise let both the upper & nether ends of the inward barres be anchored through the walls. The inward barres may be about 3 inches broad & ¾ thick. The outward barres 1 ¾ square. The pinne at the corners made wedgewise to draw the

FIGURE 23

barres together better than 2 inches broad at the top & ½ thick. Note these Irons will be best wrought at some port towne where they worke Anchors and other large worke for shipps, for I have found by experience that large worke cannot be wrought sound with litle fires and small bellowes. They will be cheapest wrought at the Iron Mills, but their fires leave the Iron brittle till it be forged againe. If this way of bandage were used in more places then towards the Top, it would prove a great security to the Spire, but I shall not insist upon more expence then necessary, and I thinke it necessary to be done towards the Top. I cannot but take notice that in my going up into the Spire I found much small Iron worke of Crampes of 8 or 10 inches long, laid out to little purpose. When a Crack is as it were sticked together with small Crampes, it leaves 3 rents for one for single stones are but torne with the Crampes when the weight streines them, but large bandages of Iron hoope in all together. It were well if the timber worke within the Spire & Tower were well repaired, for if any Timbers should fall (and some of them hang untowardly) it would give a shake to the whole Fabrick. And if the ascent to the Spire were made easy & secure, faults would sooner be espied & amended; but this may be done at leisure. I shall more urge the necessary things, & descend to the roofe of the Church.

5. The Roofe (as I said before) is made after the old way of Rafteringwithout Principalls, which though it be light yet hath it 2 great faults, that the beames instead of being tucked up to the roofe, are forced to helpe support ye roofe, and therefore often bend or breake, & a worse fault is, that it is apt to runne an end, that is, all ye rafters from one end to another to set, & decline *(fol. 8)* one way, which is a terrible mischiefe, & troublesome to prevent if it be far gone. Both these errours have had their effects, in the Roofe, besides what time, weather, & ill workemen have done. I shall reckon the principall I observed.

6. Above one halfe of the roofe of the west body sets away to the west & hath driven out the end wall of the west front. The way to cure at once the roofe & the wall will be this. Under the braces fasten 2 peeces of streight small Timber that may reach from the wall to the 8th or 10th rafter then from the set-off of the wall at the very Coines bring up 2 shores of streight stiff timber both mortised & toothed into the first Timbers, to which Timbers the braces of the 10 rafters must be pinned down, and lastly they must be anchored through the wall. This will hold the Rafters from running an end & the wall both.

ABC the end wall.

AC the Setoff at the Coines.

FIGURE 24

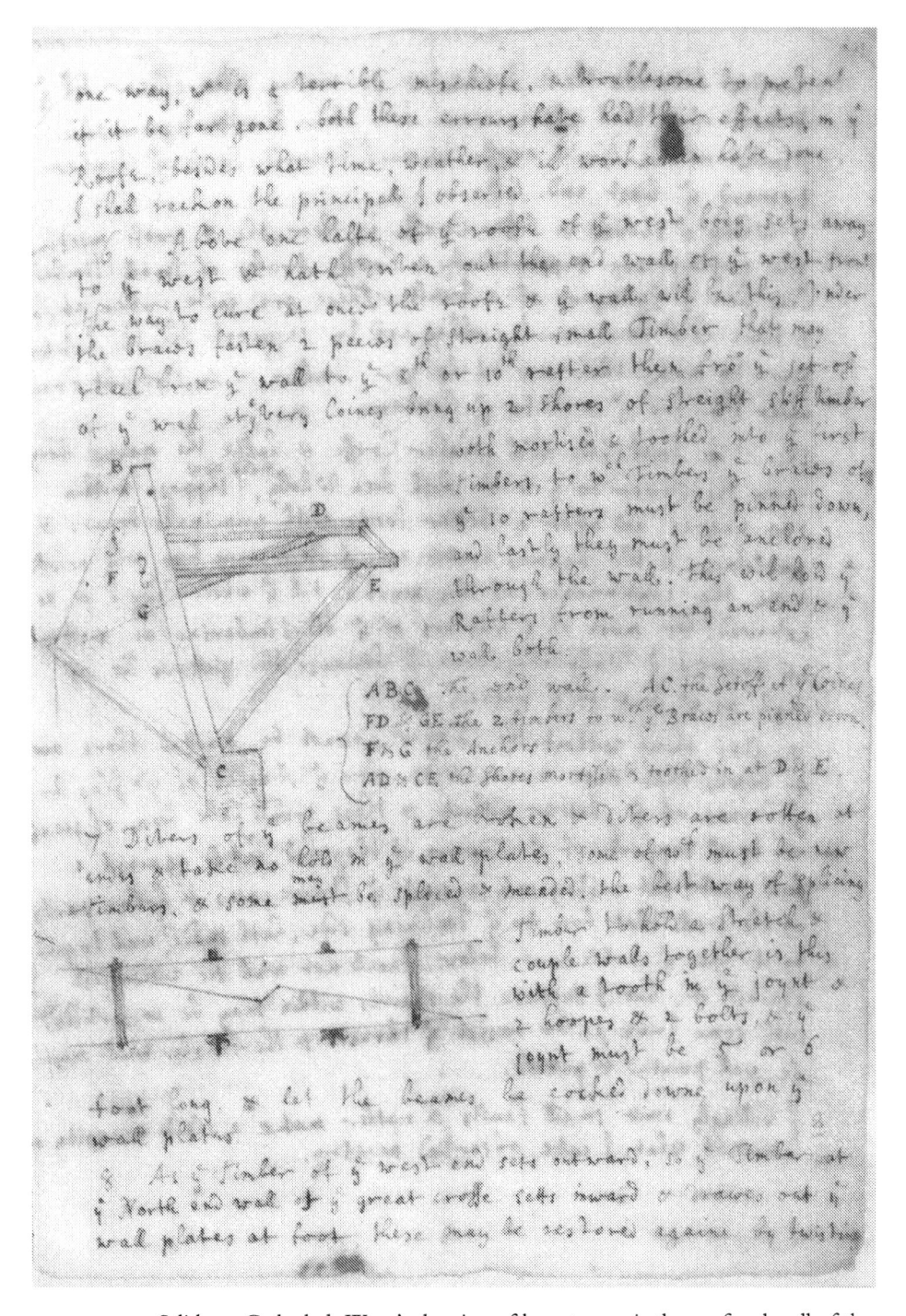

FIGURE 24. Salisbury Cathedral, Wren's drawing of how to repair the roof and wall of the west end and a detail of how to splice timber, 1668 (Salisbury Cathedral MS 192, fol. 8r). By kind permission of the Dean and Chapter of Salisbury.

FIGURE 24

FD & GE the 2 Timbers to which the Braces are pinned down.
F & G the Anchors.
AD & CE the Shores mortised & toothed in at D & E.

7. Divers of the beames are broken & divers are rotten at endes & take no hold in the wall plates, some of which must be new Timbers, & some <may>[30] be spliced & mended. The best way of splicing Timber to hold a Stretch & couple walls together is this with a tooth in the joynt & 2 hoopes & 2 bolts, & the joynt must be 5 or 6 foot long, & let the beames be cocked downe upon the wall plates.

8. As the Timber of the west end sets outward, so the Timber at the North end wall of the great crosse setts inward & drawes out the wall plates at foot, these may be restored againe by twisting *(fol. 8v)* Cordes between the 2 beames, & so winding them closer till the tenons of the Wall plates come into their Mortises againe. The timber of this North Crosse is much decayed, so is the Timber toward the East end.

9. Where the second & lesser Crosse is there, the 2 roofs meeting the rafters are supported by 2 Crosse Arches of small timber laid like the Springers of a Vault. These are quite rotten at foot & there hath been much cobling used to support them, the best way were to make them new of larger Timber, & 4 streight braces under them from the wall to the Center.

10. The South Ende of the greater Crosse & halfe the maine body from the Tower to the west hath been wholly <made new> I suppose within 100 yeares, and after a better forme, with principalls braces & purloines, & the beames tuckt up. A little more time will necessitate the continuance of this worke till the whole Church be so covered; for most of the rafters of the old Timbering are rotten at foot & the Wallplates decayed because the gutters lie as high as the feet of the rafters.

11. One thing without the Tower cannot be omitted there are 4 bowes that rise arace-wise,[31] from the Angles of the Iles to the Coines of the Tower without, & these would have been of great use to the support of the Tower if they had butted against a solid part, but resting only against the Stairecases & hollow parts of the wall that bow to the declining side, hath made <the> wall to yeeld to it upon the settlement below. I could not well see within just against it, but I suppose the staires within may be so fortified with some Iron, as to resist the thrust & the frushed wall must be well pointed & puttied.

I willingly omitt small faults, & rather make a short recapitulation of what I have observed necessary.

(fol. 9)

In the Steeple

The bracing the Spire towards the Top with Iron.

The putting in of some new stone heer & there where it is much frushed.

The mending of the shaken pinnacle and the Jamb of the dore into it.

The Wedging pointing & puttying of the Cracks & open Joynts.

The mending of the Timbers within the Tower & Steeple.

The frequent plumbing it exactly to see if it decline farther.

In the Roofe

The Shores to stay the wall & roofe at the West End.

The Splicing mending & putting in new beames where necessary.

The putting in new timber Arches at the Easterne Crosse of the Roof.

The continuance of the new roofing by parts.

Without

The mending the South west Bow. I shall adde

The looking to the Gutters and the wedging & pointing the feet of the Buttresses where needfull.

Many things I beleeve may have escaped my eye in a few howres inspection: soe large a pile of so great age would require a more exact surveigh, & yet I thinke I have taken <in> the most necessary things, in which all delay will prove ver[y][32] ill husbandrie, & the most clamorous decayes I have marked with an Asteriske.[33]

The other buildings adjoyning as the Chapter-house & Cloyster are worth the preserving.

(fol. 9v) The Chapterhouse is an Octagone or 8 sided Figure with a pillar in the Center: it wants butment & therefore the Vault is secured by 8 Irons that tie the Center to the walls; they are fastened like curtaine rods upon hookes; the hookes are yeoted[34] into the walls with lead, but the force of the Vault hath broken the Stones into which they are yeoted, & drawn out 5 of the 8, by which meanes the walls and Vaults are spread, & cleft with many great cracks. It seems the hookes were too short & they should have been Yeoted into hardstone not Freestone; the remedy will be to take out those Hooks & to bore cleane through the Coines,

& to put in hookes with long stemms, & anchor them on the outsides & this can never faile.

The Cloyster was made at first very slight & weake for the breadth, the butment is much too litle. The sure remedy will be to tye the walls together above the Vault with the beames anchored through the walls, & to adde about 2 foot ½ to the bottome of the buttresses, & to carry this addition to the buttresse about 4 foot high and this will repaire it firmely, many of the litle pillars may be contrived to be spared to mend the rest, & yet leave the Cloyster more handsome & open then before.

(fol. 10v)

> Dr Christofer Wren his
> Stating of the Condition of
> the Cathedral Church of Sarum
> propriâ manu.[35]

Report on Westminster Abbey to Francis Atterbury, Dean (1713)[1]

Source
  Original manuscript missing. *Parentalia* (London, 1750), "The Life of Sir Christopher Wren, Knt.," pt. 2, sec. 7, 295–302 (transcript in *WS*, 11:15–20)

Other Manuscript Versions
  RS MS 249, fols. 339–409, with a few differing words and with a diagram of the section through the aisle
  AS MS 313, fols. 534–54
  Westminster Abbey 66895*, "Sr Chr Wren's Acct of ye repairs of Westminster Abbey," in the hand of W. Gayfere, "An Historicall and Architectonicall Account of the Collegiate Church of St. Peter in Westminster, & of the Repairs thereof. In a Letter from Sr Chrisr Wren to the Ld Bishop of Rochester (Bp Atterbury)." It bears the note "Manuscript in the hand of W. Gayfere, many years mason employed on the repairs of the Abbey." This is possibly Thomas Gayfere senior (c. 1721–1812) or junior (1755–1827), both master masons at Westminster Abbey.[2] The text consistently uses words and phrases that differ from the text in *Parentalia*, but are similar in meaning. It includes a sketch of the aisle section on fol. 18.

Date
  1713[3]

(page 295)
When I had the Honour to attend your Lordship to congratulate your Episcopal Dignity, and pay that Respect which particularly concerned myself as employed in the chief Direction of the Works and Repairs of the Collegiate[4]-church of St. *Peter* in *Westminster*; you was pleased to give me this seasonable Admonition, that I should consider my advanced Age; and as I had already made fair Steps in the Reparation of that ancient and ruinous Structure, you thought it very requisite for the publick Service, I should leave a Memorial of what I had done; and what my Thoughts were for carrying on the Works for the future.

(page 296) In order to describe what I have already done, I should first give a State of the Fabrick as I found it; which being the Work of 500 Years, or more, through several Ages and Kings Reigns, it will come in my Way to consider the Modes of Building

FIGURES 25–26

FIGURE 25. Westminster Abbey, view of west facade, drawn by Wenceslas Hollar, 1655. By courtesy of the Dean and Chapter of Westminster.

in those Times, and what Light Records may afford us; such as at present I am able to collect, give me leave to discourse a little upon.

That a Temple of *Apollo* was here in *Thorny island* (the Place anciently so called, where the Church now stands) and ruined by an Earthquake in the Reign of the Emperor *Antoninus Pius*,[5] I cannot readily agree. The *Romans* did not use, even in their Colonies, to build so slightly; the Ruins of ancienter Times shew their Works to this Day; the least Fragment of Cornice, or Capital, would demonstrate their Handy-work. Earthquakes break not Stones to Pieces,

FIGURE 26. Westminster Abbey, view of north side, drawn by Wenceslas Hollar, 1654. By courtesy of the Dean and Chapter of Westminster.

nor would the *Picts*[6] be at that Pains: but I imagine the Monks finding the *Londoners* pretending to a *Temple of Diana*, where now St. *Paul*'s stands;[7] (Horn of Stags, Tusks of Boars, &c. having been dug up there in former times, and it is said also, in later Years) would not be behind Hand in Antiquity: but I must assert, that having changed all the Foundations of Old *Paul*'s, and upon that Occasion rummaged all the Ground thereabouts, and being very desirous to find some Footsteps of such a Temple, I could not discover any, and therefore can give no more Credit to *Diana* than to *Apollo*.

To pass over the fabulous Account, that King *Lucius*[8] first founded a little Church here, A.D. 170, out of the Ruins of the Temple of *Apollo*, destroyed by an Earthquake a little before: but it is recorded with better Authority,[9] that *Sebert*, King of the *East-Saxons*,[10] built a Monastery and Church here in 605, which being destroyed by the *Danes*, was about 360 Years after repaired by the pious King Edgar.[11] This, it is probable, was a strong good Building, after the Mode of that Age, not much altered from the *Roman*. We have some Examples of this ancient *Saxon* Manner,[12] which was with Peers or round Pillars, much stronger than *Tuscan*, round headed Arches, and Windows; such was *Winchester* Cathedral of old;[13] and such at this Day the Royal Chapel in the *White-tower* of

London;[14] the Chapel of *St. Crosses*;[15] the Chapel of *Christ-church* in Oxford,[16] formerly an old Monastery; and divers others I need not name, built before the *Conquest*; and such was the old Part of St. *Paul*'s built in King *Rufus*'s[17] Time.

King *Edward the Confessor*[18] repaired, if not wholy rebuilt this Abbey-church of King *Edgar*,[19] of which a Description was published by Mr. *Camden* in 1606,[20] from an ancient Manuscript, in these Words: *Principalis area domûs, altissimis erecta fornicibus quadrato opere, parique commissura circumvolvitur; ambitus autem ipsius ædis duplici lapidum arcu ex utroque latere hinc inde fortiter solidata operis compage clauditur. Porrò crux templi quæ medium canentium domino chorum ambiret, & sui gemina hinc inde sustentatione mediae turris celsum apicem fulciret, humili primùm & robusto fornice simpliciter surgit; deinde cochleis multipliciter ex arte ascendentibus plurimis intumescit; deinceps vero simplici muro usque ad tectum ligneum plumbo diligenter vestitum pervenit.*

The Sense of which I translate into Language proper to Builders, as I can understand it.

"The principal Aile or Nave of the Church being raised high, and vaulted with square and uniform Ribs, is turned circular to the East. This on all sides is strongly fortified with double Vaulting of the Ailes in two Stories, with their Pillars and Arches. The Cross-building fitted to contain the Quire in the Middle, and the better to support the lofty Tower, rose with a plainer and lower Vaulting; which Tower then spreading with artificial *(page 297)* Winding-stairs, was continued with plain Walls to its Timber Roof, which was well covered with Lead."[21]

These ancient Buildings were without Buttresses, only with thicker Walls: the Windows were very narrow, and latticed, for King *Alfred*[22] is praised for After-invention of Lanterns to keep in the Lamps in Churches.

In the Time of King *Henry* the Third,[23] the Mode began, to build Chapels behind the Altar to the *Blessed Virgin*: what this Chapel here was, is not now to be discovered, I suppose the Foundations of it, are under the Steps of King *Henry* the Seventh's Chapel, and this Work probably semicircular (as afterwards four more were added without the Ailes) was also intended for his own Sepulture; some of his own Relations lying now, just below those Steps, and may be supposed to have been within his Chapel: of this he laid the first Stone, *Anno* 1220,[24] and took down the greatest Part of St. *Edward*'s Church to rebuild it according to the Mode, which came into Fashion after the Holy War.[25]

This we now call the *Gothick* Manner of Architecture (so the *Italians* called what was not after the Roman Style) tho' the *Goths* were rather Destroyers than Builders; I think it should with more

Reason be called the *Saracen*[26] Style; for those People wanted neither Arts nor Learning; and after we in the West had lost both, we borrowed again from them, out of their *Arabick* Books, what they with great Diligence had translated from the *Greeks*.[27]

They were Zealots in their Religion, and where-ever they conquered, (which was with amazing Rapidity) erected Mosques and Caravansara's in Haste; which obliged them to fall into another Way of Building; for they built their Mosques round, disliking the *Christian* Form of a Cross, the old Quarries whence the Ancients took their large Blocks of Marble for whole Columns and Architraves, were neglected, and they thought both impertinent. Their Carriage was by Camels, therefore their Buildings were fitted for small Stones, and Columns of their own Fancy, consisting of many Pieces; and their Arches were pointed without Key-stones, which they thought too heavy.

The Reasons were the same in our Northern Climates, abounding in Free-stone, but wanting Marble.

The *Crusado*[28] gave us an Idea of this Form; after which King *Henry*[29] built his Church,[30] but not by a Model well digested at first; for, I think, the Chapels without the Ailes were an After-thought, the Buttresses between the Chapels remaining being useless, if they had been raised together with them; and the King having opened the East-end for St. *Mary*'s Chapel, he thought to make more Chapels for Sepulture; which was very acceptable to the Monks, after Licence obtained from *Rome* to bury in Churches, a Custom not used before.

The King's Intention was certainly to make up only the Cross to the Westward, for thus far it is of a different Manner from the rest more Westward built after his Time, as the Pillars and Spandrils of the Arches shew.

I am apt to think the King did not live to compleat his Intention, nor to reach four Inter-columns West of the Tower; the Walls of this Part might probably be carried up in his Time, but the Vaulting now covering the Quire, tho' it be more adorned and gilded, is without due Care in the Masonry, and is the worst performed of all done before. This Stone Vault was finished 23 Years after his Decease, in the Reign of King *Edward* the First,[31] so that the old Verse is not punctually right,

Tertius Henricus est templi conditor hujus.[32]

(page 298) But alas! it was now like to have been all spoiled; the Abbots would have a Cloyster,[33] but scrupled, I suppose, at moving some venerable Corpses laid between the Outside Buttresses; then comes a bold, but ignorant Architect, who undertakes to build the Cloyster, so that the Buttresses should be without the Cloyster spanning over it, as may be seen in the Section.

This was a dangerous Attempt. It is by due Consideration of the Statick Principles, and the right Poising of the Weights of the Butments to the Arches, that good Architecture depends; and the Butments ought to have equal Gravity on both Sides. Altho' this was done to flatter the Humour of the Monks, yet the Architect should have considered that new Works carried very high, and that upon a newer Foundation, would shrink: from hence the Walls above the Windows are forced out ten Inches, and the Ribs broken. I could not discern this Failure to be so bad, till the Scaffold over the Quire was raised to give a close View of it; and then I was amazed to find it had not quite fallen. This is now amended with all Care, and I dare promise it shall be much stronger, and securer than ever the first Builders left it.

After what had been done by King *Henry* the Third and his Successor, it is said, the Work was carried further by the Abbots and Monks toward the West, and I perceive also the contiguous Cloyster after the Manner it was begun by King *Henry* the Third with Butments spanning over the Cloyster, which they were necessitated to proceed upon, according as it had been begun, tho', by Error, not to be amended till it was carried beyond the Cloyster; but then they proceeded with regular Butments answerable to the North-side, till they came to the West-front. This West-vault was proceeded on with much better Care[34] and Skill, and was a Work of many Years, during the Reigns of the three succeeding *Edwards*, and King *Richard* the Second.[35] I suppose there was a great Intermission or Slackness of Work, till the *Lancastrian*[36] Line came in; for then, in the very first Bay of this Work, I find in the Vaulting, and the Key-stones, the Rose of *Lancaster*.

In the tumultuous and bloody Wars between the two Houses of *York* and *Lancaster*,[37] little was done to the Abbey, but by the Zeal of the Abbots, who drove the Work on as well as they were able, tho' slowly, to the West-end, which was never compleatly finished.

When King *Henry* the Eight[38] dissolved the Monastery, the Cloyster was finished, and other Things for the Convenience of the Abbey.

The *Consistory* (no contemptible Fabrick) was, I think, done in the Time of King *Edward* the First,[39] and, in order to join it to the Church, the East-side of the Cloyster was taken out of the West-side of the cross Part of the Church, (by ill Advice) for it might have otherwise been done by a more decent Contrivance, but it may be the King was to be obeyed, who founded this octagonal

Fabrick: the Abbot lent it to the King for the Use of the House of Commons,[40] upon Condition the Crown should repair it, which, tho' it be now used for Records, hath lately been done.

The *Saracen* Mode of Building seen in the East, soon spread over *Europe*, and particularly in *France*; the Fashions of which Nation we affected to imitate in all Ages, even when we were at Enmity with it. Nothing was thought magnificent that was not high beyond Measure, with the Flutter of Arch-buttresses,[41] so we call the sloping Arches that poise the high Vaultings of the Nave. The *Romans* always concealed their Butments, whereas the *Normans* thought them ornamental. These I have observ'd are the first Things that occasion the Ruin of Cathedrals, being so much exposed to the Air and Weather; the Coping, which cannot defend them, first failing, and if they give Way, the Vault must spread. Pinnacles are of no use, and as little Ornament. The Pride of a very high Roof raised above reasonable Pitch is not for Duration, *(page 299)* for the Lead is apt to slip; but we are tied to this indiscreet Form, and must be contented with original Faults in the first Design. But that which is most to be lamented, is the unhappy Choice of the Materials, the Stone is decayed four Inches deep, and falls off perpetually in great Scales. I find, after the *Conquest*, all our Artists were fetched from *Normandy*; they loved to work in their own *Caen*-stone, which is more beautiful than durable. This was found expensive to bring hither, so they thought *Rygate*-stone in *Surrey*, the nearest like their own, being a Stone that would saw and work like Wood, but not durable, as is manifest; and they used this for the Ashlar of the whole Fabrick, which is now disfigur'd in the highest Degree: this Stone takes in Water, which, being frozen, scales off, whereas good Stone gathers a Crust, and defends itself, as many of our *English* Free-stones do. And though we have also the best Oak Timber in the World, yet these senseless Artificers in *Westminster-hall*, and other Places, would work their Chesnuts from *Normandy*; that Timber is not natural to *England*, it works finely, but sooner decays than Oak. The Roof in the Abbey is Oak, but mixed with Chesnut, and wrought after a bad *Norman* Manner, that does not secure it from stretching, and damaging the Walls, and the Water of the Gutters is ill carried off. All this is said, the better, in the next Place, to represent to your Lordship what has been done, and is wanting still to be carried on, as Time and Money is allowed to make a substantial and durable Repair.

First, in Repair of the Stone-work, what is done shews itself: beginning from the East-window, we have cut out all the ragged Ashlar, and invested it with a better Stone, out of *Oxfordshire*, down the River, from the Quarries about *Burford*. We have amended and secured the Butresses in the Cloyster-garden, as to the greatest Part; and we proceed to finish that Side; the Chapels on the South-side are done, and most of the Arch-buttresses all along as we proceeded. We have not done much on the North-side, for these Reasons[42]: the Houses on the North-side are so close, that there is not Room left for the raising of Scaffolds and Ladders, nor for Passage for bringing Materials: besides, the Tenants taking every Inch to the very Walls of the Church to be in their Leases, this Ground already too narrow, is divided as the Backsides to Houses, with Wash-houses, Chimnies, Privies, Cellars, the Vaults of which, if indiscreetly dug against the Foot of a Buttress, may inevitably ruin the Vaults of the Chapels (and indeed I perceive such Mischief is already done, by the Opening of the Vaults of the octagonal Chapel on that Side) and unless effectual Means be taken to prevent all Nusances of this Sort, the Works cannot proceed, and if finished, may soon be destroyed. I need say no more, nor will I presume to dictate, not doubting but proper Means will be taken to preserve this noble Structure from such Nusances, as directly tend to the Demolition of it.

And now, in further Pursuance of your Lordship's Directions, I shall distinctly set down, what yet remains to finish the necessary Repairs for Ages to come. And then, in the second Place, (since the first Intentions of the Founders were never brought to a Conclusion) I shall present my Thoughts and Designs, in order to a proper compleating of what is left imperfect, hopeing we may obtain for this, the Continuance of the Parliamentary Assistance.

I have yet said nothing of King *Henry* the Seventh's Chapel, a nice embroidered Work, and performed with tender *Caen*-stone, and tho' lately built, in Comparison, is so eaten up by our Weather, that it begs for some Compassion, which, I hope, the sovereign Power will take, as it is the regal Sepulture.

I begin, as I said, to set down what is necessary for compleating the Repairs, tho' Part thereof at present I can only guess at, because I cannot as yet come at the North-side to make a full Discovery of the Defects there, but I hope to *(page 300)* find it rather better than the South-side; for it is the Vicissitudes of Heat and Cold, Drought and Moisture, that rot all Materials more than the Extremities that are constant, of any of these Accidents: this is manifest in Timber, which, if always under Ground and wet, never decays, otherwise *Venice* and *Amsterdam* would fall: it is the same in Leadwork, for the North-side of a steep Roof is usually much less decayed than the South; and the same is commonly seen in Stone Work: besides, the Buttresses here are more substantial than those of the South-side, which I complained before were indiscreetly altered[43] for the sake of the Cloyster; and I find some Emendations have been made about eighty Years since, but not well. Upon the whole Matter I may say, that of the necessary Repairs of the outward Stone Work, one third Part is already compleated. The most dangerous Part of the Vaulting over the Quire now in Hand will be finished in a few Months, but the Roof over it cannot be opened till Summer. The Repairs of the Stone Work, with all the Chapels, Arch-buttresses, Windows, and Mouldings of the North-side are yet to be done, excepting Part of the North-cross Aile: a great Part of the Expence will be in the North Front, and the great Rose Window there, which being very ruinous, was patched up for the present to prevent further Ruin, some Years since, before I was concerned, but must now be new done: I have prepared a proper Design for it. The Timber of the Roof of the Nave, and the Cross, is amended and secured with the Lead; and also the Chapels: but the whole Roof, and Ailes from the Tower Westward, with Lead and Pipes to be new-cast, remains yet, with all the Timber Work, to be mended, as hath been done Eastward of the Tower already. The Chapels on the North-side must have their Roofs amended, when we can see how to come at them, after the Removal of one little House.

And now having given a summary Account of what will perfect the meer Repairs, let me add what I wish might be done to render those Parts with a proper Aspect, which were left abruptly imperfect by the last Builders, when the Monastery was dissolved by King *Henry* the Eighth. The West-Front is very requisite to be finished, because the two Towers are not of equal Height, and too low for the Bells, which hang so much lower than the Roof, that they are not heard so far as they should be: the great West-window is also too feeble, and the Gabel-end of the Roof over it, is but Weatherboards painted.

The original Intention was plainly to have had a Steeple, the Beginnings of which appear on the Corners of the Cross, but left off before it rose so high as the Ridge of the Roof; and the Vault of the Quire under it, is only Lath and Plaister, now rotten, and must be taken care of.

Lest it should be doubted, whether the four Pillars below, be able to bear a Steeple, because they seem a little swayed inward, I have considered how they may be unquestionably secured, so as to support the greatest Weight that need be laid upon them; and this after a Manner that will add to their Shape and Beauty.

It is manifest to the Eye, that the four innermost Pillars of the

Cross are bended inward considerably, and seem to tend to Ruin, and the Arches of the second Order above are cracked also: how this happened, and how it is to be secured, I shall demonstrate.

I conceive the Architect knew very well, that the four Pillars above the Intersection of the Cross-nave would not prove a sufficient Butment to stand against the Pressure of so many Arches, unless they were very much bigger than the other Piers; but that could not be without cumbering up the principal Part of the Church: but tho' these angular Pillars could not be made bigger, yet they could be made heavier to stand against the Pressure of the several *(page 301)* Rows of Arches, which might prove an Equivalent, as may appear thus:[44]

FIGURE 27

Let A B C be an Arch resting at C, against an immoveable Wall K M, but at A upon a Pillar A D, so small as to be unable to be a sufficient Butment to the Pressure of the Arch A B: what is then to be done? I cannot add F G to it to make it a Butment, but I build up E so high, as by Addition of Weight, to establish it so firm, as if I had annexed F G to it to make it a Butment: it need not be enquired how much E must be, since it cannot exceed, provided A D be sufficient to bear the Weight imposed on it: and this is the Reason why in all *Gothick* Fabricks of this Form, the Architects were wont to build Towers or Steeples in the Middle, not only for Ornament, but to confirm the middle Pillars against the Thrust of the several Rows of Arches, which force against them every Way. The Architect understood this well enough, but knowing that it might require Time to give such a Butment as the Tower to[45] his Arches, which was to be last done; and lest there should be a Failing in the mean Time, he wisely considered, that if he tied these Arches every Way with Iron, which were next to the Middle of the Cross: this might serve the Turn,[46] till he built the Tower to make all secure, which is not done to this Day. These Irons which were hooked on from Pillar to Pillar have been stolen away; and this is the Reason of the four Pillars being bent inward, and the Walls above cracked; but nothing can be amended, till first the Pillars are restored, which I have considered how to perform, and represented in a Model. This must be first done, otherwise the Addition of Weight upon that which is already crooked and infirm, will make it more so: but the Pillars being once well secured from further Distortion, it will be necessary to confirm all by adding more Weight upon them, that is, by building a Tower according to the original Intention of the Architect, and which was begun, as appears by the Work, but left off before it rose to the Ridge of the Roof. In my Opinion the Tower should be continued to at

SIR CHRISTOPHER WREN, KNT. 301

veral Rows of Arches, which might prove an Equivalent, as may appear thus:

Let A B C be an Arch resting at C, against an immoveable Wall K M, but at A upon a Pillar A D, so small as to be unable to be a sufficient Butment to the Pressure of the Arch A B: what is then to be done? I cannot add F G to it to make it a Butment, but I build up E so high, as by Addition of Weight, to establish it so firm, as if I had annexed F G to it to make it a Butment: it need not be enquired how much E must be, since it cannot exceed, provided A D be sufficient to bear the Weight imposed on it: and this is the Reason why in all *Gothick* Fabricks of this Form, the Architects were wont to build Towers or Steeples in the Middle, not only for Ornament, but to confirm the middle Pillars against the Thrust of the several Rows of Arches, which force against them every Way. The Architect understood this well enough, but knowing that it might require Time to give such a Butment as the Tower to his Arches, which was to be last done; and lest there should be a Failing in the mean Time, he wisely considered, that if he tied these Arches every Way with Iron, which were next to the Middle of the Cross: this might serve the Turn, till he built the Tower to make all secure, which is not done to this Day. These Irons which were hooked on from Pillar to Pillar have been stolen away; and this is the Reason of the four Pillars being bent inward, and the Walls above cracked; but nothing can be amended, till first the Pillars are restored, which I have considered how to perform, and represented in a Model. This must be first done, otherwise the Addition of Weight upon that which is already crooked and infirm, will make it more so: but the Pillars being once well secured from further Distortion, it will be necessary to confirm all by adding more Weight upon them, that is, by building a Tower according to the original Intention of the Architect, and which was begun, as appears by the Work, but left off before it rose to the Ridge of the Roof. In my Opinion the Tower should be continued to at least as much in Height above the Roof, as it is in Breadth; and if a Spire be added to it, it will give a proper Grace to the whole Fabrick, and the West-end of the City, which seems to want it.

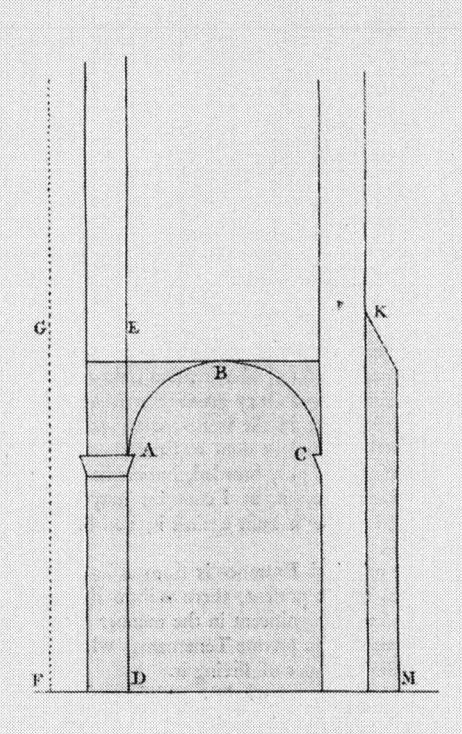

FIGURE 27. Westminster Abbey, Wren's diagram showing the section through the aisle, with weight of tower at E, 1713 (Christopher Wren, Jr., *Parentalia* [London, 1750], p. 301). The Ohio State University Libraries, Rare Book and Manuscripts.

FIGURE 28. Westminster Abbey, Wren's design for the central tower and spire, 1722 (WAM (P) 909, Westminster Abbey). By courtesy of the Dean and Chapter of Westminster.

least as much in Height above the Roof, as it is in Breadth; and if a Spire be added to it, it will give a proper Grace to the whole Fabrick, and the West-end of the City, which seems to want it.

(page 302) I have made a Design, which will not be very expensive but light, and still in the *Gothick* Form, and of a Style with the rest of the Structure, which I would strictly adhere to, throughout the whole Intention: to deviate from the old Form, would be to run into a disagreeable Mixture, which no Person of a good Taste could relish.

I have varied a little from the usual Form, in giving twelve

Notes and Reports on Gothic Churches

Sides to the Spire instead of eight, for Reasons to be discerned upon the Model.

The Angles of Pyramids in the *Gothick* Architecture, were usually inriched with the Flower the Botanists call *Calceolus*,[47] which is a proper Form to help Workmen to ascend on the Outside to amend any Defects, without raising large Scaffolds upon every slight Occasion; I have done the same, being of so good Use, as well as agreeable Ornament.

The next Thing to be considered is, to finish what was left undone at the West-front.

It is evident, as is observed before, the two West-towers were left imperfect, and have continued so since the Dissolution of the Monastery, one much higher than the other, though still too low for Bells, which are stifled by the Height of the Roof above them; they ought certainly to be carried to an equal Height, one Story above the Ridge of the Roof, still continuing the *Gothick* Manner, in the Stone-work, and Tracery.

Something must be done to strengthen the West-window, which is crazy; the Pediment is only boarded, but ought undoubtedly to be of Stone. I have given such a Design,[48] as I conceive may be suitable for this Part: the *Jerusalem-Chamber* is built against it, and the Access from *Tothill-street* not very graceful.

The principal Entrance is from *King-street*, and I believe always will continue so, but at present, there is little Encouragement to begin to make this North-front magnificent in the manner I have designed, whilst it is so much incumbered with private Tenements, which obscure and smoke the Fabrick, not without danger of fireing it.

The great North-window had been formerly in danger of Ruin, but was upheld, and stopt up, for the present, with Plaister. It will be most necessary to rebuild this with *Portland*-stone, to answer the South-rose-window, which was well rebuilt about forty Years since; the Stair-cases at the Corners must be new ashlar'd, and Pyramids set upon them conformable to the old-Style, to make the Whole of a Piece. I have therefore made a* Design in order to restore it to its proper Shape first intended, but which was indiscreetly tamper'd with some Years since, by patching on a little *Dorick* Passage before the great Window, and cropping off the Pyramids, and covering the Stair-cases with very improper Roofs of Timber and Lead, which can never agree with any other Part of the Design.

For all these new Additions I have prepared perfect Draughts and Models, such as I conceive may agree with the original Scheme of the old Architect, without any modern Mixtures to shew my

FIGURE 29
*This Front, commonly called Solomon's Porch, *the Surveyor lived to finish in the Year 1722.*

FIGURE 29. Westminster Abbey, Wren's design for the north transept, 1719 (WAM (P) 900, Westminster Abbey). By Courtesy of the Dean and Chapter of Westminster.

own Inventions: in like manner as I have among the Parochial Churches of *London* given some few Examples, (where I was oblig'd to deviate from a better Style)[49] which appear not ungraceful, but ornamental, to the East part of the City; and it is to be hoped, by the publick Care, the West part also, in good Time, will be as well adorned; and surely by nothing more properly then a lofty Spire, and Western-towers to *Westminster-abbey*.

CHAPTER 3

Letter from Paris

INTRODUCTION

French architecture of the sixteenth and seventeenth centuries, the only contemporary European architecture Wren was able to study at first hand, was one of the several forms of building that played an important part in establishing his theoretical outlook. For eight months in 1665/6 Wren was in Paris. There he met French scientists and attended meetings of their private scientific academies, but also observed buildings. The primary record of his trip is his letter from Paris "to a particular Friend." It provides not only an interesting look at the scientific culture of Paris during this period, but, most importantly, reveals the French sources that influenced Wren's own designs and helped to determine the development of his theoretical attitudes toward architecture.

Although it is undated, Wren's letter must have been written sometime between the beginning of October and mid-December 1665. The earlier date is determined by a letter written by Edward Browne to his father. In it he describes his excursion with Wren to the north of Paris, made at the end of September 1665, and records their visits to châteaux, all listed by Wren in his letter.[1] And, as Wren proposes in his letter to return to England with Lord Berkeley by Christmas, it must have been written by mid-December.[2]

The letter is unaddressed as well as incomplete. According to Christopher Jr., this letter was preceded by another text, "wherein he returns Thanks for his Recommendation of him to the Earl of St. Albans, who in the Journey, and ever since, had us'd him with all kindness and Indulgence imaginable, and made good his Character of him, as one of the best Men in the World."[3] Although the earl of St. Albans can be identified as Henry Jermyn, an earl since 1660 and the new English ambassador to France, it is unknown who provided Wren's introduction.[4]

Traveling with the earl of St. Albans, Wren had been in Paris since the end of June or the beginning of July, fortuitously escaping the bubonic plague that ravaged London that summer. He had proposed, however, to make this trip as early as March 1665. Several of his friends knew of this plan. It was reported to Christiaan Huygens by Robert Moray in his letter dated 27 March,[5] and to John Evelyn by Sir Joseph Denham sometime before 4 April.[6] On June 22, Wren himself wrote to

Ralph Bathurst of the architects "Mons. Mansard, or Signor Bernini, both which I shall see at Paris within this fortnight."[7] Leaving around the end of June, he remained eight months abroad and, despite his plan to return by Christmas, reappeared in London as late as 6 March 1666.[8]

On the eve of his trip Wren had just completed his first architectural work, Pembroke College Chapel at Cambridge, and had his second, the Sheldonian Theater at Oxford, under construction. Although he certainly looked forward to this opportunity to study French architecture at first hand, Wren's daily activities were those not just of an enthusiastic young architect, but of a distinguished natural philosopher. Apart from engagements with various English diplomats and aristocrats living in Paris, some probably introduced to him by Evelyn as promised, Wren had almost daily close association with important members of the *académies privées* in Paris, including Henri Justel, Abbé Bourdelot, Melchisédec Thévenot, and Adrien Auzout, some of whom had contacts with the Royal Society. Many of the private scientific academies had been recently created following the collapse in 1664 of the Montmor Academy, the savants and amateurs who had met regularly at the home of Henri Louis Habert de Montmor since about 1654.[9]

In January 1666, Henri Justel (1620–93), scholar and secretary to Louis XIV, wrote of "Mr. Wren, whom I see practically every day as well as many other English gentlemen,"[10] probably at the *conférences* he held in his own home. Justel was not a scientist but a collector and disseminator of scientific news, particularly in his capacity as the Royal Society's official correspondent for France from 1664 until his death. He also had a wide correspondence with learned men in France, Italy, Holland, and Germany. His *conférences* were another means of spreading information, for these were attended not only by the scientists and scholars of Paris, but also by gentlemen, noblemen, professional men, and clergymen living in the capital and the provinces. Among the foreigners present were the same sorts of people, in addition to secretaries attached to embassies, students, and young gentlemen on the Grand Tour. According to Le Gallois, "There are assemblies in his house several times a week. . . . these assemblies are composed of the most illustrious and learned men of Paris, who go to converse agreeably of everything which the occasion may offer."[11] The conversations at these meetings and the newsletters from Justel's numerous foreign correspondents, which were read aloud to the assembly, recorded the latest scientific discoveries and inventions and, more, current events in different countries involving political, military, and economic affairs. Contemporary literature was also discussed, thus placing Justel's *conférences* in the tradition of a literary academy. He had inherited from his father, a historian, a large library of books, manuscripts, and medals, which he expanded by collecting scientific and travel books.

Although Justel was not a scientist, he would have had many interests in common with Wren, including the collection of information on the practical arts. In 1667 he was proposing a book on the "commodités de la vie," much in the spirit of the Royal Society's projected history of trades, in which Wren played a significant role.[12] Their acquaintance continued over the next several decades, particularly after Justel, a Huguenot, emigrated to England in 1681. That year Wren put his name forth for election as fellow of the Royal Society and he was admitted.

In his letter, Wren reports that he attended meetings at the home of the Abbé Bourdelot: "Abbé *Burdelo* keeps an Academy at his House for Philosophy every Monday Afternoon." Formerly Pierre Michon (1610 or 1620–85), Bourdelot was a physician who for most of his life served the Prince de Condé, but also briefly Louis XIII (as *médecin du roi*), and Queen Christina of Sweden. From 1664 until his death in 1685 he played host in his home to the most prominent scientific thinkers of the day.[13] During his visit to Bourdelot's academy, however, Wren was not completely satisfied with proceedings. An unknown French correspondent, possibly Justel, reported to Oldenburg that "I took him [Wren] to Mr. Bourdelot's where today many fine things were said. He much approved what was said, but wished that they made experiments. . . ."[14]

In August 1665, Oldenburg was able to report to Boyle that "Dr Wren is well receaved at Paris, and conducted to some of their meetings; and made acquainted with Mrs Auzout, Petit and Thévenot."[15] These particular meetings were probably those of the Compagnie des Sciences et des Arts that met at the home of Melchisédec Thévenot (1620/1–92) in Issy, outside of Paris. Thévenot began these meetings after about 1662 to provide additional opportunities for discussion and experimentation outside the Montmor Academy, which by now was beset by numerous problems and disagreements among its membership. Thévenot kept in residence a mathematician, anatomist, and chemist, and pursued his own scientific studies with the help of, among others, Pierre Petit and Adrien Auzout, both also prominent members of the Montmor Academy. After the Montmor Academy closed in 1664, the Compagnie continued a year or two longer, until the high cost of experiments and apparatus forced Thévenot to close his doors. The legacy of this group is found in the Académie Royale des Sciences, established in 1666 in part due to a proposal, written by Thévenot, Auzout, Petit, and others around 1663 or 1664, for a *compagnie*, supported by the king, for the "perfection of the sciences and the arts and, in general, to search for all that can bring utility or convenience to the human race, and particularly to France."[16]

It is unclear whether Wren met Thévenot, Auzout, and Petit in the context of the Compagnie or at some other scientific meeting. According to his letter, Wren did visit the château at Issy, perhaps while attending one of the last meetings of the Compagnie at Thévenot's country house.[17] Wren shared many interests with these gentlemen. Thévenot was an amateur scientist, best remembered for his invention of a bubble level that was later improved upon by Robert Hooke and Christiaan Huygens, and for his *Relations de divers voyages curieux* (1663–72), a collection of travel accounts.[18] Pierre Petit (1594 or 1598–1677), although he had a career in the government, devoted most of his attention to investigations in astronomy and physics. Neither of these men was selected by Colbert to be a member of the Académie des Sciences in 1666. Although Thévenot was finally admitted in 1685, Petit never was. This blow, however, was softened by his election in April 1667 as one of the first foreign fellows of the Royal Society. Petit had been a regular correspondent of Henry Oldenburg and had a strong interest in English science, which would have naturally brought him into contact with Wren during his visit to Paris.[19]

Wren's statement in his letter that "Mons. Abbé Charles" introduced him to Gianlorenzo Bernini, indicates that he may have met another participant in the meetings of the Compagnie, the former Charles de Bryas, who upon becoming a Carmelite adopted the name Charles de l'Assomption. Known by his contemporaries, including Auzout and Huygens, as a collector of optical instruments, he had attended meetings of the Montmor Academy during its last days, and thereafter those of the Compagnie.[20] However, because a connection to Bernini cannot be substantiated, the identity of the "Abbé Charles" remains uncertain.[21]

The member of the Compagnie with whom Wren had most in common was the astronomer Adrien Auzout (1622–91), elected to the Royal Society in May 1666 and to the Académie des Sciences later that year. Auzout told Oldenburg at the beginning of July 1665, "I am very glad that we shall soon see your learned Mr. Wren here."[22] The two men may already have known of one another through their shared scientific interests, possibly from as early as 1659.[23] Auzout wrote to Oldenburg of his plans to take Wren to the meetings of the Compagnie, although he modestly stated, "I fear that he will not find our Company in very good shape, but if he sees nothing very splendid here at least we shall learn much from him." Auzout's subsequent letters indicate that his and Wren's frequent conversations ranged over a wide variety of scientific topics, including the Peak of Teneriffe, observations of comets, and the design of optical lenses,[24] but they probably also included architecture. Auzout, wrote Martin Lister in 1698, "was very Curious and Understanding in Architecture; for which purpose he was 17 Years in Italy by times." Unfortunately, very little evidence remains of his architectural work. It is possible that he made an early design for the Observatoire in Paris, sending a sketch of the building to Oldenburg in 1668.[25] He apparently "made an exact criticism" of Claude Perrault's translation of Vitruvius (1673), "noticing more than three hundred errors in it."[26] By the end of his life, according to Lister, he "had about 80 difficult Passages in Vitruvius, which he had Commented and Explained; and the Correction of a great number of Errata in the Text."[27] The friendship between Wren and Auzout was apparently mutually gratifying. After Wren's departure for England, Auzout wrote to Oldenburg, "We await news of Mr. Wren's arrival." Oldenburg, telling Boyle of Wren's return, reported that Wren was "very well satisfied with the civilities, he has received in France, and commends particularly Mr Auzout."[28]

Not only did Wren attend meetings of scientific academies in Paris, but he also visited at least one important "cabinet of curiosities" that included objects of scientific interest. He wrote, "Abbé Bruno keeps the curious Rarities of the Duke of Orlean's Library, well fill'd with excellent Intaglio's, Medals, Books of Plants, and Fowls in Miniature." The collection of Gaston d'Orléans (1608–60), brother of Louis XIII, was first established at the château at Blois, to which he was more or less exiled in late 1634.[29] Here the prince set up a small court of minor poets and artists as well as scientists, including the comte de Pagan, astronomer, and the Scottish naturalist Robert Morison (1620–83), who served as steward of the prince's botanical garden. His cabinet contained a huge library, with rare manuscripts and maps. In addition there were numerous items of artistic and scientific interest. These included medals, ancient bronzes and statues, engraved stones, objets d'art, weapons, agates, shells, and paintings of birds and flowers by Stefano della Bella (1610–64) and Nicolas Robert (1614–85), done presumably from specimens in the prince's garden. In 1644 John Evelyn saw the collection at the Palais du Luxembourg in Paris. The library, "rarely furnish'd with excellent bookes," the "6 Cabinets of Medails; and an incomparable collection of shells and Achates, whereof some are prodigiously rich & glorious," led Evelyn to conclude that the duke was "very learn'd in Medails, and Plants, nothing of that kind escapes him."[30]

After Gaston's death, the coins and medals in his cabinet were passed on to the king to become part of the Cabinet des Médailles du

Roi. The natural history specimens were purchased by Colbert to form the foundation of the Cabinet d'histoire naturelle. Gaston's librarian, Bénigne Bruneau (d. 1666), the "Abbé Bruno" mentioned by Wren, continued to oversee the collection and in 1664 was named *intendant* by the king. Visiting in 1666, Wren would have seen the cabinets in their new location at the Louvre. He was not the only distinguished visitor to do so that year. Bernini, accompanied by Chantelou, went to see "the King's medals," on 14 October and met "the abbé Bruneau, who is in charge of them." They examined several medals, according to Chantelou, including "two of agate, one large and one small," and some in bronze "of great beauty." Unfortunately, Bernini "could not see the Greek examples as the case was warped and could not be got open." They also looked at the shells, which Bernini "thought were very pretty."[31]

Despite the many scientific activities that occupied Wren during his visit to Paris, his letter records almost exclusively the buildings he observed in and around Paris, as well as the architects, painters, and sculptors active in France at the time. Some of these artists he may have met, for he implies that he attended meetings of the Académie Royale de Peinture et de Sculpture: "An Academy of Painters, Sculptors, Architects, and the chief Artificers of the Louvre, meet every first and last *Saturday* of the Month." The academy was founded in 1648 and reorganized by Colbert in 1663.[32]

As early as June 22, Wren had written that he planned to see "Mons. Mansard, or Signor Bernini" while in Paris. Although there is no record that he ever met François Mansart, he was introduced to Gianlorenzo Bernini, the greatest artist in Europe at the time. Bernini had been in Paris since 2 June 1665 to complete the Louvre and to sculpt a bust of Louis XIV. An additional record of Wren's famous meeting with Bernini comes from Oldenburg's unknown French correspondent, who relates, "We also took him to the house of that great architect, Chevalier Bernini. He saw the marble bust of the king and the view which Bernini has made of the Louvre which he will tell you of."[33] Oldenburg transcribed this information in a letter dated 24 August, and this meeting could not have taken place before 11 August, when the bust was removed from the Louvre to Bernini's new lodgings at the Palais Mazarin.[34] How the Englishman and the Italian communicated is unknown. Introductions were made, according to Wren, by a "Mons. Abbé Charles." This person may have been one of three clerics: Charles de l'Assomption, the amateur scientist, discussed earlier; the Abbé François, that is, Francesco Butti, secretary of Cardinal Mazarin; or the nuncio, Monsignor Carlo Roberti de' Vittori. Only the last two are known to have had contact with Bernini.[35]

Wren provides in his letter some record of the buildings he observed in Paris. He visited the Louvre every day to watch the construction, which impressed him profoundly, getting to know on what days Colbert made his weekly inspection and the workers were paid. Frequently he went inside to view the artwork and rarities, including those from the duc d'Orléans's cabinet and others located in the summer apartment of the Queen Mother under the Petit Galerie, decorated in 1655–7 by G. F. Romanelli.[36] Across from the Louvre on the other side of the Seine stood the Collège des Quatre-Nations (1662–74), its dome still under construction, designed by Le Vau to be on axis with the Louvre's Cour Carrée in a manner of which Wren did not approve, but which would later influence his own work. One quarter of a mile to the north of the Louvre stood the Palais Mazarin, formerly the Hôtel de Chevry-Tubeuf, built from 1635 with numerous subsequent additions and now part of the Bibliothèque Nationale. It housed Mazarin's extensive art collection, which after his death in 1661 was presumably passed down to his family along with the property. Wren was deeply impressed by what he saw during at least one visit.[37] The Palais Mazarin was also the site of his meeting with Bernini, who was lodged there from 8 August.

Although in his letter Wren does not mention any domed churches, he knew and studied them. Immediately after his return to London he proposed a domed crossing for Old St. Paul's and in his report assured the commissioners that he knew this form of building, "having had the Opportunity of seeing several Structures of greater Expense than this, while they were in raising, conducted by the best Artists, Italian and French, and having had daily Conference with them, and observing their Engines and Methods."[38] Wren would have known not only François Mansart's Val-de-Grâce and Ste-Marie de la Visitation, as well as Jacques Lemercier's Oratoire and Church of the Sorbonne,[39] but also Ste-Anne-la-Royale, under construction during the years of his visit, by Guarino Guarini. Guarini, a mathematician and member of the Theatine order, was in Paris from 1662 to early 1666 to teach mathematics and to design and supervise the construction of the Theatine church.[40] All of these domed churches would have a lasting influence on Wren's architectural work.

For Wren, none of these buildings in and around Paris were as impressive as the embankments along the Seine River. Edward Browne relates in a letter to his father:

> I asked him which hee took to bee the greatest work about Paris, he said the Quay, or Key upon the river side, which he demonstrated to me, to be built with so vast expense and such great quantity of materialls, that it exceeded all manner of ways the building of the two greatest pyramids in Egypt.[41]

By the year of Wren's visit, the quays, built during various periods since the thirteenth century to prevent flooding and to provide landings for river traffic, did not extend far beyond the vicinity of the Louvre and the western tip of the Ile de la Cité. Wren would have known the quais de l'Horloge (completed 1607) and des Orfèvres (begun 1608), which formed part of the monumental complex of the place Dauphine and Pont Neuf built under Henri IV.[42] On the Right Bank was the recently built quai de Gesvres (1644–9), located between the Pont du Change and the Pont Notre Dame and remarkable for its system of arcades sheltering a covered market.[43] It was joined on the west by the mid-sixteenth-century quai de la Mégisserie and, continuing farther, the paved embankment running along the river south of the Louvre and the Grande Galerie of Henri IV. On the Left Bank, the medieval quai des Augustins extended westward to the quai de Conti, and on into the new embankment in front of the Collège des Quatre-Nations (quai Malaquais), which Wren could have observed under construction at this time.[44] Coming from London, where timber wharfs still stood along the banks of the Thames, Wren was well aware of the great benefits, both aesthetic and functional, provided by the Parisian quays. About six months after his return from Paris, he included quays along the Thames as part of his design for the City of London after the Great Fire.

Wren's list of châteaux in his letter indicates that he made several excursions outside of Paris, some brief and some more extensive (see Fig. 30). He records that he went twice to Versailles, and it might have been on one of these occasions that he stopped along the way at Issy. A definitive record of one tour is provided by Edward Browne in his letter to his father written at the end of September.[45] He relates that the previous week he spent three days in the country "tempted out by so good company" of Wren and Henry Compton (1632–1713), later bishop of London and an amateur botanist.[46] On the first day they traveled to Chantilly, on the second to Liancourt and Verneuil, and after spending the night in Senlis, on the third day they visited Le Raincy during their return to Paris.

Browne's letter reflects his own fascination with the wonders and noble inhabitants of the houses they visited. Fortunately, he found that "Dr. Wren's discourse is very pleasing and satisfactory to mee about all manner of things," and he saw fit to record some of Wren's comments on buildings. At Verneuil, "Dr. Wren guest that the same man built this which built the Louvre, there being the same faults in one as in the other." At Le Raincy, "the house is small but extremely neat, and the modell pleased Dr. Wren very much." Wren's own letter also provides a record of some of his reactions to the sixteenth- and seventeenth- century buildings he viewed in and around Paris.

Even before he had returned home, Wren was already digesting the new knowledge he had gathered abroad. He stated in his letter that he hoped to give "a very good Account of all the best Artists of *France*," and that he was making it his business now "to pry into Trades and Arts." He planned to bring back "almost all *France* in Paper," that is, architectural drawings, engravings, and treatises. His project, which he had "on the Anvil," for "Observations on the present State of *Architecture, Arts,* and *Manufactures* in *France*" was probably formulated for the Royal Society's history of trades.

The only outcome of Wren's proposal appears to be his description of "chariots" in France, presented to the Royal Society in March 1666.[47] Nevertheless, his experience in France had an immediate and lasting impact on his architectural designs and influenced the development of his theoretical ideas. About two months after his return, he wrote his "Report on Old St. Paul's before the Fire," proposing to replace the tower – "a Heap of Deformities" – with "a spacious *Dome* or *Rotundo*, with a *Cupola*, or hemispherical Roof," inspired by the domed churches he had admired in Paris (Figs. 13–15). This was a conception he would return to during the course of his career in the design of the new St. Paul's and the City churches. At the same time, as is indicated by his designs for buildings such as the palace at Winchester and the Royal Hospital at Greenwich, Wren would never forget the lessons he had learned from French palaces and châteaux.

Although Wren certainly admired and emulated contemporary French architecture, in his few existing theoretical remarks he assessed it negatively. He described it as a "fashion" that the English were habitually borrowing, beginning with French Gothic.[48] Contemporary French Classical architecture, like French clothing and speaking, had feminine rather than masculine qualities. Furthermore, the French, in a competition of 1671, invented a *"Gallick Order,"* with fleurs-de-lis instead of acanthus, which could never "come up to the Grace of the old Form of the *Cor-*

inthian Capital."[49] Wren recognized the changing nature of French architecture, its particular feminine character, and, ultimately, its existence as a national style. The French Classical style was therefore another culturally specific form of architecture, which, along with the Gothic style, had to be accounted for in Wren's theory of architecture.

Letter to a Friend from Paris (late September/October 1665)

Source
  Original manuscript missing. *Parentalia* (London, 1750), "The Life of Sir Christopher Wren, Knt.," pt. 1, sec. 3, number 4, 261–2 (transcript in *WS*, 13:40–2)
Other Manuscript Versions
  RS MS 249, fols. 294–6
  All Souls MS 313, fols. 431–5
Date
  late September/October 1665

(page 261)
[1]'I have busied myself in surveying the most esteem'd Fabricks of *Paris*, and the Country round; the *Louvre* for a while was my daily Object, where no less than a thousand Hands are constantly employ'd in the Works; some in laying mighty Foundations, some in raising the Stories, Columns, Entablements, &c. with vast Stones, by great and useful Engines; others in Carving, Inlaying of Marbles, Plaistering, Painting, Gilding, &c. Which altogether make a School of Architecture, the best probably, at this Day in *Europe*.[2] The College of *The four Nations*[3] is usually admir'd, but the Artist hath purposely set it ill-favouredly, that he might shew his Wit in struggling with an inconvenient Situation. – An Academy of Painters, Sculptors, Architects, and the chief Artificers of the *Louvre*,[4] meet every first and last *Saturday* of the Month. Mons. *Colbert*,[5] Surintendant, comes to the Works of the *Louvre*, every *Wednesday*, and, if Business hinders not, *Thursday*. The Workmen are paid every *Sunday* duly. Mons. Abbé *Charles*[6] introduc'd me to the Acquaintance of *Bernini*, who shew'd me his Designs of the *Louvre*, and of the King's Statue. – Abbé *Bruno*[7] keeps the curious Rarities of the Duke of *Orleans's*[8] Library, well fill'd with excellent Intaglio's, Medals, Books of Plants, and Fowls in Miniature. Abbé *Burdelo*[9] keeps an Academy at his House for Philosophy every *Monday* Afternoon. – But I must not think to describe *Paris*, and the numerous Observables there, in the Compass of a short Letter. – The King's Houses I could not miss; *Fontainbleau*[10] has a stately Wildness and Vastness suitable to the Desert it stands in. The antique Mass of the Castle of St. *Germains*,[11] and the Hanging-gardens are delightfully surprising, (I mean to any Man of Judgment) for the Pleasures below vanish away in the Breath that is spent in ascending. The Pal-

FIGURE 30

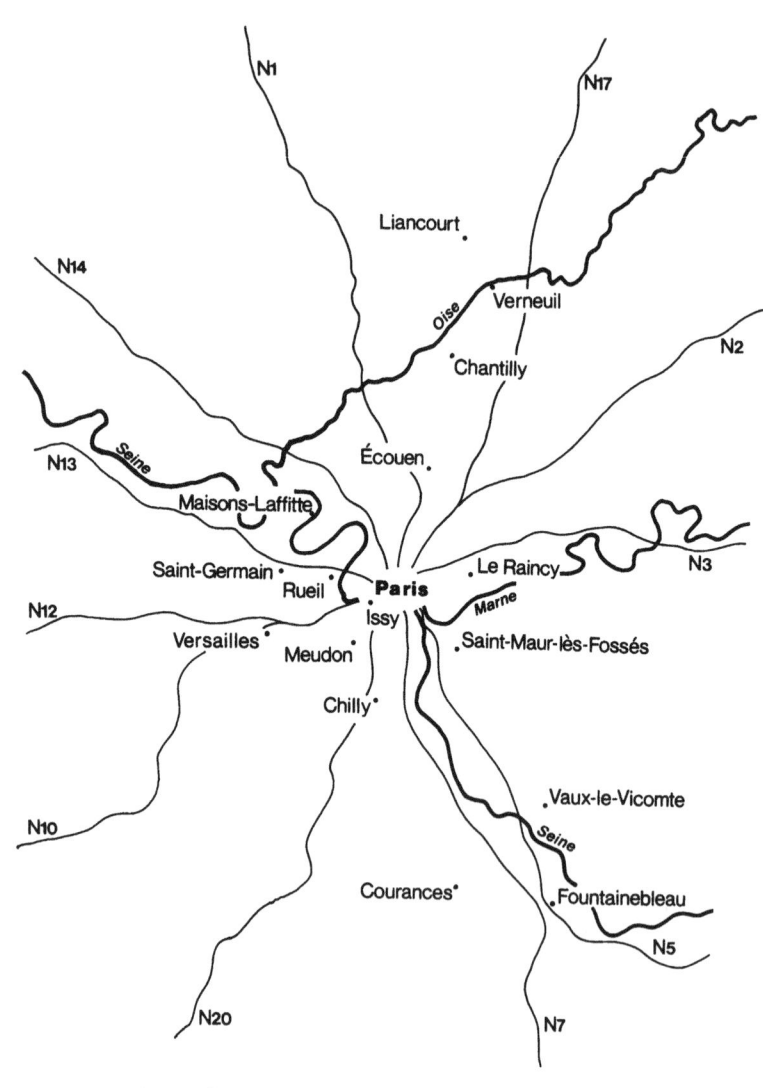

FIGURE 30. Map of sites around Paris visited by Wren in 1665–6. (Author.)

ace, or if you please, the Cabinet of *Versailles*[12] call'd me twice to view it; the Mixtures of Brick, Stone, blue Tile and Gold make it look like a rich Livery: Not an Inch within but is crouded with little Curiosities of Ornaments: the Women, as they make here the Language and Fashions, and meddle with Politicks and Philosophy, so they sway also in Architecture; Works of Filgrand, and little Knacks are in great Vogue; but Building certainly ought to have the Attribute of eternal, and therefore the only Thing uncapable of new Fashions. The masculine Furniture of *Palais Mazarine*[13] pleas'd me much better, where is a great and noble Collection of antique

Statues and Bustos, (many of Porphyry) good Basso-relievos; excellent Pictures of the great Masters, fine Arras, true Mosaicks, besides *Pierres de Raport*[14] in Compartiments and Pavements; Vasas of Porcelain painted by *Raphael*, and infinite other Rarities; the best of which now furnish the glorious Appartment of the *Queen Mother* at the *Louvre*,[15] which I saw many Times. – After the incomparable Villas of *Vaux*[16] and *Maisons*,[17] I shall but name *Ruel, Courances,* **(page 262)** *Chilly, Essoane,* St. *Maur,* St. *Mande, Issy, Meudon, Rincy, Chantilly, Verneul, Lioncour,*[18] all which, and I might add many others, I have survey'd; and that I might not lose the Impressions of them, I shall bring you almost all *France* in Paper, which I found by some or other ready design'd to my Hand, in which I have spent both Labour and some Money. *Bernini*'s Design of the *Louvre* I would have given my Skin for, but the old reserv'd *Italian* gave me but a few Minutes View; it was five little Designs in Paper, for which he hath receiv'd as many thousand Pistoles; I had only Time to copy it in my Fancy and Memory; I shall be able by Discourse, and a Crayon, to give you a tolerable Account of it. I have purchas'd a great deal of *Taille-douce*,[19] that I might give our *Countrymen* Examples of Ornaments and Grotesks, in which the *Italians* themselves confess the *French* to excel. I hope I shall give you a very good Account of all the best Artists of *France*; my Business now is to pry into Trades and Arts, I put myself into all Shapes to humour them; 'tis a Comedy to me, and tho' sometimes expenceful, I am loth yet to leave it. Of the most noted Artisans within my Knowledge or Acquaintance I send you only this general Detail, and shall inlarge on their respective Characters and Works at another Time.

ARCHITECTS.

Sig. Cavalier *Bernini,* Mons. *Mansart,* Mons. *Vaux,* Mons. *Gobert,* Mons. *Le Pautre.*[20]

Messieurs *Anguiere* and *Sarazin;*[21] Sculptors and Statuaries.

Mons. *Perrot;*[22] famous for Basso-relievos.

Van Ostal, Mr. *Arnoldin;*[23] Plaisterers, perform the admirable Works at the *Louvre.*

Mons. *Orphelin,* Mons. *de Tour;*[24] Gravers of Medals and Coins.

PAINTERS in HISTORY.

Mess. *Le Brun, Bourdon, Poussin, Ruvine, Champeine, Vilcein, Loyre, Coypel, Picard.*[25]

Miniard,[26] in History and Portraits.

Mons. *Beaubrun;*[27] in Portraits for Women.

Mess. *Baptist, Robert,*[28] for Flowers.

Mr. *Matthews*,[29] an *English* Painter, at the *Rue-Gobelins*; works for the Arras-weavers; where Mons. *Bruno*[30] is the Designer, and an excellent Artist. – There I saw Goldsmiths working in Plate admirably well.

Abbé *Burdelo*[31] works in Enamel.

Mons. *de la Quintinye*,[32] has most excellent Skill in Agriculture, Planting, and Gardening.

My Lord *Berkley*[33] returns to *England* at *Christmass*, when I propose to take the Opportunity of his Company, and by that Time, to perfect what I have on the Anvil; Observations on the present State of *Architecture, Arts*, and *Manufactures* in *France*.

CHAPTER 4

Letter on Building Churches

INTRODUCTION

In 1711, a few years before his retirement, Wren was given the opportunity to reflect upon his personal contribution to the history of church design. In a letter to a friend and fellow member of the Commission for Building Fifty New City Churches, preserved in *Parentalia*, he created the only complete record of the issues he addressed in the design of churches in and near the City of London after the Great Fire, stating the general principles of his solution for the English Protestant church.

As Colvin and Downes have discussed, the Commission for Building Fifty New Churches resulted from an act of Parliament passed in 1711 that imposed a new coal duty for "Building . . . fifty new churches of Stone and other proper Materials, with Towers or Steeples to each of them; and for purchasing of Sites of Churches and Church-Yards, and Burying-places, in or near the Cities of London and Westminster, or the Suburbs thereof."[1] In addition, the tax would support the conversion of chapels into parish churches and the building of parsonages.

This grandiose scheme began simply enough with the petition of the parishioners of St. Alphege, Greenwich, who, after the roof of their medieval church had collapsed on 28 November 1710, requested funds for rebuilding out of what remained of the coal tax that financed the new St. Paul's. The Tories, in control of the House of Commons for the first time in twenty-two years, took this as a cue to do much more – to create a monument to their recent political victory and their High Church principles. A committee appointed to "consider what churches are wanting within the Cities of London and Westminster, and Suburbs thereof"[2] concluded that, given the growing populations of these areas, funds were needed to provide for fifty new churches serving new, smaller parishes. The committee was aware that in suburban parishes at that time only a fraction of the huge population could be accommodated in the existing medieval churches, leaving spiritual guidance beyond the reach of many, especially those who needed it most: "the Vilest People, Highwaymen, House-Breakers, Felons of all Degrees, Impudent Women, and Persons Disaffected to His Majesty's Government," according to Jonathan Swift.[3]

In the view of the committee, architecture could be used as a tool for promoting religious piety and correcting social ills.

The commission appointed under the act, composed primarily of churchmen and government officials, included a few architects: Sir Christopher Wren, his son Christopher, John Vanbrugh, and Thomas Archer. A working committee was also formed, made up of these men and two other architects appointed as surveyors, Nicholas Hawksmoor and William Dickinson, both of whom had assisted Wren at St. Paul's and on the City churches. The duty of the commissioners was to request information from each parish about its population, the number of churches needed, and possible sites. The surveyors' task was to examine and survey these sites, sometimes with the assistance of other members of the working committee. The working committee was to produce drawings and models of designs, which were reviewed by the commission. The surveyors had the additional responsibility of executing the designs as approved and managing all aspects of construction.

The commissioners' evaluation and selection of the designs were based on a series of guidelines, formulated by the committee and approved by the commission in July 1712, for "one general design or forme" for all fifty churches. Many of these precepts had their origin in the advice of Wren, presented by him in a letter to a friend as "my Sentiments, after long Experience" about building the City churches. His recommendations are eminently practical in addressing urban and architectural issues. Churches should be located in well-populated areas. The unwholesome and inconvenient practice of burying in and near churches should be prohibited in favor of cemeteries located on the cheaper, open ground in the suburbs, creating the added benefit of a graceful and salubrious border around the city. As early as 1666, in his plan for rebuilding London after the Great Fire, Wren had proposed improvements to the design of the city as a whole, an idea that interested many other members of the Royal Society, especially John Evelyn.[4]

In his recommendations for the architecture of churches, Wren discussed the issues that he himself had considered in those built after the fire. Included are comments on the selection of proper materials and methods for purchasing sites and, most importantly, on the design of the church in terms of its site and its function as an auditory. The site should be selected within a more populated area rather than on cheaper, vacant land on the outskirts of the suburbs to provide for the convenience of "better Inhabitants" who, in addition, could provide more substantial contributions in support of the church. The building should be placed on the site so that it fronted onto the main thoroughfare, a precise east–

west orientation being of secondary importance. Although the facade should be adorned by porticoes and a handsome spire should rise above the surroundings as an ornament to the city, the rest of the exterior should remain plain.

In his designs for the City churches, Wren followed these precepts consistently, despite the fact that the sites were generally very cramped, irregularly shaped, and had limited street frontage.[5] In addition, existing foundations and outside walls often had to be reused. The result was a whole series of plan configurations of basically three types – aisleless halls, basilicas with nave, side aisles, and galleries, and centralized designs – most with geometries deviating slightly from strictly straight lines and right angles. By cleverly manipulating the relationship between the main space, the entrance, and the tower, Wren was able, in all but a few, to place the altar on the east end, with the entrance opposite, although not necessarily on axis.[6] Every design was given a more prominent facade along the main street, ranging from elaborate classical temple fronts defining the entire facade, the main window, or the entry, to minimal classical moldings and quoins articulating window openings and wall planes. In many of the churches, however, this facade had no doorway, the actual entry being on the side, and sometimes accessible only from a narrow passage or a churchyard. Each church tower was designed to be different from the next, resulting in a great deal of variety within the skyline of the City. Wren's concern for the design of the street facade and the tower reflects his discussion of "perspective" found in Tract I, where he describes how a building must be designed in terms of how it will be seen within the context of the site and from various primary viewpoints. In the City churches, Wren states in his letter, the visitor would catch sight of the individual church tower, "rising in good Proportion above the neighbouring Houses," as an "Ornament to the Town." As he approached the location marked by the tower, he would recognize the church by its facade, "open in View" along the main street and "adorned with Porticos."[7]

Inside the church, Wren recommended that the space should be capacious enough to hold the large suburban congregations, but not over two thousand people, because beyond this capacity it would be difficult for everyone to hear and see the preacher. In order for the church to function as an "auditory," by considering the distance and area a voice carries, Wren recommended that the main space should be approximately 60 feet wide and 90 feet long. It should not be so crowded with pews that the poor could not see and hear from the aisles; preferably, the congregation should sit on benches. Wren's concern for the acoustics of the space reflects the emphasis on preaching in the liturgy of the Church of England of this period, as well as his own scientific interest in the subject.[8] Of Wren's City churches, almost all were auditories – a single, open room, the altar or communion table placed against the eastern wall, with no screen dividing the space into nave and chancel.[9] Wren cited his design for St. James, Piccadilly, in the suburb of Westminster, built from 1676 to 1684, with a rectangular nave flanked by aisles and galleries on each side and a tower and shallow chancel at opposite ends, as an ideal solution: "I think it may be found beautiful and convenient, and as such, the cheapest of any Form I could invent" (Figs. 31–2). Although a large number of Wren's churches follow this rectilinear, three-aisled, symmetrical model, there are others where there is an irregular rectangle, or even a square or polygon, for the main space, with only a single galleried aisle to one side, or even none at all. Although this great variety of form might suggest otherwise, Wren conceived of all of his church designs as auditories.

The commission heard recommendations on church design not only from Wren, but also from John Vanbrugh.[10] Although he and Wren agreed on many points – building on open sites, using porticoes and spires, planning according to liturgical needs, placing burials on the outskirts of town – Vanbrugh's concept of "Temples" with "the most Solemn & Awfull Appearance both without and within, that is possible" was very different from Wren's "beautiful and convenient" "auditory." Ultimately, in discussions of 1712 the commission adopted Wren's recommendations for convenience, but was much more influenced when approving designs by Vanbrugh's call for "Grandure" and "Magnificence." Some plans exist, drawn on site surveys, that follow the model of Wren's St. James, Piccadilly, but neither this nor any standard church plan was ever adopted in the only twelve churches that were completed by the time the surveyors were dismissed in 1733.

After the fall of the Tory government in 1714, the grandiose vision of fifty new churches in and around London was abandoned, with only the individual churches, especially those by Hawksmoor, Archer, and Gibbs, remaining behind to form fragments of that vision. They are characterized, not by Wren's dignified, modest auditory ideal, but by that grandeur and magnificence called for in Vanbrugh's proposal and found in much of the architecture of the first two decades of the eighteenth century. By this point in his career, Wren could take only an indirect, although significant, role in this achievement – as teacher, advisor, church designer, and leading architect of the previous generation. Therefore the primary value of Wren's letter on the design of churches is as a record of his theoretical approach to one of the major challenges of his career: the creation of a new form of church architecture that responded to the liturgical needs of High Church worship and met the classical standards of beauty he sought to establish, through his theory as well as his practice, for Restoration England.

Letter to a Friend on the Commission for Building Fifty New City Churches (1711)

Source
    Original manuscript missing. *Parentalia* (London, 1750), "The Life of Sir Christopher Wren, Knt.," pt. 2, sec. 9, 318–21 (transcript in *WS*, 9:15–18)
Other Manuscript Versions
    RS MS 249, fols. 428v–432v
    All Souls MS 313, fols. 600–10
Date
    1711

(page 318)

Since Providence, in great Mercy, has protracted my Age, to the finishing the cathedral Church of *St. Paul*, and the parochial Churches of *London*, in lieu of those demolished by *the Fire*; (all which were executed during the Fatigues of my Employment in the Service of the Crown, from that Time to the present happy Reign;) and being now constituted one of the Commissioners for Building, pursuant to the late *Act, Fifty* more Churches in *London* and *Westminster*; I shall presume to communicate briefly my Sentiments, after long Experience; and without further Ceremony exhibit to better Judgment, what at present occurs to me, in a transient View of this whole Affair; not doubting but that the Debates of the worthy Commissioners may hereafter give me occasion to change, or add to these Speculations.

    1. First, I conceive the Churches should be built, not where vacant Ground may be cheapest purchased in the Extremities of the Suburbs, but among the thicker Inhabitants, for Convenience of the better sort, although the Site of them should cost more; the better Inhabitants contributing most to the future Repairs, and the Ministers and Officers of the Church, and Charges of the Parish.

(page 319)

    2. I could wish that all Burials in Churches might be disallowed, which is not only unwholesom, but the Pavements can never be kept even, nor Pews upright. And if the Church-yard be close about the Church, this also is inconvenient, because the Ground being continually raised by the Graves, occasions, in Time, a Descent by Steps into the Church, which renders it damp, and the Walls green, as appears evidently in all old Churches.

3. It will be enquired, where then shall be the Burials? I answer, in Cemeteries seated in the Out-skirts of the Town; and since it is become the Fashion of the Age to solemnize Funerals by a Train of Coaches, (even where the Deceased are of moderate Condition) though the Cemeteries should be half a Mile, or more, distant from the Church, the Charge need be little or no more than usual; the Service may be first performed in the Church: But for the Poor, and such as must be interred at the Parish Charge, a publick Hearse of two Wheels and one Horse may be kept at small Expence, the usual Bearers to lead the Horse, and take out the Corpse at the Grave. A Piece of Ground of two Acres in the Fields will be purchased for much less than two Roods among the Buildings: This being inclosed with a strong Brick Wall, and having a Walk round, and two cross Walks, decently planted with Yew-trees, the four Quarters may serve four Parishes, where the Dead need not be disturbed at the Pleasure of the Sexton, or piled four or five upon one another, or Bones thrown out to gain Room. In these Places beautiful Monuments may be erected; but yet the Dimensions should be regulated by an Architect, and not left to the Fancy of every Mason; for thus the Rich, with large Marble Tombs, would shoulder out the Poor; when a Pyramid, a good Bust, or Statue on a proper Pedestal, will take up little Room in the Quarters, and be properer than Figures lying on Marble Beds: The Walls will contain Escutchions and Memorials for the Dead, and the Area good Air and Walks for the Living. It may be considered further, that if the Cemeteries be thus thrown into the Fields, they will bound the excessive Growth of the City with a graceful Border, which is now encircled with Scavengers Dung-stalls.

4. As to the Situation of the Churches, I should propose they be brought as forward as possible into the larger and more open Streets, not in obscure Lanes, nor where Coaches will be much obstructed in the Passage. Nor are we, I think, too nicely to observe East or West in the Position, unless it falls out properly: Such Fronts as shall happen to lie most open in View should be adorned with Porticos, both for Beauty and Convenience; which, together with handsome Spires, or Lanterns, rising in good Proportion above the neighbouring Houses, (of which I have given several Examples in the City of different Forms) may be of sufficient Ornament to the Town, without a great Expence for inriching the outward Walls of the Churches, in which Plainness and Duration ought principally, if not wholly, to be studied. When a Parish is divided, I suppose it may be thought sufficient, if the Mother-church has a Tower large enough for a good Ring of Bells, and the other Churches

smaller Towers for two or three Bells; because great Towers, and lofty Steeples, are sometimes more than half the Charge of the Church.

5. I shall mention something of the Materials for publick Fabricks. It is true, the mighty Demand for the hasty Works of thousands of Houses at once, after the Fire of *London*, and the Frauds of those who built by the great, have so debased the Value of Materials, that good Bricks are not to be now had, without greater Prices than formerly, and indeed, if rightly made, will deserve them; but Brick-makers spoil the Earth in the mixing and hasty burning, till the Bricks will hardly bear Weight; though the Earth about *London*, rightly managed, will yield as good Brick as were the *Roman* Bricks, (which I have often found in the old Ruins of the City) and will endure, in our Air, beyond *(page 320)* any Stone our Island affords; which, unless the Quarries lie near the Sea, are too dear for general Use: The best is *Portland*, or *Rochabbey* Stone; but these are not without their Faults. The next Material is the Lime; Chalk-lime is the constant Practice, which, well mixed with good Sand, is not amiss, though much worse than hard Stone-lime. The Vaulting of *St. Paul*'s is a Rendering as hard as Stone; it is composed of Cockle-shell-lime well beaten with Sand; the more Labour in the beating, the better and stronger the Mortar. I shall say nothing of Marble, (though *England*, *Scotland*, and *Ireland*, afford good, and of beautiful Colours) but this will prove too costly for our Purpose, unless for Altar-pieces. In Windows and Doors *Portland* Stone may be used, with good Bricks, and Stone Quoyns. As to Roofs, good Oak is certainly the best; because it will bear some Negligence: The Church-wardens Care may be defective in speedy mending Drips; they usually white-wash the Church, and set up their Names, but neglect to preserve the Roof over their Heads: It must be allowed, that the Roof being more out of Sight, is still more unminded. Next to Oak is good yellow Deal, which is a Timber of Length, and light, and makes excellent Work at first, but if neglected will speedily perish, especially if Gutters (which is a general Fault in Builders) be made to run upon the principal Rafters, the Ruin may be sudden. Our Sea-service for Oak, and the Wars in the North-sea, make Timber at present of excessive Price. I suppose 'ere long we must have recourse to the *West-Indies*, where most excellent Timber may be had for cutting and fetching. Our Tiles are ill made, and our Slate not good; Lead is certainly the best and lightest Covering, and being of our own Growth and Manufacture, and lasting, if properly laid, for many hundred Years, is, without question, the most preferable; though I will not deny

but an excellent Tile may be made to be very durable; our Artisans are not yet instructed in it, and it is not soon done to inform them.

6. The Capacity and Dimensions of the new Churches may be determined by a Calculation. It is, as I take it, pretty certain, that the Number of Inhabitants, for whom these Churches are provided, are five times as many as those in the City, who were burnt out, and probably more than 400,000 grown Persons that should come to Church, for whom these fifty Churches are to be provided, (besides some Chapels already built, though too small to be made parochial.) Now, if the Churches could hold each 2000, it would yet be very short of the necessary Supply. The Churches therefore must be large; but still, in our reformed Religion, it should seem vain to make a *Parish-church* larger, than that all who are present can both hear and see. The *Romanists*, indeed, may build larger Churches, it is enough if they hear the Murmur of the Mass, and see the Elevation of the Host, but ours are to be fitted for Auditories. I can hardly think it practicable to make a single Room so capacious, with Pews and Galleries, as to hold above 2000 Persons, and all to hear the Service, and both to hear distinctly, and see the Preacher. I endeavoured to effect this, in building the Parish Church of *St. James's, Westminster*,[1] which, I presume, is the most capacious, with these Qualifications, that hath yet been built; and yet at a solemn Time, when the Church was much crowded, I could not discern from a Gallery that 2000 were present. In this Church I mention, though very broad, and the middle Nave arched up, yet as there are no Walls of a second Order, nor Lanterns, nor Buttresses, but the whole Roof rests upon the Pillars, as do also the Galleries; I think it may be found beautiful and convenient, and as such, the cheapest of any Form I could invent.

FIGURES 31–2

7. Concerning the placing of the Pulpit, I shall observe———
———A moderate Voice may be heard 50 Feet distant before the Preacher, 30 Feet on each Side, and 20 behind the Pulpit, and not this, unless the Pronunciation be distinct and equal, without losing the Voice at the last Word of the Sentence, which is commonly **(page 321)** emphatical, and if obscur'd spoils the whole Sense. A *French* Man is heard further than an *English* Preacher, because he raises his Voice, and not sinks his last Words:[2] I mention this as an insufferable Fault in the Pronunciation of some of our otherwise excellent Preachers; which School-masters might correct in the young, as a vicious Pronunciation, and not as the *Roman* Orators spoke: For the principal Verb is in Latin usually the last Word; and if that be lost, what becomes of the Sentence?

8. By what I have said, it may be thought reasonable, that the

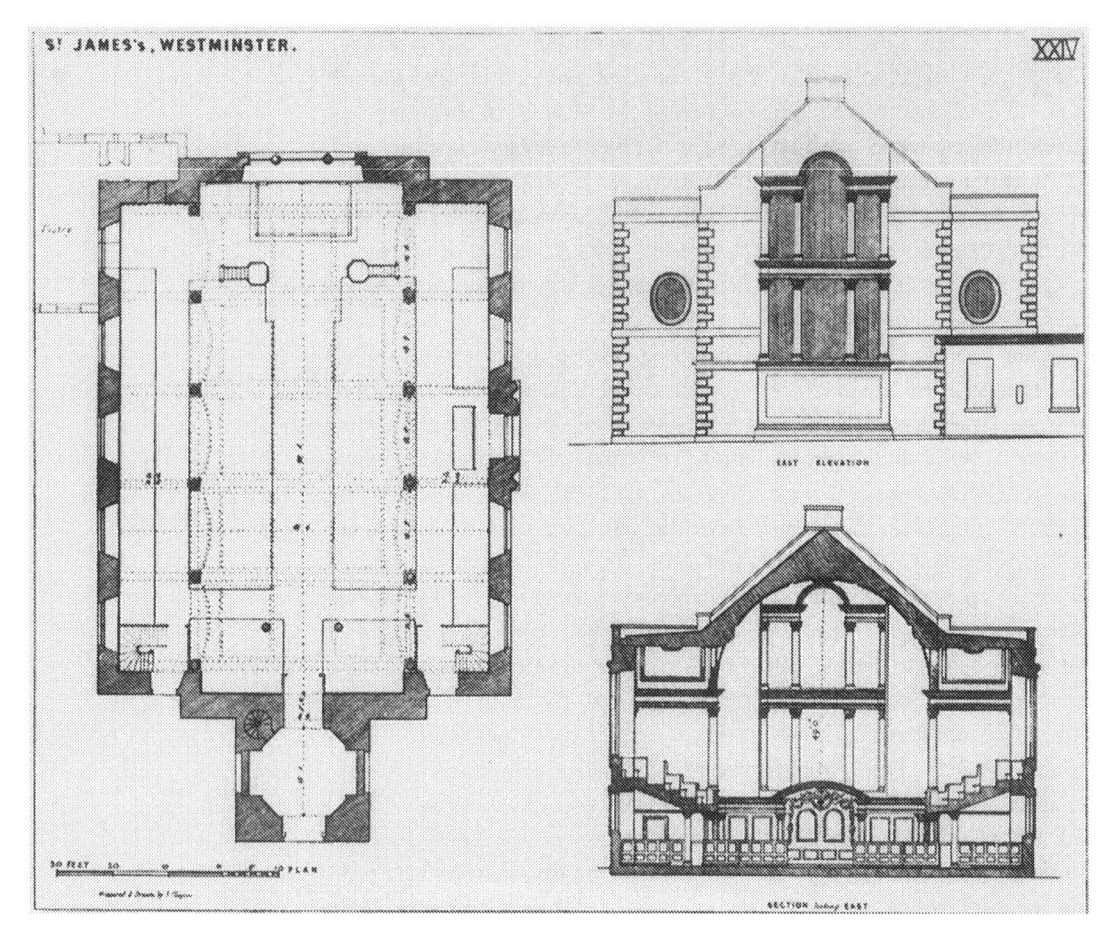

FIGURE 31. London, St. James, Piccadilly, plan, east elevation, and section, 1676–84, drawn by John Clayton, 1848 (John Clayton, *The Dimensions, Plans, Elevations, and Sections of the Parochial Churches of Sir Christopher Wren* [London, 1848–9]). Special Collections Library, The University of Michigan.

new Church should be at least 60 Feet broad, and 90 Feet long, besides a Chancel at one End, and the Bellfrey and Portico at the other. These Proportions may be varied; but to build more room, than that every Person may conveniently hear and see, is to create Noise and Confusion. A Church should not be so fill'd with Pews, but that the Poor may have room enough to stand and sit in the Alleys,[3] for to them equally is the Gospel preach'd. It were to be wish'd there were to be no Pews, but Benches; but there is no stemming the Tide of Profit, and the Advantage of Pew-keepers; especially too since by Pews, in the Chapels of Ease, the Minister is chiefly supported. It is evident these fifty Churches are not enough for the present Inhabitants, and the Town will continually

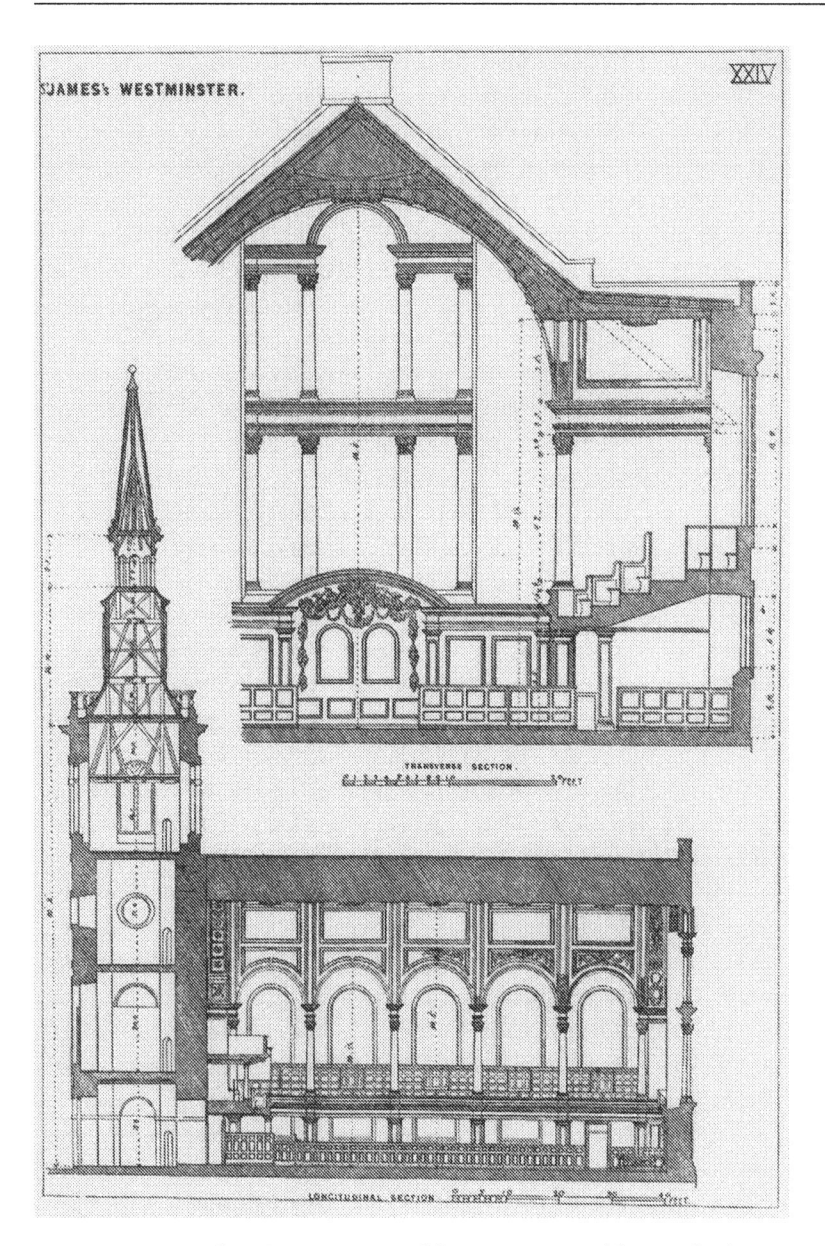

FIGURE 32. London, St. James, Piccadilly, transverse and longitudinal sections, 1676–84, drawn by John Clayton, 1848 (John Clayton, *The Dimensions, Plans, Elevations, and Sections of the Parochial Churches of Sir Christopher Wren* [London, 1848–9]). Special Collections Library, The University of Michigan.

grow; but it is to be hoped, that hereafter more may be added, as the Wisdom of the Government shall think fit; and therefore the Parishes should be so divided, as to leave room for Sub-divisions, or at least for Chapels of Ease.

I cannot pass over mentioning the Difficulties that may be found, in obtaining the Ground proper for the Sites of the Churches among the Buildings, and the Cæmeteries in the Borders without the Town; and therefore I shall recite the Method that was taken for purchasing in Ground at the North-side of *St. Paul*'s Cathedral, where in some Places the Houses were but eleven Feet distant from the Fabrick, exposing it to the continual Danger of Fires.[4] The Houses were seventeen, and contiguous, all in Lease-hold of the Bishop or Dean alone, or the Dean and Chapter, or the Pettycanons, with divers Undertenants. First we treated with the superior Landlords, who being perpetual Bodies were to be recompens'd in Kind, with Rents of the like Value for them and their Successors; but the Tenants in Possession for a valuable Consideration; which to find what it amounted to, we learn'd by diligent Inquiry, what the Inheritance of Houses in that Quarter were usually held at: This we found was fifteen Years Purchase at the most, and proportionably to this the Value of each Lease was easily determin'd in a Scheme, referring to a Map. These Rates, which we resolv'd not to stir from, were offered to each; and, to cut off much Debate, which may be imagin'd every one would abound in, they were assur'd that we went by one uniform Method, which could not be receded from. We found two or three reasonable Men, who agreed to these Terms: Immediately we paid them, and took down their Houses. Others who stood out at first, finding themselves in Dust and Rubbish, and that ready Money was better, as the Case stood, than to continue paying Rent, Repairs, and Parish Duties, easily came in. The whole Ground at last was clear'd, and all concern'd were satisfied, and their Writings given up. The great Debate was about their Charges for fitting-up their new Houses to their particular Trades: For this we allow'd one Year's Purchase, and gave leave to remove all their Wainscote, reserving the Materials of the Fabrick only. This was happily finish'd without a Judicatory or Jury; altho' in our present Case, we may find it perhaps sometimes necessary to have recourse to Parliament.

CHAPTER 5

Tracts on Architecture

INTRODUCTION

Despite their fragmentary nature, Wren's five Tracts provide the most coherent statement of his theory of architecture. Because they address traditional themes found in architectural treatises since the Renaissance, it has been suggested that Wren intended to make his own contribution to this genre, preparing the tracts at the end of his long career, that is, in the early 1700s, as the draft for a projected four-part treatise.[1] Each part would have addressed a by now familiar subject. The first would have been on beauty, covering most of the material in Tract I. Part 2 would have been on the origin of building and the orders, discussed in Tracts I, II, and III. The third would have been on classical antiquities with drawn reconstructions, including the descriptions in Tracts IV and V of buildings recorded in the Bible and by Josephus, as well as the classical monuments described by Pliny the Younger and Herodotus. The fourth and final part of the projected treatise would have concerned structure, based on material contained in Tract II.

It is unknown if Wren intended to produce a finished treatise. Evidence does show, however, that his investigation of the subjects contained in the undated Tracts began early, rather than late, in his career. From as early as 1663, and continuing particularly during the 1670s, as shown in Hooke's diary and other sources that will be discussed, Wren was busy drawing reconstructions and studying ancient buildings. Around the same time at the Royal Society, as the group's minutes show, he and Hooke investigated problems of structures. This suggests that Wren wrote the Tracts in the mid-1670s, as his career was shifting into full gear rather than slowing to a halt. Wren had certainly formulated most of his important theoretical ideas by the 1690s. Roger North (1653?–1734), a lawyer turned architect and "a dabbler" in mechanics and mathematics, relates in his unpublished "Of Building" (1690s) that on Saturdays he and his brother visited St. Paul's and got "a snatch of discourse" from Wren. Wren, in a manner "obliging and communicative," "gave short but satisfactory answers" to their questions.[2] In a "discourse with him upon the subject of beauty,"

> He (for argument sake), held the contrary, that there were things naturally handsome or deformed, which were so to

all eys, learned or unlearned. And instanc't in tryangles, that all approved an equilater, and disliked a scalene; and so the comon demensions of columes, which were aggreable to all.[3]

Similar ideas are found in Wren's Tract I in reference to the natural causes of beauty.[4]

Although he was concerned with theoretical issues traditionally treated in architectural treatises, Wren approached them in a completely new way based on his particular understanding of architecture as a natural philosopher. He applied the values and methods of seventeenth-century science to detailed investigations of buildings of all types and periods, and consequently collected a unique body of data that compelled him to rethink inherited precepts and formulate new ones. As a result, he presents in the five Tracts: (1) a new hypothesis of the origin of the Classical style, (2) the first history of architecture, (3) one of the first dualistic definitions of beauty, and (4) one of the earliest statical investigations of structures. Before treating each of these subjects, it is necessary to investigate the unique nature of Wren's architectural knowledge, combining various sources and interpretations, both old and new, which provided the foundation for his new theoretical ideas.

Wren had no formal training in architecture, but by the time he began to practice at the age of thirty it is clear that he was already an astute observer of buildings. He continued to examine them over the course of his entire life – sometimes as the direct result of his official duties as Surveyor General, sometimes simply as opportunities presented themselves. In all instances this work was driven by his own intense interest in the subject. Whether it was during excavations for new buildings in London, surveys and repairs of Gothic cathedrals, travels to new building sites, or a visit to Paris, in every situation Wren seems to have taken the time to gather data on some form of architecture never before observed by him. At the same time, beginning early in his career, Wren attempted to describe and reconstruct biblical and ancient classical buildings based on literary sources. For him it was an activity as important as the design of actual buildings. In a letter of 1663 he rejected the making of architectural drawings as part of a demonstration to Charles II during an upcoming visit to the Royal Society, declaring, "Designs in architecture are only considerable as they are appropriated to some work in hand, or else, as they are a kind of criticism and search into antiquity."[5]

Wren's examination of past buildings took place not only as a part of his practice as an architect but also as a part of his activities as a Royal Society fellow. Wren was one of several at the society who carried on discussions of building practices, antiquities, structures, and other architectural matters, which often were continued in more informal social settings. Wren and his close circle of friends, particularly Robert Hooke, his closest collaborator in his practice of architecture, met in their homes and in the London coffeehouses to enjoy lively discussions of all manner of things, ranging from the philosophical to the curious, among them a wide variety of architectural matters. Together they observed buildings at first hand, talked to travelers, examined written sources, made drawn reconstructions, and debated the structure, form, and style of diverse monuments.

Wren's knowledge of a broad range of architecture, formed over many years within a variety of settings, provided the foundation for his writings, not only in the form of data for his descriptions of past buildings, but as the stimulus for his new theoretical ideas. The Tracts show his interest in more traditional classical antiquities, but also in biblical monuments and other buildings found in the area of the Mediterranean that preceded, as well as followed, those of the ancient Greeks and Romans. At the same time, there is evidence that Wren went further, to study other forms of past architecture – local antiquities (pre-Roman, Roman, and medieval), as well as building practices outside Europe in the Near East, Far East, and New World.

The core of Wren's investigation of classical monuments is found in the Tracts. In Tract IV he discusses four: the Temple of Diana at Ephesus, the Temple of Peace (i.e., the Basilica of Maxentius and Constantine), the Temple of Mars Ultor, and the Mausoleum of Halicarnassus; Porsenna's Tomb is treated in Tract V. These discussions appear to be related to the activities of Wren's circle, which often sought out the latest information on classical buildings, particularly those not recorded in treatises or topographic works. For example, on 23 May 1676 Hooke records, "At Sir Chr. Wren with him to Mr. Montacues, then to Corners. Saw scetches of Athens." On 6 December 1679 he "Dined with Sir Ch. Wren. Saw his Septizonium Severi. See figure A."[6] This was probably an engraving owned by Wren of the early-third-century Septizonium on the Palatine in Rome, demolished in 1588.[7]

Some of these exchanges involved the drawing of reconstructions. According to Hooke's diary, in October of 1677 he and Wren speculated on the form of the tomb of Porsenna, historically an Etruscan king from the late sixth century B.C. Both used the evidence of Varro's description of the monument as quoted by Pliny the Younger, but disagreed on its true form. Hooke wrote in his diary on 4 October: "at the Crown. Discoursd of Porsennas tomb of which Sr Ch: Wren gave a description but comparing it with the Words it agreed not. I found the form of it quite otherwise and Described it."[8] On 17 October, Hooke again saw the drawing of Wren's reconstruction and made a sketch of it in his diary (Fig. 45): "to Sr Chr. Wrens. Discoursed with him long of Porcena's tomb which he had thus drawn. a. signifying the Labyrinth & ground plat. b. the upright &c of which see the figures."[9] The next day Hooke "Drew a rationall porcenna," his own scheme.[10] They continued their debate on October 20 at Mans coffeehouse.[11] The drawing that Hooke saw at Wren's home may have been the same one that John Aubrey had heard of and hoped to see: "desire him [Wren] to show me *his* excellent draught of Porsenna's monument."[12] Aubrey wrote that "Sir Christopher Wren hath made a Draught of it about four foot long, which I could not (yet) obtain the favour to see."[13] Although Wren's drawing was never heard of again, Hooke's scheme was presented on 9 July 1684 to the Royal Society and is recorded in a sketch by Aubrey.[14]

Wren made reconstruction drawings of at least two other classical buildings discussed in the Tracts. As has been mentioned before, a plan and elevation of the Temple of Diana at Ephesus, dating from 356 B.C. and celebrated as one of the Seven Wonders of the World, are published with Tracts I through IV in the appendix of the 1750 *Parentalia* and are probably based on original sketches by Wren (Figs. 35–6). Another of the Seven Wonders, the Greek Mausoleum of Halicarnassus, completed c. 349 B.C., influenced Wren's design of the Great Model of St. Paul's, where he used the stepped pyramid motif as the lantern of the domed vestibule (Fig. 53). The Great Model was completed from as early as the spring of 1673, and certainly by August of 1674.[15] The drawing preserved in Tract V, which coincides with Wren's description, is by Nicholas Hawksmoor, but there may well have been one made by Wren to accompany his description (Fig. 44).

Wren's study of biblical monuments is represented primarily in the Tracts, where he discusses a total of nine. In the published Tract IV are descriptions of the Temple of Dagon that Samson destroyed, the "sepulchre" of Absalom, and the Temple of Solomon; the manuscript Tract V includes the city of Enos, the two columns constructed by the sons of Seth, Noah's Ark, the Tower of Babel, the pyramids of Egypt, and, repeating some of the material in Tract IV, the "pillar" of Absalom and the Temple of Solomon, followed by the city of Babylon. Apparently, Wren also drew reconstructions of some of these monuments. The minutes of the Royal Society meeting on 25 June 1712 record that "A letter was read from Dr. [William] Musgrave concerning Dr. Hudson's new designed Edition of Josephus. Mr. [Abraham] Hill said that Sir Christopher Wrenn had made severall draughts of Buildings mentioned in Josephus."[16] Of the buildings discussed in the Tracts, all except for the city Enos are found in *The Antiquities of the Jews* by the ancient Roman Jewish historian Josephus.[17] Of these, however, only one is known from outside evidence to have been drawn by Wren: the tomb or pillar of the biblical figure Absalom, son of David. John Aubrey noted, in part 3 on mausolea in *Monumenta Britannica,* that he had seen Wren's reconstruction: "*Absalom's Pillar,* which was cutt out of a rock; which Sir Christopher Wren says 'twas a pretty thing. Insert his draught of it here."[18] Unfortunately, the drawing is now lost. There is no further evidence for reconstructions of biblical buildings by Wren, although it is possible that they once existed. His description of the Tower of Babel in Tract V possibly included a reconstruction that was known to Hooke, who in later years went on to make his own drawings, some of which were presented to the Royal Society.[19]

It is very likely that Wren's passages on biblical buildings in the Tracts are related to discussions among his circle of friends. According to Hooke's diary, the Temple of Solomon was the subject of a dinner party on 6 September 1675. "At Mr Storys coald venison and coadling. With Sr Chr. Wren. Long Discourse with him about the module of the temple at Jerusalem."[20] This was probably the model made by Jacob Jehudah Leon, a Dutch rabbi. A letter of introduction, written by Constantine Huygens and dated 7 October 1674, tells Wren of the bearer, a Jew who intends to show his model of the Temple of Solomon that he has been constructing for many years. This man has been identified as Leon, who had studied and published on the temple since the 1640s and traveled to London to exhibit his model in 1675.[21]

Taken as a whole, Wren's presentation of architectural monuments in Tracts IV and V goes much further than the undifferentiated catalog of Roman antiquities found in Renaissance treatises, for example, Serlio's book 3 of 1540. Extending his scope of investigation beyond the ancient Roman world, Wren includes biblical buildings, which had been neglected by all previous writers except those of biblical exegesis, most notably Villalpando and Kircher. He presents them in conjunction with classical buildings in a more or less chronological discussion, thus creating a sequence beginning with many of the most important monuments of biblical antiquity followed by those of Greece and Rome. Further, Wren demonstrates how this development arose logically out of the origins of architecture, presenting a new hypothesis of the original forms and how they were developed and changed over time in biblical and then classical architecture. In his Tracts, Wren joined the tradition of the antiquarian with the methods of the scientist, applying a new and more rigorous approach borrowed from the New Science that ultimately led him to challenge architectural traditions adhered to for centuries.

Scientific method demanded that the investigator question all received knowledge on his subject, which for the studies of both nature and architecture during this period was derived from the ancient Greeks and Romans.[22] Hence Wren could not accept as given the precepts presented by the traditional ancient authorities for the Classical style – Vitruvius and the Roman remains. Instead he acknowledged a problem avoided by architects and theorists since the fifteenth century: that these authorities did not agree on the forms and proportions of the orders. During Wren's time this fact was definitively proven by Antoine Desgodets (1653–1728) in his *Les edifices antiques de Rome* (1682). Desgodets demonstrated not only that the ancients used a variety of measures for a single order but also that the Renaissance theorists had made errors in recording them.[23] Wren, recognizing the "great Differences" among the forms and measures of the orders, concluded that they had been "arbitrarily used" by the ancients.[24]

In addition, scientific method demanded the gathering of data – directly, comprehensively, systematically, and critically – to form a "natural history" to be used as the basis for formulating new, true laws of a phenomenon. Therefore, Wren examined not only the traditional literary and material sources for past buildings but also a variety of new sources. Before accepting any of the data they provided, he assessed all of them for their accuracy and reliability.[25] As a result of applying the methods of science, Wren went beyond earlier studies to examine a much broader range of architecture, past and present, than ever before. Most importantly, Wren, unlike his predecessors, no longer ignored the ample architectural evidence existing by the seventeenth century that contradicted the Vitruvian myth of the origin of architecture and the classical orders, as well as the accepted history of its development starting with the Egyptians and passing to the Greeks, the Romans, and on to the present.

Among Wren's evidence was a wide range of buildings, never before considered by architects, that came to his attention. At Wren's home on 17 October 1677, he and Hooke "Discoursed also of Persepolis,"[26] the capital of the Persian Empire erected during the late fifth century B.C. A few years later, in 1680, Hooke, Wren, and John Evelyn on several occasions visited the French traveler John Chardin to hear his descriptions and possibly see his drawings of the ruins there, none of which were published until 1711.[27] On 14 November 1677 Hooke recorded "To Sir Chr Wr. at Mans with him and Mr. Smith, a description of Sta Sophia."[28] Their discussion of Hagia Sophia, dedicated in 537, must have been with Thomas Smith, a fellow of the Royal Society and Oxford divine who lived in Constantinople for two years from 1669 while in the service of the English ambassador. Smith had visited the building and described it in his travel account published in the *Philosophical Transactions*,[29] although the inaccuracy of Hooke's sketch of the plan indicates how little he understood its form. Wren mentioned "St. Sophia" in Tract II, noting the form of its vaulting, which he also found used in "the Mosques and Cloysters of the *Dervises*" as well as "the present Seraglio, which was the episcopal Palace of old; the imperial Palace, whose Ruins still appear, being farther eastward."[30] Wren's interest in the vaulting used in Constantinople is confirmed by Roger North, who records that Wren sought information on "their covering their vaults with lead" from his brother Sir Dudley North, who had the greatest knowledge of "the manner of the Turkish buildings."[31]

Wren's interests also went beyond Europe and the Near East to include more distant lands and times. He knew about Chinese architecture, most certainly from travel books, telling Aubrey that "The *Chineses* have great Mausolea of Earth, which fashion is more ancient than the Romans."[32] Closer to home, and available for his direct examination, were prehistoric stone circles of heatedly debated origins. According to John Stukeley, who had the information from John Harwood, F.R.S., "Sir Christopher Wren says, there are such works as Stonehenge in Africa & that they are temples dedicate[d] to Saturn[.] He well may mean they were made by the Phoenicians, and by Saturn Shadi is meant."[33]

Some of the material cited above was collected by Wren as a part of the Royal Society's natural and mechanical history program. Through this program information on all types of architecture was solicited and collected in the form of reports and travel books, some illustrated. Many were printed or reviewed in the *Philosophical Transactions*. These sources showed that primitive dwellings of all kinds continued to be built every place outside of Europe.[34] In the former territories of the Egyptian, Persian, and Roman empires there were architectural remains that had classical attributes but clearly constituted other modes of building.[35] In the Near East and the Far East there were long-established monumental forms of building unlike any elsewhere – Islamic and Chinese architecture.[36] The most conspicuously inexplicable architectural evidence was found among the material antiquities of Great Britain, in primitive megalithic structures such as the stone circles at Stonehenge and Avebury. Examined at first hand by Royal Society fellows, in particular John Aubrey in his unpublished *Monumenta Britannica* (written primarily 1663–72), and discussed at meetings,[37] they were not easily placed within recorded history.

In gathering evidence on all forms of building, Wren was limited by his sources. As for any natural phenomenon, Wren as a scientist would have preferred his own direct observations, or those of a reliable witness. Due, however, to the difficulties of travel and, upon arrival, of finding anything recognizable, he had to depend on written records. The most up-to-date information was provided by travel books, which often included descriptions of biblical and classical buildings, some even the eyewitness accounts of natural philosophers and therefore of immense value. In addition Wren relied on the descriptions of ancient writers that he deemed authentic and reliable. As the Tracts indicate, he considered among the most important Pliny the Younger and Herodotus, who described famous monuments of early antiquity such as the Seven Wonders of the World, presumably based on their own observations. For the monuments of Old Testament times the primary sources were the histories of Josephus and the Bible. For the original forms of building, created during the earliest age of mankind, the only records available were the accounts found in the Bible and in Vitruvius's *De architectura*.

Wren's reliance upon ancient literary sources, in particular Vitruvius and the Bible, may seem to contradict the skepticism that guided seventeenth-century science, but in fact it is a reflection of its particular nature. Despite the fact that it was ancient, and therefore suspect, Wren accepted Vitruvius's text: "*Vitruvius* hath led us the true Way to find the Originals of the Orders."[38] Although he does not state his reasons, he probably considered it, based on his scientific judgment, an old enough and reliable enough record, to say nothing of its being the *only* surviving classical account. At the same time he could not ignore, as Renaissance theorists had, the conflicting source of the Bible. Wren was among the scientists of the seventeenth century who, despite their skepticism, were Christians. They accepted the authority of the Bible, often stating how in the search for knowledge there were two books to read: Nature and Scripture, both revealing divine laws.[39]

Although as an architect Wren had inherited the notion that the Renaissance precepts of classical architecture were absolute and universal, given by nature and God, Wren as a scientist had to confront what his investigation of the architecture of all times and places revealed: that a wide variety of past and present building practices existed which contradicted them. Nevertheless, he was confident that, as in the study of natural phenomena, the true principles of architecture would ultimately be revealed after one gathered and analyzed as large a body of data as possible. That data, created by Wren's active investigation of ancient and more recent buildings around the world, is recorded in his history of biblical and classical architecture in Tracts IV and V, as well as in his notes on London antiquities, reports on Gothic churches, and observations on

French architecture. Wren went on to develop reasoned explanations for the architectural phenomena he observed. In Tract V he writes:

> I judge it not improper to endeavour to reform the Generality to a truer tast in Architecture by giving a larger Idea of the whole Art, beginning with the reasons and progress of it from the most remote Antiquity; and that in short, touching chiefly on some things, which have not been remark'd by others.[40]

In the course of doing so, Wren wrote, he hoped to discover "the Grounds of Architecture"[41] or fundamental theoretical principles. In his investigation of the "reasons" and "Grounds" behind the origin and history of architecture, beauty, and structure, he was forced to consider the question of the true nature of architecture – whether it is a phenomenon based on the absolute, universal laws of nature and, by extension, God, or on the laws of society and man.

In formulating his hypothesis of the origin of architecture and the orders, Wren had no material evidence available to him and thus had to depend on the accounts of Vitruvius and the Bible. He considered both accurate historical documents; the Bible's authority was indisputable. Despite the mythological nature of these accounts, and the fact that they did not agree with one another, Wren conflated and amended them to create a single origin and time line that could include all known architecture.

In his myth of origins, Vitruvius described the original primitive dwelling as made out of natural materials to provide protection from the elements.[42] Wren accepted this as a plausible hypothesis, and went on to expand it by speculating on the origin of the first temple, where, according to Vitruvius, the classical orders had developed.[43] However, he rejected Vitruvius's demonstration that the orders were based on the forms and proportions of the human body[44] and focused instead on his implication that the first column was a tree. Wren writes:

> The first Temples were, in all Probability, in the ruder Times, only little *Cellæ* to inclose the Idol within, with no other Light then a large Door to discover it to the People, when the Priest saw proper, and when he went in alone to offer Incense, the People paying their Adorations without Doors; for all Sacrifices were performed in the open Air, before the Front of the Temple; but in the southern Climates, a Grove was necessary not only to shade the Devout,

but, from the Darkness of the Place, to strike some Terror and Recollection in their Approachers; therefore, Trees always [were] an Adjunct to the *Cellæ*.[45]

The idea of an original tree column was common since the Renaissance, based on Vitruvius's description of "forked stakes" in the original primitive hut, as well as of entasis imitating the figure of tree trunks.[46]

Due to their uneven growth and eventual decay, Wren continued, the trees surrounding the cella were later "represented with Stone Pillars, supporting the more durable Shade of a Roof," although the ornaments still recalled the original "Arbour of spreading Boughs." In the same manner, the first fora in cities, for protection from the sun, were "planted round with Walks of Trees," which were subsequently replaced by "Porticoes of Marble" where "both Architraves and Roofs were of Timber."[47] Later on, in both the temple and the forum, the elements of the superstructure came to be built in stone. Wren's idea of stone ornament copying the leaves of trees parallels Vitruvius's description of the origin of the Corinthian capital from acanthus leaves. His idea of the wooden superstructure transferred into stone derives directly from Vitruvius's description of the origin of the Doric entablature copying exactly in stone carpentry details formed "by an exact fitness deduced from the real laws of nature."[48] For Vitruvius, these myths of origin demonstrated not only that the details of the orders imitated nature's forms but also that they embodied her physical laws.

Wren called the first primitive, thick column based on the mature tree the Tyrian or Phoenician order because it was used by workers from Tyre, a city in Phoenicia, to build the Temple of Solomon. " 'Tis most probable *Solomon* employed the *Tyrian* Architects in his Temple, from his Correspondency with King *Hiram*; and from these *Phœnicians* I derive, as well the Arts, as the Letters of the *Grecians*. . . ."[49] In his history of architecture, Wren described the use of the Tyrian order in other monuments of biblical antiquity and how it was later adopted by the Greeks, who refined it into the slenderer Doric, Ionic, and Corinthian orders.

Wren's hypothesis of the Tyrian order represents a radical departure from Renaissance architectural theory for several reasons. First, although it reiterates the idea of the first column as a tree trunk, it dismisses the idea that the orders were based on human proportions. "This [the tree] I think the more natural Comparison," Wren writes, "than that to the Body of a Man, in which there is little Resemblance of a cylindrical Body."[50] The idea of human proportions as the basis for architecture had been crucial to Renaissance theorists in proving that architecture was based on natural law. Second, Wren's hypothesis dismisses the Vitruvian idea of the spontaneous appearance of the Doric order in all of its perfection by postulating a rude and thick primitive order, the Tyrian, as a root classical order. However, Wren did reinforce Renaissance thinking by demonstrating that the Tyrian, and the Greek and Roman orders that developed from it, had an origin in nature as described by Vitruvius.

Furthermore, by placing the Tyrian order at the Temple of Solomon, whose design, according to the Bible, was dictated by God,[51] Wren implied that the orders had a divine origin. In doing so he participated in a very old tradition concerning the divine architecture of the Temple of Solomon,[52] as well as a more recent one involving a protoclassical, Solomonic order. The exegetical writer Villalpando, in his famous 1604 reconstruction of the Temple of Solomon, gave the building a Corinthian order of palm leaves, and thus was able to reconcile Vitruvian and biblical authority. His order was widely accepted in the seventeenth century, proclaimed by Fréart de Chambray, for example, as being "as near as one can approach to that divine *Idea*." A related seventeenth-century tradition held that the Temple had spiral or twisted columns, a notion based on the columns originally located at Old St. Peter's in Rome that since the late Middle Ages were thought to be from the Temple.[53] Wren rejected both theories, describing Villalpando's order as "mere Fancy" and ignoring the spiral column in favor of a new form. Wren's rude order may still have been based on passages in the Bible and Josephus, leading him to conclude that the temple had "thick Pillars of the groser Proportions."[54] Although he never made claims to its divinity, Wren's Tyrian order reflected a long-standing idea about a Solomonic order of classical form and with origins in nature and God.

Wren's hypothesis of a thick column based on the proportions of the mature tree may have been influenced by recent discoveries, some made through the work of the Royal Society, of certain preclassical remains. By stating that "from these *Phœnicians* I derive, as well the Arts, as the Letters of the *Grecians*, though it may be the *Tyrians* were Imitators of the *Babylonians*, and they of the *Ægyptians*,"[55] Wren suggested that after its origin in the remote past, the Tyrian order was transferred from the Egyptians, to the Babylonians, to the Phoenicians (from whom it derived its name), and then to the Greeks. Since the Renaissance, scholars had accepted the Egyptians as the precursors of Greek culture, the diffusion of knowledge taking place through one or more of the other ancient eastern empires.[56] Wren knew monuments of these early civilizations, including immense Egyptian obelisks and columns and the thick, nonclassical columns at Persepolis, the capital of the Persian Empire.[57]

Similar in form were the huge megalithic columns of the stone circles in Britain, the origins of which were the subject of great debate from the mid-seventeenth century on. Whereas Inigo Jones believed the builders were Romans who used a Tuscan/Ionic order, Aylett Sammes favored Phoenician colonists and John Aubrey the Druids, the priests of the ancient Britons. According to Aubrey, Wren's friend and colleague at the Royal Society, the Druids, who might also have been Old Testament patriarchs, erected the stone circles to replace the groves of trees where they had once worshipped.[58] Many of these ideas are reflected in Wren's hypothesis of the Tyrian order, which in turn, could account for the existence of these and other prehistoric monuments.

With his idea of the Tyrian order, Wren implied a development beginning with its origin as a tree in nature, to a rude column of divine origin used in buildings like the Temple of Solomon, to the orders used by the early eastern empires, and then to the Doric, Ionic, and Corinthian orders of classical Greece and Rome. In this sequence Wren shifted from the concept of the orders as natural and divine to that of the orders as the unique products of specific cultures. This becomes even clearer in his discussion of biblical and classical buildings in Tracts IV and V. After describing the monuments cited in Genesis – the first city Enos, the two columns erected by the sons of Seth, Noah's Ark, the Tower of Babel, and the Great Pyramids of Egypt – Wren continues with several "Tyrian" monuments cited elsewhere in the Bible – the Temple of Dagon destroyed by Samson, the Sepulchre of Absalom, and the Temple of Solomon. He goes on to the city of Babylon, which is followed by early classical buildings: the tomb of the Etruscan king Porsenna, which, according to Wren, used the "Tyrian" order, the Mausoleum of Halicarnassus, which used "the exactest Form of the *Dorick*," and the Temple of Diana at Ephesus, which "introduced the *Ionick* Order."[59] Finally Wren discusses the "Temple of Peace" (Basilica of Maxentius and Constantine) and the Temple of Mars Ultor.

Wren assumes a chronology that begins with the first temple and forum in the remote past, initially using tree trunks as columns and then stone replicas, and continues with monuments from Old Testament times, using the stone tree-trunk column, now called the Tyrian order, through the Egyptian, Babylonian, Greek, Etruscan, and Roman periods, each developing its own order on the basis of what had come before. Although this chronology suggests a single path of diffusion of architectural knowledge, Wren demonstrates the uniqueness of the form of each building example, attempting to make a verbal or drawn reconstruction that would verify its form and structure, as well as the uniqueness of the conditions of its creation: the feasibility of its construction and how the form would fulfill the building's intended function. For example, he discussed the Egyptian pyramids in terms of the particular economic conditions that led to their creation, and Greek and Roman buildings in terms of the proportions and optical refinements that had an impact on their designs.

Wren's description of the origin and development of architecture in Tracts IV and V can be called the first "history" of architecture because it demonstrates, for the first time, a historical consciousness. This understanding of buildings as the product of particular cultural circumstances is not evident in earlier discussions of past buildings. Since the beginning of the Renaissance, artists had produced sketchbooks and published treatises with descriptions and illustrations of ancient buildings, but until the last quarter of the seventeenth century these constituted catalogs of examples undifferentiated by time or place.[60] Texts that treated the subject of past architecture, including Alberti's treatise of around 1450, the "Raphael" letter to Pope Leo X of 1520, and Vasari's prefaces to his *Vite* of 1550, presented critical rather than historical approaches to past art and architecture. Within the framework of periods or styles — the "good" antique, followed by the decline into the "barbarous" German or Gothic, and thereupon the rebirth of the antique with Brunelleschi and others — buildings were occasionally cited, but not discussed in terms of their forms or the circumstances that led to certain forms, beyond the placement of each within one of the periods.[61] Furthermore, by presenting a biological approach, these accounts conveyed the idea of a growth in antiquity, followed by decay during the Middle Ages, and then the resumption of growth with the Renaissance and continuous growth thereafter, promoting the concept of the ultimate timelessness and perfection of the Classical style.

Wren, by considering as much as possible the physical evidence of past buildings and examining the particular circumstances surrounding their creation, recognized that each culture produced its own characteristic forms as the result of a particular time and place. At the same time, by giving a chronological treatment of past monuments that was divorced from earlier value judgments, and therefore allowed a comparative study of the architecture of different periods, Wren understood the nature of architecture to be evolutionary and changing, subject to improvement but also decline. Because of his sense of history, Wren went on to postulate a new theory of beauty that acknowledged the impact of custom and society.

Wren's historical consciousness, recognizing past architecture and by extension present and future architecture as the product of society, could logically lead him to abandon the Renaissance ideal of the perfection and eternal validity of the Classical style. Within his history, however, exists another conception that contradicts his belief in cultural specificity in favor of universality: the diffusion of the Classical orders from a single natural and divine root order. The idea of diffusion from a single source is an old one, figuring most prominently in the Bible but found also in other writings modeled upon it: freemasonic history and universal history.[62] For Wren, however, the root, Tyrian order had not passed unchanged over the course of history, but each successive society had modified it into many other orders – "not only *Roman* and *Greek*, but *Phœnician, Hebrew*, and *Assyrian*." As they had been handed down, the orders not only retained their authority based on their origins, but gained added authority as the legitimate inventions of these great civilizations: "being founded upon the Experience of all Ages, promoted by the vast Treasures of all the Great Monarchs, and Skill of the greatest Artists and Geometricians, every one emulating each other."[63] This echoes earlier ideas on the development of classical architecture as stated by Alberti, "Building . . . enjoyed her first gush of youth . . . in Asia, flowered in Greece, and later reached her glorious maturity in Italy."[64] For Wren, the Classical orders stood as the "Principals," "uncapable of Modes and Fashions,"[65] certainly because of their origins, and even more so because of the greatness of the cultures that perpetuated them. Paradoxically, Wren used the evidence and methods of reasoning founded on contemporary science to create a new hypothesis of the orders not only as originating in nature and God, but also as products of society, which did not reject but rather reaffirmed the long-held belief in the eternal validity and universal applicability of the Classical style.

There are important parallels between Wren's approach to the past and that of his contemporary Johann Bernhard Fischer von Erlach (1656–1723), architect to Leopold I, Holy Roman Emperor, and author of *Entwurff einer historischen Architektur* (1721). In his history of architecture, the first of its kind to be published, Fischer utilized many of the same types of sources as Wren, included most of the same buildings, and furthermore presented others in which Wren had an interest – Stonehenge (presented as Roman), Hagia Sophia, mosques in Constantinople, and Chinese buildings – thus encompassing buildings of all times and cultures. Similarly, while Fischer exhibits a historical consciousness, he also maintains the idea of diffusion from a single source. He presents the Temple of Solomon as the root of Greek, Roman, and all subsequent architecture, each following the taste of the nation that made it, but all ultimately derived from the perfection of the original source. Fischer concludes from his history that "tho' Custom may indeed authorize certain Whims in the Art of Building; . . . there are certain general Principles in Architecture, which can by no Means be laid aside, without offending the Eye," including symmetry and strength.[66] In his definition of beauty, Wren, despite his recognition of custom, also retained the idea of "natural causes": geometry, uniformity, and proportion.

The framework for Wren's discussion of beauty and structure is established at the beginning of Tract I. Accepting the Vitruvian tripartite definition of architecture, Wren writes: "Beauty, Firmness, and Convenience, are the Principles." He amends this statement, however: "the two first depend upon geometrical Reasons of *Opticks* and *Staticks*; the third only makes the Variety."[67] Wren did not elaborate any further on the principle of convenience, which "only makes the Variety." For the other two principles he applied the epistemology of seventeenth-century science. For beauty he rejected traditional beliefs that viewed geometry as an absolute value, given by nature and God, and attempted to establish "geometrical Reasons of *Opticks*," borrowing from the analytical methods of empiricism. For firmness, which will be discussed at the end of this introduction, he attempted to establish, for the first time, "geometrical Reasons of *Staticks*" on the basis of rationalism.

Wren states that "Beauty is a Harmony of Objects, begetting Pleasure by the Eye."[68] The initial part of his definition, which formed the basis of Renaissance theory and practice, was first established by Alberti: "Beauty is that reasoned harmony of all the parts within a body, so that nothing may be added, taken away, or altered, but for the worse."[69] In contrast, the second part of Wren's definition, "begetting Pleasure by the Eye," has its origin in seventeenth-century scientific thought, reflecting the empirical approach to the study of phenomena. According to Francis Bacon, it was the senses "from which all knowledge in nature must be sought."[70] Similarly, Wren wrote that beauty is based on "geometrical Reasons of *Opticks*," and that it "is begotten by the Use of our Senses to . . . Objects."[71] Therefore, for Wren the aesthetic experience had less to do with the reality of the object itself, and more to do with the visual appearance of the object that resides in the viewer. The effect of beauty is triggered by two kinds of outside stimuli that he called "causes," the "natural" and the "customary."[72] Whereas the natural causes relate to the physiology of the eye, the customary relate to the psychology of the mind.

The "natural" causes are "*Geometry*, consisting in Uniformity (that is Equality), and Proportion." Rather than specifically architectural qualities, Wren is speaking about geometrical shapes, and goes on to cite the square and circle as the most beautiful, having the greatest uniformity, as well as the simplest proportions, followed next by the "parallelogram" and oval. Beauty being a matter of "Opticks," however, geometry has no value in and of itself, but only as a *cause* of beauty in the perception of the viewer. All viewers would agree to the effect of geometry on the visual sense: "Geometrical Figures are naturally more beautiful than other irregular; in this all consent as to a Law of Nature." Wren recognizes that there exist not only the senses, but also the mind, "the Judgment," which is the seat of the "Pleasure" produced by "the Eye."[73] The optical sense forms an image of the object and perceives it, depending on its particular geometry, as having a greater or lesser degree of beauty. This perception made by the eye is then conveyed to the mind, which then judges or understands the object accordingly.

Wren's discussion of geometry, as it does or does not relate to the object itself, and as it relates to the perception and judgment of the viewer, reflects two different philosophical traditions – one artistic, the other scientific. The first is the theory of Alberti, who postulated the existence of real and innate qualities of beauty in architecture, determined by the rational laws of mathematics, underlying nature and residing in God. Borrowing from Platonic/Neoplatonic thought, Alberti believed that beauty is produced "by invention and the working of the intellect" – specifically, abstract principles of geometry, proportion, and symmetry, each of which constitutes "some inherent property, to be found suffused all through the body."[74] These abstract principles could be found in nature and, because the ancients discovered them there, in classical architecture.

Although Alberti admitted that the properties of beauty were perceived by the senses, where they gave some pleasure, of greatest importance was the understanding of these properties, especially musical proportions, which takes place in the mind: "when the mind is reached by way of sight or sound, or any other means, *concinnitas* [harmony or congruity] is instantly recognized."[75] Therefore, the judgment of beauty was based on "the workings of a reasoned faculty that is inborn in the mind." "For within the form and figure of a building," he writes, "there resides some natural excellence and perfection that excites the mind and is immediately recognized by it."[76] Reflecting Augustinian ideas, Alberti believed that, through the pleasure and delight that results from recognizing beauty, divinity is revealed. Particularly in the design of temples, the rules of beauty must be applied, because "There is no doubt that a temple that delights the mind wonderfully, captivates it with grace and admiration, will greatly encourage piety."[77] Beauty from geometry and proportion was essential for revealing the wisdom of God, who had created the universe based on mathematical laws.

Wren's idea of the natural causes of beauty in architecture echoes the tradition of Alberti and adopts his rules for beauty – "harmony," "geometry," "proportion," "uniformity," and, from his description of facade design, the idea of symmetry. Wren does not, however, follow Alberti in conceiving these as qualities resulting in an absolute beauty innate in the object and instantly understood by the mind. Wren assigned the primary role in the aesthetic experience to the visual sense, which views the object, determines whether it has the geometrical qualities of beauty, and then conveys its assessment to the mind. Whereas Wren would agree with Alberti that the geometrical qualities could be found underlying nature, this did not make them an absolute value with overriding authority.

Furthermore, there is no indication that Wren believed in divine beauty. In his study of biblical buildings, including the Temple of Solomon, he placed no special significance upon their particular forms. Although he gave the Classical orders a natural and divine origin in the Tyrian, these orders were constantly subject to change due to culture. Even in the design of churches, he presented no formal requirements that would ensure beauty and the cognition of God. It does seem that Wren shared the belief of many of his contemporaries that, like a priest, the scientist made discoveries in nature that revealed God – the beauty, elegance, and harmony found in nature's works, from the heavens to raw stones, being a testament to His wisdom.[78] As for beauty in architecture, however, Wren believed that though it had a foundation in nature and God, it was ultimately determined by society and man.

Wren's conception of geometry in architecture is related to the belief, held by many seventeenth-century scientists investigating the physical sciences, that mathematics was central to conceiving and working out theories.[79] In his 1657 inaugural speech to Gresham College, Wren declared: "Mathematical Demonstrations being built upon the impregnable Foundations of Geometry and Arithmetick, are the only Truths, that can sink into the Mind of Man, void of all Uncertainty; and all other Discourses participate more or less of Truth, according as their Subjects are more or less capable of Mathematical Demonstration."[80] Whereas the primacy that Wren placed on mathematics as a key to understanding nature may seem to reinforce Alberti's conception of absolute beauty, Wren's phrase "Mathematical Demonstrations" indicates a very different understanding, which separates it from not only Alberti but also from Wren's fellow scientists. As J. A. Bennett has discussed, in his own scientific work Wren's theories were not mathematical derivations based on high-level principles but "demonstrations" based on observations.[81] To explain a phenomenon in astronomy or physics he studied the sensible data and then ordered it in the form of a simple series of mathematical or geometrical rules, often validated by a preconceived notion of neatness. Wren believed that to prove a theory, a scientific problem should be "order'd into a geometrical Way of reasoning from Ocular Experiment."[82]

An example of Wren's approach is provided by his theory of motion, formulated from 1668 on the basis of repeated collision experiments conducted with Laurence Rooke. It states: "The proper and most truly natural velocities of bodies are reciprocally proportional to the bodies."[83] While Wren believed that this simple mathematical description represented a true "philosophical" explanation of the phenomenon, his colleagues at the Royal Society disagreed. William Neile complained that Wren was "against finding a reason" for the experimental results and instead claimed "that the appearances carry reason enough in themselves as being the law of nature."[84] Disapproving of this approach, Neile declared, "to conclude that the aparence is the reality and that the aparence must not be denied to be really true under pretence that it is an axiome mee thinks is not very philosophicall."[85] For Wren, the "appearances," that is, a mathematical "view" of the sense data, to use Bennett's phrase, was the best guide to the truth of nature. For other scientists, however, this description or model in neat, mathematical terms provided only empirical rules that did not constitute a true scientific explanation of reality.

The notion of mathematical appearances that guided Wren's scientific thinking is reflected in his "natural causes" of beauty. Certainly geometry, uniformity, and proportion were linked to the real, sensible qualities of the object itself and the physical relationships of its parts; but, as in Wren's theory of motion where the *appearance* of geometry took priority, the aesthetic experience is a phenomenon of the senses, based on the "geometrical Reasons of *Opticks*." Wren's idea of the natural causes of beauty, however, is much more than a simple adaptation of his scientific thinking. He was aware that a geometrical appearance that created an aesthetic experience in architecture was completely different from a neat, mathematical demonstration of a natural phenomenon. The phenomenon of architectural beauty was dependent upon the unique physical conditions under which an individual person would view the building, making it impossible to formulate absolute laws concerning the geometrical appearance, despite the fact that these appearances also depended upon a phenomenon of nature – the physiology of the human eye.

As a result, in Tract I, Wren called for the architect to be "well skilled in Perspective" and to design buildings as three-dimensional entities seen from "principal Views," considering their specific angles and distances. He presented very general guidelines for the architect, limiting the overall proportion of a facade, describing how its parts should be composed for both frontal and angular views, and prescribing the amount and size of ornaments depending on whether the primary viewing position was close or far.[86] Although his discussion is related to the old concept of optical adjustments, discussed by Vitruvius[87] and used by the ancients, as Wren himself described for the Basilica of Maxentius and the Temple of Mars Ultor,[88] Wren was less concerned with making corrections to compensate for the failure of the visual sense and more with giving general proportional and compositional guidelines that would ensure a geometrical appearance that would *never* need corrections.[89]

Wren's awareness of the important role of visual perception in architecture probably was related to his work on the theory of optics and on vision, especially in terms of its application to dioptrics or optical lenses for telescopes. From the mid-1650s he made studies on refraction, light, and vision, including the anatomy of the eye, which unfortunately are not recorded.[90] With his understanding of the physiology of the eye, he was able to formulate certain rules for the natural causes of architecture. In this case, however, these were variable rules, not laws that can be applied to every situation, because although human perception might be subject to natural law, the perception of buildings was linked to their uncontrolled and changing environment – that is, society.

Beauty in architecture was subject to society and man in even more profound ways. For Wren, the visual sense determines out of the natural causes whether or not an object is beautiful, leading the mind or the "Judgment" to accept or reject it. Certain natural causes – irregularity, oblique lines, extreme proportions, and so forth – are known to the mind, via the eye, as having little beauty. Unfortunately, it is possible for the mind not to reject but instead to accept them as having beauty due to the "customary causes." The customary causes are outside influences that disturb the mind of the perceiver – "Familiarity," "novelty," "particular inclination," and "custom" – that "breed a Love to Things not in themselves lovely." Although the mind understands from the senses that an object lacks beauty, these causes take hold and the "Fancy blinds the Judgment"[91] – that is, the imagination, which works without rules or authority, overrules what the senses have determined and forces the mind to accept the object as beautiful. Therefore the customary causes do not affect the physiological perception of the sense data but rather the mind's interpretation of that data. They have no foundation in nature but are based solely on the observer as an individual and as a member of society.

Wren was not the first theorist to recognize that the judgment of beauty could be influenced by factors related less to the object in question and more to human psychology. In his treatise Alberti showed his awareness of arguments that beauty should be judged according to "relative and variable criteria" that followed "individual taste" rather than rules.[92] He rejected them, however, stating that "When you make judgments on beauty, you do not follow mere fancy, but the workings of a reasoned faculty that is inborn in the mind."[93] Wren, as a natural philosopher, believed that the impact of individual preconceptions and cultural norms on the reason had even greater importance because of its occurrence in the investigation of natural phenomena. J. A. Bennett has recognized the similarity between Wren's idea of customary causes and Francis Bacon's "Idols" or "false appearances." In the study and interpretation of nature, Bacon cautioned against "a corrupt and ill-ordered predisposition of the mind" that "perverts and infects... the intellect." The idols, according to Bacon "force and overrule the understanding" and lead men into "idle fancies."[94]

In architecture the customary causes had a detrimental effect on the viewer. They led him to accept as beautiful certain physical qualities of objects that were not naturally beautiful. These qualities, approved by the individual through their familiarity, novelty, or personal appeal, and by society through their repeated usage, constituted "Modes and Fashions," and represented, for the present moment, the "Taste" of a particular individual or society. For example, Wren observed that "Persons of otherwise a good Genius" could not be persuaded "to think anything in Architecture could be better than what they had heard commended by others, and what they had view'd themselves." Gothic cathedrals seen abroad "they lik'd the better for being not much differing from Ours in England."[95] The approval created by the customary causes had led the English to adopt the rude Gothic style from France, and now, Wren feared, to copy a French, very feminine mode of decoration.[96] For Wren, the approval of new orders, including Villalpando's Solomonic order of 1604 and a "*Gallick Order*" of 1671 for the attic story of the Cour Carrée at the Louvre, was attributable to nothing more than their novelty, and he concluded, "Neither will the Flower-de-luce of the *French*, nor the Palms of *Villalpandus*, ... come up to the Grace of the old Form of the Corinthian Capital."[97] Certain modes and fashions created by the ancients – for example, certain proportions for columns and the "Affectation... to judge nothing beautiful, but what was adorned with Columns, even where there was no real Use of them" – still persisted into the present day because of the customary causes. "Because they were found in the great Structures (the Ruins of which we now admire)," Wren wrote, "we think ourselves strictly obliged still to follow the Fashion."[98]

Although he criticized these fashions resulting from the psychological influences on a viewer's judgment of what is beautiful, Wren did not intend to eliminate the customary causes. He did not follow the example of science, where, according to Bacon, it was necessary to eradicate the "idols" and separate the mind from the fancy so that the judgment would be cleansed and free to discover the truth of nature. In the architect's creative process, Wren believed, the customary causes were essential. Although in some cases they could have a negative result, in others they were what brought about progress in architecture.

The impact of the customary causes on the mind of the architect could result in the creation of "novelties." These were innovations that resulted when the "Fancy blinds the Judgment" – when the architect's imagination or intuition prevails over his judgment and makes him succumb to his own personal inclinations and the customs of society. The value of novelties to both the viewer and the architect was solely from their newness, which could not last: "That which is commendable now for Novelty, will not be a new Invention to Posterity, when his Works are often imitated, and when it is unknown which was the Original."[99]

At the same time, however, although in customary beauty "lies the great Occasion of Errors," there also "is tried the Architect's Judgment." That is, a novelty could prove to be an "invention" as long as the architect's judgment maintained control over the forces of custom, personal preference, and the imagination and guided the design toward functional utility, structural stability, as well as "the true Test," "natural or geometrical Beauty." As a result, instead of creating novelties that constituted transient "Modes and Fashions" approved solely for their newness, the architect made inventions that, because "the Glory of that which is good of itself is eternal," survived beyond their initial novelty. By "think[ing] his Judges, as well those that are to live five Centuries after him, as those of his own Time," the architect created a standard of "good Taste,"[100] recognized in the present and for posterity.

The influence of the customary causes on the architect's design thinking had led to the great inventions of past civilizations. Wren observed how "Great Monarchs are ambitious to leave great Monuments behind them; and this occasions great Inventions in the mechanick Arts."[101] Among these inventions were the Classical orders that developed out of the root natural and divine order. Initially "Experiments" of the architects and cultures that produced them, existing as novelties, they could have ended up as passing fashions, as Wren predicted would be the fate of the Gallic order. Instead, the orders had lasted through the centuries as the "Principals" "uncapable of Modes and Fashions." They had been refined and shaped by the "greatest Artists and Geometricians"[102] in each ancient civilization according to their own customs and fancies, and with the help of the experience of previous cultures and the wealth of their own. As Wren demonstrated in his history of architecture, the Greek orders had their birth in the most magnificent buildings of their age, some considered Wonders of the World. At the same time, the orders not only retained the natural and divine essence of their originals, but also continued to follow natural law by retaining the logic of post and lintel construction and employing "the comon demensions of columes, which were aggreable to all."[103] That is, although each was initially created by an architect at the instigation of his fancy and the customary causes, and had won approval as novelties, the orders, particularly the Greek and Roman, proved to be inventions based on the architect's judgment and his application of fundamental principles. Other decorative forms and proportions might be created for the orders, but these would prove only to be "the Modes and Fashions of those Ages wherein they were used."[104] The essentials of the orders, however, would remain lasting inventions that formed the basis of two of the great national styles, and collectively an eternal and universal style.

For his own time, Wren was very cautious about the creation of new inventions. In terms of the orders he was adamantly against the new versions, finding "Experiments in this kind . . . greatly expenceful, and Errors incorrigible." This "is the Reason the Principles of Architecture are now rather the Study of Antiquity than Fancy." It would seem therefore, that by stating in Tract I that "Architecture aims at Eternity," Wren supported the idea of creating buildings today based on the "Principles" of "Beauty, Firmness, and Convenience," but also based on the "principals, the Orders" – that is, the Classical style. At the same time, however, Wren begins his Tracts with the statement, "Architecture has its political Use; publick Buildings being the Ornament of a Country; it establishes a Nation, draws People and Commerce; makes the people love their native Country."[105] This statement demonstrates that he believed buildings should also be designed to reflect the particular culture that made them, and furthermore to represent that culture to its own people and to the world.

According to Wren's theory, it should be possible today, as it had been in the past, for the architect to achieve both goals. The architect, based on his understanding of history, must embrace the only eternal and universally applicable style of the past, the Classical. But he must go even further, using his imagination and judgment, to make inventions within it that will result in an architecture that is a product of his own "Nation." At the same time, he must base those inventions upon the fundamental principles of architecture derived from nature and thereby transcend current fashion and mode to produce an architecture that will last for "Eternity." In applying this prescription to his own architecture, however, Wren discovered a variety of conflicts existing between his theoretical principles and the practical realities of building in Restoration England, which forced him to create unforeseen compromises in form, structure, and style.

Wren was not the only scientist turned architect during the second half of the seventeenth century to formulate a dualistic definition of beauty that challenged inherited architectural notions on the basis of the New Science. There were two others: the Frenchman Claude Perrault (1613–88), physician, member of the Académie des Sciences and designer of the East Front of the Louvre; and the Italian Guarino Guarini (1624–83), Theatine monk, mathematician and astronomer, and architect to the duke of Savoy. Although Perrault, Wren, and Guarini were all in Paris in 1665/6, the first as a resident, the others as visitors, there is no evidence that they ever met. It is possible that Wren had direct knowledge of Perrault's theory through his publications: the commentary of his *Les dix livres d'architecture de Vitruve* (1673) and the preface of his *Ordonnance des cinq espèces des colonnes selon la méthode des anciens* (1683).[106] He could not, however, have known Guarini's treatise *Architettura civile*, which, though written from 1678 and continued until his death in 1683, was not published until 1737.

The similarity among the theories of these three men is probably due less to direct contact than to their common backgrounds as scientists on the side of the "Moderns." Like Wren, Perrault and Guarini rejected the absolute authority of the ancients at the same time as they accepted the primacy of the Classical style. As a result they, too, absorbed the lessons taught by Vitruvius and the ancient remains and reiterated by fifteenth- and sixteenth-century theorists and buildings, but went on without hesitation to accept or reject them based on their own judgment and experience. Guarini and Perrault, like Wren, had a knowledge of past architecture that made them realize that, rather than continuity, the nature of architecture involves change in relationship to cultural conditions. For example, Guarini shared Wren's interest in and appreciation for Gothic architecture and analyzed it in similar terms. In a brief history of the Goths, Guarini called them "liberal and ingenious builders," suggested an origin for their "mode of building" in the north, and listed several Gothic buildings in Spain, France, and Italy as works "built with great expense, and not without great art." The style was characterized by a "slenderness" of proportions, a "Gothic order" where colonnettes supported ribs, and vaults based on "portions of circles." By appearing to be structurally weak and to stand miraculously, Guarini concluded, Gothic buildings "astonish the intellect and render the spectators terrified."[107]

Perrault and Guarini also shared with Wren the belief that proportion is essential to the creation of beauty, but admitted, as he did, that given the evidence of past architecture, all past proportional systems have pleased and that no absolute proportions exist.[108] Perrault in particular attacked the arguments of earlier theorists who, using Vitruvius, postulated the existence of absolute proportions based on the imitation of the tree trunk in the column, wood carpentry in the cornice, and the head and torso of a human body in the capital and the shaft. Perrault pointed out that, although these were not exact imitations, they still please. Likewise, he questioned the arguments of theorists, beginning with Alberti, that musical harmonies express a natural, God-given order, and therefore must be used in architecture. While admitting that musical harmonies are fixed by nature, and that the ear is immediately offended if they are not correct, Perrault still pointed out that, though the eye is even better equipped to register differences, many other proportional systems have pleased. He concluded therefore that there are no absolute proportions based either on nature, the human body, or music.[109]

Perrault and Guarini believed, as did Wren, that architecture is akin to a phenomenon of nature, with physical qualities structured according to the absolutes of geometry and subject to empirical laws of perception. This belief led them all to formulate dualistic definitions of beauty. Natural philosophers recognized that the truth of nature could be discovered in two ways. According to Francis Bacon's empirical method, one must study nature based on observation and experiment, using the senses to collect facts that will form the basis for induction by which the laws or causes behind the infinite variety of nature will be revealed. René Descartes acknowledged that the world of material facts can be understood through the senses, but believed that the reason will discover the truth of nature and that its laws will be universal, eternal, and based on mathematics.[110] In their dualistic definitions of beauty, Perrault, Guarini, and Wren all recognize its more absolute nature, based on geometry, proportion, and symmetry, as well as its more relativistic, changeable nature, which varies according to the taste of the individual, the customs of society, and the physiology of visual perception. There are, however, important differences among the views of these three theorists on the relative importance of each aspect and their relationship to one another.

Guarini is probably the closest to Wren in that he gives priority to geometry and mathematics in architecture. Architecture "depends upon geometry," Guarini wrote, and "professes itself disciple" of mathematics.[111] In his treatise he demonstrated the geometrical basis of every element of the plan (ichnography) and elevation (elevated orthography), including the Classical orders, as well as of the vault (projected orthography). In the last he presented graphic techniques of projective geometry, derived from stereotomy, but used now, not for the purpose of stonecutting, but to demonstrate simple and complex forms of vaulting.

Guarini went on, in the same manner as Wren, to recognize the impact of the visual sense on the perception of geometry. Guarini wrote, "Architecture, although it depends on mathematics, nevertheless is an art that delights, that desires not at all by the reason to displease the sense." Architecture must follow the rules of mathematics, but "when it is a question that its observed demonstrations are to offend the view, it changes them, it leaves them, and finally contradicts the same ones."[112] Although one must start with the ancient rules of proportion, because repeated usage has shown their validity, one "can correct the antique rules and invent new ones."[113] Although he did not reject the Classical language or its proportions, Guarini believed it is necessary to modify them in order to ensure that architecture will be pleasing to the eye. He described general empirical laws for correcting two problems of perception that parallel Wren's categories of "natural" and "customary" causes.

The first relates to the physiological nature of perception, where the visual sense deceives the imagination and understanding. In general, "the power of the imagination corrects the images and appearances of the eyes," so that, for example, what appears from an angle to be an ellipse is understood to be a circle.[114] Nevertheless, Guarini described, similarly to Wren, optical illusions resulting from the object's surroundings and foreshortening resulting from the viewer's position.[115] Citing a variety of cases, he gives recommendations for corrections, demonstrating how, in order to have the illusion of proportionality, one must "depart from the rules and the true proportions."[116]

The second problem of perception has to do with the judgment of beauty in architecture, which can be disturbed by different prejudices. It is difficult, Guarini writes, to understand why proportions bring delight, and "no less difficult is the knowledge of the root of beauty of a pretty outfit," or "the discordance of sound in Music, or the variety of colors in Painting."[117] Moreover, "men change modes, and that which first was admired as beautiful, then becomes abhorred as deformed."[118] Guarini ascribed these phenomena to the personal prejudices and interests of the viewer, which prevent sound judgment. Pride causes a viewer to like only his own work; envy causes him to dislike another's. Personal inclination creates a preference for certain forms; ignorance creates inept judgments.[119]

In addition to personal prejudice, Guarini found that in judging architecture viewers are often "carried by the genius of their own country to abhor what is against their custom." As a result of custom, "what is pleasing to one nation is displeasing to another." For example, "Roman Architecture first was displeasing to the Goths, and Gothic Architecture is displeasing to ourselves."[120] Yet, Gothic architecture "had to be pleasing in those times."[121]

Paralleling Wren's arguments, Guarini called for the architect to reject custom and prejudice and design according to "a reasonable judgment and a judicious eye"[122] brought about by experience, knowledge, and an understanding of the nature of perception. At the same time, he should design only for a reasonable viewer, "judicious and free from every inclination."[123] It was up to the architect, therefore, to work against the influences of custom and prejudice on beauty in architecture and to correct the failures of the optical sense.

Whereas Wren postulated two "causes" of beauty, natural and customary, that produced an optical effect, Perrault described two "kinds" of beauty, "positive" and "arbitrary," perceived precisely by the eye and understood directly by the mind.[124] Perrault did not agree with Wren that the eye's perception of the real qualities of the object was subject to any weaknesses of the optical sensation. Instead, for Perrault the eye always perceived accurately, the visual judgment being "as a rule very certain and almost infallible."[125] He believed that "since the judgment of sight is so exact and since the certainty of the knowledge it gives us is so precise," the judgment is never "deceived by the distortions and the adverse effects that we imagine can be caused by distance and varying relative position."[126] The ability for the judgment to correct itself against foreshortening and optical illusions was not innate but acquired through experience. This hypothesis was shared by Guarini, who nonetheless believed that this ability is limited, making optical adjustments necessary. For Perrault, optical adjustments were useless in architecture, because the eye would always perceive accurately and the judgment always automatically understand any visual shortcomings.

A building, according to Perrault, is considered beautiful because of certain specific qualities, each of which pleases for different reasons. "Positive" beauties are "based on convincing reasons," and are "bound to please everyone, so easily apprehended are their value and quality." These include "the richness of the materials, the size and magnificence of the building, the precision and cleanness of the execution, and symmetry." Positive beauties are absolute, founded on "common sense and reason," which are all that are necessary to judge them.[127] Perrault's positive beauty of symmetry, involving "the relationship the parts have collectively as a result of the balanced correspondence of their size, number, disposition, and order," is equivalent to Wren's natural causes of uniformity. There are differences, however, in that Perrault is concerned with actual qualities, and Wren only with appearances. Most importantly, Perrault, unlike Wren and Guarini, does not recognize proportion as a "positive" beauty, but rather as an "arbitrary" beauty.

Perrault believed that common sense was not sufficient to judge certain qualities that were among the "arbitrary" beauties. They depended upon "custom" and "prejudice," which created a desire "to give a definite proportion, shape, or form to things that might well have a different form without being misshapen." Whereas arbitrary beauties "should cause displeasure because they contravene reason and good sense," instead they please due to association. In some cases they are associated with positive beauties, and as a result "the esteem that inclines the mind to things whose worth it knows also inclines it to things whose worth it does not know and little by little induces it to value both equally." In other cases they are approved because of their association with certain people of esteem, for example, "the regard we have for the worthiness and patronage of people at court makes us like their clothing and their way of speaking." Further, if an arbitrary beauty "is accompanied by our knowledge and good opinion of the person" who approves it, we have a "predisposition" to do so as well. Arbitrary beauties in architecture are akin to the "fashions and patterns of speech" established at court. As the love bestowed on them derives from custom and prejudice, not from anything positive, "after a time they offend us without their having undergone any inherent change."[128] Not only do modes change over time within a culture, they differ from one nation to another without any positive basis. For example, Perrault found it impossible "to demonstrate that the music of France is better than that of Italy."[129]

In architecture the primary arbitrary beauty is proportion. Perrault compared architectural proportions to the "proportions of a fashionable costume." They are not absolute and have no positive basis in nature or reason. They have pleased only because of their association with positive beauties, which cannot be altered without impairing the whole work, so that over time custom has established the belief that proportions are also beautiful and cannot be changed. Yet the inventors of proportional systems "had no rule other than their fancy to guide them, as their fancy changed they introduced new proportions, which in turn were found pleasing."[130] Other architects and theorists have continued to change the proportions up to the present time, and all of them have been approved.

Although they were based on fancy and custom, Perrault believed that arbitrary beauties played an important role in architecture. Common sense is all that is needed to create and judge positive beauty. However, "taste" is needed to do so for arbitrary beauty, and this is what "distinguishes true architects from the rest."[131] In order to achieve this standard of good taste, the arbitrary beauties need to be studied and their nature understood, requiring "the discipline of long familiarity with rules that are established by usage alone."[132]

Having established the arbitrary nature of the proportions in architecture, Perrault proposed changes for the better to be made by the architect with good taste. The ancients had made inventions in the forms of the orders, using "des genies inventifs" and "studious research" to make changes for the better.[133] Perrault approved of all that had been "introduced judiciously and with reason" up to the present.[134] All of the moderns, however, had failed "to establish fixed and certain rules." Not only did they all lack "sufficient authority" to establish unalterable laws, but their rules were neither "endowed with self-evident truth" nor "endorsed by probabilities and reasons" that made one set preferable to all others. Particularly in the proportions, the moderns had failed to achieve "something fixed, constant, and established."[135]

This is what Perrault himself proposed to do, presenting himself as the authority to establish, as law, a new proportional system for the five orders. His system was justified by its basis in reason, whole numbers and simple divisions, easily remembered and used, and, paradoxically, by its basis in ancient precedent. Because he had distilled his proportions from the systems of Vitruvius and modern writers, as well as from the multitudinous measures of the ancient monuments recorded by Desgodets, Perrault believed that he had rediscovered the original system of Vitruvius, "intended not so much to correct what is ancient as to return it to its original perfection,"[136] which had been lost due to the negligence of the workmen. Rather than a return to ancient authority, this reflected his recognition of the legitimacy of the Classical proportions gained through long-standing custom. We must follow "the usage that we have become accustomed to find pleasing in the fine works of the ancients," making sure not to "stray too far from those that are accepted and in current use."[137] With his new proportional system Perrault established a standard of good taste based on the authority of society's customs, as well as of his own individual reason and experience. By proving that the proportions of ancient architecture were arbitrary, he was able to perfect them and, by rejecting optical adjustments, establish them for all time.

Perrault, Guarini, and Wren all applied their backgrounds as scientists to the formulation of their theories of architecture. In varying degrees they applied the epistemological categories of the New Science, rationalism and empiricism, to formulate dualistic definitions of beauty. All three recognized the arbitrary qualities of past architecture and developed a historical consciousness that led them to recognize the relativistic nature of beauty based on custom. Although they rejected ancient authority, they used long-standing custom as the basis for reaffirming the legitimacy of the Classical style – for Wren a legitimacy reinforced by its natural and divine origin. All three recognized the need for an authority to establish a standard of good taste based on reason and a knowledge of the nature of architecture.

On the issues of the invention of new orders and the use of optical adjustments there is less agreement. Perrault only allowed two new orders, both of his own invention. In 1671 he proposed and then won the competition for a French order to replace the attic story of the Cour Carrée at the Louvre. Recorded in a plaster model placed in the court until the mid-eighteenth century, and in the frontispiece to his 1673 translation of Vitruvius, it was composed of a capital with plumes instead of acanthus leaves, surrounded by a circle of fleur-de-lis alternating with orbs.[138] In his Vitruvius edition, Perrault introduced the invention of coupled columns, which he had in 1667 "executed with great splendor" in the East Front of the Louvre.[139] Admitting later in his *Ordonnance* that "almost no examples of it exist in antiquity," he nevertheless pleaded, "this is one innovation that deserves to be accepted into architecture for its considerable beauty and convenience."[140] Having established the proportions and forms of the Classical orders, and perfected them with these two inventions, Perrault rejected optical adjustments, thus closing the door on any individual artistic license.[141]

With his theory Perrault intended to establish an authoritative and conservative French Classical manner for all time. Furthermore, with his design for the East Front of the Louvre, the palace of the French king, he presented this style to the world, expressly in opposition to the architecture of France's greatest cultural rival, Italy. Although Blondel and other members of the Académie d'Architecture did not agree with his reasons, Perrault was successful in promoting the idea of a single style, the image of classical authority and scientific reasoning, instituted from above and recognized by one and all as the French national style. With the approval of Louis XIV and Colbert, Perrault hoped to accomplish in architecture what they had already done for French society – the creation of a nation united under the absolutist rule of the Sun King, the greatest monarch of Europe and of the century. Just as Colbert had placed all artistic production under state control to communicate and promote this message, so Perrault showed that architecture could also be enlisted in the same program.[142]

Guarini took a very different view from Perrault on the invention of new orders and optical adjustments, which reflects certain intentions related to the milieu in which he worked. In his treatise he approved of "invenzioni" that went beyond the traditional Classical orders, presenting a whole gamut of possibilities, including Gallic and Solomonic orders and others of his own creation. He stipulated, however, that such work must be left "to the genius and industry of the virtuosi," like himself.[143] Whereas in his treatise he presented rules for correcting visual distortions, in his own work Guarini went beyond mere correction. Using mathematics, he established a complex geometrical framework created by the intersections of three-dimensional volumes, and then manipulated the geometries, less to correct than to exploit optical illusions to "delight the eye."[144] Guarini, more than either of his contemporaries, pushed the Classical style to its limits, designing and using new orders and borrowing techniques from Gothic architecture to achieve an illusory and incredible quality, particularly in his domes. By constructing a church that seemed to stand miraculously, filling worshippers with awe and delight, Guarini created an architectural setting that reinforced the dramatic ceremonies of the Theatine order, which, like the Jesuit, made use of theatrical devices to stir the emotions and inspire religious faith.[145]

Wren's position on the issues of invention and optical adjustments lies at a point between Perrault's and Guarini's. Having established the eternal validity of the Classical orders, due to their natural and divine origin and their development under great civilizations, Wren stated that they are "the only Thing uncapable of Modes and Fashions." Any new order would be a "novelty" – transient and not eternal.[146] In his discussion of "perspective," Wren describes how to ensure that the building achieves the geometrical appearance that is the most beautiful without having to resort later to optical corrections. Yet for both the orders and the natural causes Wren never prescribed specific forms or rules that would fix them in any way. Furthermore, he recognized the importance of "inventions" as a means of perfecting architecture. In the end, however, the creative process must be controlled by "the Architect's Judgment" and by the application of fundamental geometrical, functional, and structural principles. Architecture was to be neither restricted by the kind of unchangeable rules proposed by Perrault nor open to the kind of free invention pursued by Guarini.

Although both Perrault and particularly Guarini were well versed in matters involving masonry construction, Wren alone contributed new ideas to this subject in his writings on architecture. By treating technical matters he was returning to the model of fifteenth-century Italian treatises – for example, the 1489–92 treatise of Francesco di Giorgio – but also continuing a French tradition that began with Philibert Delorme in 1567 and continued into the seventeenth century with Desargues (1640), Derand (1643), and Deschales (1674).

In contrast to his empirical definition of beauty based on "geometrical Reasons of *Opticks*," Wren gave structure a rational definition as a phenomenon based on true, quantitative geometry. "Firmness," he wrote, being founded on "the geometrical Reasons of . . . *Staticks*" is, in comparison to beauty and convenience, "the most essential Part of Architecture." After establishing the basic structural concept of "position" – "no other than upright being firm" as a principle "from Nature, and consequently Necessity"[147] – Wren went on in Tract II to consider the problem of the abutment of the arch and various forms of vaults according to geometrical and mathematical principles. The problem of abutment is also discussed in his "Report on Westminster Abbey," a building where he attempted to apply his rudimentary principles to practice.

Declaring that "no Author hath given a true and universal Rule for this," Wren criticized a popular rule-of-thumb method for determining the thickness of the piers supporting an arch recorded in the treatise on stereotomy by François Derand, *L'Architecture des voûtes* (1643).[148] According to Wren, Derand's method (Fig. 33, *Fig. 1*) neglected the height of the pier itself as well as the loading of the arch, and thus was "neither true nor universal" and not "built upon any sure geometrical Theorem." "What is true," Wren declared, "will be shewn to be only determinable by the doctrine of finding the Centers of Gravity in the Parts of the proposed Design." Assuming that the reader had some knowledge of centers of gravity from Archimedes or a "modern Geometrician," perhaps having in mind his colleague the mathematician John Wallis, Wren made his own demonstration (Fig. 33, *Fig. 2*). Considering half of the arch with its supporting pier, he calculated the center of gravity for each part, the vertical pier and the "horn" of the arch. If they were "equiponderant," that is, equally balanced, "the whole Stone will stand immoveable upon the Basis."[149] In other words, if for the entire body the total weight passed through a center of gravity located within the base of the pier (to the left of AB), the arch would stand.

Although Wren's formulation for the half-arch is flawed, because he falsely assumed it would act as a rigid body in normal masonry construction and was unaware of horizontal forces, he did attempt to go beyond earlier geometrical methods and to apply mathematical principles to the design of structures. On the basis of his demonstration Wren concluded that "the Design, where there are Arcades, must be regulated by the Art of Staticks, or Inventions of the Centers of Gravity, and the duly poising all Parts to equiponderate; without which, a fine Design will fail and prove abortive."[150] Using the same principle, he went on to discuss the form and abutment of different vaults, the groin vault, the fan vault based on pointed arches "made up of Sections of Circles," and the dome on pendentives. By first describing each vault geometrically, then conceiving the spandrel of a vault as a solid body, and finally determining its center of gravity, he was able to compare them (Figs. 33–4). His analysis showed that the dome on pendentives was "the lightest Manner, and requires less Butment than the Cross-vaulting," its center of gravity being nearest to its support.[151]

Wren's work on structures found in Tract II appears to have been part of an investigation on the subject that took place at the Royal Society. Among the issues considered there during the 1670s was the problem of the arch. In December 1670, "Mr. Hooke brought in this problem of architecture; the basis of the distance of two pillars and the altitude of an arch being given, to find out the right figure of that arch, for the firm sustaining, upon the whole, or any part of it, any weight given; as also to find out the butments of that arch."[152] In January 1671, according to the minutes, Wren had a solution that was given to the president. Although it appears to have been known to his colleagues, including Isaac Newton,[153] no record of it remains except in the passages of Tract II.

At about the same time, Hooke developed a solution that he related to the president in January but did not present until December of that year. He described "a cubico-paraboloid conoid; adding, that by this figure might be determined all the difficulties in architecture about arches and butments." Four years later he published his description of the inverted catenary curve as "*The true Mathematical and Mechanical Form of all manner of Arches for Building, with the true Butment necessary to each of them. A problem which no Architectonick Writer hath ever yet attempted, much less performed."*[154] This formulation by Hooke may have had an influence on Wren's design for the dome of St. Paul's. In his diary on 5 June 1675, Hooke claimed that Wren "was making up of my principle about arches and altered his module by it." Various scholars have examined whether a catenary profile exists in the section of the cathedral.[155]

Despite the fact that they are now known to be incorrect, Wren was the first to formulate principles of applied mechanics. The passages in Tract II constitute one of the earliest attempts, predating the development of structural analysis during the eighteenth century, to analyze structural problems "philosophically," based on quantitative, mathematical analyses of force and equilibrium.[156] According to Rowland Mainstone, "No quantitative application of statical theory [to architectural design] is recorded before the time of Wren."[157]

The studies of the arch made by Wren and others at the Royal Society may seem simplistic in comparison to the complex forms of vaults presented in a series of contemporary French treatises on stereotomy, the art of cutting stones.[158] All of these works ultimately derive from Philibert Delorme's 1567 treatise on architecture where, in book 4, he presents complex forms of vaulting and instructions on how to cut the individual stones.[159] Although represented geometrically in orthographic drawings, the methods presented in the French treatises involve no mathematical analysis of vaults as the basis for structural stability. Instead they are directed to the stonecutter as a way of visualizing two-dimensionally complex spatial and geometrical relationships for the purpose of executing specific problems found in stone construction.

This tradition was continued in the seventeenth century with the most important treatise on stereotomy of this period, François Derand's *L'Architecture des voûtes, ou l'art des traits et coupes des voûtes* (Paris, 1643; new edition 1743), which contains 119 chapters of working instructions for the stonemason. At about the same time, however, more strictly mathematical descriptions were being formulated for the forms of arches and vaults, beginning with Desargues in 1640, who presented a more universally applicable method founded on basic principles of projective geometry, which was rejected by craftsmen. The mathematical approach was continued by Deschales in 1674, working from Derand's precepts. It was not until the work of Philippe de la Hire in 1695 that the subject was approached from a strictly statical viewpoint.[160] The procedures found in the treatise of Guarino Guarini, written from 1678, although they derive from the stereotomy of Derand and other French writers, are related neither to the working of stone nor to the statical analysis of structure. Instead, they are used to design complex spaces, formed by the intersections of simple geometrical bodies based on the circle as well as conic sections, where an illusion of greater spatial depth and structural lightness than actually exists is created.[161]

Wren's statical principles, albeit rudimentary, also represent an advancement beyond the geometrical methods used, as late as the end of the seventeenth century, to determine the safest forms, dimensions, and proportions for arches, vaults, and their supports. Derand's geometrical demonstration of 1643 to determine the abutment of an arch was just one of many such methods used since the Middle Ages to ensure structural stability. Much evidence has been uncovered, from the close study of contemporary drawings and the detailed measurements and analyses of monuments, indicating the use during the Middle Ages of simple geometric constructions to determine the dimensions and proportions of structural components, ranging from entire plans and sections down to the smallest details. Although they may have been initially used for practical purposes in order to systemize the design of complex structures, or even for mystical reasons in order to ensure beauty and harmony according with the geometrical order of the universe, evidence shows that these geometrical methods came to reflect and provide structural safety factors tested by experience.[162]

During the Renaissance, when these methods were adapted to the form and proportions of the Classical style, their structural significance was retained. This is clearly the intention in the quadrature methods presented by Francesco di Giorgio in his second treatise of 1489–92 and in the geometric formulas for determining arch buttresses of Rodrigo Gil de Hontañón dating from the mid-sixteenth century.[163] This tradition continued into the late seventeenth century. François Blondel presented to the Académie des Sciences complex geometrical constructions for flying buttresses and the joints of buttresses, utilizing conic sections. In his writings Carlo Fontana presented detailed graphical methods that employed geometry to determine the section of a dome in all its parts, as well as its supports.[164]

Although applied to the design of structures, none of these methods ventured outside the limits of geometry to consider statical principles. Wren appears to have been the only architect of his time to have done so. In the design of actual buildings, however, the limited evidence suggests that Wren's attempts to analyze structural problems based on statics always occurred within the framework of a more empirical approach, determined by his knowledge of other structures and his own trials.

Tracts I through IV (beginning in the mid-1670s)

Source
   Original manuscript missing. *Parentalia* (London, 1750), "The Life of Sir Christopher Wren, Knt.," pt. 2, appendix, 351–68, with four engravings: structural diagrams, the plan and elevation of the Temple of Diana at Ephesus and its shrine, and the plan of the Temple of Mars Ultor (transcript in *WS* 19: 126–39)

Other Manuscript Versions
   RS MS 249, fols. 475v–501v, with ink-and-wash drawings of the Temple of Diana at Ephesus (plan, elevation, and plan and elevation of the shrine) and of the Sheldonian Theater (plan and elevation of rafters), signed by Flitcroft
   AS MS 313, fols. 671–721

Date
   Beginning in the mid-1670s

(page 351)

APPENDIX.

Of ARCHITECTURE; and Observations on *Antique Temples*, &c.
[*From some rough Draughts, imperfect.*]

TRACT I.

ARCHITECTURE has its political Use; publick Buildings being the Ornament of a Country; it establishes a Nation, draws People and Commerce; makes the People love their native Country, which Passion is the Original of all great Actions in a Common-wealth.[1] The Emulation of the Cities of *Greece* was the true Cause of their Greatness. The obstinate Valour of the *Jews*, occasioned by the Love of their Temple, was a Cement that held together that People, for many Ages, through infinite Changes. The Care of publick Decency and Convenience was a great Cause of the Establishment of the *Low-countries*, and of many Cities in the World. Modern *Rome* subsists still, by the Ruins and Imitation of the *old*; as does *Jerusalem*, by the Temple of the Sepulchre, and other Remains of *Helena*'s Zeal.[2]

   Architecture aims at Eternity; and therefore the only Thing uncapable[3] of Modes and Fashions in its Principals, the *Orders*.

153

The *Orders* are not only *Roman* and *Greek*, but *Phœnician*, *Hebrew*, and *Assyrian*; therefore being founded upon the Experience of all Ages, promoted by the vast Treasures of all the great Monarchs, and Skill of the greatest Artists and Geometricians, every one emulating each other; and Experiments in this kind being greatly expenceful, and Errors incorrigible, is the Reason that the Principles of Architecture are now rather the Study of Antiquity than Fancy.

Beauty, Firmness, and Convenience, are the Principles;[4] the two first depend upon the geometrical Reasons of *Opticks* and *Staticks*; the third only makes the Variety.

There are natural Causes of Beauty. Beauty is a Harmony of Objects,[5] begetting Pleasure by the Eye. There are two Causes of Beauty, natural and customary. Natural is from *Geometry*, consisting in Uniformity (that is Equality) and Proportion. Customary Beauty is begotten by the Use of our Senses to those Objects which are usually pleasing to us for other Causes, as Familiarity or particular Inclination breeds a Love to Things not in themselves lovely.[6] Here lies the great Occasion of Errors; here is tried the Architect's Judgment: but always the true Test is natural or geometrical Beauty.

Geometrical Figures are naturally more beautiful than other irregular; in this all consent as to a Law of Nature. Of geometrical Figures, the Square and the Circle are most beautiful;[7] next, the Parallelogram and the Oval. Strait Lines are more beautiful than curve; next to strait Lines, equal and geometrical Flexures; an Object elevated in the Middle is more beautiful than depressed.

(page 352) Position is necessary for perfecting Beauty. There are only two beautiful Positions of strait Lines, perpendicular and horizontal: this is from Nature, and consequently Necessity,[8] no other than upright being firm. Oblique Positions are Discord to the Eye, unless answered in Pairs, as in the Sides of an equicrural Triangle:[9] therefore *Gothick* Buttresses are all ill-favoured, and were avoided by the Ancients, and no Roofs almost but spherick raised to be visible, except in the Front, where the Lines answer; in spherick, in all Positions, the Ribs answer. Cones and multangular Prisms want neither Beauty nor Firmness, but are not ancient.

Views contrary to Beauty are Deformity, or a Defect of Uniformity, and Plainness, which is the Excess of Uniformity; Variety makes the Mean.

Variety of Uniformities makes compleat Beauty: Uniformities are best tempered, as Rhimes in Poetry, alternately, or sometimes with more Variety, as in Stanza's.

In Things to be seen at once, much Variety makes Confusion, another Vice of Beauty. In Things that are not seen at once, and have no Respect one to another, great Variety is commendable, provided this Variety transgress not the Rules of *Opticks* and *Geometry*.

An Architect ought to be jealous of Novelties, in which Fancy blinds the Judgment;[10] and to think his Judges, as well those that are to live five Centuries after him, as those of his own Time. That which is commendable now for Novelty, will not be a new Invention to Posterity, when his Works are often imitated, and when it is unknown which was the Original; but the Glory of that which is good of itself is eternal.

The Architect ought, above all Things, to be well skilled in Perspective; for, every thing that appears well in the Orthography, may not be good in the Model,[11] especially where there are many Angles and Projectures; and every thing that is good in Model, may not be so when built; because a Model is seen from other Stations and Distances than the Eye sees the Building: but this will hold universally true, that whatsoever is good in Perspective, and will hold so in all the principal Views, whether direct or oblique, will be as good in great, if this only Caution be observed, that Regard be had to the Distance of the Eye in the principal Stations.[12]

Things seen near at hand may have small and many Members, be well furnished with Ornaments, and may lie flatter; on the contrary, all this Care is ridiculous at great Distances; there bulky Members, and full Projectures casting quick Shadows, are commendable: small Ornaments at too great Distance, serve only to confound the Symmetry, and to take away the Lustre of the Object, by darkening it with many little Shadows.

There are different Reasons for Objects, whose chief View is in Front, and for those whose chief View is sideways.[13]

Fronts ought to be elevated in the Middle, not the Corners; because the Middle is the Place of greatest Dignity, and first arrests the Eye; and rather projecting forward in the Middle, than hollow. For these Reasons, Pavilions at the Corners are naught; because they make both Faults, a hollow and depressed Front. Where Hollows and Solids are mixed, the Hollow is to be in the Middle; for, Hollows are either Niches, Windows, or Doors: The first require the Middle to give the Statue Dignity; the second, that the View from within may be direct; the third, that the Visto[14] may be strait. The Ancients elevated the Middle with a Tympan,[15] and Statue, or a Dome. The triumphant Arches, which now seem flat, were elevated by the magnificent Figure of the Victor in his Chariot with four Horses abreast, and other Statues accompanying it. No sort of Pinnacle is worthy enough to appear in the Air, but Statue. Pyramids are *Gothick*; Pots are modern *French*. Chimnies ought to be hid, if **(page 353)** not, to be well adorned. No Roof can have

Dignity enough to appear above a Cornice, but the circular; in private Buildings it is excusable. The Ancients affected Flatness. In Buildings where the View is sideways, as in Streets, it is absolutely required, that the Composition be square, Intercolumnations equal, Projectures not great, the Cornices unbroken, and every thing strait, equal, and uniform. Breaks in the Cornice, Projectures of the upright Members, Variety, Inequality in the Parts, various Heights of the Roof, serve only to confound the Perspective, and make it deformed, while the Breaches and Projectures are cast one upon another, and obscure all Symmetry. In this sort of Building there seems no Proportion of Length to the Heighth; for, a Portico the longer the more beautiful in *infinitum*: on the contrary, Fronts require a Proportion of the Breadth to the Heighth; higher than three times the Breadth is indecent, and as ill to be above three times as broad as high.[16] From this Rule I except Obelisks, Pyramids, Columns, such as *Trajan's*,[17] &c. which seem rather single Things than Compositions:[18] I except also long Porticoes, though seen direct, where the Eye wandering over the same Members infinitely repeated, and not easily finding the Bounds, makes no Comparison of them with the Heighth.

Vitruvius hath led us the true Way to find out the Originals of the Orders.[19] When Men first cohabited in civil Commerce, there was Necessity of Forums and publick Places of Meeting. In cold Countries, People were obliged to shut out the Air, the Cold, and the Rain; but in the hot Countries, where Civility first began, they desired to exclude the Sun only, and admit all possible Air for Coolness and Health: this brought in naturally the Use of Porticoes, or Roofs for Shade, set upon Pillars. A Walk of Trees is more beautiful than the most artificial[20] Portico; but these not being easily preserved in Market-places, they made the more durable Shades of Porticoes; in which we see they imitated Nature, most Trees in their Prime, that are not Saplings, or Dotards,[21] observe near the Proportion of *Dorick* Pillars in the Length of their Bole,[22] before they part into Branches. This I think the more natural Comparison, than that to the Body of a Man, in which there is little Resemblance of a cylindrical Body. The first Pillars were the very Boles of Trees turned, or cut in Prisms of many Sides. A little Curiosity would induce to lay the *Torus* at the Top; and the Conjecture is not amiss, to say it was first a Band of Iron, to keep the Clefts, occasioned by the Sun, from opening with the Weight above; and to keep the Weather from piercing those Clefts, it was necessary to cover it with the Plinth, or square Board. The Architrave conjoined[23] all the Pillars in Length, the Couples joined them crossways. I suppose now, that the Ends of the Couples[24] might be hollowed away, as in this Scheme.[25] ★ ★ ★ ★ ★ [*The rest is wanting.*]

TRACT II.

MODERN Authors who have treated of Architecture, seem generally to have little more in view, but to set down the Proportions of Columns, Architraves, and Cornices, in the several Orders, as they are distinguished into *Dorick, Ionick, Corinthian,* and *Composite*; and in these Proportions finding them in the ancient Fabricks of the *Greeks* and *Romans,* (though more arbitrarily used than they care to acknowledge) they have reduced them into Rules, too strict and pedantick, and so as not to be transgressed, without the Crime of Barbarity; though, in their own Nature, they are but the Modes and Fashions of those Ages wherein they were used; but because they were found in the great Structures, (the Ruins of which we now admire) we think ourselves strictly obliged *(page 354)* still to follow the Fashion, though we can never attain to the Grandeur of those Works.

Those who first laboured in the Restoration of Architecture, about three Centuries ago, studied principally what they found in *Rome,* above-ground, in the Ruins of the Theatres, Baths, Temples, and triumphal Arches; (for among the *Greeks* little was then remaining) and in these there appeared great Differences; however, they criticised upon them, and endeavoured to reconcile them, as well as they could, with one another, and with what they could meet with in the *Italian* Cities: and it is to be considered, that what they found standing was built, for the most part, after the Age of *Augustus,*[26] particularly, the Arches, Amphitheatres, Baths, *&c.* The *Dorick* Order they chiefly understood, by examining the Theatre of *Marcellus*;[27] the *Ionick,* from the Temple of *Fortuna Virilis*;[28] the *Corinthian,* from the *Pantheon* of *Agrippa*;[29] the *Composite,* from the triumphal Arch of *Titus,*[30] &c. I have seen among the Collections of *Inigo Jones,* a Pocket-book of *Pyrrho Ligorio*'s, (an excellent Sculptor, and Architect, employed by Pope *Paul* the third, in the building of the *Vatican* Church of *St. Peter* in *Rome,* about the Year 1540)[31] wherein he seemed to have made it his Business, out of the antique Fragments, to have drawn the many different Capitals, Mouldings of Cornices, and Ornaments of Freezes, *&c.* purposely to judge of the great Liberties of the ancient Architects, most of which had their Education in *Greece.*[32]

But although Architecture contains many excellent Parts, besides the ranging of Pillars, yet Curiosity may lead us to consider whence this Affectation arose originally, so as to judge nothing beautiful, but what was adorned with Columns, even where there was no real Use of them; as when Half-columns are stuck upon the Walls of Temples, or Basilicæ; and where they are hung-on, as it were, upon the Outside of triumphal Arches, where they cannot be supposed of any Use, but merely for Ornament; as *Seneca* observed in the *Roman* Baths: *Quantum columnarum est nihil sustinentium, sed in ornamentum positarum, impensæ causâ!* It will be to the Purpose, therefore, to examine whence proceeded this Affectation of a Mode that hath continued now at least 3000 Years, and the rather, because it may lead us to the Grounds of Architecture, and by what Steps this Humour of Colonades came into Practice in all Ages.

Epist. 87.[33]

The first Temples were, in all Probability, in the ruder Times, only little *Cellæ* to inclose the Idol within, with no other Light than a large Door to discover it to the People, when the Priest saw proper, and when he went in alone to offer Incense, the People paying their Adorations without Doors; for all *(page 355)* Sacrifices were performed in the open Air, before the Front of the Temple; but in the southern Climates, a Grove was necessary not only to shade the Devout, but, from the Darkness of the Place, to strike some Terror and Recollection in their Approachers; therefore, Trees being always an Adjunct to the *Cellæ*, the *Israelites* were commanded to destroy not only the Idols, but to cut down the Groves which surrounded them:[34] but Trees decaying with Time, or not equally growing, (though planted at first in good Order) or possibly not having Room; when the Temples were brought into Cities, the like Walks were represented with Stone Pillars, supporting the more durable Shade of a Roof, instead of the Arbour of spreading Boughs; and still in the Ornaments of the Stone Work was imitated, (as well as the Materials would bear) both in the Capitals, Frizes and Mouldings, a Foliage, or sort of Work composed of Leaves, which remains to this Age.

This, I am apt to think, was the true Original of Colonades environing the Temples in single or double Ailes.

People could not assemble and converse, but under shade in hot Countries; therefore, the *Forum* of every City was also at first planted round with Walks of Trees———

Lucus in urbe fuit mediâ, lætissimus umbrâ.[35]

These Avenues were afterwards, as Cities grew more wealthy, reformed into Porticoes of Marble;[36] but it is probable, at first the Columns were set no nearer than the Trees were before in Distance, and that both Architraves and Roofs were of Timber; because the Inter-columns would certainly have been too large to have had the Architraves made in Stone; but the Architects in After-ages, being ambitious to perform all in Stone, and to load the Architraves also with heavy Cornices of Stone, were necessitated to bring the Pillars nearer together; and from hence arose the Differences of the *Eustyle, Sustyle, Diastyle,* and *Pycnostyle* Disposition of Columns, by which *Vitruvius*[37] and his Followers would make a systematical Science of their Art, forming positive Rules, according to the Diameters of their Columns, for the Inter-columns, and the Proportions[38] of the Architrave, Cornice, and all the Members of which they are composed.

But, by the way, it is to be observed, the Diameters of Columns were grosser at first, though Timber Architraves did not require to be borne by a more substantial Pillar, as in the *Tuscan* Order; but, because in the Groves, the ancient Trees of large Growth (and Antiquity always carries Veneration with it) were used to be of most Esteem. So at first the Columns were six Diameters in Heighth; when the Imitation of Groves was forgot, the Diameters were advanced to seven; then to eight; then to nine, as in the *Ionick* Order; then, at last, to ten, as in the *Corinthian* and *Italick* Orders: And herein the Architects had Reason, for the great Expence is in raising and carving[39] of the Columns; and slenderer Columns would leave them more Opportunity to shew their Skill in carving and enriching their Works in the Capitals and Mouldings. Thus the *Corinthian* Order became the most delicate of all others, and though the Column was slenderer, yet bore a greater Weight of Entablature than the more ancient *Orders*.

When the old Statuaries in *Greece*, such as *Phidias,*[40] *Praxiteles,*[41] and their Disciples, began to be celebrated for their Art, and the People grew[42] fond of their Works, it is no Wonder (for *honos alit artes*)[43] they fell upon the *Corinthian* Capital, which in no After-age to this Time has been amended, though the *French* King, *Lewis* the fourteenth, proposed Rewards to such Artists as should find out a *Gallick Order*;[44] therefore *Callimachus*, the old Architect and Inventor, (according to *Vitruvius*'s Story of the Nurse and Basket)[45] must still retain the *(page 356)* Honour of it; for, neither will the Flower-de-luce of the *French*,[46] nor the Palms of *Villalpandus*,[47] in his imaginary Scheme of the Temple of *Solomon*, come up to the Grace of the old Form of the *Corinthian* Capital.

It seems very unaccountable, that the Generality of our late Architects dwell so much upon this ornamental, and so slightly pass over the geometrical, which is the most essential Part of Architecture. For Instance, can an *Arch* stand without Butment sufficient?

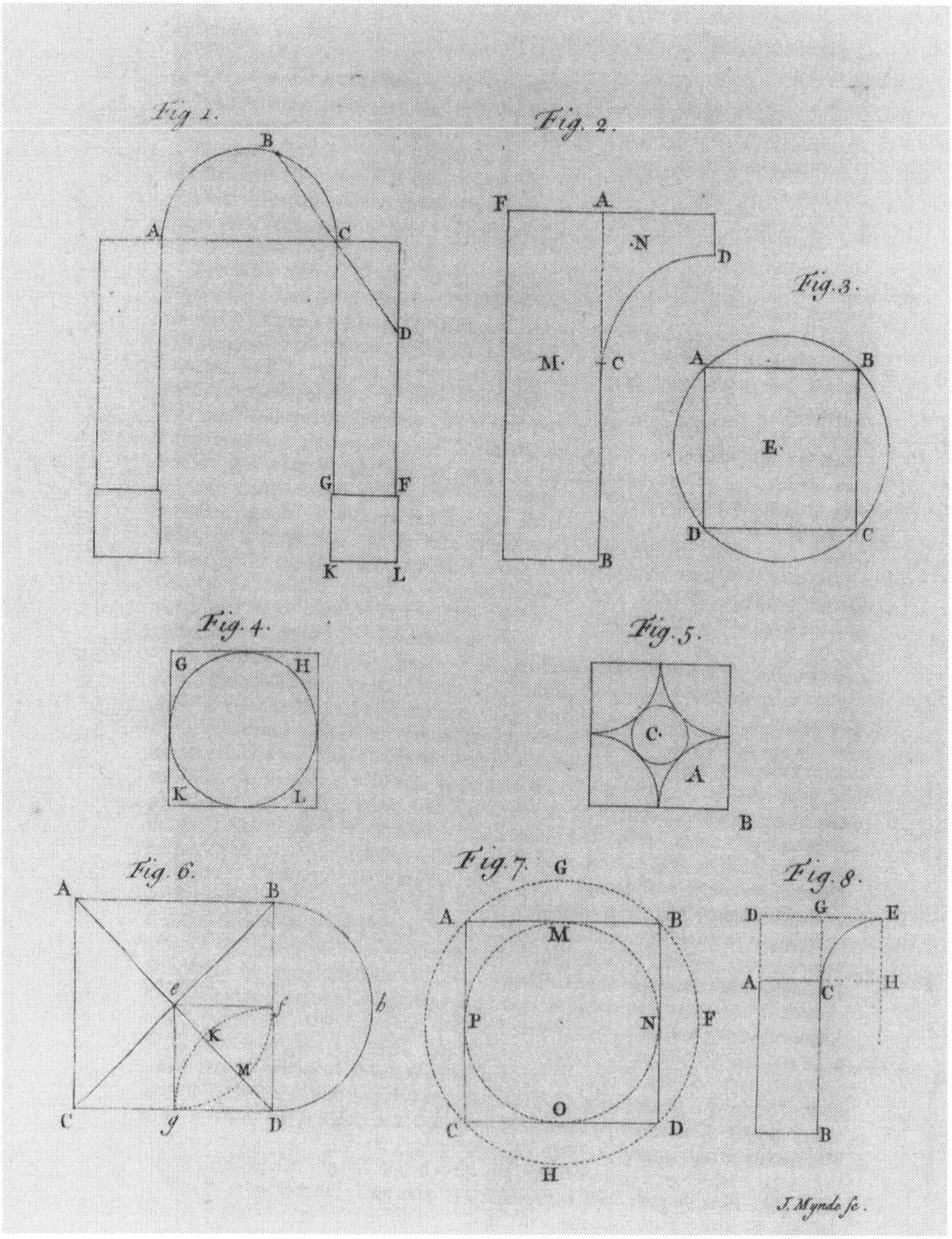
Fig. 1.
B
A
C
D
G
F
K
L
Fig. 2.
F
A
N
D
M·
C
B
Fig. 3.
A
B
E·
D
C
Fig. 4.
G
H
K
L
Fig. 5.
C·
A
B
Fig. 6.
A
B
e
f
b
K
M
C
g
D
Fig. 7.
G
A
B
M
P
N
F
O
C
D
H
Fig. 8.
D
G
E
A
C
H
B
J. Mynde sc.

If the Butment be more than enough, 'tis an idle Expence of Materials; if too little, it will fall; and so for any Vaulting: And yet no Author hath given a true and universal Rule for this; nor hath considered all the various Forms of Arches.

The Rule given by the Authors[48] for the Butment of Arches, is this: [See Figure 1.] Let A B C be the Arch, of which B is a third Part; extend the Line B C, and make C D equal to C B, and draw the Perpendicular C D F, this determines the Butment G F, (as they say) but wherefore? for add to the Bottom, as K L, the Arch then must certainly press more upon the higher Part than the lower; or if some additional Weight be added above the Arch, that must still press more than before this was added. So this Rule (if it were built upon any sure geometrical Theorem, as it is not) is neither true nor universal; and what is true will be shewn to be only determinable by the Doctrine of finding the Centers of Gravity in the Parts of the proposed Design. In demonstrating this, I will not trouble the Reader with nice geometrical Speculations, or Calculations, but by easy Inductions; supposing he hath read *Archimedes*, or the modern Geometricians,[49] who have purposely treated of Centers of Gravity; or at least, that he will give Credit to those who have established all the Principles of this Science by

FIGURE 33

FIGURE 33. Structural diagrams in Tract II, 1750: *Fig. 1*. Rule-of-thumb method for determining the thickness of the piers supporting an arch. "The Rule given by the Authors for the Butment of Arches is this: Let A B C be the Arch, of which B is a third Part; extend the Line B C, and make C D equal to C B, and draw the Perpendicular C D F, this determines the Butment G F, (as they say) but wherefore? for add to the Bottom, as K L, the Arch then must certainly press more upon the higher Part than the lower; or if some additional Weight be added above the Arch, that must still press more than before this was added." (Tract II) *Fig. 2*. Wren's method for determining the abutment of an arch by means of centers of gravity. "Let a Stone be cut in this Form, F B a Parallelogram, C D a Semicircle added, A B a Perpendicular, M the Center of Gravity of F B, and N of A C D, now if N be equiponderant to M on each Side the Perpendicular A B, it is certain the whole Stone will stand immoveable upon the Basis at B, although it be but half an Arch; add the like Stone on the opposite Side, till the Horns meet in an entire Arch, so the Whole will stand as well as the Halves. If any thing be added without M, that alters nothing, only 'tis an useless Expence; but if any thing be added above N, that alters the Center of Gravity, which therefore must be provided for, by adding more Weight to M; and the same may be shewn in all kinds of Vaulting." (Tract II) (Stephen Wren, *Parentalia*, London, 1750, facing p. 356.) The Ohio State University Libraries, Rare Book and Manuscripts.

Fig. II.
FIGURE 33

Demonstration unquestionable; so it will not be necessary to dive into the Rudiments.

Let a Stone be cut in this Form, F B a Parallelogram, C D a Semicircle added, A B a Perpendicular, M the Center of Gravity of F B, and N of A C D, now if N be equiponderant to M on each Side the Perpendicular A B, it is certain the whole Stone will stand immoveable upon the Basis at B, although it be but half an Arch; add the like Stone on the opposite Side, till the Horns meet in an entire Arch, so the Whole will stand as well as the Halves. If any thing be added without M, that alters nothing, only 'tis an useless Expence; but if any thing be added above N, that alters the Center of Gravity, which therefore must be provided for, by adding more Weight to M; and the same may be shewn in all kinds of Vaulting. So it appears that the Design, where there are Arcades, must be regulated by the Art of Staticks, or Invention of the Centers of Gravity, and the duly poising all Parts to equiponderate; without which, a fine Design will fail and prove abortive. Hence I conclude, that all Designs must, in the first place, be brought to this Test, or rejected. I have examined some celebrated Works, as the *Pantheon*, and judge there is more Butment than necessary, though it is flat and low; but I suppose the Architect provided it should stand against Earthquakes, as indeed it hath, and will. The great Fabrick of *St. Peter*'s, if it had been followed as *Bramante* had designed it, would have been as durable; but the Butment of the Cupola was not placed with Judgment: however, since it was hooped with Iron, it is safe at present, and, without an Earthquake, for Ages to come.[50] Iron, at all Adventures, is a good Caution; but the Architect should so poise his Work, as if it were not necessary.

The Free-masons[51] were not very solicitous about this, because they used Buttresses on the Outside of the Wall, which they extended as far as they guessed would be sufficient; and they had yet a farther Help, by loading the Buttress with a Pinnacle, to the Height of which they were not confined. The *Romans* never used Buttresses without, but rather within, though they cut off a Part of the Arch, but not of the Vaulting that depended on the Arch,[52] as it *(page 357)* appears in the Ailes of *Dioclesian*'s Baths, and in some respect also in the *Templum Pacis*.[53]

The different Forms of Vaultings are necessary to be considered, either as they were used by the Ancients, or the Moderns, whether *Free-masons*, or *Saracens*.[54] The *Romans*, though they sometimes used a Hemisphere, where the Room was round; or Half-hemispheres,[55] as in the *Exedræ* of the Baths, or the Tribunes of Temples and *Basilicæ*, yet generally they used a plain cylindrical Vaulting, where the Walls were parallel;[56] or Cross-vaulting, where two Cylinders intersect in Diagonals, as in the *Templum Pacis*;⁵⁷ and in all the Theatres in the Passages under the Steps. The Moderns, whose Arches were not circular, but made of Sections of Circles,⁵⁸ used commonly another sort, where the Spandrils resting upon the Pillars, sprang every way round as their Arch rose. It is not easy to give a geometrical Definition, but by calling it a circular inverted Cone (A), resting upon its Apex (B); (C) the Middle, they filled up with Tracery-work, for which this Way gave them great Opportunity of divers Variations, which I need not insist on.⁵⁹ Another Way, (which I cannot find used by the Ancients, but in the later eastern Empire, as appears at *St. Sophia*,⁶⁰ and by that Example, in all the Mosques and Cloysters of the *Dervises*,⁶¹ and every where at present in the *East*) and of all others the most geometrical, is composed of Hemispheres, and their Sections only: and whereas a Sphere may be cut all manner of Ways, and that still into Circles, it may be accommodated to lie upon all Positions of the Pillars.⁶² Let E be a Cupola or Hemisphere, resting upon four Pillars A B C D, from whence arise the four Arches, to which the Sections, being Semicircles, must join on all Sides, whether A B be equal to B C or not. Cut the Hemisphere again horizontally, the Section will be an entire Circle, touching in the Keys of the Arches, and G H K L will be Spandrils resting upon the Pillars, yet still are Parts of the Hemisphere; and if the horizontal Circle be taken away, you may build upon that Circle an upright Wall, which may bear a Cupola again above, as is done at *St. Sophia* and *St. Peter's*,⁶³ and at all the Churches at *Rome*. I question not but those at *Constantinople* had it from the *Greeks* before them, it is so natural, and is yet found in the present Seraglio, which was the episcopal Palace of old;⁶⁴ the imperial Palace, whose Ruins still appear, being farther eastward.⁶⁵ Now, because I have for just Reasons followed this way in the vaulting of the Church of *St. Paul's*,⁶⁶ I think it proper to shew, that it is the lightest Manner, and requires less Butment than the Cross-vaulting, as well as that it is of an agreeable View; and, at the same time, I shall shew how the Centers of Gravity are to be computed. To shew that it requires less Butment than the diagonal Cross-vaulting, I will compare them both together, without any perplexed Demonstration, as follows.———

It is evident that the Spandrils, or loading of the diagonal Cross-arches, where two cylindrical Vaults meet, must be an inverted Pyramid, whose Basis is a Parallelogram,⁶⁷ with two Sides strait, and two circular; and wherever it be cut horizontally, it will be cut into like Parallelograms: now, in the other eastern Way of Vaulting by Hemispheres, the Spandrils are the Solids, which are left when a Hemisphere is taken out of a Half-cube; each of these also must be

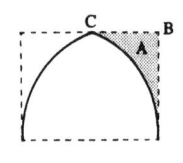

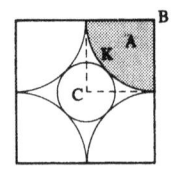

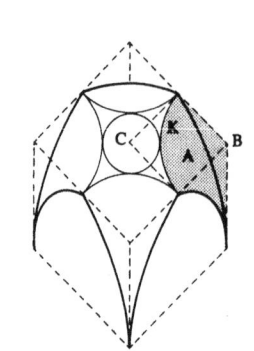

FIGURE 34. Diagrams of structural systems according to Wren's descriptions in Tract II
A. Fan vault, cf. Fig. 33, *Fig. 5*.
"It is not easy to give a geometrical Definition, but by calling it a circular inverted Cone (A), resting upon its Apex (B); (C) the Middle, they filled up with Tracery-work . . ." (Tract II). Diagram by author.

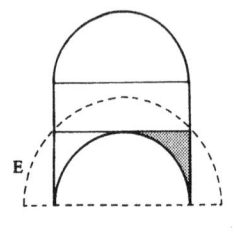

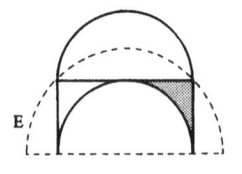

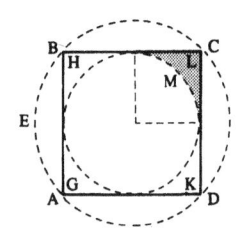

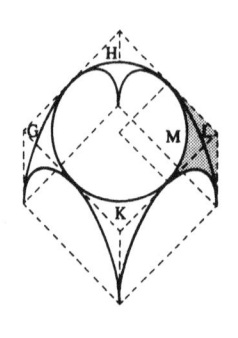

B. Dome on pendentives, including alternative with drum (*top*), cf. Fig. 33, *Figs. 3, 4*.
"Let E be a Cupola or Hemisphere, resting upon four Pillars A B C D, from whence arise the four Arches, to which the Sections, being Semicircles, must join on all Sides, whether A B be equal to B C or not. Cut the Hemisphere again horizontally, the Section will be an entire Circle, touching in the Keys of the Arches, and G H K L will be Spandrils resting upon the Pillars, yet still are Parts of the Hemisphere; and if the horizontal Circle be taken away, you may build upon that Circle an upright Wall, which may bear a Cupola again above. . . ." (Tract II). Diagram by author.

164

C. Structural system used at St. Paul's.
"I have for just Reasons followed this way in the vaulting of the Church of *St. Paul's* . . . it is the lightest Manner, and requires less Butment than the Cross-vaulting, as well as that it is of an agreeable View . . ." (Tract II). Diagram by author.

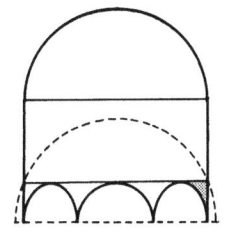

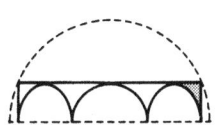

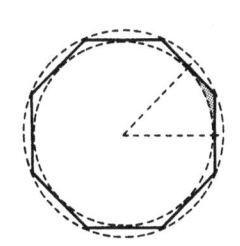

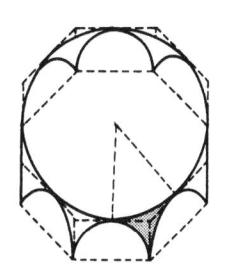

D. Cross vault, including alternative with pointed arch (*top*), cf. Fig. 33, *Fig. 6*.
"Let A B C D represent the whole Vaulting between four Pillars, then *e f g* will represent the Quarter of this Vaulting resting upon D. Now, because the solid Half-cylinder C D is cut off by the Half-cylinder B D, it is evident the whole Cross-vault will be equal to one Half-cylinder, whose Diameter is B D, the Heighth *f h*, and the Length A B; and because D *g e f* is one fourth Part, this being deducted out of the Cube of *f* D, the Remainder (supposing it filled up to the Crown) *e*, is the Body we suppose at D, for the Butment, and the Parts of this circular inverted Pyramid will bear a Proportion with the Ordinates of the Quadrant, being the Radius less the Ordinates squared: so the Ordinates of the Pyramid are known; and by the known Methods the Centers of Gravity will be known of the Whole or Part. As for the *Gothick* Vaulting, turn this Pyramid upon its Axis, and it will be a Conoide in the Whole, and in its Parts as the Circle to the Square circumscribed, and the Centers will be given of the Whole and the Parts" (Tract II). Diagram by author.

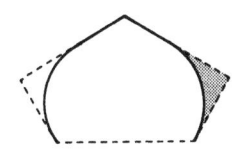

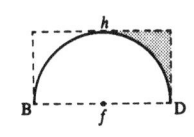

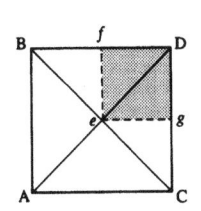

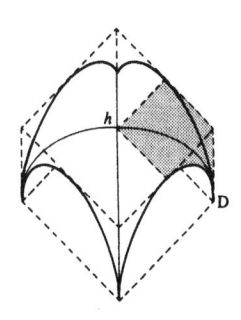

165

a sort of inverted Pyramid, whose Bases and Sides are circular, and wherever it is cut horizontally, it is cut into Pieces of Circles.⁶⁸

What these are that give the Butment of Arcades in the several Forms of Arches may be geometrically determined, for Example in the *Roman* Way of Cross-arches.

Fig. VI.
FIGURES 33, 34D

Let A B C D represent the whole Vaulting between four Pillars, then *e f g* will represent the Quarter of this Vaulting resting upon D. Now, because the solid Half-cylinder C D is cut off by the Half-cylinder B D, it is evident the whole Cross-vault will be equal to one Half-cylinder, whose Diameter is B D, *(page 358)* the Height *f h*, and the Length A B; and because D *g e f* is one fourth Part, this being deducted out of the Cube of *f* D, the Remainder (supposing it filled up to the Crown) *e*, is the Body we suppose at D, for the Butment, and the Parts of this circular inverted Pyramid will bear a Proportion with the Ordinates of the Quadrant, being the Radius less the Ordinates squared: so the Ordinates of the Pyramid are known; and by the known Methods the Centers of Gravity will be known of the Whole or Part.⁶⁹ As for the *Gothick* Vaulting, turn this Pyramid upon its Axis, and it will be a Conoide in the Whole, and in its Parts as the Circle to the Square circumscribed, and the Centers will be given of the Whole and the Parts.⁷⁰

FIGURES 34D

Fig. VII.
FIGURE 33

Now, the third Way of vaulting by Parts of Hemispheres may be thus considered. Let A B C D be four Pillars, and G F H be supposed the whole Hemisphere, before it be cut off by six Arches, and by the two horizontal Sections P O N, then is D O N one of the eight Spandrils; therefore the said Spandril is the Sphere less the Cube divided by 8, or the Hemisphere less half the Cube divided by 4, which is one Spandril, such as O N D.⁷¹ Now, let these several Spandrils in the *Roman*, the *Gothick*, or *Saracen* Way be compared together, (see Fig. VI.) *g f* D in the *Roman*, is the Basis of the square (inverted Pyramid); *g* K D in the *Gothick* is but the Quadrant of a Circle inscribed, and *g* M K D but the Remainder to the Square; which being evidently the least and lightest, and the Center of Gravity nearest to D, I have therefore followed in the Vaultings of *St. Paul's*, and, with good Reason, preferred it above any other Way used by Architects. But none of these Vaultings are in Buildings thought necessary to be filled up to the Crowns of the Vaultings, but so high as to give Butment to the Arches above the Pillars, which Architects have determined, by Practice, to be a third Part of the Heighth of the Arch.⁷² It seems necessary to consider the proper Butment of the cylindrical or strait Vaultings⁷³ upon parallel Walls, or two Pillars only of some Breadth. In order to find this by Steps, we will consider an Arch abstracted from what may be laid upon it, or affixed to it. Let A B be a Body (the Heighth

FIGURES 33, 34D

or Thickness doth not enter into this Consideration) upon the level Top, to lay the Body G E D, the Line G E being a Quadrant, D E a Tangent to it ★ ★ ★ ★ ★ [74]

[*The rest is wanting.*]

TRACT III.

THE *Tyrian* Order was the first Manner, which, in *Greece*, was refined into the *Dorick* Order, after the first Temple of that Order was built at *Argos*:[75] but if we consider well the *Dorick* Order,[76] we manifestly may trace the same to be but an Imitation in Stone, of what was usually done in Timber, in the long Porticoes they used to build in Cities, by which they tolerated the Heat of the Day, and conversed together: the Roofs of those Porticoes were framed after this Manner.

First, They laid the Timber, called Architrave, to join the Pillars in a Row, upon these they laid the Beams that joined the opposite Rows, then upon these they raised the Rafters, which *Vitruvius* calls *Capreoli*,[77] which meeting in a Triangle, made the Roof to cast off Weather; the Rafters were fastened by two Tenons into the very Ends of the Beams, by sawing aslant into the Ends of them, not as we do by Mortises. Upon the Architrave they placed a Plank, the better to join the Ends of these Architraves together upon the Pillars; then the Pins (improperly called *Guttæ*) driven upwards, would not only fix the *Capreoli* to the Beams, but stay them from sliding upon the Architraves, and gage the opposite Architraves together, to keep a strait Range in the long Porticoes: *(page 359)* and thus may be discerned the Reason of the Triglyphs, and of the whole *Dorick* Order; and these long Porticoes were the general Method of building Cities in the hot Climates.

When *Alexander* had determined to build *Alexandria*, and had settled the Place, he left *Dinocrates* his Architect to compleat the same, who drew a long Street with Porticoes on both Sides, from the Lake *Mæotis* to the Sea, and another cross it, that lead to *Pelusium*; then built Walls and large Towers, each capable to quarter five hundred Men; the noble Ruins of which remain at this Day; (a) then giving great Privileges to *Egyptians* and *Jews*, they soon filled the Quarters between the Porticoes with private and publick Buildings.[79] Thus were Cities suddenly raised, and thus was *Tadmor*[80] built, the Ruins of which shew nothing at present to Travellers, but incredible Numbers of Pillars of the *Dorick* Order, some

---

(a) Near this City stands a Pillar, erected by one of the *Ptolomys*, (but vulgarly called Pompey's Pillar) the Shaft of which consists of one solid Stone of Granate, 90 Feet high, and 38 in Compass. [Le Bruyn's *Voyage*, p. 171.][78]

Fig. VIII.
FIGURE 33

yet standing, more broken, which were certainly the Remains of long Porticoes to shade the Streets. Now, how was *Tarsus* and *Anchiala* built in a Day?[81] that is, I suppose, the Walls and Gates were set out in a Day; and this Way of setting out the principal Streets by Porticoes, occasioned that hundreds of Pillars, of all sorts, were to be bought at the Quarries ready made, where great Numbers of Artizans wrought for Sale of what they raised; and this is the Reason why even at *Rome* the Scantlings are not always found conformable to the Rules, especially in sudden Works; as to instance in the Portico of the *Pantheon*, where are scarcely two Columns of the same Diameter; some of the Columns being six★ *Roman* Palms and ten Inches [*Pollices*] in Diameter, others six Palms and five Inches. However, as it is a Coloss-work, and most wonderfully rich, consisting of sixteen huge Columns of the *Corinthian* Order, each Column being one solid Stone of oriental Granate, the Eye cannot readily discern any Disproportion. And thus in the great Pillar of *London*, the Height exceeding the due Proportion of the Order, one Module is imperceptible to the Eye.[83]

See Monsieur Desgodetz.[82]
★*The* Roman *Palm is nine Inches* English *Measure.*

Plinii Epist. Lib. 9.[84]

Pliny the younger, proposing to repair and enlarge, by the Addition of a Portico, an old Temple of *Ceres*, that stood upon his Estate in *Tuscany*, directs his Architect immediately to buy four Marble Columns, of any sort he pleased. By this Method of purchasing, at any time, Columns of all Orders and Proportions, ready formed at the Quarries, as Goods in a Shop, or Warehouse, the Ancients had an Advantage of erecting Porticoes (the stately Pride of the *Roman* Architecture) of any Grandeur, or Extent, in a very short Time, and without being over scrupulous in the Exactness of the Dimensions.

TRACT IV.

AN Example of *Tyrian* Architecture we may collect from the Theatre, by the Fall of which, *Sampson* made so vast a Slaughter of the *Philistines*, by one Stretch of his wonderful Strength.[85] In considering what this Fabrick must be, that could at one Pull be demolished, I conceive it an oval Amphitheatre, the Scene in the Middle, where a vast Roof of Cedar-beams resting round upon the Walls, centered all upon one short Architrave, that united two Cedar Pillars in the Middle; one Pillar would not be sufficient to unite the Ends of at least one hundred Beams that tended to the Center; therefore, I say, there must be a short Architrave resting upon two Pillars, upon *(page 360)* which all the Beams tending to the Center of the Amphitheatre might be supported. Now, if *Sampson*, by his miraculous Strength pressing upon one of these Pillars, moved it from its Basis, the whole[86] Roof must of necessity fall.[87]

168

The most observable Monument of the *Tyrian* Style, and of great Antiquity, still remaining, is the Sepulchre of *Absalom**:[88] the Body of this Structure is square, faced on every Side with Pillars, which bear up an hemispherical *Tholus* solid; a large Architrave, Freeze, and Cornice lie upon the Pillars, which are larger in proportion to their Heighth, than what we now allow to the *Tuscan* Order; so likewise is the Entablature larger.

*Over against Jerusalem *eastward, in the Valley of* Jehosaphat.

This whole Composition, though above 30 Feet high, is all of one Stone, both Basis, Pillars, and *Tholus*, cut as it stood out of the adjacent Cliff of white Marble.

It is to be wished, some skilful Artist would give us the exact Dimensions to Inches, by which we might have a true Idea of the ancient *Tyrian* Manner; for, 'tis most probable *Solomon* employed the *Tyrian* Architects in his Temple, from his Correspondency with King *Hiram*;[89] and from these *Phœnicians* I derive, as well the Arts, as the Letters of the *Grecians*, though it may be the *Tyrians* were Imitators of the *Babylonians*, and they of the *Ægyptians*.

Great Monarchs are ambitious to leave great Monuments behind them; and this occasions great Inventions in[90] the mechanick Arts.

What the Architecture was that *Solomon* used, we know but little of, though holy Writ hath given us the general Dimensions of the Temple, by which we may, in some measure,[91] collect the Plan, but not of all the Courts.[92]

Villalpandus[93] hath made a fine romantick Piece, after the *Corinthian* Order, which, in that Age, was not used by any Nation; for the early Ages used much grosser Pillars than the *Dorick*: in after Times, they began to refine from the *Dorick*, as in the Temple of *Diana* at *Ephesus*, (the united Work of all *Asia*) and at length improved into a slenderer Pillar, and leafy Capital of various Inventions, which was called *Corinthian*; so that if we run back to the Age of *Solomon*, we may with Reason believe they used the *Tyrian* Manner, as gross at least, if not more, than the *Dorick*, and that the *Corinthian* Manner of *Villalpandus* is mere Fancy.

Of the Temple of Diana *at* Ephesus, *according to the Account of* Pliny.

FIGURES 35–6

The Temple of *Diana* at *Ephesus*, a most surprising Example of the *Grecian* Magnificence, introduced the *Ionick* Order:[94] it was two hundred and twenty Years in building, at the joint Expence of all the States of *Asia*, each Government contributing a Pillar.[95] In this Structure the Capitals were first formed with Voluta's, and the Proportions changed from the *Dorick* to a slenderer Pillar. The De-

Front of the Temple of Diana at Ephesus

The Shrine in the Temple

The Ground Plan

FIGURE 35. Wren's reconstruction of the Temple of Diana at Ephesus, elevation, with the shrine, 1750 (Christopher Wren, Jr., *Parentalia* [London, 1750], following p. 361). The Ohio State University Libraries, Rare Book and Manuscripts.

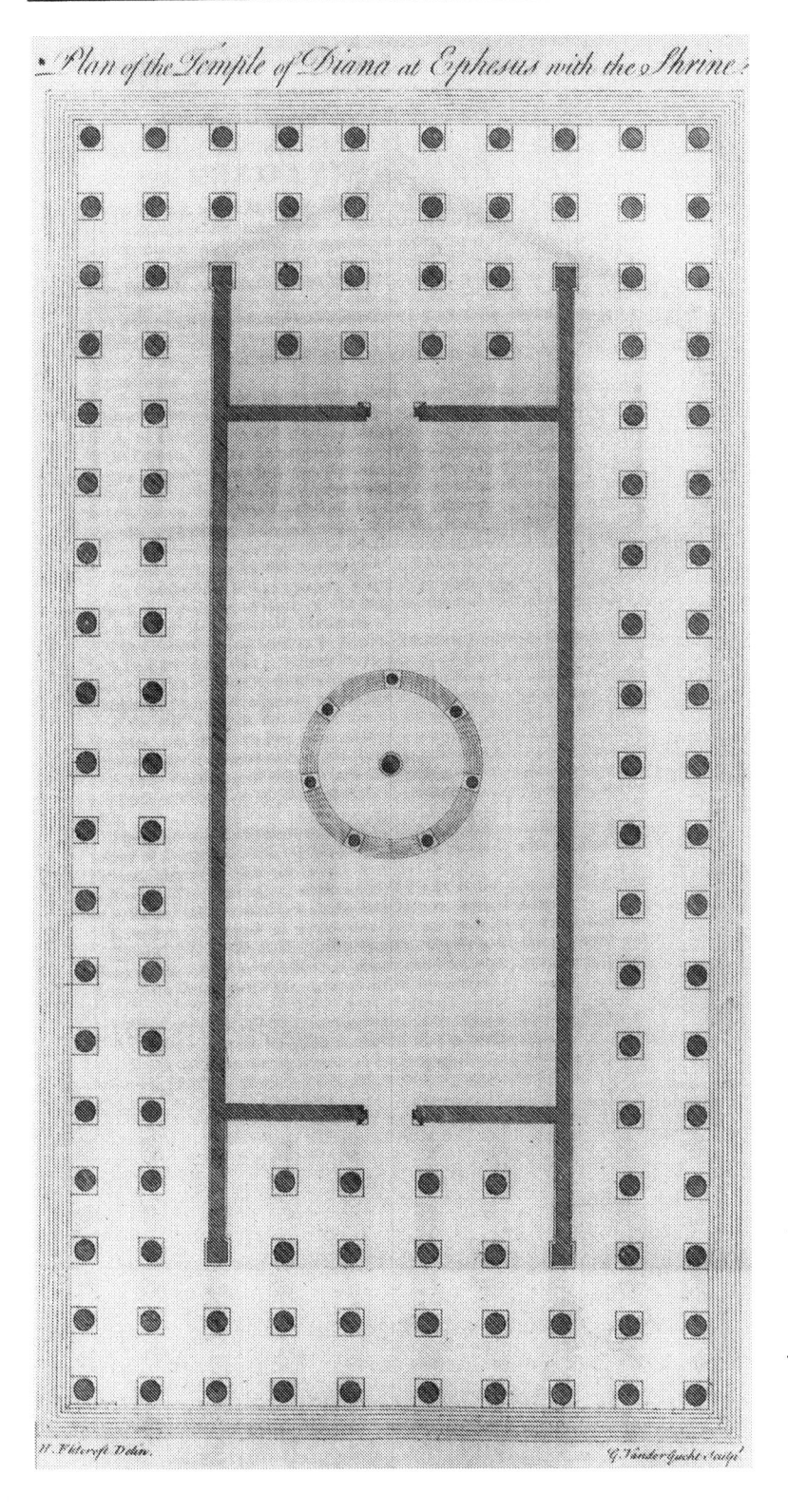

FIGURE 36. Wren's reconstruction of the Temple of Diana at Ephesus, plan, 1750 (Christopher Wren, Jr., *Parentalia* [London, 1750], following p. 361). The Ohio State University Libraries, Rare Book and Manuscripts.

scription in *Pliny*[96] is short, and what no Authors, ancient or modern, seem sufficiently to explain. The Account, therefore, of this prodigious Fabrick, the first Instance of the Use of the *Ionick* Order, requires to be as fully and clearly illustrated, as the most authentick Aid we can have from Antiquity will allow.

The Length of the whole Temple was 425 Feet, the Breadth 220 Feet. The Pillars were in Number 127, each 60 Feet high. – To make out this Number of Pillars, the Disposition must be *Decastyle-dipteron*, and the Columns thus reckoned; 40 in the Fronts, fore and aft, and 60 in the Ailes; so this *Peribole* makes just 100; besides these, are 16 in the *Pronavi*, and the 4 *Antæ*, making in all 120. The Colonade affords no more, but the Tabernacle, or *(page 361)* Shrine situated in the Middle of the *Cella*, wherein stood the Coloss Image of *Diana Multimammea*, contains seven, and answers the Number in *Pliny*.

This strange Idol, (which is represented in the Coins of *Ephesus*,[97] and other *Asiatick* Cities) of as odd a Figure as any *Indian* Pagod, (the Remains of very ancient Superstition, before the *Ionick* Migration, which, it seems, the *Greeks* would still preserve, believing it fell out of Heaven, and sent by *Jupiter*) was made of Cedar; and the *Cella* had a flat Roofing of Cedar; for vaulted it could not well be, for want of Butment, being 115 Feet broad, and near as high, and 230 Feet long. Thus was the Huntress placed, as it were, in a Grove of Marble Pillars.

All the ancient Idols were encircled with Groves; and this seems to be the Reason of the perpetual Adherence of all Architecture[98] to this Form, and no other, of Colonades about Temples; meaning to represent the original Groves, as the Capitals, and all the Ornaments carry still the Figures of Leaves.

Diana Artemis was the Moon, her Solemnities were by Night: the nineteen Pillars in the Ailes represented her Period; the seven Pillars of the Chapel in the Middle of the *Cella*, the Quarter of her menstrual Course. This, I suppose, was the ΝΑΙΣΚΟΣ, we translate the Shrine of *Diana*; the Representation of which, 'tis supposed, and not of the whole Structure, the Silversmiths of *Ephesus* formed in Models for Sale to Strangers, "which brought no small Gain to the Craftsmen." In like manner, at this Day, small Models of Wood, garnished with Mother of Pearl, of the holy Sepulchre at *Jerusalem*, are usually made for Sale to Pilgrims and Foreigners.[100]

Acts of the Apostles, c. xix. v. 24.[99]

The Columns being 60 Feet high, the Diameter, according to Rule, must be 6 Feet 8 Inches, that is, a ninth Part; thus every Column would contain at least 110 Tun of Marble, besides Base and Capital, and the vast Stones of the Entablature, but more especially of the middle Intercolumn, which being wider than the rest, to open more Way for the Entrance, as usual in the *Greek* Temples, was about 22 Feet, and could not bear its own Weight, unless the Architrave and Freeze were both of one Stone, which together would be above 150 Tun; the setting of which (for it seems the Architect despaired) was miraculously attributed to the Goddess herself, as beyond the Reach of human Skill.[101]

Thirty-six of the Columns were carved by *Scopas*, a famous Statuary of the School of *Praxiteles*; and the outward Walls of the *Cella* were adorned with Pictures, about the Time of *Apelles*.

Modern Travellers[102] tell us, there are great Heaps of Ruins at this Day, and large Vaults, which probably were the Substructions of the Colonades.

I imagine the Ascent to it was easy, and not with many Steps, that the ’ΑΠΗ'ΝΗ ‘ΙΕΡΑ`, *Thensa Sacra*, might commodiously pass: this was a covered Waggon drawn by two Mules, in which the Idol was placed, and carried through the Streets to the *Circus*, upon grand Solemnities.

> [We often see this Temple represented upon Medals, with the Figure of *Diana*; but the Frontispiece, because of the small Room left in these sort of Monuments, is never to be seen there charged with more than eight Pillars, sometimes with six, with four, or only with two.[103]]

(page 362)

Observations on the Temple of **Peace**, built by the Emperor **Vespasian**.[104]

FIGURES 37–9

1. The Greatness of this ⋆Temple, the most magnificent of old *Rome*, is prodigious; it is longer than our † *Westminster-hall*,[105] and the middle Nave only, besides the Ailes, is more than a seventh Part broader; in Heighth it exceeds the highest Cathedral now in the World.

⋆ 300 *Feet long,* 200 *Feet broad.*
† 228 *Feet long,* 66 *Feet broad.*

2. The Walls are thin, where the Roof presses not; but admirably secured where the Weight lies; first, by the Piles behind the Pillars, which are of that Thickness backward, that they are sufficient Butment to the Arch of the Ailes: (this not being observed in the *Gothick* Cathedrals, the Vault of the Ailes resting against the Middle of the Pillars of the Nave, bend them inward; and therefore, in *Westminster-abbey*, they are cramped, in some Places, cross the Aile to the outward Wall, with vast Irons, to secure the Vault of the Aile from spreading.)[106] Secondly, the Weight of the Roof above hath a mighty Butment from the slope Walls between the Windows, which answer to the Half-frontispieces of the Ailes; from

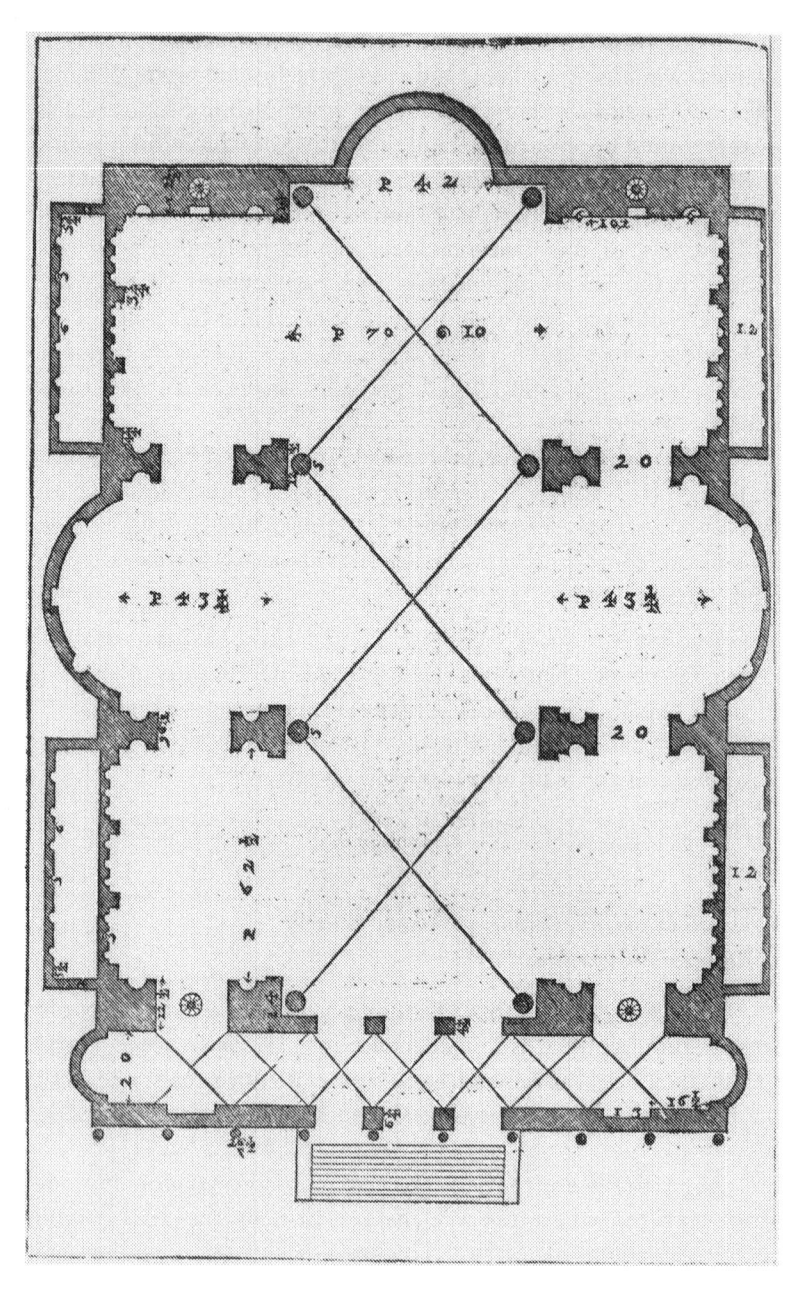

FIGURE 37. Palladio's reconstruction of the "Temple of Peace" (Basilica of Maxentius and Constantine), plan, 1570 (Andrea Palladio, *I Quattro Libri dell'architettura* [1581 (1570)], vol. 4, pl. 12). University of Illinois Library at Urbana-Champaign, Rare Book Room and Special Collections Library.

FIGURE 38. Palladio's reconstruction of the "Temple of Peace" (Basilica of Maxentius and Constantine), section and elevation, 1570 (Andrea Palladio, *I Quattro Libri dell'architettura* [1581 (1570)], vol. 4, pl. 13). University of Illinois Library at Urbana-Champaign, Rare Book Room and Special Collections Library.

whence the flying Buttresses of the *Gothick* Fabricks seem to have taken their Original.

3. This Temple ascends to its vast Heighth each Way, by three Degrees; the mighty Nave is butted by the Ailes, and the Ailes by the Tribunals, and little Rooms without; which we may well suppose to be those Archives, wherein the *Sibyll*'s Books, the Spoils of the *Jewish* Temple, and the Records of *Rome*, the most sacred for Antiquity, were kept.[107]

4. Thus it rises to be equal in Heighth to half the whole Breadth between the side Tribunals; and a Line drawn from the Key of the Vault of the Nave, to the Key of the Arch of the Aile, determines the Breadth of the Aile: so that in the farthest Part you see always half the Vault of the Nave; which makes it seem free and spacious, containing more than an Acre of Ground in its Pavement, and might well contain an Assembly of 20,000 Persons; the common Use of it being a Hall of Justice, and for that Reason it was made very light-some; whereas the consecrated Temples were generally very obscure.

5. I have admired the Greatness and Firmness of this Pile, but I cannot commend the Architect's Judgment for obscuring the majestick Stature of it with an humble Portico, and low Wings, which cause the visual Ray to cut off very much of the Height; so that in Perspective the Front will look exceeding broad and flat, and, to those that approach the Entrance, will seem as it were grafted upon the low Portico; though the Grace in the double Frontispiece and Acroteria, doth something make amends, distinguishing the mighty Breadth into several Parts.

6. But shall I accuse Antiquity for want of Skill in Opticks, of which every where it shews such admirable Proofs? since particularly here the Architect hath given great Testimony of it in the Contrivance of his Cornice, wherein he hath left out the *Corona*, or Hanging-square, by an unusual Example.[108] The *Corona* seems an essential Part in all Cornices, as that which gives Denomination to the whole, and is necessary to the Beauty of a Cornice; because, by its Projecture, it shadows all the lower Members, receiving upon its plane Surface a terse Light from above; this gives the Eminence and distinct Appearance which we see in the Parts of a Cornice at distance; but the Artist here ingeniously apprehending that his Lights in this Fabrick stood level with his Cornice, and therefore it would want the Effect for which it is used, and that the Hanging-face of it *(page 363)* would be fore shortened to nothing, to the Eye which beholds it from beneath, wisely left out this Member, which, if these optical Reasons did not prevail, would never have been used, since, of all Members, this is that which most loads the

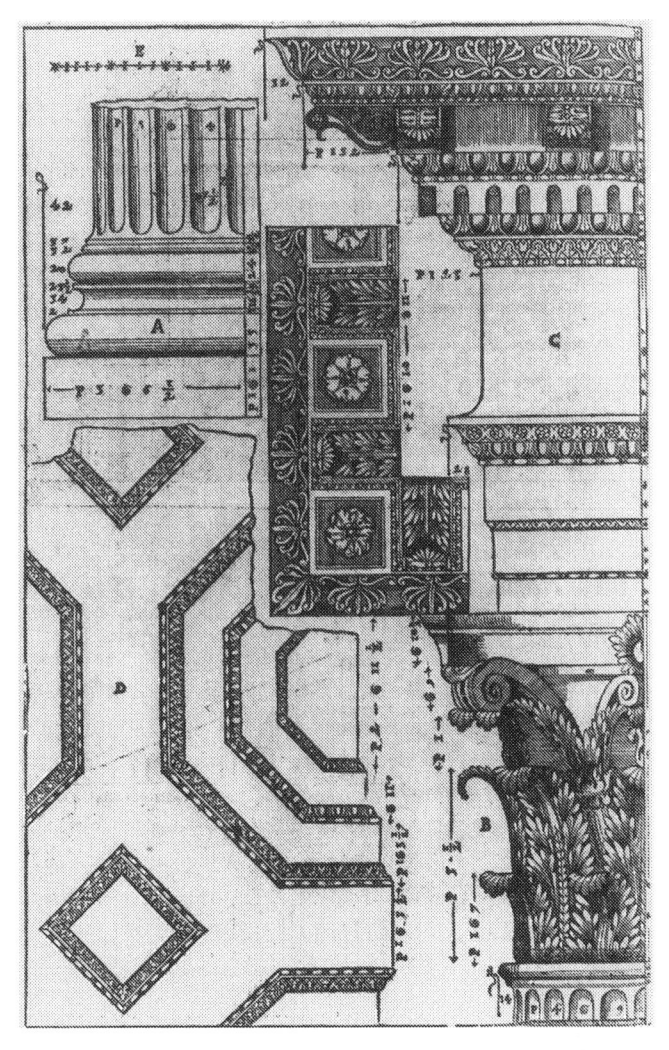

FIGURE 39. Palladio's reconstruction of the "Temple of Peace" (Basilica of Maxentius and Constantine), interior order, 1570 (Andrea Palladio, *I Quattro Libri dell'architettura* [1581 (1570)], vol. 4, pl. 14). University of Illinois Library at Urbana-Champaign, Rare Book Room and Special Collections Library.

Cornice, and makes us, for want of Stones of such Vastness, and Money to move them, despair, in these Days, of coming near the Greatness of such a Pillar and Entablement as is here used, where the Projecture of the Cornice is near 5 Feet.[109]

7. It was not therefore Unskilfulness in the Architect that made him chuse this flat kind of Aspect for his Temple, it was his Wit and Judgment. Each Deity had a peculiar Gesture, Face, and Dress

hieroglyphically proper to it; as their Stories were but Morals involved: and not only their Altars and Sacrifices were mystical, but the very Forms of their Temples. No Language, no Poetry can so describe Peace, and the Effects of it in Men's Minds, as the Design of this Temple naturally paints it, without any Affectation of the Allegory. It is easy of Access, and open, carries an humble Front, but embraces wide, is luminous and pleasant, and content with an internal Greatness, despises an invidious Appearance of all that Heighth it might otherwise justly boast of, but rather fortifying itself on every Side, rests secure on a square and ample Basis.

8. I know very well the Criticks in Architecture will scarce allow this Temple to be accurate, doubting a Decay of the Art in the Time of *Vespasian*, who finished this Temple; but it was *Claudius* who began it, when we need not suspect Corruption.[110] Nor need we scruple that the Entablement of the Columns is not continued, but that the Arches of the Ailes break higher than the Architraves; for these Arches resemble so many Tribunals, which are usually made in the Form of Niches, with the vaulted Head, adorned with a reticulate Work, but are not frequently set upon any Imposts, like the Arches of a Gate: but in the Inside of the best Works, the whole Entablement is seldom precisely kept; sometimes the Architrave is not expressed, as within the Portico of the Temple of *Vesta* at *Tivoli*;[111] most frequently is the Freeze omitted, and always in the Inside of the Porticoes of Temples is the Cornice omitted, unless you will call the Mouldings of the Listels a Cornice. Within the Portico of the *Pantheon*, over the Capitals, runs a compound Moulding of Architrave and Cornice combined in one, yet all together make not the due Bigness of the Cornice: in the open Air it is as well the Protection from Weather[112] as the Crown of the Pile, and therefore not to be interrupted nor broken forward, without just Reason; within, where it is an Impediment, 'tis often omitted, as in this Case, by its great Projection, it would have obscured the Descent of the Light. The same Order of Arches without Imposts is observed throughout, in the Portico before the Temple, in the Windows of the Fronts, in the Passages through the Tribunals, in the Niches; and though we have not extant more Examples of the like, yet I am apt to believe the *Basilicæ*, which were vaulted with Stone, followed this kind of Fabrick; and as it is vast, and well poised, so it is true, well proportioned, and beautiful, and was deservedly esteemed by the *Romans* themselves, as one of the most considerable Structures of *Rome*.

(page 364)   FIGURE 40

Observations on the Temple of Mars Ultor,[113] *built by* Augustus; *the Ruins of which are seen near the Torre de Conti, at Rome.*[114]

> *Templa feres, et me victore, vocaberis* Ultor.
> OVID, FAST. L. 5.[115]

I.

As studiously as the Aspect of the Temple of *Peace*[116] was contrived in Allusion to Peace and its Attributes, so is this of *Mars* appropriated to War: a strong and stately Temple[117] shews itself forward; and, that it might not lose any of its Bulk, a vast Wall of near 100 Feet high is placed behind it; (because, as *Vitruvius* notes, Things appear less in the open Air),[118] and though it be a single Wall, erected chiefly to add Glory to the Fabrick, and to muster up at once a terrible Front of Trophies and Statues, which stand here in double Ranks, yet an ingenious Use is made of it, to obscure two irregular Entrances, which come from a bending Street: and to accommodate itself as well to the Situation, as to give Firmness to the Wall but 5 Feet thick, it is built in various Flexures, (because a strait Wall is easier ruined by Tempests): these Flexures give Opportunity to form two other Frontispieces, in which are seen Niches much greater *(page 365)* than ordinary, and may be supposed to contain the Trophies.—Thus stands the Temple like the *Phalanx*, while the Walls represent the Wings of a *Battalia*.

> *Prospicit armipotens operis fastigia summi,*
>   *Et probat invictos summa tenere Deos.*
> *Prospicit in foribus diversæ tela figuræ,*
>   *Armaque terrarum milite victa suo.*
> *Hinc videt Æneam oneratum pondere sacro,*
>   *Et tot Iüleæ nobilitatis avos.*
> *Hinc videt Iliaden humeris ducis arma ferentem,*
>   *Claraque dispositis acta subesse viris.*
> *Spectat et* Augusto *prætextum nomine templum,*
>   *Et visum, lecto Cæsare, majus opus.*[119]
> *Digna gigantèis hæc sunt delubra trophæis,* &c.[120]
> OVID. FAST. L. 5.

II.

In this Court we have an Example of circular Walls; and certainly no Enclosure looks so gracefully as the circular: 'tis the Circle that equally bounds the Eye, and is every where uniform to itself;

THE LIFE OF

A Plan of the Temple of Mars Ultor

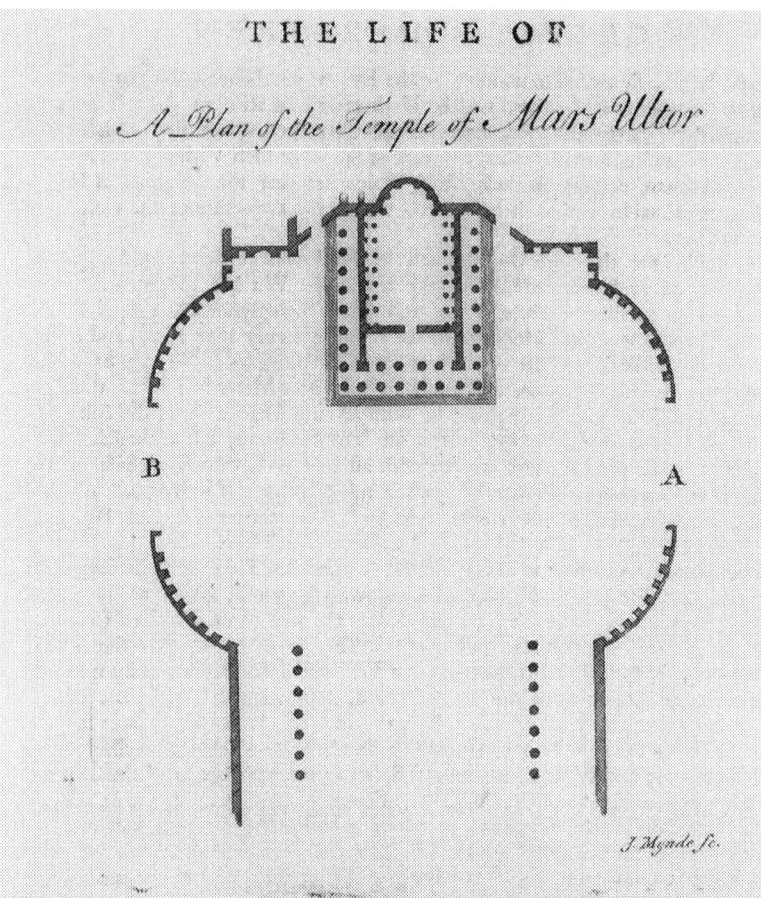

J. Mynde sc.

Observations on the Temple of Mars Ultor, *built by* Augustus; *the Ruins of which are seen near the* Torre de Conti, *at* Rome.

Templa feres, et me victore, vocaberis Ultor.   Ovid. Fast. L. 5.

I.

AS studiously as the Aspect of the Temple of *Peace* was contrived in Allusion to Peace and its Attributes, so is this of *Mars* appropriated to War: a strong and stately Temple shews itself forward; and, that it might not lose any of its Bulk, a vast Wall of near 100 Feet high is placed behind it; (because, as *Vitruvius* notes, Things appear less in the open Air) and though it be a single Wall, erected chiefly to add Glory to the Fabrick, and to muster up at once a terrible Front of Trophies and Statues, which stand here in double Ranks, yet an ingenious Use is made of it, to obscure two irregular Entrances, which come from a bending Street: and to accommodate itself as well to the Situation, as to give Firmness to the Wall but 5 Feet thick, it is built in various Flexures, (because a strait Wall is easier ruined by Tempests): these Flexures give Opportunity to form two other Frontispieces, in which are seen Niches much greater than

FIGURE 40. Plan of the Temple of Mars Ultor in *Parentalia*, 1750 (Christopher Wren, Jr., *Parentalia* [London, 1750], p. 364). The Ohio State University Libraries, Rare Book and Manuscripts.

180

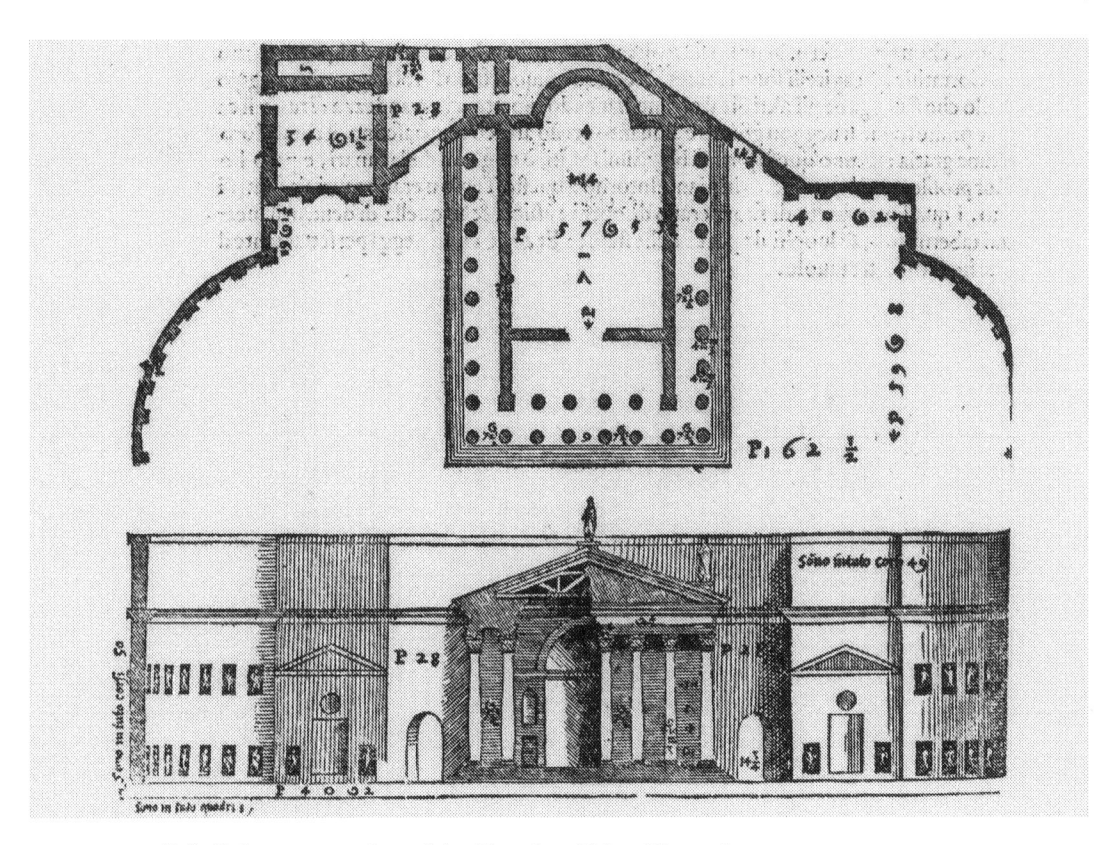

FIGURE 41. Palladio's reconstruction of the Temple of Mars Ultor, plan and elevation, 1570 (Andrea Palladio, *I Quattro Libri dell'architettura* [1581 (1570)], vol. 4, pl. 16). University of Illinois Library at Urbana-Champaign, Rare Book Room and Special Collections Library.

but being of itself perfect, is not easily joined to any other Area, and therefore seldom can be used: a Semicircle joining to an Oblong, as in the Tribunal at the End of this Temple, is a graceful Composition.

III.

If I might divine in Architecture, I would say, that the two Porticoes that made up the Court were directly opposite to the two Side-frontispieces, and that the Walls of the Court might continue on the other Side of a Street, leaving open the Passages A B; and this might be the Reason that *Palladio*[121] sought no farther for them, finding Foundations to end at A and B. By this means, those that walk in either Portico, will have the Prospect of a Side-frontispiece before them; those that walk in the Ante-temple, will have that goodly Tour of Statues diffused about them; and those that enter

FIGURES 41–3

FIGURE 42. Palladio's reconstruction of the Temple of Mars Ultor, detailed elevation and section, 1570 (Andrea Palladio, *I Quattro Libri dell'architettura* [1581 (1570)], vol. 4, pls. 18 and 19). University of Illinois Library at Urbana-Champaign, Rare Book Room and Special Collections Library.

the Court, have an excellent Perspective of the Whole; those that come down from the Temple, will have the View of the Temple of *Neptune*, which *Palladio* says, stood over-against it.[122] The *Romans* guided themselves by Perspective in all their Fabricks; and why should not Perspective lead us back again to what was *Roman*? If I presumed, 'twas *Tully*[123] that animated me, who assures us, that Reason is the best Art of Divination.

    I cannot omit commending the Fronts of the Porticoes: the Listels are invented to make Roofs, too narrow for a Vault, rise airy and light; the Ornaments between, consisting of a Trayle of Fillets continuing in square Angles, seem to me to have been borrowed from Beds of Gardens, and very properly would suit to that End.[124]

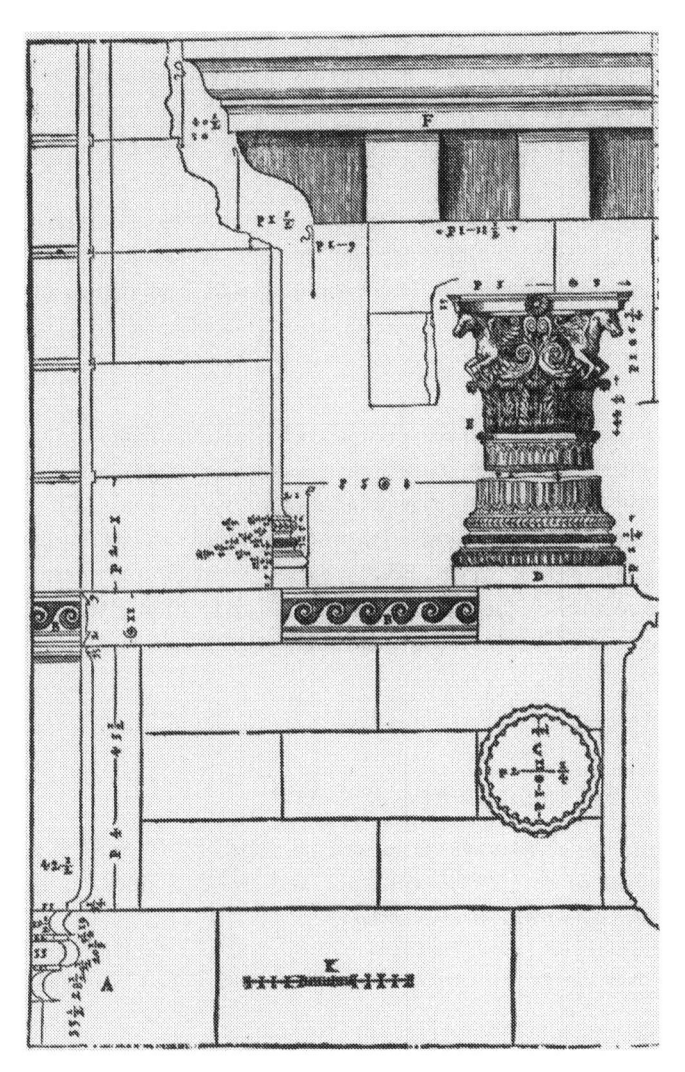

FIGURE 43. Palladio's reconstruction of the Temple of Mars Ultor, interior order, 1570 (Andrea Palladio, *I Quattro Libri dell'architettura* [1581 (1570)], vol. 4, pl. 22). University of Illinois Library at Urbana-Champaign, Rare Book Room and Special Collections Library.

IV.

The Cornice of the Wall advises us what Cornice to use in plainer Works; and gracefully is the Basis of the Columns made a continued Basis to the whole Temple. But the Pillar with the Capital of Horses-heads, (supposed by *Palladio (page 366)* to be one of the inward Ornaments)[125] belongs not to this, but the other neighbouring Temple of *Neptune*; for, 'twas *Neptune* who was called

Dominator Equorum. This, and the Temple of *Peace*, and the *Pantheon*, are those which *Pliny*[126] particularly mentions among the most remarkable Works of *Rome*.

V.

The Squares in the Wall of the *Cella* opposite to the Intercolumnations, tell us how extremely the Ancients were addicted to square and geometrical Figures,[127] the only natural Foundation of Beauty.

VI.

We find the most adorned Temples of the *Corinthian* Order have the Walls of the *Cella* channelled; so much they affected the Ostentation of great Stones, that where there were Joints, they would not seem to obscure them, that the Shafts of the Pillars might the better appear entire, and to give a darker Field behind them: the right Proportion of them is double in Length to their Breadth: the Appearance is best where there is much together.

(page 367)

Of the Sepulchre of **Mausolus** King of **Caria.**[128]

FIGURE 44

The Sepulchre of *Mausolus* is so well described by *Pliny*,[129] that I have attempted to design it accordingly, and also very open, conformable to the Description in *Martial*.[130]

Aëre vacuo pendentia Mausolèa.

And yet it wanted not the Solidity of the *Dorick* Order, which I rather call the *Tyrian*, as used in that Age.

The Skill of four famous Artists, *Scopas, Briaxes, Timotheus,* and *Leochares*, all of the School of *Praxiteles*, occasioned this Monument to be esteemed one of the seven Wonders of the World. These Architects living before the Time of *Alexander*, and before the Beginning of the Temple of *Diana* at *Ephesus*, (for *Mausolus* died,

* Aliter 106[131]

according to *Pliny*, in the second Year of the * hundredth Olympiad, which was before the *Ionick* Order was first in Use) I conclude this Work must be the exactest Form of the *Dorick*.[132] It appeared from the City *Halicarnassus* to the Sea, that is, North and South, 64 Feet, and so much every way; for, each Artificer took his Side: and being hexastyle, contained in all 36 Pillars; that is to say, 20 for the four Fronts, and 16 within, which supported the *Pteron*, (as *Pliny* calls it) in the Manner expressed in the Plan.

Pteron is an unusual Term, and not, I think, to be found in the Authors we have. *Harduin*, in his Notes on *Pliny*,[133] and others consider the Word, as in the plural Number, *Ptera*, (ΠΤΕΡΑ`) *Alæ*,[134] and think it imports the same Meaning as *Pteromata* in *Vitruvius*;[135] *Muri duo in altitudinem consurgentes alarum instar*.[136] But if we take it, as it is, in the singular Number, it cannot bear here that Signification; but may relate, as I conclude, to what we now call an *Attick* Order, and what rose above the Cornice,[137] to have been called by this Term, in *Greek* Authors of Architecture, now lost.[138]

This *Pteron* was here raised as high again[139] as the Order below, to bear the triumphal Chariot of King *Mausolus*. Like the *Romans* did in their triumphal Arches; but in this, it is raised so high, because it stands upon a second Range of Columns within, and that the Chariot might be seen at Sea; for such was the Situation of *Caria*, where all the Ships that doubled this South-west Cape of *Asia* must keep the usual Tract to *Rhodus*.

Supposing then in the Order, which *Vitruvius* calls *Systyle*,[140] (where the Inter-column is double to the Diameter of the Column) if the Column is 4 Feet Diameter, and the Inter-column 8 Feet, the whole Facade will be 64 Feet. The Heighth of the Columns of 7 ½ Diameter will be 30 Feet, and with the *Dorick* Entablature of a fourth Part of the Column, will make 37 ½ Feet, which is just 25 Cubits; as *Pliny* makes the Heighth of the first Story: above the *Cyma* of the Cornice must be a *Zocle* of 2 ½ Feet, for fixing the Statues, which will make in all 40 Feet from the Floor. Upon the 16 inward Columns rose the *Pteron*, (the ancient *Greek* Term, as I have noted, for whatever was erected above the Cornice, which we now call an *Attick* Story) the Pilasters whereof, that they might be visible, were supported on a Substructure, or Pedestal, of 20 Feet, so elevated to be seen above the Statues of 7 Feet, and being 14 Feet behind the *Cyma* of the outward Columns, could not well be lower. The Pilasters then of the *Pteron* being 24 Feet, made with their Cornice 30 Feet more; and upon this the Stone Covering rising 24 Feet more, *in metæ cacumen*,[141] (as *Pliny* phrases it) made the whole *Pteron* 74 Feet. Now, if round about the lower Colonade is added an Ascent in Steps of 10 Feet, (the third of the Pillar) there will be to the Platform on the Top 124 Feet, upon which stood the triumphal Chariot **(page 368)** of *Mausolus*, in Marble, 16 Feet high; so the whole Heighth will be 140 Feet, as by *Pliny*.—The whole Circumference I have computed 416 Feet, which exceeds *Pliny's* by 5 Feet. The Bottom and Facade, *Pliny* reported as he was informed by *Greek* Measure, I have computed by just Proportions, will appear half the Face, or like the Facade of a Tuscan Temple, to which the Breadth of the Brim of the Petasus, & the Bells, supply the Place of an Entablature.

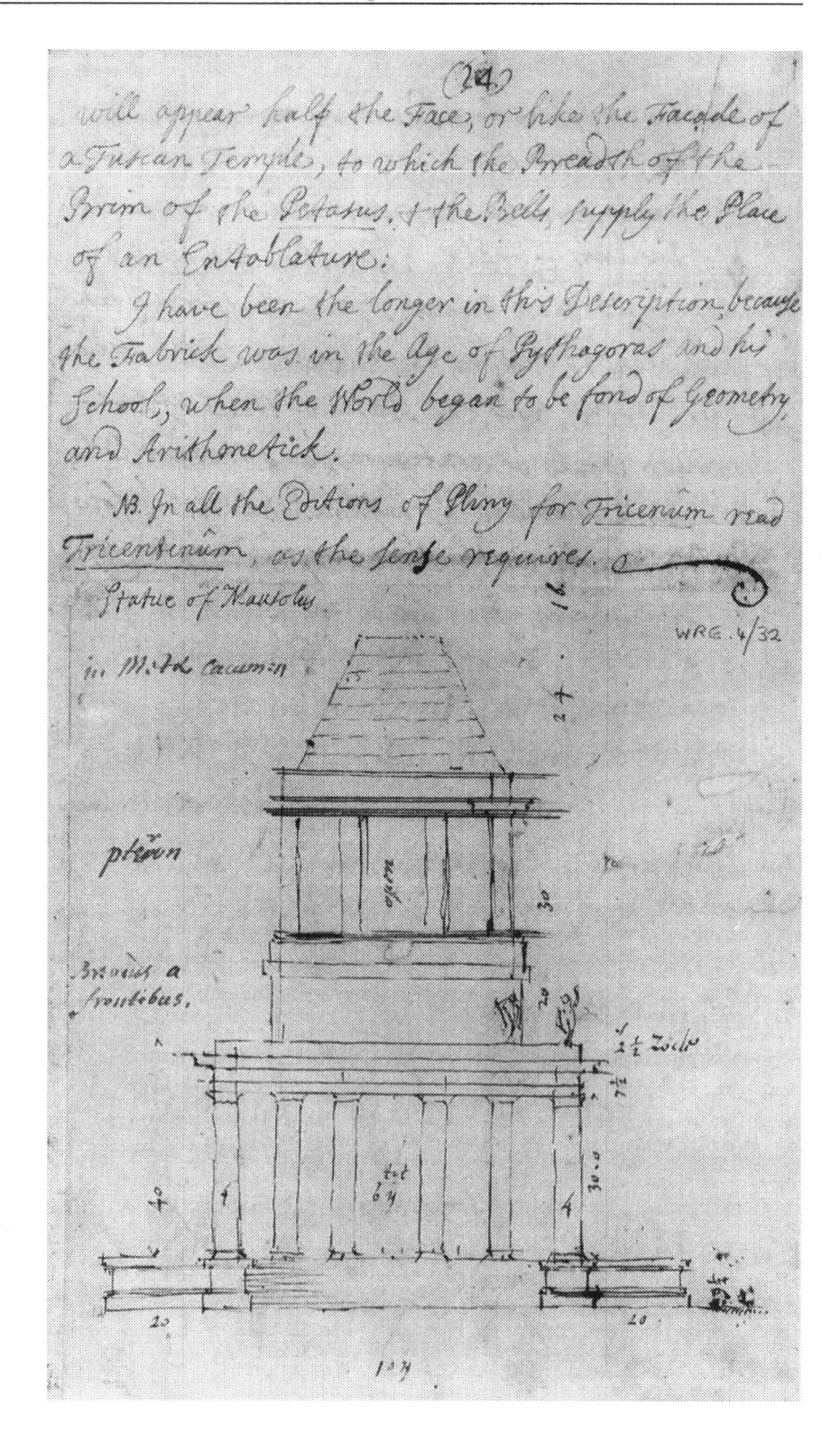

I have been the longer in this Description, because the Fabrick was in the Age of Pythagoras and his School, when the World began to be fond of Geometry and Arithmetick.

13. In all the Editions of Pliny for *Tricenum* read *Tricentenum*, as the sense requires.

Statue of Mausolus

which indeed are very fine. First, the Ascent in Heighth is a third Part of the Pillar; then the Column with the Architrave being 32, will be half the Facade 64, and the Face of the *Pteron* and Pedestal, will have the Appearance of being as high as broad over the Heads of the Statues. The Ascent of Steps up to the Platform, is only the proper Stone Covering, the Stones being 12 Inches high, and 6 Inches saile.[142] The Breadth at the lower Steps to the whole Heighth, is as 3 to 4, which is the Sides of *Pythagorick* rectangular Triangles. The Ordinance of the Whole falls out so wonderfully, and the Artists being contemporary with the School of *Plato*, I know not but they might have something to practise from thence, in this harmonick Disposition. I have joined the 16 inward Pillars into four Solids, and continued the same to the Top; opening also the middle Inter-column of the *Pteron*, that Solid may be upon Solid, and Void upon Void; so all is firm, yet airy. I have omitted *Triglyphs* in the Freeze, which I take to be the only Place for the Inscription, and Monuments were never without. I believe Triglyphs are proper for Porticoes chiefly, as in Imitation of Timber Entablatures. There might be round upon the first Order 20 Statues; 16 more below upon the Solids in Niches; and 12 in Niches of the *Pteron*, in all 48, each Statuary taking 12. *Pythis*, a fifth Artist, (says *Pliny*) made the Coloss Figure of *Mausolus*, in a Chariot drawn by four Horses.

The Plate of the above is omitted, on account of the Drawing being imperfect.

FIGURE 44 *(facing page)*. Wren's reconstruction of the Mausoleum of Halicarnassus, elevation, drawn by Nicholas Hawksmoor, date unknown ("Discourse on Architecture" (tract V), p. 14, in "Heirloom" copy of Christopher Wren, Jr., *Parentalia* [London, 1750]). British Architectural Library, RIBA, London.

Tract V, "Discourse on Architecture" (beginning in the mid-1670s)

Source
   Original manuscript missing. Manuscript in Christopher Wren, Jr.'s hand in RIBA "Heirloom" copy of *Parentalia* (London, 1750), with drawing of the elevation of the Mausoleum of Halicarnassus by Nicholas Hawksmoor (transcripts in WS, 19:140–5, and in Lucy Phillimore, *Sir Christopher Wren: His family and times* [London, 1881], appendix 2, 245–50)

Date
   Beginning in the mid-1670s

(page 1)

DISCOURSE ON ARCHITECTURE. BY SIR C: W:

Whatever a mans sentiments are upon mature deliberation it will be still necessary for him in a conspicuous Work to preserve his Undertaking from general censure, and to aim to accommodate his Designs to the Gust of the Age he lives in, though it appears to him less rational.

I have found no little difficulty to bring Persons of otherwise a good Genius, to think anything in Architecture could be better then what they had heard commended by others, and what they had view'd themselves. Many good Gothick forms of Cathedrals were to be seen in our Country, and many had been seen abroad, which they lik'd the better for being not much differing from Ours in England: this humour with many is not yet eradicated, and therefore I judge it not improper to endeavour to reform the Generality to a truer tast in Architecture by giving a larger Idea of the whole Art, beginning with the reasons and progress of it from the most remote Antiquity; and that in short, touching chiefly on some things, which have not been remark'd by others.

The Project of Building is as natural to Mankind as to Birds, and was practis'd before the Flood. By Josephus[1] we learn that Cain built the first City *Enos*, and enclos'd it with Walls and Rampires; and that the Sons of Seth the other Son of Adam erected *(page 2)* two Columns of Brick <and> Stone, to preserve their Mathematical Science to Posterity, <so well built that though the one of

Brick was destroy'd by the Deluge, the other of Stone was standing in the time of Josephus.>[2]

The first Peece of Naval Architecture we read of in Sacred History was the *Arke* of *Noah*,[3] a work very exactly fitted and built for the Purpose intended. It was by measure just 6 times as Long as Broad, and the Heighth was ⅗ of the Breadth: This was the Proportion of the *Triremes*[4] afterwards. The Dimentions, and that It was 3 Stories high, and that It had a Window of a Cubit Square is only mention'd; but many other things sure were of necessity to be contriv'd for use, in this Model of the whole Earth.

First, One small Window was not sufficient to emit the Breath of all the Animals; It had certainly many[5] other Windows as well for Light as Air. It must have Scupper-Holes, and a large Sink, and an Engin to Pump it; for It drew, as I compute, with all its Cargo and Ballast at least 12 foot Water. There must be Places for Insects the only Food of some Birds and Animals. Great Cisterns for Fresh-Water not only for Land Animals, but for some Water-Fowl and Insects. Some Greens must grow in Tubs, the only food of Tortoises, and some Birds and Insects; since we certainly have learnt that nothing is produced by spontaneous Generation, *(page 3)* and we justly beleive there was no new Creation. I need not mention Stairs to the several Stories; with many other things absolutly necessary for a years Voyage, for Men and Animals, though not mention'd in the Story; and Providence was the Pilot of this little World, the Embrio of the Next.

Most certainly Noah was divinely qualified, not only as a Preacher of Righteousness, but the greatest Philosopher in the *Historia Animalium* that ever was; and it was Work enough for his whole Family to feed them, and take care of the young Brood; for in a years time there must be a great increase in the Ark, which was food for the Family, and the Beasts of Prey.

The first Peece of Civil Architecture we meet with in Holy Writ is the Tower of Babel.[6] Providence scatter'd the first Builders, so the Work was left off, but the Successors of Belus the son of Nimrod probably finish'd It, and made it His Sepulchre upon his Deification. It was built of Burnt Brick Cemented with Bitumen. Herodotus[7] gives us a surprizing Relation of it, which being set down by measure, is not beside our Subject to observe.

It consisted of Eight several Stories; the First was one Stade, or 625 foot square, and of the same *(page 4)* measure in Height; upon which were rais'd seven more, which if they were all equal with the First would amount to 2,500 foot, which is not credible: the Form must be therefore Pyramidal; and being adorn'd on the Outside with Rows of Galleries in divers Stories, diminish'd in Height in Geometrical Proportion; so the whole Mass would have the Aspect of Half an Octaedron, which is that of all the Egyptian Pyramids.

These Corridores being Brick wasted in more than *1600* years: and it was These which Alexander actually began to Repair, not the whole Bulk, as I suppose.

How Herodotus had his Measures, I question, for He flourish'd <but> *100* years before Alexanders Conquest of Babylon, so It was then *1500* years old.

I proceed next to those mighty Works of Antiquity, the Wonderful *Pyramids* of Egypt, yet remaining without considerable decay after almost *4000* years; for 2000 years agoe, they were reckon'd by Historians of uncertain Original.

I cannot think any Monarch however Despotick could effect such things meerly for Glory; I guess there were reasons of State for it.

Egypt was certainly very early Populous, because so productive of Corn by the help of the Nile, in a *(page 5)* manner without labour. They deriv'd the River, when it rose, all over the Flat of the Delta, and as the People increas'd, over a great deal of Land that lay higher. The Nile did not always Flow high enough for a great Part of the then inhabited Country, and without the Nile They must either starve or prey upon those who had Corn; This must needs create Mutiny and Bloodshed, to prevent which it was the Wisdom of their Ancient Kings and Priests to Exact a certain Proportion of Corn, and lay it up for those who wanted the benefit of the River when it disappointed their sowing. Thus Joseph[8] lay'd up for Seven Years; and sur'ly He was not first; this Provision being ever so essentially necessary to support the Popularity, and consequently the Grandure of the Kingdom; and continu'd so in all Ages, till the Turks neglected all the upper Canales, except one which still supply's Alexandria. Now what was the consequence? It was not for the Health of the Common people, nor Policy of the Government, for them to be fed in Idleness; great Multitudes were therefore imploy'd in that which requir'd no great Skill, the Sawing of Stone square to a few different Scantlings; nor was there any need of Scaffolding or Engins, for hands only would raise them from Step to Step: a little teaching serv'd to make them set by Line: and thus these great Works in *(page 6)* which some Thousands of hands might be imploy'd at once, rose with Expedition: the difficulty was in Mustering the men to move in order under proper officers, and probably with Musick; as Amphion[9] is say'd, much about the same Age, to have built the Walls of Thebes with his

Harp; that is, Musick made the Workmen move exactly together, without which no great weight can be mov'd, as Seamen know, for the Sheet-Anchor will by no means move without a fiddle to make men exert their united force in equal time; otherwise they pull one against another, and lose great part of their force.

The next observable Monument of great Antiquity, which yet remains, is the *Pillar of Absolom*.[10] By the description given of it, and what I have learnt from Travellers who have seen it, we must allow it to be very Remarkable, though not great. It is compos'd of seven Pillars, six about in a Hexagon, and one in the middle, which Bear up an Hemispherical Tholus solid; a large Architrave, Frize and Cornice lie upon the Pillars, which are larger in proportion to their height then what we now allow to the Tuscan Order, so likewise is the Entablature larger.

This whole Composition though at least *30* foot high is all of One Stone, both Basis, Pillars and Tholus cut as it stood out of the adjacent Cliff of white Marble.

I could wish some skilfull Artist would give us the *(page 7)* exact dimentions to inches, by which we might have an idea of the Antient Tyrian manner for, it was probable Solomon, by his correspondance with King Hiram, employ'd the <Tyrian> Artists in his Temple:[11] and from the Phœnicians I derive as well the Arts as the Letters of the Græcians, though it may be, the Tyrians were Imitators of the Babylonians, and They of the Egyptians.

Great Monarchs are ambitious to leave great Monuments behind them, and this occasions great Inventions and Mechanicks Arts.

What the Architecture was that Solomon used we know little of, though Holy Writ hath given us the general dimentions of the Temple,[12] by which we may in some manner collect the Plan, but not of all the Courts.

Villalpandus[13] hath made a fine Romantick Piece after the Corinthian Order, which in that Age was not used by any Nation: for the First Ages used grosser Pillars then Dorick. In after Times They began to refine from the Dorick, as in the Temple of Ephesus (the united Work of all Asia) and afterwards improv'd into a Slenderer Pillar, and Leavy Capital of various inventions, which they call'd Corinthian. So that if we run back to the Age of Solomon, we may with reason beleive They used the Tyrian Manner, as gross at least as the Dorick, and that the Corinthian Manner of Villalpandus is meer fancy: Nay when long after *(page 8)* Herod built the *Atrium Gentium,* he that carefully considers the description in Josephus[14] will find it to be a Tripple Portico, and thick Pillars of the groser Proportions, Which being whole stones of an incredible Bulk, our

Saviours Disciples admir'd them: *Master,* said they, *see what Stones are here!*[15] Titus would have sav'd this Noble Structure, but a soldier throwing a torch upon the Roof which was Cedar Planks cover'd with Bitumen, it easily took fire and consum'd the whole Building.

All the City was thus cover'd flat with Bitumen (easily gather'd from the Lake of Sodom) and upon the flat roofs, the Jews celebrated under booths of Palm-boughs the Feast of Tabernacles.

The Body of the <first> Temple was gilt upon Bitumen, which is good Size for gilding and will preserve the timber. The Roof, and Cedar Wainscot within being carv'd with Knotts was gilded all over with a thick leaf, so I understand the word, *Overlay'd*,[16] for if it was cover'd with plate apply'd over the knots and Imbossments, the gold nails to fix it on would have exceeded the Weight of the plate, whereas the quantity of the Nails is reckon'd but small in proportion. The Doors might be plated over and naild, and the Hinges and Bars, call'd *Chains*,[17] might be solid for these were afterwards stripp'd when the Egyptians pillaged the Temple in the Reign of Rehoboam.

That[18] Herod did more than the <upper> Portico doth not appear, for the substruction under this Portico was *(page 9)* certainly Solomons Work: the whole Hill Moriah was Wall'd upright by him from the bottom of the Valley, which render'd a broad Area above for all the Buildings of the Courts: This is the Work in which were used stones of *10* and *12* Cubits, call'd (as well they might) *Costly-Stones*.[17]

Now It may well be inquir'd how in an uneven Craggy Country as it is about Jerusalem, such mighty Loads of Stone could be brought: I shall give my thoughts. Solomon had an Army of Labourers in his Works; now suppose a Stone *12* Cubits long, *2* broad, and one thick, this would amount to *648* of our solid feet, which in Marble would be *64* Tun's and more; Eight men will draw a Tun, but the ground being hilly, we will allow *10* men to a Tun, which will be *640* men: now how all these men can be brought to draw together I show as follows. First *10* men draw in a Rope, (as Bargemen with us) at the end of this rope is a Spring-tree, (as our Coachmen use for the *2* fore-horses) to each end of which is a rope, so *20* men draw in the second rank; each rope hath again its Spring-tree,[20] and so on to a sixt rank, <each rank doubling the number:> and supposing *10* men to govern the rest, (possibly with Musick) makes the number *640* men:[21] and this will be found readier then Capsterns, and by this means much vaster stones may be mov'd, and even by Barbarous People, without Engins. I cannot otherwise see what need Solomon had of such great multitudes of Labourers, as Threescore and ten Thousand Bearers of burdens, *(page 10) and Fourscore Thousand Hewers of Stone in the Mountains*, &c.[22] probably <too> they were employ'd by Months, and the rest were by turns to Till the ground and bring food for the Labourers, that[23] the Country Work <might> proceed.[24]

The Walls of Babylon were most stupendious Works built with Brick and cemented with Bitumen: the Height of them, according to Herodotus,[25] was Two hundred Royal Cubits, and the Breadth Fifty; which in our Measure, (reckoning every Royal-Cubit with Herodotus, 1 foot 9 inches, which is 3 inches above the Common Cubit measure) makes the height *375* foot; and the Breadth *93* ft *9* in.

In these Walls were One hundred Gates of Brass, with Ornaments in[26] Architecture of the same Metal. Besides the first Wall, (which was encompass'd with a wide and deep Foss always supply'd with water, the sides of which were Lin'd with Brick,) was an Inner Wall built of near the same strength, though not altogether of the same Breadth.

The Extent of the City must add to the Surprise, which being a Square contain'd a Front on every Side of One hundred and Twenty Stadia, that is, Fifteen of our Miles, and makes up in the whole Threescore miles.

Another stupendious Fabrick, of I think also Tyrian Architecture, was the Monument of Porsenna, King of Etruria.[27] This Sepulchre we have describ'd by Pliny[28] with the particular Dimension's in Feet which I have accordingly Delineated. *(page 11)* First, a Basis of squar'd stone Fifty foot high rais'd the Pile above any vulgar contiguous Buildings, which being solid only in those Parts that bore weight, was so contriv'd withinside as to form a very intricate Labyrinth, into which whoever enter'd without a clew of thread would not be able to find the way out.

Upon this Basis stood Five Pyramids of *150* foot high; Four in the Angles, and one in the Center; Bodies call'd Pyramids, though it is manifest They must have been <so> cut off as to have a large space on the Top to carry a Second Story of Four more lofty Pyramids of *100* ft high; and over Them a 3d Order of Five more. Now how These could be borne is worth the consideration of an Architect. I conceive it might be thus perform'd secur'ly.

Set half Hemispherical Arches, such as we make the heads of Niches, but lay'd back to back, so that each of these have its Bearing upon 3 Pyramids of the Lower Order, that is 2 Angular ones and the Middle Pyramid; and These cuting one another upon the Diagonals will have a firm Bearing for all the Works above.

Pliny mentions a Brass Circle and Cupola, lay'd upon the Five Lower Pyramids, not I suppose to bear any thing, but chiefly for

FIGURE 45

FIGURE 45. Wren's reconstruction of Porsenna's Tomb, plan and elevation, drawn by Robert Hooke, 17 October 1677 (Robert Hooke, *Diary*, MS 1758). Guildhall Library, Corporation of London.

Ornament, and to Cover the Stone Work of the Arches, upon the strong Spandrells *(page 12)* of which if another Platform were rais'd, upon That might the upper Structure be built; and the whole have a stupendious effect, and seemingly very Open.

Pliny took his Description of this extraordinary Pile from the Measures set down by *Varro,*[29] a diligent and therefore credible Author, who probably might have taken his[30] Dimensions when it was standing before the absolute conquest of Etruria by the Romans: the Summary then of this prodigious Edifice, (erected to show the Vanity of the Eastern Monarchs could be exceeded by the Italians) may be thus compriz'd.

The Basis of the whole was *300* ft square, and *50* ft high; upon which stood Five Pyramids, each *75* ft square, and *150* ft high; upon which rested the Brasen Circle and Cupola, stil'd by Pliny *Petasus*, (which I take to be a Brass-Covering securing the Arches) from which hung little Bells by chains, which sounded as they were mov'd by the Winds.

The Four Pyramids of the Second Order of *100* ft high, standing upon the Circle or Brim of the *Petasus* as upon an Entablature, were evidently the Four First Angular Pyramids continu'd to an Apex, or near to a Point, so each will be in all from the Basis *250* ft high, and rise as high as the *Petasus;* above which was again a Platform,[31] containing the Third Order of Five more Pyramids, *(page 13)* of which the 4 Angular Pyramids rested firmly upon the Keys of the Diagonal Sections of the half Hemispherical Vaultings, which were call'd by the Ancients, *Conchæ*, resembling the heads of Niches joyn'd back to back. This Platform I take to have been round, as being the Horizontal Section of the *Petasus;* and the Bases of the 5 upper Pyramids would be contiguous, and thus would be of the same shape and as high as the same below as Varro asserts with some suspicion, fearing how they would stand, but I with confidence, the Proportions perswading, which indeed are very fine.

The Heighth to the Breadth of the Basis is 6 to 1. The Heighth of the Pyramids to the Brass *Petasus* is 2 to 1, but taking in their whole height it would have 4 to 1 but allowing the Point of the Pyramid to be taken off (as it ought) and allowing for the Brasen Brim and Bells it will be *250* ft above which was the Floor that bore the Five upper Pyramids of 4 to 1. So the Heighth is *550* ft as 6 to 11.

I have ventur'd to put some Ornaments at the Top, belonging to the Tuscan Superstition. (They then us'd not Statues.) They are Golden Thunderbolts so the Whole will be *600* ft high, that is double to the Basis; and the Heighth to the Brass Circle *(page 14)* will appear half the Face, or like the Facade of a Tuscan Temple, to which the Breadth of the Brim of the *Petasus,* and the Bells, supply the Place of an Entablature.

I have been the longer in this Description, because the Fabrick was in the Age of Pythagoras and his School, when the World began to be fond of Geometry and Arithmetick.

N.B. In all the Editions of Pliny for *Tricenûm* read *Tricentinûm,* as the sense requires.[32]

Conclusion: Wren's Method of Design

Architectural historians have long been aware of the importance of Wren's writings as a possible key to understanding the genesis and nature of his designs and built works. In practice, however, this has proven to be problematic, because Wren's writings are primarily analytical rather than prescriptive in nature. That is, apart from the functional issues generally described in his letter on the design of national churches, the recommendations related to perspectival viewing in Tract I, and the diagrammatic descriptions for determining the abutment of arches and vaults in Tract II, these writings are concerned with discovering the principles underlying past and present architecture, principles that do not necessarily translate directly into a method for creating new buildings. Furthermore, although the evidence of his writings on architecture can be used to establish a link between Wren's scientific background and his architectural thinking, it is for the most part in terms of his approach to the study of history and his empirical definition of beauty. Determining a definite link between his mind-set as an experimental scientist and as a practicing architect is much more difficult.

A first step toward resolving these problems has been made by recognizing that seventeenth-century natural and mechanical philosophy, as a whole and within Wren's own work, was much more broadly based than is contemporary science, and included the application of theoretical precepts to practical matters – what today would be considered engineering or technology. There were two related interpretations of the nature of architecture that placed it within this category, and hence within the realm of science in general. First, it was considered a mechanical art, where nature is "put in constraint, moulded, and made as it were new by art and the hand of man."[1] Second, it was considered a mathematical science, one of the arts "which taste of the Mathematicalles" – that is, involves the practical application of geometry.[2] Because of the existence of a single broad realm of intellectual endeavor during the seventeenth century, the difference between Wren as a "scientist" and as an "architect" may not have been that great.

There is, however, an important divergence between the objectives of the scientist and those of the architect. Whereas the scientist studies a natural phenomenon in order to establish underlying laws, the architect creates a building by applying a method of design, doing so in response to particular requirements as well as general theoretical principles. The architect's work is perhaps more analogous to the scientist's making of instruments, an activity within the realm of the mathematical sciences, and one essential for creating the tools to gather the data necessary for broader theoretical investigations. Wren himself worked to develop an improved telescope for investigating particular problems in astronomy, instruments for finding longitude at sea, a microscope for studying particles of matter, as well as a perspectograph, a weather-clock, and other instruments.[3] All involved the application of geometry and arithmetic, in accordance with real or postulated physical laws, to fulfill a specific purpose. In a sense, Wren's design of buildings can be understood in the same way.

The parallel between the design of instruments and the design of buildings, however, still does not account for the fundamental difference between applied science and architecture – that architecture involves decisions that go beyond issues of function and stability, where correctness can be more or less clearly determined, to include the much more uncertain issues of beauty, form, style, and precedent, which can generally be called aesthetic matters. Wren's own writings demonstrate that he fully appreciated the aesthetic problems the architect faced. He investigated them by studying buildings through history and, out of his analysis, postulated a set of principles that explained, primarily for his own satisfaction, the ways in which these issues had operated in the past.

Unfortunately, how Wren applied these aesthetic lessons, in conjunction with pragmatic considerations, to create his own designs is much more difficult to determine. As a result, it is necessary to hypothesize on the nature of Wren's method of design by examining his written statements about making architecture and by considering them in relationship to the specific building projects that reveal his process of design, in particular, St. Paul's Cathedral. For Wren, the question he faced as an architect was twofold. First, how to create, by applying fundamental principles, an eternal architecture that was simultaneously useful, visually beautiful, and structurally sound. Second, how to create, through the selection and employment of a historical style, an architecture that was the most appropriate expression of English society under the restored Stuarts.

Wren's fundamental definition of architecture, which underlies his method of design, is found in Tract I: "Beauty, Firmness, and Convenience, are the Principles." In designing buildings Wren sought to fulfill all three of these goals, and never one at the expense of another. From documents relating to specific projects and from the letter on the building of churches, which of all his writings represents the closest thing to a functional program or brief, it is clear that Wren conceived design as a problem that involved fulfilling specific practical requirements inside and out, in relationship to the site. At the same time, Wren writes in his report on Westminster Abbey, "It is by due Consideration of the Statick Principles that good Architecture depends." Unless it is "regulated by the Art of Staticks," he states in Tract II, "a fine Design will fail and prove abortive." Therefore, "All Designs must, in the first place, be brought to this Test, or rejected."[4] In his discussion of structural principles and specific examples of structure it is important to note that Wren was solely concerned with masonry arches and vaults.

Despite his recognition of the importance of function and structure as criteria of design, Wren did not believe that either should be the overriding determinant of form, even in projects where pragmatic considerations were of great importance. For example, in his discussion of churches Wren recommended, to fulfill both the functional and acoustical needs of Anglican worship, a design "at least 60 Feet broad, and 90 Feet long, besides a Chancel at one End, and the Bellfrey and Portico at the other," citing St. James, Piccadilly, as the prime example.[5] Yet in the over fifty churches he designed, he created many variations on the basic design of a nave flanked by side aisles and galleries, transforming the rectilinear, longitudinal *parti* in some cases to the point that it became centralized, domed, and even polygonal in form. In Tract II, Wren discussed different vaulting types, determining on the basis of statics that the dome on pendentives was the "lightest manner."[6] Yet in the design of the dome of St. Paul's, for example, where structural stability was of utmost importance, he explored a wide variety of shapes and combinations, which indicates that he was guided as much by formal considerations as by structural ones.

In fact, Wren believed the goal of creating beauty was equally important to, and integral with, that of function and structure. At the same time, beauty was no more the product of discrete or precise rules than they were. In Tract I, Wren states that the natural causes of beauty are "geometry," including "uniformity" or "equality," and "proportion." For each quality he neither calls for nor prohibits the use of any specific forms or arrangements but acknowledges a broad range of possibilities. Therefore Wren did not believe in only two alternatives – an absolute and complete beauty or an absence of beauty. Rather, there could be varying degrees of beauty in between.

For geometry and uniformity, Wren presents various qualities that have greater or lesser beauty: "Geometrical Figures are naturally more beautiful than other irregular. . . . Of geometrical Figures, the Square and the Circle are most beautiful; next, the Parallelogram and the Oval. Strait Lines are more beautiful than curve; next to strait Lines, equal and geometrical Flexures." Among straight lines, the most beautiful are "perpendicular and horizontal." "Oblique Positions are Discord to the Eye, unless answered in Pairs, as in the Sides of an equicrural Triangle," that is, an equilateral or isosceles triangle. For uniformity, at one end of the scale of beauty there was "Deformity, or a Defect of Uniformity," but also, at the other extreme, "Plainness, . . . the Excess of Uniformity." In between deformity and plainness lay "Variety," which caused the greatest beauty: "Variety of Uniformities makes compleat Beauty: Uniformities are best tempered, as Rhimes in Poetry, alternately, or sometimes with more Variety, as in Stanza's." Thus Wren established a scale of qualities for uniformity ranging from plainness, through variety, to deformity, with beauty found not on either extreme but with the mean, which in itself could vary toward "more" or "much" variety.[7]

In contrast to theorists of the previous two centuries, who presented long and detailed discussions on how proportion should be used in architecture, Wren said very little about it. In only one instance in his writings did he discuss proportions in plan – for the design of the parish church. Although he recommended that the plan be 60 feet wide and 90 feet long, he qualified this by "at least" and declared, "these Proportions may be varied." His dimensions were based not on reasons of beauty – that is, a preference for the proportions 2 to 3 – but on functional need, calculated according to how far a voice could carry and be heard by everyone.[8] However, there are a few instances where Wren discusses the proportions found in the section of a building. For example, on the basis of Palladio's reconstruction of the Basilica of Maxentius, he discovered that the nave "rises to be equal in Heighth to half the whole Breadth," and "a Line drawn from the Key of the Vault of the Nave, to the Key of the Arch of the Aile, determines the Breadth of the Aile" (Fig. 38).[9] Yet he says nothing about the resultant proportions of 1 to 2 or the geometry of the triangle, or how they might relate to the beauty of the building. For the orders in particular, Wren clearly had no interest in discussing or establishing proportional rules. According to his friend Roger North, Wren believed that "there were things naturally handsome or deformed, which were so to all eyes, learned or unlearned," including "the comon demensions of columes, which were aggreable to all."[10] Nonetheless, in Tract II he criticized "Modern Authors" who "have reduced them into Rules, too strict and pedantick" and ignored the fact that these proportions were "more arbitrarily used than they care to acknowledge" by the ancients.[11]

Given the wide range of geometries and qualities of uniformity that Wren accepted, as well as the virtual absence of any discussion of proportion, it is perhaps of no surprise that he did not go on to discuss how these causes of beauty should be directly applied to the design of buildings. Most notably, he seems to have had little interest in how geometry and proportion should be applied in plan, section, and elevation, which had been the substance of design methods since the fifteenth century, beginning with the treatises of Francesco di Giorgio. In contrast, Wren believed the design must first and foremost be considered in terms of the "Perspective" of the completed building – "for, every thing that appears well in the Orthography, may not be good in the Model, . . . and every thing that is good in Model, may not be so when built." In Tract I he discusses the composition of a building in terms of three aspects relating to the "principal Views" that must be considered when designing it for a pleasing geometrical appearance: the angle of view, "whether direct or oblique," the relationship between different views, and the distance to the building, close or far.[12]

For a building viewed primarily from the front, the facade should be elevated in the middle, because "an Object elevated in the Middle is more beautiful than depressed," and should not be elevated at the ends. In addition, it should project forward in the middle, not recede. Wren gives the example of ancient buildings that have in the middle a pediment, statue, or dome, adding that there should be "no Roofs almost but spherick raised to be visible." At the same time, when using alternating "Hollows and Solids," the former – a window, door, or niche – should be placed in the middle. Because the building should not be elevated at the ends, it should not have corner pavilions. Except for the raised center, the rest of the roofline should be flat, as in ancient buildings, with the exception of houses, where a roof can appear above the cornice. There should be no pinnacles, "Gothick pyramids," or chimneys, although if there must be chimneys, they should be "well adorned," as, for example, the "pots" of the "modern *French*." As for the proportions of the facade, Wren recommends that the width to the height be no more vertical than 1 to 3, and no more horizontal than 3 to 1, thus allowing a wide range within these limits.

When a building was seen principally at an angle, for example, down a street, Wren prescribed a different formal composition. "It is absolutely required, that the Composition be square, Intercolumniations equal, Projectures not great, the Cornices unbroken, and every thing strait, equal, and uniform." For this kind of viewpoint, Wren seems to have preferred the use of long colonnades or porticoes, believing that "the longer the more beautiful in *infinitum*." As a result there were no recommended facade proportions, because "in this sort of Building there seems no Proportion of Length to the Heighth."

For Wren these precepts on the oblique view seem to apply as well to the viewing of interior spaces, for example, down the nave of a church, where the two sides are seen at an angle. In his report on Old St. Paul's, he found that "The excessive Length of Buildings is no otherwise commendable, but because it yields a pleasing Perspective by the continu'd optical Diminution of the Columns" (Figs. 11–12). Unfortunately, at the cathedral Wren observed that the intercolumniations adjacent to the crossing were narrower than the rest, resulting in "Deformities" – a lack of uniformity. Furthermore, at the crossing the colonnades were "cut off by Columns ranging within their Fellows," so that "the Grace that would be acquir'd by the Length is totally lost." With the new domed crossing of his Pre-Fire Design, all of these defects would be removed, creating two continuous, uniform colonnades seen in a "pleasing Perspective" (Figs. 13–15).[13]

The forms created on the interior to give a pleasing appearance to the viewer were what determined the geometry and proportion of the building's section, not vice versa. A good demonstration of Wren's orientation is given by a comparison of Salisbury Cathedral and Old St. Paul's. At Salisbury, Wren admired the interior for "the naturall beauty which arises from proportion of the first dimensions," specifically how "the breadth to the highth of the Navis, and both to the Shape of the Iles beare a good proportion," and how "the pillars and the intercolumnations ... are well suited to the highth of the arches."[14] In contrast, he criticized the nave of Old St. Paul's for being "much too narrow for the Heighth,"[15] although in fact a comparison of their sections reveals that its proportions are slightly *less* vertical than Salisbury's (Figs. 14, 20). This suggests that Wren's judgment of the quality of proportions was based, not on a study of a drawn section, but on his visual impression while in the space. Similarly, he took notice of the proportions in the section of the Basilica of Maxentius only because they created a particular visual effect: "in the farthest Part you see always half the Vault of the Nave; which makes it seem free and spacious."[16]

The design of a building was determined not only by the angle of the principal views but also by whether these views were closely related or completely separate. Wren wrote that "In Things to be seen at once, much Variety makes Confusion, another Vice of Beauty." This would seem to apply to a single principal view of a building or object seen in its entirety, for example, a main facade, but also to a sequence of different views seen in close succession, such as the front followed by the side. In contrast, Wren found, "In Things that are not seen at once, and have no Respect one to another, great Variety is commendable." Completely separate, unrelated views of an object would include the front and the back, as well as the exterior and the interior. Whether or not the quality of "much" or "great Variety" of form or composition would cause beauty depended on the views. It would lead only to "Confusion" in closely related views, but would be "commendable" in separate ones, as long as "the Rules of *Opticks* and *Geometry*"[17] were still followed.

The distance from which an object was viewed determined how it should be articulated. When seen "near at hand," it could have "small and many Members," and "lie flatter." "All this Care is ridiculous at great Distances," however, where "bulky Members, and full Projectures casting quick shadows, are commendable." These precepts applied to the ornamentation of a building. When seen primarily close up, it could be "well furnished with Ornament" that was small and flat. At a distance, however, such ornament would "serve only to confound the Symmetry, and take away the Lustre of the Object, by darkening it with many little Shadows."

The issue of determining the size and projection of the building's smaller components relative to distance extended to its overall massing. For example, "In the remoter Aspect," Wren's Pre-Fire Design for St. Paul's would appear "to swell in the Middle by Degrees, from a large Basis rising into a Rotundo bearing a *Cupola*, and then ending in a *Lantern*," which gave "incomparable more Grace" than "the lean Shaft of a Steeple" of the old cathedral (Figs. 7–9).[18] As a part of the larger whole, the more massive form of a dome was preferable to a thin tower. Still, Wren did not object to towers seen at great distances as isolated entities in the skyline. For the towers of the City churches, he stated that "handsome Spires, or Lanterns, rising in good Proportion above the neighbouring Houses, . . . may be of sufficient Ornament to the Town."[19] He did not offer any further specifics for the design of towers, although he might have believed that similarly to "Obelisks, Pyramids, Columns, such as *Trajan*'s," because they "seem rather single Things than Compositions,"[20] they were not subject to proportional rules.

It appears that Wren did not believe in a set of preferred, precise, and invariable geometries or proportions or in the need to adhere strictly to those ultimately selected. Although historians have attempted to demonstrate the systematic application of geometry and proportion in the

Conclusion: Wren's Method of Design

plans and elevations of many of Wren's buildings, his writings show that he was not interested in applying regulating lines or geometrical methods to orthographic drawings to ensure a pleasing form.[21] For Wren, geometry had importance less as a design tool than as an end result – the geometrical, uniform, and proportioned appearance of the final building from the primary views. The achievement of the greatest possible beauty certainly did depend upon the observance of broad geometrical parameters formulated on the basis of Wren's own experience as an architect and his understanding of the work of other architects. Nevertheless, even more critical to creating beauty was the application of the architect's judgment within the context of the particular problem at hand. Wren recognized that the architect had the difficult and complicated task of reconciling the goal of creating beauty with specific pragmatic considerations: the functional program, the site, and the structural requirements, which could often call for very different kinds of geometrical relationships.

Among Wren's buildings are examples where the specific interior spatial needs and restrictions of the site led him either (1) to compromise his preferred geometrical appearance or (2) to create devices that maintained a geometrical appearance while concealing the true formal relationships. Wren's parish churches provide an example of the first case, where the "ideal" design, represented by his description in his letter on churches and by St. James, Piccadilly (1676–84) (Figs. 31–2), can be contrasted with the reality of the other built churches. Touted in his letter to a friend as both "beautiful and convenient," the simple geometry and composition of the basic plan were well suited for accommodating, seeing, and hearing the ceremonies: a regular rectangle, at least 60 by 90 feet, with chancel and entrance tower directly opposite one another on the east–west axis, arranged as a nave with side aisles and galleries above. Because of their unrestricted sites, in Christ Church, Newgate Street (1677–87), and St. Clement Danes (1680–2) even more so than in St. James, Piccadilly, Wren was able to achieve this ideal and, because each site opened onto a major street to the west, was able to optimize it even further. In these two churches a straight east–west axis runs from the entry from the street through the vestibule beneath the tower and down the center of the nave to the chancel. Furthermore, the site allowed Wren to give the main facade of each church a regular, symmetrical composition centered on the entry and tower, embellished by a "portico," or at least by a greater amount of decoration than is found on the other sides of the church.

In the vast majority of the City churches, however, an oddly shaped and cramped site, combined with the need to reuse existing foun-

FIGURE 46. Cambridge, Trinity College Library, exterior from west, 1676–84. (Photo by author).

dations, mediated against the regular, geometrical appearance of the optimum design. In some cases the tower was shifted off-center or was pushed back to the rear, the entrance was set off-axis to the chancel or even at right angles to it within a side wall, and the aisles and galleries were placed on only one side of the nave. In addition, the side or back of the church often faced the main street and therefore was given the most decoration, even though it had no entry. The basic plan became highly irregular and often had few right angles, the only sense of a regular geometry occurring within the space of the nave and, if it existed, in the primary facade. The way in which the particular site and needs of each church resulted in a wide range of variations on the basic design, which represented a kind of geometrical and functional ideal, gives some suggestion of what Wren meant in Tract I by "Convenience . . . makes the Variety."[22]

In other instances, instead of compromising the preferred geometrical appearance, Wren used visual devices that allowed it to coexist with the arrangement required by the function and/or the site. At Trinity College Library in Cambridge (1676–84) (Figs. 46–7), Wren needed to

FIGURE 47. Cambridge, Trinity College Library, exterior from east, 1676–84 (National Monuments Record). Photo RCHME © Crown Copyright.

resolve the conflicts between the spatial needs of the interior, the desired exterior formal expression, and the existing buildings.[23] For the interior, he designed a traditional form of reading room, a long, narrow, but tall space. Along each side were bookshelves arranged in alcoves, illuminated by clerestories above. By means of this geometrical volume, Wren was able to fulfill the need to store and read books in a simple and direct way. In terms of the site, this room was placed above an open ground-level walkway, together forming a range that closed the end of an existing courtyard. The building has two facades, one facing Nevile's Court as the edge of an open space, the other facing the river as a three-dimensional block. Because of the site, both facades are viewed frontally and therefore rise high enough to have proportions no broader than Wren's recommended 1 to 3. Reflecting the interior functions and the need for large windows, the upper story of both facades is filled with large arched windows. On the river side, they are framed by flat vertical and horizontal bands of wall, forming an upper story that rests on a solid ground floor that is articulated by small rectangular windows and large Doric portals.

The courtyard facade is composed as two equal arcaded stories, in the tradition of Palladio's double-arcaded designs, and those of his inheritors, including Sansovino's Library of San Marco in Venice (1536–60) and Inigo Jones's Royal College of Physicians in London (1651–3), destroyed in the Great Fire.[24] At Trinity College this composition creates some overall conformity with the older ranges surrounding the space.

In response to different site conditions, and because they are not seen together or in close succession, the facades are treated quite differently. Furthermore, neither one expresses directly the horizontal divisions of the interior. Because of the requirement that the reading room be placed at the same level as the second floor of the existing buildings, Wren was forced to drop the floor level of the reading room to a point below the ground floor entablature of the facade. On the river facade, the true floor level falls to a point above the windows but below the lintels of the portals, making it necessary to add solid transoms above the actual doors. On the courtyard side, the floor level corresponds to the imposts of the ground-floor arcade, making it necessary to fill in the lunettes. As a result, the double arcade composition is retained, at the same time that the lowered floor level of the reading room is accommodated. Furthermore, on the interior the upper arcade now becomes a clerestory above the bookshelves and reading alcoves. Wren was able to maintain the geometrical appearance of the library's exterior while fulfilling the specific requirements of the site and of the interior functions.

The solid lunettes at Trinity were a device, Wren related, "of which I have seen the effect abroad in good buildings." He was probably thinking of examples in France where a mezzanine floor was inserted within the lunettes of arches.[25] At Trinity, however, there is not a separate floor level but a single, continuous space that rises from impost level through the lunettes into the arcades of the upper level. The true nature of the interior space is belied in the facade by the lower entablature, which in the Classical language represents the location of a floor or ceiling. Wren used a similar expedient in the Fountain Court of Hampton Court, begun after 1689, where the arches of the ground-floor walkway are filled in with recessed segments, the upper profile matching the semicircle of the arch, the lower profile a segmental arch.[26]

In houses of this period it was not uncommon for architects to create a regular facade composition that had little connection to the functional arrangement of rooms immediately behind. Although this occurred for the most part only in plan, there are some instances where it is found in section.[27] In examples of Mannerist and Baroque architecture in Italy, the discontinuity between exterior and interior was expressed by using

Classical motifs in an unorthodox or inconsistent way, disregarding the rules for the use of the orders established by Vitruvius and Renaissance theorists based on their origin in wooden construction and post and lintel structure. Wren saw no need to adhere to the structural metaphor of the Classical orders. But unlike some architects who manipulated Classical motifs to reveal their true nature, as decoration applied separately from the actual structure and interior divisions, Wren did so to conceal it and to create an illusion of continuity.

In the same way as the requirements of function and site, the need for a stable structure in a building could dictate certain forms that contravened the regular, geometrical appearance sought for the sake of beauty. Wren did believe, however, that in masonry vaulted construction there was the potential for achieving a harmonious relationship between form and structure. In the repairs at Old St. Paul's he sought "to neglect nothing that may conduce to a decent uniform Beauty, or durable Firmness in the Fabrick." He hoped, therefore, "to enumerate as well the Defects of Comeliness as Firmness, that the one may be reconcil'd with the other in the Restitution."[28]

In Tract II, Wren presented a series of different vault types that were based on geometrical forms and would be understood visually as such: the dome, the half-dome, the barrel vault, the cross vault, the pointed cross vault, the fan vault, and the dome on pendentives. Although he considered the last to be "so natural," being "the most geometrical," "the lightest Manner" requiring less abutment, and "of an agreeable View,"[29] Wren accepted all of them as possible choices. The real issue was not the geometry of the vaults, all of which had some degree of beauty, but solving the problem of the abutment that could seriously impinge upon the appearance of the geometry. Wren did not believe concealed iron ties were a good substitute, although they could, by eliminating the need for massive abutment, preserve the basic geometrical form. He observed the use of iron in Gothic buildings, including Salisbury Cathedral, and in the dome of the new St. Peter's, but recommended it only as an added safety: "The Architect should so poise his Work, as if [iron] were not necessary."[30] In his opinion, "this way of tying walls together with Iron, instead of making them of that substance and forme, that they shall naturally poyse themselves upon their butment is against the Rules of good Architecture."[31]

The problem of buttressing vaults was solved in different ways by ancient and medieval architects. Wren asserted that "The *Romans* always concealed their Butments."[32] What he meant by this statement is indicated in his description of the Basilica of Maxentius, where the nave was covered by three cross vaults and the aisles by barrel vaults placed laterally to the nave (Figs. 37–8):

> The Walls are thin, where the Roof presses not; but admirably secured where the Weight lies; first, by the Piles behind the Pillars, which are of that Thickness backward, that they are sufficient Butment to the Arch of the Ailes.... Secondly, the Weight of the Roof above hath a mighty Butment from the slope Walls between the Windows, which answer to the Half-frontispieces of the Ailes.... This Temple ascends to its vast Heighth each Way, by three Degrees; the mighty Nave is butted by the Ailes, and the Ailes by the Tribunals, and little Rooms without....[33]

Different parts of the building were used to abut others, and any additional abutment was concentrated where it was most needed in the form of thickened walls or added segments of wall. Therefore the structural system did little to negatively alter the geometrical appearance of the building. The basilica, Wren concluded, "as it is vast, and well poised, so it is true, well proportioned, and beautiful."

In contrast to the Roman, Gothic vaults were supported by "Arch-buttresses," or flying buttresses, connected to pier buttresses, as abutment. Gothic architects "used Buttresses on the Outside of the Wall, which they extended as far as they guessed would be sufficient; and they had yet farther Help, by loading the Buttress with a Pinnacle, to the Height of which they were not confined."[34] For Wren this system of buttressing had fundamental flaws. Although the vaults of the nave were equally supported on both sides by the flying buttresses, for the aisle vaults this was not the case: "they are indeed supported on the outside by the buttresses, but inwardly they have no other stay but the pillars themselves which ... if they stood alone without the weight above, could not resist the spreading of the Iles one minute."[35] At the crossing there was an even greater problem with the tilting of each pier toward the center because "the angular arches that rest upon that pillar ... both conspire to thrust it inward toward the Center of the Crosse." Wren believed that the weight of the nave vaults in the first case, and the weight of the crossing tower in the second, should "confirme the Pillars in their perpendicular Station," and hence "there should be no need of butment inward." He had to admit, however, that "there is scarce any Gothick Cathedrall, that I have seen at home or abroad, wherein I have not observed the Pillars to yield, and bend inward from the weight of the Vault of the Isle."[36] He thus concluded that, although theoretically a lateral thrust could be counteracted by increasing the vertical load, experience had proven this was not the case for aisle vaults, as demonstrated in his sectional diagram of Westminster Abbey (Fig. 27).

The Gothic system of buttressing had additional problems. It lacked durability due to poor materials and construction techniques. Flying buttresses "are the first Things that occasion the Ruin of Cathedrals, being so much exposed to the Air and Weather; the Coping, which cannot defend them, first failing, and if they give Way, the Vault must spread." Most importantly, this system of buttressing had little beauty. "*Gothick* buttresses are all ill-favoured" due to their oblique angles. Pinnacles, placed on top of pier buttresses to load them against the lateral thrust of the flyers, "are of no use, and as little Ornament."[37]

Wren's goal of designing a building for a pleasing geometrical view, and at the same time for stability based on geometrical laws, has inherent conflicts. Structural stability often required the placement or addition of buttressing that could significantly alter the geometrical appearance. In many of his own buildings, Wren appears to have solved this dilemma by concealing the true nature of the structure – its form and/or its material – in a manner that maintained the appearance of the preferred geometry or material. In the City churches, what appear to be masonry vaults are actually of wood, and are built according to a conventional method using timber framing sheathed in plaster on wooden lathing. Despite his focus on masonry vaults in Tract II, Wren must have been aware of the advantages of this form of construction. Spans could be achieved with less weight and lateral thrust, allowing the desired geometrical appearance to be preserved without added abutment. Furthermore, skilled craftsmen capable of creating the desired forms in timber were readily available, in contrast to those working in stone. Although stonemasons still made Gothic fan vaults during the seventeenth century, it appears that, until the dome of St. Paul's, their skills had not yet been applied in the construction of Classical forms of vaulting.[38]

Although it was not unusual by this period to conceal the true nature of a structure, Wren went further to exploit the formal qualities made possible by the lightness or spanning capabilities of a hidden structure. The spacious, light-filled interior of St. Stephen Walbrook in London, for example, achieved by means of a large wooden dome resting on slender supports, could not have been achieved in masonry. Similarly, the span of almost 70 feet at the Sheldonian Theater in Oxford (1664–9), one of the longest of the period, was made possible only by Wren's timber truss, concealed behind a flat wooden ceiling.[39] For St. Paul's, as will be discussed, Wren used unconventional materials and forms to create a form of dome that would have been much more difficult to achieve using more traditional solutions.

It is clear that in his writings Wren did not provide rigid rules or formulas for achieving convenience, beauty, and stability. Instead, as is suggested by his own designs, he believed in applying general pragmatic and aesthetic parameters according to the architect's own judgment and experience, and in response to the unique conditions and goals of the particular project. This method of design should not be considered contradictory to his goal of creating buildings in accordance with natural law – "the geometrical Reasons of *Opticks* and *Staticks*" that lie behind beauty and structure. Rather, it suggests that Wren's principles should be interpreted as relative criteria always subject to the variables inevitably introduced by the individual architect and his culture. As a result, although "Architecture aims at Eternity"[40] through the application of fundamental principles, this goal can never be entirely achieved. Because the architect must accommodate all the divergent formal implications of the principles of beauty, stability, and convenience in the process of designing a particular building, none can ever be fulfilled absolutely.

Wren's awareness of the impact of culture on architecture is demonstrated not only by his particular way of applying aesthetic and pragmatic principles to create a building but also by his acknowledgment of the selection and application of a historical style as part of the design process. The issue of styles, specifically the Classical and the Gothic, underlies every subject addressed in his writings. For example, in describing the most beautiful of the natural causes Wren lists the forms and compositions typical of the Classical style; the least beautiful, the Gothic. His discussion of vaults and their abutment is made in terms of the relative qualities of the structural systems associated with each style. Furthermore, he made designs in both the Classical and the Gothic styles, in at least one case as alternatives for the same project. Clearly, for Wren an important issue of design involved determining which style should be used in architecture today and, further, adapting authoritative examples of that style to new circumstances – namely, applying precedent. Because he never wrote explicitly on the subject, Wren's attitude toward style must be reconstructed from scattered remarks, outside evidence, and his own buildings.

By Wren's time, the concept of style was an old one. Renaissance architects beginning with Alberti had rejected the characteristic forms of the "poor" Gothic in favor of those of the "good" antique. Wren was one of the first to reconsider this appraisal. On the basis of his study of past architecture, he developed a historical consciousness, understanding past styles as products of specific cultures, and hence each legitimate in its own right. He believed that within a culture each style evolves not only through successive applications of the fundamental principles of geometrical beauty, functional utility, and structural stability, but also as a result of the changing forces of custom. As a result, each style bears the imprint of the character of the particular society that created it, its unique values and ideas. This notion underlies Wren's initial statements in Tract I:

> Architecture has its political Use; publick Buildings being the Ornament of a Country; it establishes a Nation, draws People and Commerce; makes the People love their native Country, which Passion is the Original of all great Actions in a Common-wealth. The Emulation of the Cities of *Greece* was the true Cause of their Greatness. The obstinate Valour of the *Jews*, occasioned by the Love of their Temple, was a Cement that held together that People, for many Ages, through infinite Changes. The Care of publick Decency and Convenience was a great Cause of the Establishment of the *Low-countries*, and of many Cities in the World. Modern *Rome* subsists still, by the Ruins and Imitation of the *old*; as does *Jerusalem*, by the Temple of the Sepulchre, and other Remains of *Helena's* Zeal.

Wren understood, as indicated in these passages, that the concept of style as specific forms representing the values of a specific culture had several implications for contemporary architecture. First, the selection of a past style was in effect an act of identifying contemporary society with a particular culture of the past. Second, by adopting that style, the values of the past culture that made it would be reconstituted and turned into those of the present age. Furthermore, because of these associated meanings, understood by viewers, architecture could be the means of maintaining or even promoting the well-being of the society that created it. By making references to the past, architecture could express the true character of a society, as well as its aspirations, becoming a symbol that would unify its own people and challenge other nations.

Wren's understanding of the power of the meanings associated with an architectural style is clearly evident in his arguments over which style, Classical or Gothic, was the most appropriate for the society of the restored Stuart monarchy. During the initial years of Charles II's reign and of Wren's practice in architecture, both styles were established forms of building in England. The Classical had been imported to England from abroad, first by Inigo Jones under Charles I.[41] Even by the early 1660s, however, it continued to coexist with the native Gothic style surviving in general building practice. Most houses, churches, and collegiate buildings, despite the use of Classical ornamentation by foreign as well as native craftsmen based on examples in Italian, French, and Dutch architectural treatises, continued to be designed according to Gothic traditions.[42] As someone new to the practice of architecture, and by 1669 as Surveyor General, Wren was compelled to give serious consideration to the question of style, in particular, whether or not the Classical and its various associated meanings were appropriate for contemporary England – an England of the restored Stuarts, but also of the Royal Society and the New Science.

The Classical was recognized in Restoration England as the style introduced into England by the early Stuarts and as the style of the leading nations of Europe, Italy and France. Most importantly for Wren and other prominent figures of the period, it was an ancient style used by all the great civilizations of the past, the greatest being the Roman Empire under Augustus. During the early 1660s members of Wren's circle argued for the Classical style by making a parallel between the London of Charles II and the Rome of Augustus. The virtuoso John Evelyn, F.R.S., who on several occasions discussed architecture with the king, evoked the image of Augustan Rome in speaking about contemporary architecture. In his *Fumifugium* (1661), he called for reforms in London, so that "this Glorious and Antient City . . . from Wood might be rendred Brick; and (like another *Rome*) from Brick made Stone and Marble."[43] In 1664, in the dedication of his English edition of Fréart de Chambray's *Parallèle de l'architecture antique et de la moderne*, Evelyn declared that Charles II was a "paragon" to "the great Augustus," to whom Vitruvius dedicated his own treatise. He praised Sir John Denham, Wren's predecessor as Surveyor General, for paving the streets of London in much the same spirit as "the Reformation of Rome."[44]

In his *Observations* of 1665, written as a letter to Wren, Thomas Sprat, F.R.S., who later wrote the official history of the Royal Society, recorded that he and Wren "have sometimes debated together, what place and time of all the past, or present, we would have chosen to live in, . . . we both agreed, that *Rome*, in the *Reign* of *Augustus*, was to be preferr'd before all others." But now, with the restoration of the king, "we need not search into antient History for a reall Idea of happinesse," for his reign had brought with it peaceful ways, a liberal government, and virtuous people, but also great achievements in science and "wonderful progress" in "the Beauty of our Buildings." "This last," Sprat continued, "was the peculiar honour of *Augustus*, who is said *to have found Rome of Brick, and to have left it of Marble*," and it was now to be Charles II's. Sprat declared that, after Augustus in Rome, "never any Nation in the world has proceeded by swifter degrees, to excell in Convenience and Magnificence," because of "the powerfull influence of a *Royal Example*" and the work of Christopher Wren – "to you your Country is to owe very much of its Ornament, as well as experimental knowledge."[45]

Evelyn, Sprat, and many others believed there was a Golden Age dawning under the restored Stuarts, during which England would rise to challenge the supremacy of Louis XIV's France, not only in science through the work of the Royal Society, but also in architecture. Wren was the architect to make their hopes real. When the works quoted above were written, he was just beginning to extend his work beyond science into architecture, taking on his first building commissions. For him to accept the mission set forth by Evelyn and Sprat – to emulate Augustan Rome through the design of contemporary buildings in the antique manner – was no simple matter. Wren was still first and foremost a scientist who could not unquestioningly accept the authority and superiority of the ancients. By the second half of the seventeenth century, the scientific precepts of the ancients, preserved in classical texts and accepted for centuries as law, were being seriously challenged in the public debate known as the Quarrel of the Ancients and Moderns.[46] Out of it came the conclusion that the Moderns were the victors over the Ancients – recent scientific discoveries, made from the direct observation of nature and verification by experiment, proved that the Greeks and Romans had not known everything and indeed had often been wrong. The work of the ancients had to be rejected and surpassed; "Plus Ultra" was to replace the "Non Ultra" written by the ancients on the Pillars of Hercules, beyond which there was to be no sailing and no further discovery.[47]

Wren and his friends stood among the Moderns in science. When the quarrel came to other fields, however, their position was not so clear. These men, and most of their colleagues at the Royal Society, were gentlemen educated in the humanities, taught to accept Classical writings as the touchstone for all learning. Although new discoveries and experiments had proven the ancients wrong in science, in the realm of literature, the fine arts, and architecture they continued to be revered and admired. Classical architecture was considered to have a perfection and superiority demonstrated, according to Vitruvius, by its foundation in the laws of nature and, according to Alberti, by the ideal society of classical antiquity, a Golden Age, which had created it. As a result, both sides of the quarrel accepted the superiority of the ancients in the literary and artistic disciplines, disagreeing only on whether further progress could be beyond them. The Ancients declared that the Classical works had reached the absolute height of perfection, using the simile of the Ancients as a giant and the Moderns as a dwarf to indicate the decay of knowledge. The Moderns, however, claimed that the dwarf stood on the shoulders of the giant – that is, contemporary works, using ancient works as a basis, could equal or even surpass them.[48]

As an architect and classically educated gentleman, Wren was predisposed to accept the belief in the superiority of the Classical style over the Gothic and in the possibility of attaining a perfection beyond the ancients. As a natural philosopher, however, he could not do so solely on the basis of the style's associationed meanings and reputed superiority. In his writings on architecture, Wren sought to uncover convincing reasons by analyzing the two styles on the basis of certain more absolute criteria – that is, the statical laws of structures and the natural causes of beauty, but also on more relative criteria – the customary causes of society.

As has been discussed earlier, Wren concluded that, in terms of the principles of statics, ancient architecture had the greatest stability, compared to the Gothic with its serious structural defects. Furthermore, the Classical style had the greatest beauty based on the natural causes. From his study of a broad range of ancient examples – Roman, Greek, and biblical or Hebraic buildings, and the protoclassical temple and forum – as well as modern – the works of Inigo Jones and sixteenth- and early seventeenth-century French architecture – Wren was led to characterize its forms as the most beautiful: the geometries of the circle and square, right angles, uniform divisions, symmetry, and ratios of small whole numbers. Finally, because the orders had their origin in nature and God, and were perfected by the great cultures of the past, they possessed both geometrical beauty and structural stability.

In comparison to the ancient, Gothic buildings employed the kinds of geometries that created less beauty. From the examples he knew at first hand, English medieval buildings of various periods and French Gothic cathedrals, Wren characterized the style as having oblique angles and vertical elements, like the pinnacle and the "lean Shaft of a Steeple,"[49] which had less or no beauty. He did recognize that some features were acceptable on the basis of beauty and structure: "Cones and multangular Prisms want neither Beauty nor Firmness."[50] Furthermore, certain medieval buildings could have qualities of natural beauty on the higher end of the scale. He wrote approvingly of the "good proportion" found in the nave of Salisbury Cathedral, and its ornaments: "the Mouldings are decently mixed with large planes" and the marble colonnettes, although

214

they are "so long & slender," have "a stately and rich Plaineness."[51] Nevertheless, Gothic architecture could never surpass the beauty of the Classical.

Wren concluded that the "good *Roman* Manner" was preferable over "*Gothick* Rudeness,"[52] a mode or fashion not "naturally" beautiful or stable. Nevertheless, he recognized that, despite its fundamental flaws, the Gothic was still a legitimate style that had gained approval out of the customary causes. Custom had perpetuated it over the centuries – from its invention by the "Saracens" or Arabs, to its introduction to western Europe by the returning Crusaders, to its adoption by the English from the French – and could even demand its usage in the present. Similarly, the Classical had also lasted through the ages, not only because of its aesthetic and structural superiority but through custom. Succeeding civilizations had consciously decided to continue or borrow the Classical style of an earlier age. The orders, the "*Phoenician, Hebrew,* and *Assyrian*" as well as the "*Roman* and *Greek,*" were created by "every one emulating each other." The Classical style was revived intentionally by "those who first laboured in the Restoration of Architecture, about three Centuries ago." Further, "Modern *Rome* subsists still, by the Ruins and Imitation of the *old.*"[53] In England, according to Wren's friend John Aubrey, "old Roman Architecture" was "first revived" under Edward VI, who "sent for the Architects and Workmen out of Italie." "The next Step of Roman Architecture" came with the work of Inigo Jones.[54]

Wren was aware that, regardless of its associationed meanings and fundamental qualities, the choice of a style for Restoration England would ultimately depend on custom. In Tract V he wrote: "Whatever a mans sentiments are upon mature deliberation it will be still necessary for him in a conspicuous Work to preserve his Undertaking from general censure, and to aim to accommodate his Designs to the Gust of the Age he lives in, though it appears to him less rational."[55] Furthermore, he realized that the taste of his culture, whether represented by the clients, the users, the general public, or the king, could change from one situation to the next. As a result, Wren designed buildings in both the Classical and Gothic styles, depending on what custom demanded in the particular circumstances. Within the culture of the king and his court the demand was for the style that would turn London into a New Rome. Occasionally, however, Wren found it necessary "to deviate from a better Style"[56] and employ the Gothic. Usually it was used as a practical solution to the problem of completing or adding to already existing Gothic structures, a solution that nevertheless achieved the classical goal of "a Harmony of Objects"[57] or conformity. The north transept facade of Westminster Abbey must be finished, Wren wrote, using forms "conformable to the old-Style, to make the Whole of a Piece." For the tower "to deviate from the old Form, would be to run into a disagreeable Mixture, which no Person of good Taste could relish."[58] In a few situations, however, the Gothic style was employed in response to the demands of society, as will be seen in the example of St. Paul's.

Having selected a style, Wren was faced with the problem of how to apply it in the design of the buildings of his own time. This involved not only the use of its characteristic decorative motifs but also the adaptation of its common forms and compositions, demonstrated in authoritative examples, to the taste and needs of contemporary society. The use of precedent had been fundamental to the idea of the Renaissance since the mid-fifteenth century in Italy, when architects began to revive antiquity by adapting ancient motifs and compositions to suit new circumstances.[59] The idea of historical precedent therefore is consistent with Wren's concept of "inventions." Existing architectural models are modified based on the architect's imagination, but also his judgment, which regulates any innovations according to the fundamental principles of beauty, structure, and function.

Wren's knowledge of history would have provided him with many building examples demonstrating typical compositional organizations in plan, elevation, massing, and interior space, as well as ornamental details. Whether he deliberately used these as a repertory of forms on which to model new designs, and how he might have actually used them, is difficult to determine. Studies of his ornament have revealed that Wren created sensitive and imaginative variations based on standard examples.[60] There has only been limited success in identifying the ancient models Wren used for the planning and overall composition of his designs.[61] The facade of Pembroke College Chapel at Cambridge (1663–5) combines an ancient temple front, possibly the one illustrated in Serlio's book 3 on antiquities (1562), with a triumphal arch, possibly one of the several also included in this book.[62] A major feature of both examples, however, is missing – an entry in the center. The suggestion in *Parentalia* that the Sheldonian Theater (1664–9) was a recreation of the Theater of Marcellus is supported by the ceiling illusionistically painted as an ancient velarium.[63] The plan, however, is not D-shaped but U-shaped, and oriented not toward the flat wall but toward the middle of the semicircle where the vice chancellor's seat is located.

Three of Wren's buildings are related to monuments he discusses in the Tracts. For St. Mary-le-Bow (1670–2), *Parentalia* stated, "The Model is after that of the *Templum* Pacis."[64] True, the church has a wide

Conclusion: Wren's Method of Design

three-bay nave flanked by narrow side aisles covered by transverse barrel vaults, and uses Corinthian columns, now engaged, supporting impost blocks at a level lower than the keystones of the aisle arches, but these similarities are scarcely noticeable. Wren seems to have used the Mausoleum of Halicarnassus as a model for the lantern over the vestibule of the Great Model for St. Paul's, built in 1674.[65] In comparing it to Wren's verbal reconstruction, drawn by Hawksmoor, there is very little in common, other than the attic story and stepped pyramid, on which stands, instead of Mausolus and the quadriga, St. Paul (Figs. 44, 53). The model for the wooden catafalque or "mausoleum" for the body of Queen Mary II as it lay in state at Westminster Abbey on 5 March 1695, can be identified as Porsenna's tomb[66] (Fig. 45). There was, however, a complete change in scale and materials, as well as in essential details: four pyramids or obelisks, forming a square, were interrupted at their midpoint, not by a dome supporting additional pyramids, but by a canopy from which bells hung.

In these few examples where a precise historical model or prototype can be identified, it is clear that each served only as a point of departure. Wren invariably changed the model almost beyond recognition in order to suit the given circumstances – the functional program, site conditions, materials, structure, and so forth. He was less interested in reusing existing types or in making designs with a recognizable model than in creating inventions that applied the formal lessons he had learned from ancient examples in an imaginative but also judicious manner – that is, in accordance with fundamental principles. For example, the Mausoleum of Harlicarnassus demonstrated how to design a monumental base for a statue that was at once structurally solid and visually light. Furthermore, in using ancient precedent Wren did not hesitate to disregard or manipulate it without regard to the meaning or formal integrity of the original source.

The same can be said for Wren's use of medieval precedent. Among his schemes in the Gothic style, some involve simply the application of ornament, which he was able to do skillfully and accurately. For example, in the design for the north transept facade of Westminster Abbey, which he made in collaboration with William Dickinson, the deputy surveyor, he restored some of the elements from the original early English facade, visible in Hollar's 1654 engraving, and borrowed other decorative elements from the western facade, also engraved by Hollar (Figs. 29, 26, 25). Wren made a design for the west front, which does not survive in drawing, that was also to continue "the *Gothick* Manner, in the Stonework, and Tracery."[67] At St. Mary Aldermary, because the Tudor Gothic outer walls survived the Great Fire, this style was continued for the tower and the interior, where there are plaster fan vaults ascribed to Wren.[68]

In other designs by Wren a specific medieval model can be identified. The tower of St. Dunstan's-in-the-East is based on a Gothic steeple type known as an imperial crown, an engineering tour de force that would have appealed to Wren: four flying buttresses springing from the corners of the tower and meeting in the center to support a spire. This type was used in the steeples of several English Gothic churches, including the medieval St. Mary-le-Bow, of unknown date, as well as St. Nicholas, Newcastle, dating from the fifteenth century, which has the greatest similarity to St. Dunstan's, particularly to an earlier version of the design.[69] In its final form, Wren's tower is much lighter and more vertical than St. Nicholas and has changes in details. The tower of St. Alban's, Wood Street, a square shaft rising into eight pinnacles, was probably modeled after Magdalen College at Oxford University, which dates from the late fifteenth century, and Merton College Chapel, from the mid-fifteenth century. In his version, however, the form and ornaments are much more simplified.

Despite their recognizably Gothic ornamentation and overall proportions, Wren composed all of his Gothic schemes so that the parts within the whole have a geometrical order and uniformity much more characteristic of Classical architecture. At Westminster Abbey, he recommended that the two towers of the west facade be made equal. Furthermore, the tower added at the crossing, according to his report, should be as high as it is wide, and with either a tall Gothic spire or, as Wren's drawing shows, a pointed dome on a short drum (Fig. 28). For the Gothic towers of his City churches Wren articulated the overall vertical massing with strongly projecting horizontal string courses, which reduced the tall shaft into smaller geometrical and horizontally proportioned parts.

Wren's designs in the Gothic style are truly inventions, with characteristics that make them unlike any real medieval building. This is particularly the case for Tom Tower, the entry gate to Christ Church College, Oxford (1681–2). Wren "resolved it ought to be gothic to agree with the Founders worke, yet I have not continued soe busy as he began" (Fig. 48).[70] He designed a massive vertical tower, imitating the two existing medieval bastions below, but greatly enlarged. It is composed as three simple monumental masses overlaid with minimal Gothic ornament – a square tower supporting an octagon, crowned by a dome based on the section of an ogive arch. Into Tom Tower and all of his Gothic designs Wren infused elementary geometries and their proportions, sym-

FIGURE 48. Oxford, Christ Church, Tom Tower, 1681–2. Photo by author.

metry, and uniformity – the natural causes of the greatest beauty. In other words, although he accepted the demands of custom and created an overall Gothic mass with Gothic ornament, he worked to imbue it with characteristics that are significant as a reflection of Classical norms, but, even more, as embodiments of fundamental and enduring qualities derived from nature.

Wren's design method was described by John Summerson in 1936 as an "empirical" or "arbitrary" approach. As the antithesis to "imaginative" design, it involved the "conscious selection of formal relationships" rather than unconscious, and "the formation of judgments in light of previous experience rather than of established principles."[71] From the evidence of his writings and buildings, it is clear that Wren, by applying a scientific viewpoint to existing artistic traditions, reformulated established principles of architecture and followed a method of design that was not made up of strict design rules or preconceived notions of form but of general pragmatic and aesthetic guidelines based on experience, to be applied according to the unique conditions and goals of the particular problem. He did not reject the "fancy" or imagination, but he subjected the "novelties" it produced to the regulation of the "judgment." As a result, Wren produced creative solutions for the architecture of his age that responded to society's demands for a particular style and models of design, but also to his own desire to design in accordance with nature and her principles of beauty, convenience, and stability. Although embodying a precarious balance of all these divergent factors, Wren's architecture nevertheless succeeds, to greater and lesser degrees, in existing for "Eternity" and for the "Nation," manifesting nature's principles as well as society's character.

The complex history of St. Paul's best demonstrates Wren's empirical method, as well as its furthest consequences: a discontinuity within the same building organism between exterior and interior form, and between form and structure. Although this phenomenon is not unprecedented in the history of architecture, and can be found in many examples in Italy and France of this period, for Wren it was less a deliberate artistic device than an outcome of his empirical design approach. Furthermore, this discontinuity conforms to his empirical definition of beauty stated in Tract I.

Wren's work at St. Paul's[72] began in 1661 when he was consulted about repairs for the old medieval Latin-cross cathedral. After almost six centuries, the building was a wreck from the abuses of nature and man – most recently during the Interregnum when Cromwellian soldiers used it as a stable and tradespeople hacked holes for timbers into the columns of Inigo Jones's Corinthian portico, built only a few decades earlier (Figs. 6–12).[73] After his return from Paris in 1666, Wren was invited again to make recommendations. In his scheme known as the Pre-Fire Design, Wren went far beyond simple repairs to create "a decent uniform Beauty" and a "durable Firmness" within a building that was, to his thinking, wanting in both. Two proposals were involved (Figs. 13–15). The first was to extend the recasing, executed by Jones on the exterior of the Romanesque nave and transepts, into the interior, thereby strengthening the walls and giving them "a good *Roman* Manner." The second was to replace the "Heap of Deformities" – the Romanesque crossing with its tower, "most defective both in Beauty and Firmness, without and within" – with "a spacious *Dome* or Rotundo, with a *Cupola*, or hemispherical Roof."[74]

With a new crossing Wren hoped to bring greater convenience and beauty to the existing fabric. The functional focus of the interior was shifted from the nave to the crossing, which was "a very proper Place for a vast Auditory," so important to the preaching that took place during Anglican services, leaving the nave as more of an introductory or processional space. The crossing also became the aesthetic focus of the interior, improving the form of the old cathedral, both inside and out. Inside, Wren removed the agglomeration of piers and arches at the crossing, which were added in later medieval times to help stabilize the sinking tower, but blocked the view. In addition, the spacing between these piers and the older supports was narrower than in the rest of the church. In their place he provided four new massive piers, occupying the first bays of the nave, the transept arms, and the choir, and defining an octagonal space that extended the full distance between the exterior walls.

The Pre-Fire Design was influenced by several diverse sources. The idea of an octagonal crossing within a Latin-cross plan seems to have come from the cathedral of Ely, from the fourteenth century, which has a crossing spanning 70 feet, rising to a stone and timber lantern, and with piers as wide as the side aisles.[75] Wren's idea of a centrally planned auditory rather than the rectilinear one he later used in the design of the City churches may have been inspired by the excellent acoustics at Ely, and by the centrally planned, sometimes octagonal chapter houses of England designed for reciting and hearing the Rules and used also for council meetings.[76] For the domed rotunda, Wren was inspired by the Early Baroque churches he had recently observed in Paris. These sources were now combined in accordance with Classical standards of beauty. The interior was given a "clear thorough View of the Nave," and the proportions of the original, "much too narrow for the Height," now would be "render'd spacious in the Middle," "where it had been more graceful to have been rather wider than the rest." Outside, the old cathedral now had a raised, pointed dome, giving it "incomparable more Grace" than the original tower and making the building "seem to swell in the Middle by Degrees."[77]

Wren's new crossing posed a serious structural problem: how to create a dome that could be perched high above a space about 85 feet wide on four supports. Although Wren selected the dome on pendentives, which according to his statical analysis was "the lightest Manner," requiring less buttressing than cross vaults,[78] he realized that a better guide would be provided by past experience, as demonstrated by the domes of French churches. These he had seen "while they were in raising, conducted by the best Artists, *Italian* and *French*," with whom he "had daily Conference, ... observing their Engines and Methods."[79] Wren borrowed many structural features from the church of the Sorbonne by Lemercier, built from 1635, which had a two-shell dome resting on a drum and spanning about 40 feet.[80] The inner was of masonry, opening at the apex to a lantern contained within the interstitial space of the two domes. The outer was framed in timber and covered in lead, and crowned by its own lantern. This design solved the visual problem of creating a domed space scaled to the interior and a domed mass scaled to the city.

For St. Paul's, Wren used all of these features but made modifications to ensure stability in a dome twice the size (Figs. 14–15). To reduce the overall weight, the outer shell, framed in timber, was crowned by a lantern in the form of a curious openwork pineapple- or pinecone-shaped metal spire. Furthermore, as in the Sorbonne, the loads of the lantern and timber shell did not rest on the inner masonry shell but were diverted to the drum, thus allowing the inner shell to be thinner. Because both domes were relatively light and furthermore were pointed in section – the inner very slightly, the outer much more so – the lateral thrusts were countered sufficiently by the surcharge at the haunches of the inner dome. The overall reduction in weight and lateral thrust meant that the piers did not require as much mass and abutment. Although the structural solution for the dome resulted in two obviously separate shells of very different form, Wren used ornament on the exterior and interior surfaces – concave fluting and horizontal moldings – to create the visual impression of continuity.

Wren's design soon came to nothing when the Great Fire destroyed the old cathedral, but it established two conceptions that would continue to be debated in the new St. Paul's. The first was the medieval nave of Old St. Paul's, with the classicized decoration added by Inigo Jones, representing the religious and architectural traditions of England. The second was the Classical, domed rotunda, derived from the latest monuments in France and Italy and representing the modernity and greatness of those countries. John Evelyn, who supported Wren's Pre-Fire Design over the objections of others on the commission, recognized this conception as a major turning point for English architecture: "we had a mind to build it with a noble Cupola, a form of Church-building, not as yet known in England, but of wonderfull grace."[81] With it, Wren hoped England would counter "the Opinion of our *Neighbours*" that "It is pity [London] should longer continue the most unadorn'd of her Bigness in the World."[82]

Ten days after the fire, in his plan for rebuilding the City of London, Wren produced his first sketch for a new St. Paul's where these elements appear again – a portico leading to a rectangular nave followed by a domed rotunda – the introductory nave and the circular "auditory," the functional and formal center of the Pre-Fire Design.[83] A few years later, in the First Model, finished in 1670, these two elements were reformulated in an awkward and unexpected fashion. The auditory was now rectangular, with a long barrel-vaulted nave, galleries, and side aisles transformed into external loggias, a scheme closely related in form and function to the parish churches Wren was designing. The rectangular auditory was *preceded* by a domed vestibule space, at least 60 feet in diameter, with three porticoes, a drum surrounded by coupled columns, and a dome.[84] Although the design now provided for function with the nave and for beauty with the domed rotunda, the joining and unexpected reversal of these two disparate parts were highly criticized on the grounds of custom. For some, according to *Parentalia*, it was too unlike "the old *Gothick* Form of cathedral Churches;" for others it was "not stately enough." That is, the design followed neither old medieval traditions nor the modern classical norms. As a result, "in order to find what might satisfy the World, the *Surveyor* drew several Sketches meerly for Discourse-sake."[85]

In the Greek Cross Design of 1672 Wren responded to the second criticism: "observing the Generality were for Grandeur, he endeavour'd to gratify the Taste of the *Connoiseurs* and Criticks, . . . with a Design . . . conformable to the best Stile of the *Greek* and *Roman* architecture."[86] Returning to the idea of a circular auditory, Wren created a Classical, centrally planned domed scheme, the four equal arms linked by concave quadrants (Figs. 49–51). Soon this scheme was modified by the addition of a small, circular, domed vestibule with a large, freestanding portico to form the Great Model, designed in 1673 and built in 1673–4 (Figs. 52–3). Similar to its predecessor, the exterior was articulated by Corinthian pilasters, with shallow pedimented porticoes fronting the transept and choir facades. Wren derived these two designs from the fifteenth-century projects for St. Peter's in Rome, specifically the centrally planned schemes of Bramante, Michelangelo, and Antonio da Sangallo the Younger, which included, as did the Great Model, a domed vestibule that gave the exterior the overall appearance of a Latin-cross scheme.[87]

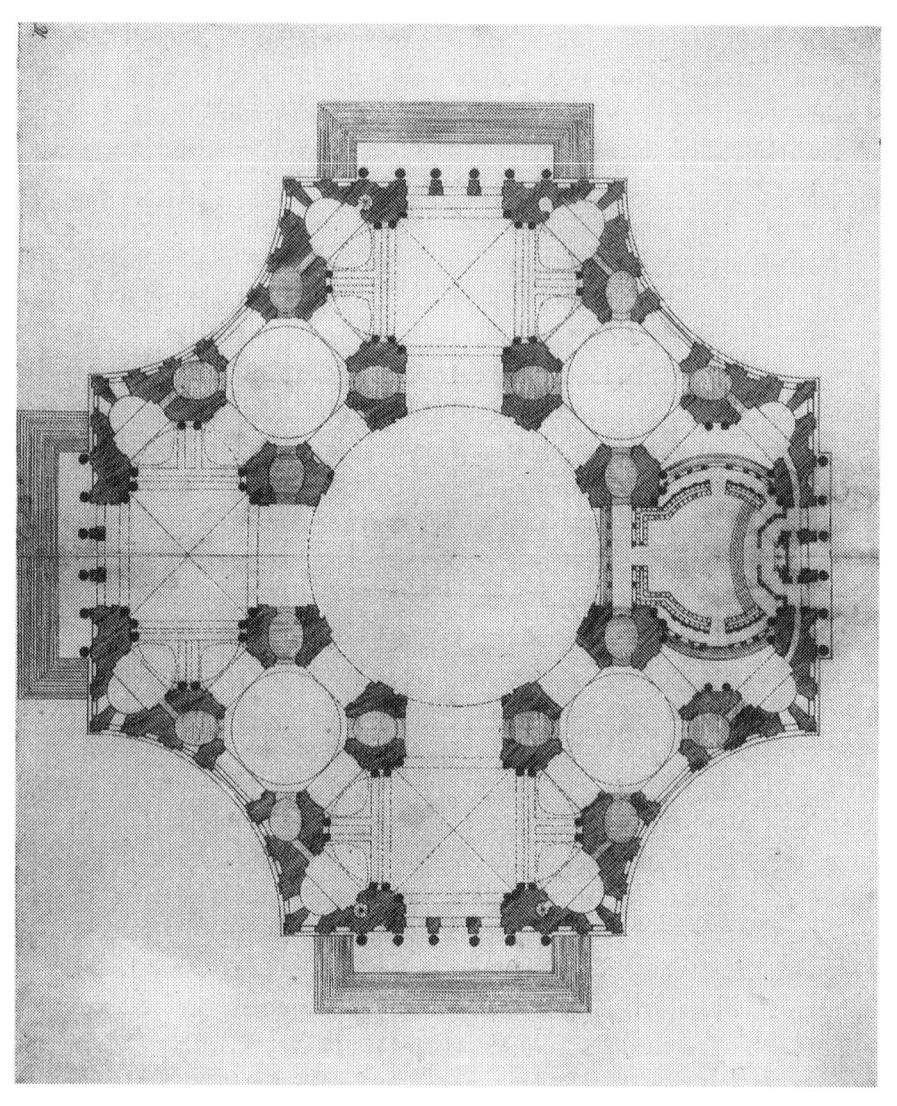

FIGURE 49. Greek Cross Design for St. Paul's, plan, 1672 (AS II. 21. All Souls College, Oxford). The Warden and Fellows of All Souls College, Oxford.

In the design of the dome for both schemes, Wren used French sources. As in the Pre-Fire Design, there were two domes, but now both were of masonry: an outer dome that was pointed and had decorative ribs; an inner dome that was semicircular and smooth. Each was a separate structure with its own ornamental system, but joined at their bases to rest on a short colonnaded drum. Most importantly, the inner dome was brought into close proximity to the outer and was given an oculus that allowed a view to its inner surface, illuminated by a ring of windows.

This motif of the cut-off dome, where the lower surface of the outer dome was viewed through the oculus of an inner dome, derived from the design of François Mansart for the Bourbon Chapel at St. Denis, conceived in 1663. Wren, who was in Paris and planned to meet Mansart, probably saw final drawings of the design during the summer of 1665, before the project was abandoned.[88]

The sources for the planning and imagery of the Great Model were clearly recognizable to the public, but the connotations were mixed. On one hand it represented popery, the domed, centralized classical composition derived from *the* monument of the Catholic church. On the other hand it represented the rationalism of the New Science, based on reason rather than faith, the abstract geometry and the biaxial symmetry expressing, not religious beliefs, but universal, natural laws.[89]

Neither of these images was acceptable to the Anglican clergy, who immediately returned to the earlier criticism, finding that the Great Model was "not enough of a Cathedral-fashion."[90] In response to the demands of custom, Wren produced a scheme during the first half of 1674 in the "Cathedral-form . . . but so rectified, as to reconcile, as near as possible, the *Gothick* to a better Manner of Architecture" – the Warrant Design (Figs. 54–8). This was a Latin-cross scheme, now derived from Old St. Paul's as remodeled by Jones and redesigned by Wren before the fire (Figs. 6–15). In place of the centralized plan of the Great Model, Wren used the old Latin-cross plan, with a basilican section of high nave and low side aisles. Above the octagonal crossing, now even more closely modeled on Ely Cathedral with the use of eight piers, rose a hybrid structure that combined a Gothic tower and spire with the Pre-Fire Design's classical domed rotunda, an idea Wren could not abandon.

In the Gothic nave of the Warrant Design, Wren continued the classicizing that had been implemented at Old St. Paul's. On the exterior Wren replicated Jones's "quasi-Tuscan" ornament – plain arched windows separated by Romanesque wall buttresses, now treated as broad flat pilasters, which he crowned with pinnacles in the form of stepped pyramids. On the west he created a close version of Jones's design, with the wall of the high nave articulated by a pediment and three arched windows, joined by scrolls to the lower side aisles and preceded by a giant Corinthian portico.[91]

Wren took Jones's approach even further in the Warrant Design by applying ancient models to classicize the traditional massing and proportions of a medieval cathedral. The section of the high nave and low side aisles, covered with cross-vaults, was based on the Basilica of Maxentius, which Wren so greatly admired in Tract IV for its beauty and

FIGURE 50. Greek Cross Design for St. Paul's, section, 1672 (AS II. 23. All Souls College, Oxford). The Warden and Fellows of All Souls College, Oxford.

firmness. At the crossing Wren created a traditional medieval tower, but one that was essentially a smaller version of the Pre-Fire dome, now crowned by a timber spire. The spire, however, was transformed into a series of stepped stages, each a progressively smaller octagonal pavilion, resulting in a pagoda-like form. Furthermore, the tower acted as a huge lantern by being placed at the apex of a pendentive dome rising from the octagonal crossing. The form of the dome was modeled after the Pantheon, complete with stepped buttressing, although here it served only as the support for the timbers of the outer shell.[92] The dome's structure, slightly pointed, double-shelled, and ribbed, each of the eight ribs supporting a pier buttress of the domed tower/lantern, owed more to Michelangelo's St. Peter's dome as built by della Porta.[93]

226

Conclusion: Wren's Method of Design

FIGURE 51. Greek Cross Design for St. Paul's, west elevation, 1672 (AS II. 22. All Souls College, Oxford). The Warden and Fellows of All Souls College, Oxford.

By using ancient and more modern Classical models, Wren created an assemblage of simple geometrical and horizontally proportioned masses and spatial volumes that nevertheless, as a whole, had the spatial arrangement, massing, and overall proportions of a Gothic cathedral. In other words, Wren was able, through a manipulation of geometry and proportion, to give a Classical character to a Gothic conception. Just as Jones had classicized a traditional Gothic cathedral for the first Stuarts, so Wren did for the restored Stuarts. Despite the complete absence of Gothic ornament, the design was recognized as an English and Protestant cathedral and was given a warrant on 14 May 1675.

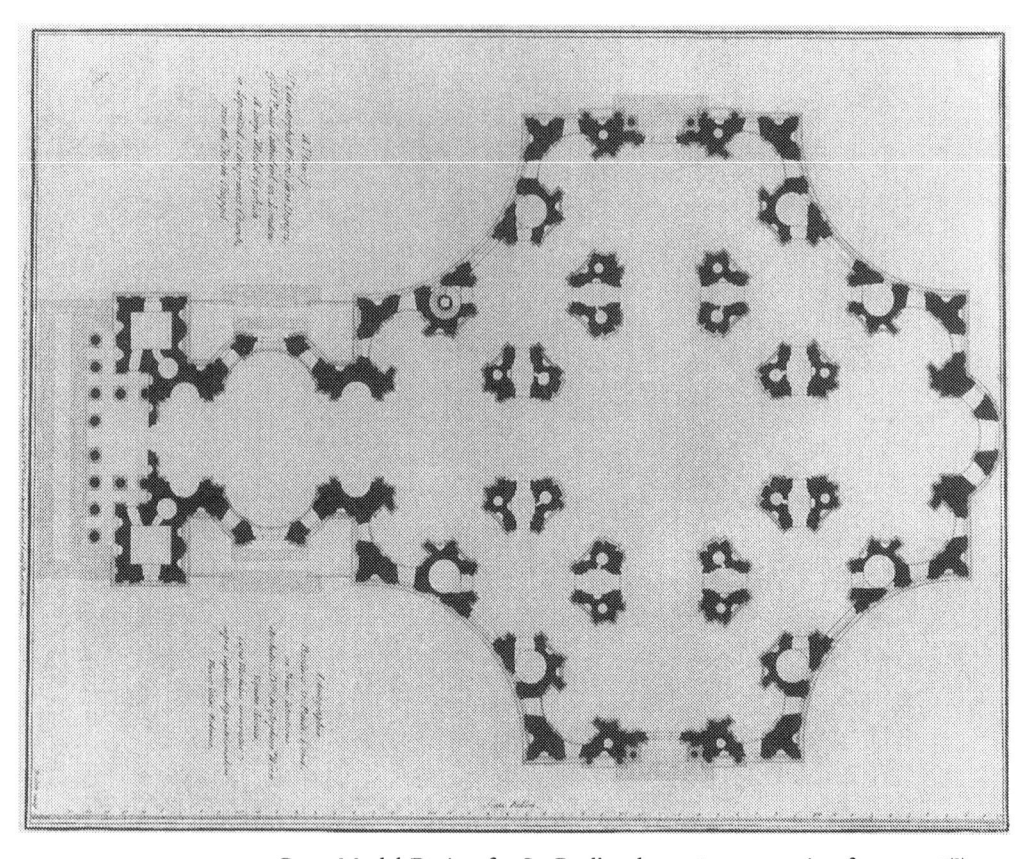

FIGURE 52. Great Model Design for St. Paul's, plan, 1673, engraving from 1726(?). (Christopher Wren, *A catalogue of the churches of the city of London: royal palaces, hospitals, and publick edifices, built by Sr. Christopher Wren . . . during fifty years: viz. from 1668 to 1718* (London: printed for S. Harding [1726?]). Photograph courtesy of the Art Institute of Chicago.

In the sequence of designs for St. Paul's, Wren did not hesitate to produce schemes that were more "Classical" in response to the aspirations of the Crown, but also more "Gothic" in response to the demands of the Church of England. Based on his knowledge of their origins and particular characteristics, Wren understood both styles to be as much products of custom as nature. In his judgment, however, the Classical style had primacy because it utilized the most beautiful geometries among the natural causes, and also the orders, legitimized by their natural and biblical origins and by the great civilizations that had adopted and made them their own. Furthermore, based on the customary causes, it was the style selected as the most appropriate for a monument to the restored Stuarts. This belief in the priority of the Classical style is expressed in the

Conclusion: Wren's Method of Design

FIGURE 53. Great Model Design for St. Paul's, view of model, 1673 (National Monuments Record). By courtesy of St. Paul's Cathedral.

Great Model. Wren's society, however, had an equally legitimate claim for the Gothic as the most appropriate style for a monument of the Church of England, and the Warrant Design expresses this belief. In both designs, by instilling the "most beautiful" geometries, Wren ensured that St. Paul's, no matter what style had been imposed by different customs, would survive the "true Test" of the natural causes.

Although he respected the customary causes, Wren was forced in the end to make a difficult choice of the kind he had cautioned against when describing the vicissitudes of "customary beauty" in Tract I: "Here lies the great Occasion of Errors; here is tried the Architect's Judgment...."[94] Wren, acting on his authority as Surveyor General and, more, as an architect with a reasonable judgment and "Fancy" informed by "the Study of Antiquity," determined in the end that the appropriate solution for St. Paul's was a compromise between the divergent forces of custom. Two months after the warrant was granted, the Definitive Design was established, probably the result of rethinking that Wren had begun a year before, soon after the drawings of the Warrant Design were sub-

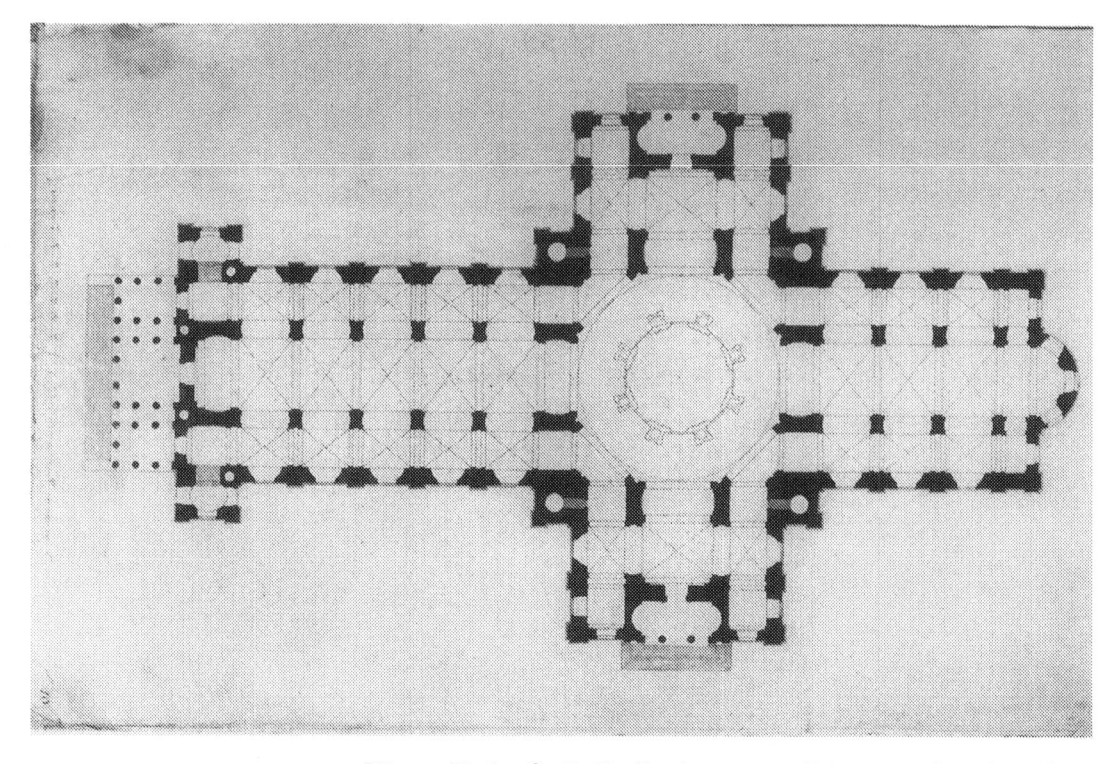

FIGURE 54. Warrant Design for St. Paul's, plan, 1674–5 (AS II. 10, All Souls College, Oxford). The Warden and Fellows of All Souls College, Oxford.

mitted.[95] Changes to the Definitive Design continued until the completion of the construction in 1710. The design of the dome was not finalized until the late 1690s.

The final design is a compromise between the Gothic and the Classical. Working from the Warrant Design's Gothic Latin-cross plan and nave section, Wren guided the design back to the Great Model's exterior massing and vaulting, and the Warrant's tower back to the Pre-Fire Design's centralized dome. As a result of his empirical approach, combining various features from his earlier schemes, some selected for functional reasons, others for formal ones, the final design of St. Paul's has discontinuities between exterior form and interior space and between form and structure (Figs. 59–63).

In response to the clergy's demand for function and tradition, Wren kept the Warrant Design's Latin-cross plan and exterior massing. However, in order to approach more closely the centrally planned ideal of the Great Model, he added a domed vestibule that allowed him to reduce the number of bays in the nave to equal those of the choir, thus creating a sense of centrality around the crossing. The Warrant Design's medieval section of high nave and lower side aisles was preserved, but was given the Great Model's Classical interior arcade, articulated by a giant order of Corinthian pilasters supporting an entablature, covered by saucer-domes. Whereas the interior retained the spatial configuration of a typical Gothic church, serving the needs of the Anglican liturgy, the exterior was modified based on different goals. On the exterior, the true massing is concealed by extending the one-story-high exterior walls of the aisles upward to create a freestanding screen, thus returning to the massing of the Great Model, a blocky base crowned by a hemispherical dome. Furthermore, Wren created the geometrical appearance appropriate for a building approached not just from the front but from all sides.

Although the exterior mass and interior space had very different forms due to the unique requirements of each, Wren attempted to create an impression of continuity between them. The massive block of the exterior is articulated as two stories of coupled, superimposed pilasters. The lower story, with arched windows opening to the aisles, loosely corresponds to the giant order of the nave, and the upper story, decorated by aedicules, to the zone of the vaults. However, because the upper wall is freestanding, Wren had to replace what logically would be a window within each aedicule with a solid niche. Then, because light was needed in the low gallery above the aisle, he inserted, as unobtrusively as possible, a real window beneath the niche.[96]

Although discontinuities between exterior form and interior space are not new in Baroque architecture, in Wren's case they result less from the pictorial approach of an artist, who designs each setting for its maximum visual effect, and more from the empirical approach of a scientist, who solves problems of function, site, structure, and visual form separately and thus creates a building characterized less by unity than by compromise among different elements. These discontinuities also reflect a consciously empirical conception of beauty. For Wren, beauty was a visual phenomenon based on customary but also natural causes. The natural causes were concerned with the appearance of geometry for the primary "perspectives," which could exist as separate views where things "are not seen at once, and have no Respect one to another."[97] Therefore the geometry of parts not seen together need not coincide. On the basis of this empirical definition of beauty, Wren did not hesitate to create separate systems of interior and exterior form, as well as ornament, each system responding to different requirements, both practical and aesthetic.

Wren's empirical definition of beauty is reflected at St. Paul's in another by-product of his design method: a discontinuity between

FIGURE 55. Warrant Design for St. Paul's, cross-section, 1674–5 (AS II. 12, All Souls College, Oxford). The Warden and Fellows of All Souls College, Oxford.

visual form and structure. Whereas beauty was caused by the appearance of geometry, Wren considered structure to be based on "geometrical Reasons of *Staticks*."[98] As a result he became aware that the creation of firmness in his buildings could be treated as a problem separate from that of beauty, and that real structure and materials did not have to be

Conclusion: Wren's Method of Design

FIGURE 56. Warrant Design for St. Paul's, west elevation, 1674–5 (AS II. 11, All Souls College, Oxford). The Warden and Fellows of All Souls College, Oxford.

expressed formally, but could be concealed. At St. Paul's, this conception allowed him to develop structural solutions for the problems of abutting the nave vaults and covering the crossing for the most part independently of considerations of visual form.

For the nave, spanning 41 feet, Wren chose to build brick vaults covered with stucco, creating a monumental interior in a relatively light

FIGURE 57. Warrant Design for St. Paul's, longitudinal section, 1674–5 (AS II. 14, All Souls College, Oxford). The Warden and Fellows of All Souls College, Oxford.

material, but still requiring substantial abutment (Fig. 62). Based on his studies of Gothic architecture, Wren knew flying buttresses to be a sound solution to the problem of counteracting the thrusts of the nave's saucer-domes. Although he accepted them on the ground of the geometrical reasons of statics, he rejected them, because of their oblique angles, on the grounds of the geometrical causes of beauty. Because beauty was a visual phenomenon, however, Wren saw no contradiction in utilizing flying buttresses to solve the structural problem of the interior and then hiding them behind a freestanding screen. Wren could have believed that this wall, which recently has been determined to have no structural purpose,[99] provided the additional vertical load necessary to withstand the lateral thrusts. However, according to Wren's hypothesis, the vertical load was needed only at the base of each flyer, as demonstrated by pinnacles at that location in Gothic buildings, and at St. Paul's by the two-foot-

FIGURE 58. Warrant Design for St. Paul's, south elevation, 1674–5 (AS II. 13, All Souls College, Oxford). The Warden and Fellows of All Souls College, Oxford.

thick strip buttresses placed there on the inside of the screen wall. Therefore, it appears that the use of a continuous, freestanding wall was primarily for visual reasons – to present a proper geometrical appearance to the viewer – and for the most part was unrelated to the structural reality of the building.

At the crossing Wren faced his most challenging structural problem, one never before encountered in England: the construction of a dome, 112 feet in diameter, poised over 92 feet above the octagonal crossing. After the hybrid dome of the Warrant Design, Wren made a whole series of schemes that took him back in the direction of the dome of the Pre-Fire Design.[100] In each alternative Wren maintained the same basic features: eight piers, eight pendentives, a high drum, and a dome of more than one shell, each with a particular visual purpose. First, there was an outer steeply pointed dome, in some schemes of masonry but in most timber-framed for lightness, which was to be seen in relationship to

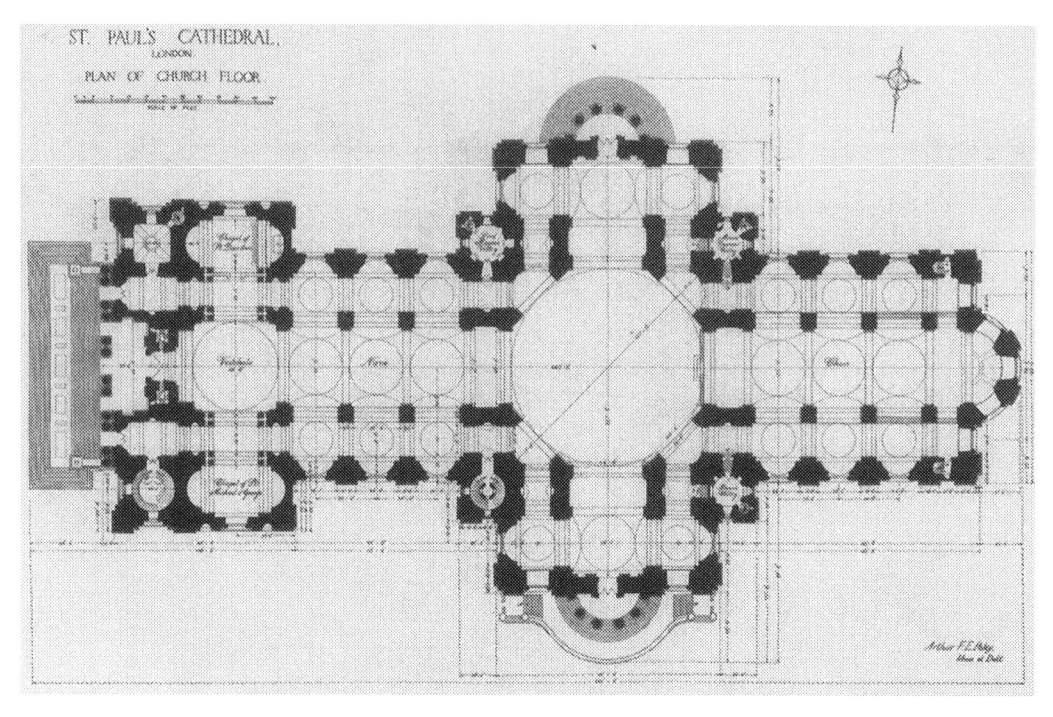

FIGURE 59. St. Paul's Cathedral, London, plan, 1675–1710, drawn by Arthur Poley, 1927 (Arthur Poley, *St. Paul's Cathedral London, Measured, Drawn, and Described* [London, 1927], pl. 23). British Architectural Library, RIBA, London.

the city. Second, there was an inner masonry dome, only slightly pointed, scaled in relationship to the interior space, with an oculus looking on to the surface of the outer dome – that is, a cut-off dome. After the Warrant Design, Wren began to explore the idea of a third shell, designed solely for structure and hidden between the other two. A triple-shell dome had several advantages over the double. In the double-shell system, in order to maintain the separate function and form of each, the outer dome had to be designed so that its loads were diverted to the drum rather than resting on the inner dome, which would affect this dome's form and structure. With the triple shell, the form and structure of the outer and inner shells could remain independent of one another.

From the exterior, the dome of St. Paul's appears to be a single hemispherical form and a single structural entity. From the interior, the dome is revealed to have a separate interior shell, seemingly hemispherical in form, that opens through its oculus into the illuminated zone beyond. In reality it is a three-shell dome, where the inner 18-inch-thick brick cone has the primary structural role (Fig. 63). Stabilized by the heavy

FIGURE 60. St. Paul's Cathedral, London, interior nave, 1675–1710. Photo © Woodmansterne.

lantern, the cone exerts very little lateral thrust, and requires, in contrast to the dome of St. Peter's, the addition of only one iron chain. Wren's use of the cone, in conjunction with a drum that tapers inward, may have been prompted by an idea first given to him by Robert Hooke – the catenary curve, which, when inverted, works in compression.[101]

The geometry of the cone is solely for structural, not visual, purposes. It is hidden between an outer lead-encased timber shell, which is

FIGURE 61. St. Paul's Cathedral, London, exterior from southeast, 1675–1710. Photo by author.

supported by the cone, and an inner brick shell 18 inches thick.[102] Slightly pointed in section, each with its own decorative system – the exterior has ribs, the interior was designed to have mosaics[103] – the outer and inner shells were each designed to create a geometrical appearance for the particular view. As for the conical dome, for Wren it did not lack geometrical beauty – "Cones," he writes in Tract I, "want neither Beauty nor Firmness" – but it was "not ancient."[104] As a result, Wren hid the geometry of the true conical structure within two shells that present the viewer with a proper geometrical, as well as Classical, appearance, thus complying with both natural law and the demands of custom.

With the completion of St. Paul's, Wren fulfilled his vision, first proposed in 1666 with the Pre-Fire Design, to create "an Ornament to his Majesty's most excellent Reign, to the Church of *England*, and to this great City."[105] Wren's writings on architecture show that, from the very beginning of his career, he believed that the goal of architecture was twofold. Because

Conclusion: Wren's Method of Design

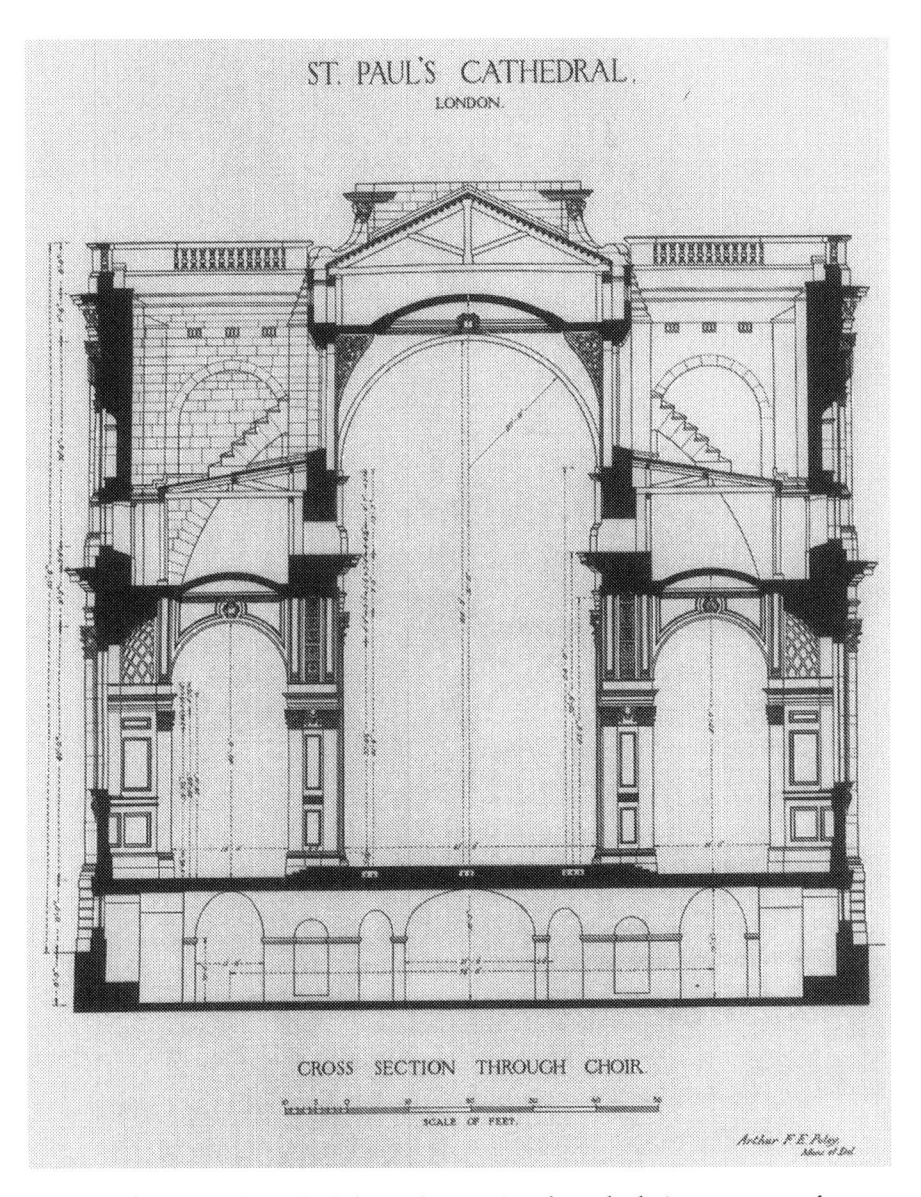

FIGURE 62. St. Paul's Cathedral, London, section through choir, 1675–1710, drawn by Arthur Poley, 1927 (Arthur Poley, *St. Paul's Cathedral London, Measured, Drawn, and Described* [London, 1927], pl. 12). British Architectural Library, RIBA, London.

"Architecture aims at Eternity," and "the Glory of that which is good of itself is eternal," the architect must create "Beauty, Firmness, and Convenience." But because "Architecture has its political Use; publick Buildings being the Ornament of a Country,"[106] the architect must also create a cultural symbol. As Surveyor General, Wren conceived of an architec-

Wren's "Tracts" on Architecture and Other Writings

FIGURE 63. St. Paul's Cathedral, London, section through crossing, 1675–1710, drawn by Arthur Poley, 1927 (Arthur Poley, *St. Paul's Cathedral London, Measured, Drawn, and Described* [London, 1927], pl. 10). British Architectural Library, RIBA, London.

ture that reflected and promoted the glories of the restored Stuart monarchy and established its greatness for posterity.

As a result of this double goal, Wren understood architecture as a phenomenon dependent on society as well as nature. In Tract I, he posited a dualistic, empirical definition of beauty, determined by the natural causes of geometry and the customary causes of individual inclination and societal custom. Because these causes did not create an absolute beauty, but only an appearance that was constantly subject to the vagaries of man's perception and understanding, Wren set out in his writings to establish "a truer tast in Architecture."[107] In his theory, based on the studies of London antiquities and Gothic churches, as well as the investigation in his Tracts of the origin and history of architecture, he concluded that this standard of good taste should not be the Gothic, but the superior style, the Classical. In the discussions among his close circle, Wren agreed that the Classical was the only appropriate style for the restored Stuarts, whose standing was equal to that of the Roman emperors.

In his architecture, Wren achieved this Classical standard, but was sometimes forced by custom to deviate from it, utilizing Gothic motifs and compositions. Nevertheless, all of his buildings, no matter what style, were designed with an underlying *visual* order of simple geometries. Wren's architecture succeeded in creating an image of a classical ideal that fulfilled the aspirations of Restoration England for political status in the present. At the same time, this image went beyond an ideal of the classical to an ideal of the universal. By standing on the shoulders of the giant, Wren and his society hoped, through the perfection of their architecture, to surpass all past cultures and to be remembered for all time.

Because of Wren's empiricism, in some buildings, particularly at St. Paul's, the image coexisted separate from the reality – the functional plan, formed according to specific social or religious traditions, together with the structural system, formed according to nature's laws of statics. Although a design with such disparities might represent a failure to most architects, it was completely logical to one who was also a natural philosopher. As his writings show, Wren understood architecture as a phenomenon in which, as in all of nature's productions, the outward appearance often hides the underlying real order. Because of his scientific viewpoint, Wren was able to create an architecture that accommodated all the multiple and often contradictory forces of nature and society. The result was neither an ideal harmony nor an unresolved compromise, but, closer to Wren's empirical understanding of natural phenomena, an intricate correlation between vision and reality.

APPENDIX

Comparison of Tracts IV and V

A. Comparison of Tract IV in *Parentalia*, 360, and Tract V, 6–7, in RIBA *Parentalia*

The most observable Monument of the *Tyrian* Style, and of great Antiquity, still remaining, is the Sepulchre of *Absalom*:	The next observable Monument of great Antiquity, which yet remains, is the *Pillar* of *Absolom*. By the description given of it, and what I have learnt from Travellers who have seen it, we must allow it to be very Remarkable, though not great.
the Body of this Structure is square, faced on every Side with Pillars,	It is compos'd of seven Pillars, six about in a Hexagon, and one in the middle,
which bear up an hemispherical *Tholus* solid; a large Architrave, Freeze, and Cornice lie upon the Pillars, which are larger in proportion to their Heighth, than what we now allow to the *Tuscan* Order; so likewise is the Entablature larger.	which Bear up an Hemispherical Tholus solid; a large Architrave, Frize and Cornice lie upon the Pillars, which are larger in proportion to their height then what we now allow to the Tuscan Order, so likewise is the Entablature larger.
This whole Composition, though above 30 Feet high, is all of one Stone, both Basis, Pillars, and *Tholus*, cut as it stood out of the adjacent Cliff of white Marble.	This whole Composition though at least *30* foot high is all of One Stone, both Basis, Pillars and Tholus cut as it stood out of the adjacent Cliff of white Marble.
It is to be wished, some skilful Artist would give us	I could wish some skilfull Artist would give us

the exact Dimensions to Inches, by which we might have a true Idea of the ancient *Tyrian* Manner; for, 'tis most probable *Solomon* employed the *Tyrian* Architects in his Temple, from his Correspondency with King *Hiram*; and from these *Phœnicians* I derive, as well the Arts, as the Letters of the *Grecians*, though it may be the *Tyrians* were Imitators of the *Babylonians*, and they of the *Ægyptians*.	the exact dimentions to inches, by which we might have an idea of the Antient Tyrian Manner for, it was probable Solomon, by his correspondance with King Hiram, employ'd the Tyrian Artists in his Temple: and from the Phœnicians I derive as well the Arts as the Letters of the Græcians, though it may be, the Tyrians were Imitators of the Babylonians, and They of the Egyptians.
Great Monarchs are ambitious to leave great Monuments behind them; and this occasions great Inventions in mechanick Arts.	Great Monarchs are ambitious to leave great Monuments behind them, and this occasions great Inventions and Mechanicks Arts.
What the Architecture was that *Solomon* used, we know little of, though holy Writ hath given us the general Dimensions of the Temple, by which we may, in some measure, collect the Plan, but not of all the Courts.	What the Architecture was that Solomon used we know little of, though Holy Writ hath given us the general dimentions of the Temple, by which we may in some manner collect the Plan, but not of all the Courts.
Villalpandus hath made a fine romantick Piece, after the *Corinthian* Order, which, in that Age, was not used by any Nation; for the early Ages used much grosser Pillars than the *Dorick*: in after Times, they began to refine from the *Dorick*, as in the Temple of *Diana* at *Ephesus*, (the united Work of all *Asia*) and at length improved into a slenderer Pillar, and leafy Capital	Villalpandus hath made a fine Romantick Piece after the Corinthian Order, which in that Age was not used by any Nation: for the First Ages used grosser Pillars then Dorick. In after Times They began to refine from the Dorick, as in the Temple of Ephesus (the united Work of all Asia) and afterwards improv'd into a Slenderer Pillar, and Leavy Capital

Appendix

of various Inventions,	of various inventions,
which was called *Corinthian*;	which they call'd Corinthian.
so that if we run back	So that if we run back
to the Age of *Solomon*,	to the Age of Solomon,
we may with Reason believe	we may with reason beleive
they used the *Tyrian* Manner,	They used the Tyrian manner,
as gross at least, if not more,	as gross at least
than the *Dorick*, and that the	as the Dorick, and that the
Corinthian Manner of	Corinthian Manner of
Villalpandus is mere Fancy.	Villalpandus is meer fancy:

B. Comparison of Tract IV in *Parentalia*, 360–1, and Tract V, 24, text under drawing of Mausoleum of Halicarnassus in RIBA *Parentalia*

The Temple of *Diana* of *Ephesus*, a most surprizing Example of the *Grecian* Magnificence, introduced the *Ionick* Order: it was two hundred and twenty Years in building, at the joint Expence of all the States of *Asia*, each Government contributing a Pillar.	The Temple of Diana of Ephesus of great Magnitude introduc'd the Ionick Order. It took [illegible] 220 years in Building, at the joint expense of all the States of Asia, and was justly esteem'd among the Wonders of the World.
In this Structure the Capitals were first formed with Voluta's, and the Proportions changed from the *Dorick* to a slenderer Pillar.	In this the Capitals were first made Voluta's and the Proportions chang'd from the gross Dorick to a slenderer Pillar.
The Description in *Pliny* is short, and what no Authors, ancient or modern, seem sufficiently to explain.	The Description in Pliny is but short, and what no Authors Ancient or Modern seem to make [illegible] sufficiently.
The Account, therefore, of this prodigious Fabrick, the first Instance of the Use of the *Ionick* Order, requires to be as fully and clearly illustrated, as the most authentick Aid we can have from Antiquity will allow.	This being so Wonderfull a Fabrick, and the First Example of the Ionick Order, I thought requir'd to be well considered.
The Length of the whole Temple was 425 Feet, the Breadth 220 Feet.	The Length was 425 feet, the Breadth 220 ft.

245

Appendix

The Pillars were in Number 127, each 60 Feet high.	It contained 127 Pillars of 60 ft. high. Each prince [illegible] Republick of Asia contributing a Pillar.

Abbreviations

Alberti, *DRA*	Leon Battista Alberti, *On the Art of Building in Ten Books (De re aedificatoria)*, trans. J. Rykwert, N. Leach, R. Tavernor (Cambridge, MA: MIT Press, 1988)
AS	All Souls College, Oxford University
Aubrey, *MB*	John Aubrey, *Monumenta Britannica*, Bodleian MS Top. Gen. c. 24 and c. 25. Facsimile ed. Rodney Legg, William Hoade, Robert J. Briggs, and John Fowles, 2 vols. (Sherborne, Dorset: Dorset Publishing, 1980 and 1982)
Birch	Thomas Birch, *History of the Royal Society of London*, 4 vols. (London, 1756–7). Facsimile ed. (New York: Johnson Reprint, 1968)
BL	British Library, London
Bodleian	Bodleian Library, Oxford University
CHO	*The Correspondence of Henry Oldenburg*, ed. A. R. Hall and M. B. Hall, 11 vols. (Madison, WI: University of Wisconsin Press, 1965–77)
DBA	Howard Colvin, *A Biographical Dictionary of British Architects 1600–1840*, 3d ed. (New Haven, CT: Yale University Press, 1995)
DNB	*Dictionary of National Biography*
DSB	*Dictionary of Scientific Biography* (New York: Scribner, 1976)
Hooke, *Diary 1672–80*	Robert Hooke, *The Diary of Robert Hooke: 1672–1680* (Guildhall Library, MS 1758), ed. H. W. Robinson and Walter Adams (London: Taylor and Francis, 1935)
Hooke, *Diary 1688–93*	*Diary*, 1688 to 1693 (BL MS Sloane 4024), in R. T. Gunther, ed., "Life and Work of Robert Hooke (Part IV)," vol. 10 of *Early Science in Oxford* (Oxford: for the author, 1935)
JBO	*Journal Book of the Royal Society*, Royal Society, London
OED	*Oxford English Dictionary*
PAR	Christopher Wren, Jr., *Parentalia: or, Memoirs of the Family of the Wrens* (London, 1750). Facsimile ed. (Farnborough: Gregg, 1965)

Abbreviations

PT	*Philosophical Transactions of the Royal Society of London*, 30 vols., 1665–1715. Facsimile ed. (New York: Johnson Reprint, 1963)
RIBA	British Architectural Library, Royal Institute of British Architects
RS	Royal Society, London
Vitruvius	Vitruvius, *On Architecture (De architectura)*, trans. Frank Granger, 2 vols. (Cambridge, MA: Harvard University Press, Loeb Classical Library, 1983)
WA	Westminster Abbey, Cathedral Library
WS	*Wren Society*, ed. A. T. Bolton and H. D. Hendry, 20 vols. (Oxford: for Wren Society at Oxford University Press, 1924–43)

Notes

INTRODUCTION

1. For information on fifteenth-, sixteenth-, and seventeenth-century architectural treatises, see Dora Wiebenson, *Architectural Theory and Practice from Alberti to Ledoux* (Architectural Publications, 1982). For information on English treatises, see Eileen Harris, *British Architectural Books and Writers 1556–1785* (Cambridge: Cambridge University Press, 1990).
2. Wren's library included Claude Perrault's 1684 French edition of Vitruvius; the 1512 edition of Alberti's *De re aedificatoria*, printed in Paris; the 1663 Venice edition of Serlio's Books I through VII; and the 1601 Venice edition of Palladio. See *A Catalogue of the Curious and Entire Libraries of that ingenious Architect Sir Christopher Wren, Knt., and Christopher Wren, Esq., his Son* (London, 1748), facsimile in *Sale Catalogues of Libraries of Eminent Persons*, ed. A. N. L. Munby, 12 vols. (London: Mansell with Sotheby Parke-Bernet, 1971–5), vol. 4: "Architects," ed. D. J. Watkin (1972), 1–39 (hereafter cited as Wren's Library). Wren would also have had access to other editions of these books.
3. John Evelyn, *The Diary of John Evelyn*, ed. E. S. de Beer, 6 vols. (Oxford: Clarendon, 1955), 3:106 (10 July 1654). For a more detailed discussion of Wren's early life and scientific career, see: Kerry Downes, *The Architecture of Wren* (New York: Universe Books, 1982); J. A. Bennett, *The Mathematical Science of Christopher Wren* (Cambridge: Cambridge University Press, 1982); Michael Hunter, "The Making of Christopher Wren," *London Journal* 16, no. 2 (1991): 101–16; and Bryan Little, *Sir Christopher Wren: A Historical Biography* (London: Robert Hale, 1975).
4. Wren's Library, Lots 545, 443.
5. Ibid., Lots 529, 540.
6. Bodleian, Sevile E. 7, among a group of books given by Wren to the Savile Library in 1673. See J. A. Bennett, "Studies in the Life and Work of Sir Christopher Wren," Ph.D. diss., Cambridge University, 1976, appendix, for a complete listing.
7. Wren's Library, Lot 561, lists the 1708 English edition of John James, but it is probable that Wren knew the original French edition.
8. Wren's Library, Lots 563 and 562.
9. Books on antiquities in Wren's Library include: Johannes Jacobus Boissardus, *Romanae Urbis Topographiae et Antiquitates*, 6 pts. (Frankfurt, 1597–1602) (Lot 528); O. Panvini, B. Marliani, P. Victoris, and J. J. Boissardi, *Antiquitates Romanae Topographia Romae*, 8 pts., 2 vols. (Frankfurt, 1627?) (Lot 532); Antonio Bosio, *Roma Sotterranea* (Rome, 1632) (Lot 555); Francisco Perrier, *Icones & Segmenta illustrium e Marmore Tabularum quae Romae* (Rome, 1645) (Lot 533), and "Figures, Antiques, Designes à Rome, Par François Perrier, Par." (Lot 210); Giovanni Pietro Bellori, *Columna Antoniana M. Aurelii Antonini* (Rome, 1672?) (Lot 553), and *Columna Trajano* (Rome, 1673) (Lot 554); Raffaello Fabretti, *De aquis et aquaeductibus veteris Romae* (Rome, 1688 [1680?]) (Lot 369); Giovanni Giacomo Rossi, *Admiranda romanorum antiquitatum ac veteris sculpturae vestiga*, notis J. Pietro Bellori (Rome: Johannes Jacobus de Rubeis,

1685?) (Lot 537), and *Insignium Romae Templorum Prospectus* (Rome, 1684) (Lot 551); Hildebrandus F. Rosini, *Antiquitates Potissimum Romanae e Rosino Allisque . . . contractae notis Dempsteri* (Amsterdam, 1685) (Lot 80). An unknown work is cataloged as "Roma Vetus, Capitolii, Templorum, Amphitheatrorum, Theatrorum, Circi, &c. fig. ex Officina D. de Rubeis" (Lot 568).

10. Antoine Babuty Desgodets, *Les edifices antiques de Rome* (Paris, 1697?) (Wren's Library, Lot 547).
11. Wren's Library, Lots 401, 536, 566. Lot 28 of "Prints."
12. Ibid., Lots 109, 318, 114, 207 and 367, 145, 143, 140, 471.
13. For example, William Hacke, ed., *A collection of original voyages* (London, 1699) (Wren's Library, Lot 207) and *A collection of voyages undertaken by the Dutch East-India Company* (London, 1703).
14. *Bibliotheca Hookiana* (London, 1703), facsimile in *Sale Catalogues of Libraries of Eminent Persons*, ed. A. N. L. Munby, 12 vols. (London, Mansell with Sotheby Parke-Bernet, 1971–5), vol. 11: "Scientists" (1972), 57–116.
15. The natural histories and topographies contained in Wren's Library include: Robert Plot, *Natural History of Oxfordshire* (Oxford, 1677) and *Natural History of Staffordshire* (Oxford, 1686) (Lots 105, 106); William Dugdale, *Antiquities of Warwickshire* (London, 1656), *The History of St. Paul's Cathedral in London* (London, 1658), *Monasticon Anglicanum abridged* (London, 1693), and *Monasticon Anglicanum*, 3 vols. (1718; orig. ed. 1673) (Lots 252, 251, 254, 253); Charles Leigh, *The natural history of Lancashire*, (Oxford, 1700) (Lot 277); Aylett Sammes, *Antiquities of Great Britain*, (London, 1676) (Lot 287); John Webb, *Vindication of Stoneheng Restored* (London, 1665) (Lot 530).
16. For a general discussion of the study of natural history at the Royal Society, see Michael Hunter, *Science and Society in Restoration England* (Cambridge: Cambridge University Press, 1981): 13, 37, 91.
17. See Harris, *British Architectural Books*, 503–4, for a detailed account of the publishing history of this work.
18. J. A. Bennett, "Christopher Wren: The Natural Causes of Beauty," *Architectural History* 15 (1972): 5–8; idem, "A Study of *Parentalia* with two unpublished letters of Sir Christopher Wren," *Annals of Science* 30, no. 2 (June 1973): 130–2.
19. BL MS Add. 25,071, fol. 55v.
20. Ibid., fol. 60.
21. Ibid., fol. 55v.
22. See Bennett, "Study of *Parentalia*," 141–2, and *WS*, 19:x.
23. BL MS Add. 25,071, fol. 101.
24. *PAR*, 274.
25. Christopher Wren, Jr.–J. Ward, 14 Feb. 1739, BL MS Add. 6209, fol. 207.
26. *PAR*, 351–68.
27. Christopher Wren, Jr.–J. Ward, 17 Jan. 1740, BL MS Add. 6209, fol. 215. Bennett, "Natural Causes," 7.
28. For example, the discussion of the origin of building occurs at the end of Tract I, then reappears in the middle of Tract II.
29. BL MS Add. 25,071, fol. 101.
30. BL MS Lansdowne 698, no. 4, fol. 136v. The same catalog is found in the RIBA "Heirloom" copy of *Parentalia*.
31. *PAR*, 264–7, 283–7, 271–80. See below the excerpts from "Of *London* in ancient

Times," "Of the taking down of the vast Ruins of the *old Cathedral*," and "Of the ancient cathedral Churches of St. *Paul*."

32. Bodleian, Tanner 145, fols. 129–130v.
33. Salisbury Cathedral Library MS 192.
34. Bodleian MS Aubrey 2, fol. 72v, quoted in Michael Hunter, *John Aubrey and the Realm of Learning* (New York: Science History Publications, 1975), 64. Aubrey's *Wiltshire* MS is RS MS. 92; the report on Salisbury Cathedral appears on fol. 273.
35. In BL MS Add. 25,071, fol. 55v, Christopher Wren, Jr., states that it was printed in *History and Antiquities of the Cathedral-Church of Salisbury; and the Abbey-Church of Bath* (London: E. Curll, 1719). The letter is also printed in a later edition, Richard Rawlinson, *The History and Antiquities of the Cathedral Church of Salisbury, and the Abbey Church of Bath* (London: W. Mears and J. Hooke, 1723).
36. BL MS Add. 25,071, fol. 55v, lists "An Architectonical Account of the Cathedral Church of Salisbury."
37. Ibid., fols. 60, 66.
38. See Lawrence Weaver, "Notes on an interleaved heirloom copy of Wren's *Parentalia*," *Proceedings of the Society of Antiquaries of London*, 2d ser., 22 (17 June 1909): 524; facsimile edition of RIBA copy (Farnsborough: Gregg, 1965).
39. This copy, acquired for St. Paul's Cathedral Library in 1870, includes a manuscript on the Order of the Garter written in 1631 by Matthew Wren. Kerry Downes and J. A. Bennett, *Sir Christopher Wren*, exh. cat., Whitechapel Art Gallery (London: Trefoil Books, 1982), 43.
40. See Weaver, "Notes."
41. Scientific papers include a deaf and dumb language, weather clock, anatomy of a river eel, rising of sap in trees, and solution to the problem of the ellipse – the last two in the hand of a copyist.
42. Also the dedication plate, endpaper, and small illustration of the facade of St. Paul's.
43. On Flitcroft, see *DBA*; John Summerson, *Architecture in Britain 1530–1830* (New Haven, CT: Yale University Press, 1993), 337; and *WS*, 19:121, n. 2. On Vandergucht, see *Bryan's Dictionary of Painters and Engravers*, ed. George C. Williamson, 5 vols. (New York: Macmillan, 1905).
44. BL Royal Kings MS 283. Perhaps his work for the *Parentalia* inspired Flitcroft to make the other reconstructions found in his manuscript, imitating the buildings selected by Palladio in *I Quattro Libri*, and to combine them with his other drawings of the orders and his own designs for a projected treatise on architecture.
45. No original drawings of the Sheldonian Theater exist. *WS*, 19:91. The RIBA copy has three windows drawn in ink and pasted on this engraving, of unknown origin.
46. *Bryan's Dictionary*, 3:393.
47. Wren, "Tract IV," 184–5, 187.
48. Kerry Downes, *Hawksmoor* (London: Zwemmer, 1959), 21, 284 item 555. See also Lawrence Weaver, "Memorials of Wren," *Architectural Review* 26, no. 155 (Oct. 1909): 175–83, where he compares these sketches to the 1893 rendering by J. E. Goodchild, a pupil of C. R. Cockerell, supposedly based on sketches by Wren.
49. AS IV. 61–4. See Downes, *Hawksmoor*, 278, item 152–5.
50. Harris, *British Architectural Books*, 188–90. See Bernard Adams, *London Illustrated 1604–1851* (London: Library Association, 1983), 96–104, where he describes the derivation of this book from William Maitland's *History of London* (1756).
51. For example, the following views: choir of St. Paul's, from Henry Overton, *Prospects*

(c. 1720–30); Westminster Abbey, from William Maitland, *History of London* (1739 and 1756); Chapel of Henry VIII, from Robert West and William H. Toms, *Perspective Views of All the Ancient Churches* (London, 1739); St. Clements in the Strand, from John Maurer, *Nine London Views* (1752); St. Mary-le-Bow, from *Nouveau théâtre de la Grande Bretagne* (London, 1724–9); St. Stephen Walbrook, from John Boydell, *A Collection of One Hundred Views in England and Wales* (London, 1770); and Winchester Palace, from Samuel and Nathaniel Buck, *Buck's Antiquities* (1726–52). See Adams, *London*.

52. See Downes, *Architecture*, 20. These engravings of St. Paul's and other buildings were possibly made as the basis for a complete edition of Wren's work (see *WS*, 14:xii and *Walpole Society* 22 [1934]: 136); reprinted in *WS*, 14, pls. 2–4.
53. E.g., in BL Map Library, Kings Top. 21.59 (view of London), 29.14-kl (Hampton Court), and 43.39.h (Salisbury Cathedral).
54. See Adams, *London*, xvii.
55. Lucy Phillimore, *Sir Christopher Wren: His family and times* (London, 1881), 340–1.
56. They follow after page 351.

    Engraving of ruins in landscape, source unknown.
    Elevation and plan of five orders, source unknown.
    View of ruins of Palmyra, from *A New Geographical Dictionary*, 2 vols. (London, 1759–60).
    Perspective of Noah's Ark, with three details, source unknown.
    View of Tower of Babel under construction, source unknown.
    Two views of pyramids of Egypt and perspective of Absalom's Tomb, from Cornelius de Bruyn (Le Brun), *Voyage au Levant* (Delft, 1700; London, 1702).
    Plan of Temple of Solomon, source unknown.
    View of Babylon, possibly from E. Sale, G. Psalmanazar, A. Bower, G. Shelvoche, J. Campbell, J. Swinton, et al., *An Universal History: From the earliest account of time to the present* (Dublin, 1744).

57. E.g., Hans Reuther, "Das Modell des Salomnischen Tempels im Museum für Hamburgische Geschichte," *Niederdeutsche Beitrage zur Kunstgeschichte* 9 (1980): 180.

CHAPTER 1. NOTES ON THE ANTIQUITIES OF LONDON

Introduction

1. *PAR*, 264–7.
2. *PAR*, 285–6.
3. For example, at Winchester, while building the palace there, Wren discovered mosaic tesserae, coins, and the hearth from a Roman bath. See Aubrey, *MB*, 2:942, 978, and 25 January 1688, *JBO*, 7.
4. *JBO*, 9.
5. This work appeared separately and in Thomas Hearne's edition of Leland's *Itineraries*. Joseph M. Levine, *Dr. Woodward's Shield: History, Science, and Satire in Augustan England* (Berkeley: University of California Press, 1977), 144.
6. John Woodward, *An account of some Roman Urns and other Antiquities lately digg'd up near Bishopsgate* (London, 1713), 13–14. Letter to Wren, i–xii.
7. John Strype, "Of divers Roman and other antique curiosities found in London,

before and since the great fire," in John Stow, *A Survey of the Cities of London and Westminster*, ed. John Strype, 2 vols. (London, 1720), 2, appendix, 21. See also Levine, *Dr. Woodward's Shield*, 93, 102; Arthur MacGregor, "Collectors and collections of rarities in the sixteenth and seventeenth centuries," in *Tradescant's Rarities*, ed. A. MacGregor (Oxford: Clarendon, 1983), 86–7.

8. Nehemiah Grew, *Musaeum Regalis Societatis or a Catalogue and Description of the Natural and Artificial Rarities belonging to the Royal Society* (London, 1681).
9. John Bagford, "A Letter to the Publisher, written by the ingenious Mr. John Bagford, in which are many curious Remarks relating to the City of London, and some things about Leland," John Leland, *Collecteana*, ed. Thomas Hearne (Oxford: At the Theatre, 1715), 1:lx.
10. Aubrey, *MB*, 1:500.
11. Also material from Wren in John Aubrey's *A Perambulation of Surrey*, Bodleian MS Aubrey 4.
12. Michael Hunter, *John Aubrey and the Realm of Learning* (New York: Science History Publications, 1975), 76–7.
13. Bagford, "Letter," lxiii.
14. Aubrey, *MB*, 1:511.
15. BL MS Sloane 958, fols. 105–9. Reproduced in part in *The Victoria History of London*, ed. William Page (London: Constable, 1909), 124.
16. Bagford, "Letter," lviii–lxxxvi. See Donald Grayson, *The Establishment of Human Antiquity* (New York: Academic Press, 1983), 7, and Levine, *Dr. Woodward's Shield*, 139–40.
17. Strype, "Of divers Roman and other antique curiosities," in Stow, *Survey* 2: Appendix, 21–4. See Levine, *Dr. Woodward's Shield*, 139, and John J. Morrison, "Strype's Stow: The 1720 Edition of 'A Survey of London,'" *London Journal* 3, no. 1 (May 1977): 40–54.
18. See Hunter, *John Aubrey*, 148–208. See also Michael Hunter, "The Royal Society and the Origin of British Archaeology," *Antiquity* 65 (1971): 113–21, 187–92.

"Of *London* in ancient Times"

1. Julius Caesar unsuccessfully invaded Great Britain in 55 and 54 B.C.
2. Tacitus, *Agricola* 13 (Cambridge, MA: Harvard University Press, Loeb Classical Library, 1953): "It was, in fact, Julius of happy memory who first of all Romans entered Britain with an army: he overawed the natives by a successful battle and made himself master of the coast; but it may be supposed that he rather discovered the island for his descendants than bequeathed it to them."
3. Lucan, 2.572 (Cambridge, MA: Harvard University Press, Loeb Classical Library, 1977): "... turned his back in panic to the Britons whom he had gone out of his way to attack."
4. One of the many fanciful etymologies proposed for the name *London* during this period. William Camden, for example, also suggested the meaning of "*Ships*, call'd by the British *Lhong*; so that *London* is as much as a *Harbour* or *City of Ships*." William Camden, *Britannia*, ed. Edmund Gibson (London, 1695), 311.
5. Claudius, reigned A.D. 41–54.
6. Nero, reigned A.D. 54–68.
7. Wren was made Surveyor of His Majesty's Works on 28 March 1669.

8. Located on Cheapside at Bow Lane. Construction began in 1671.
9. Wren's find was recorded by John Aubrey: "they knew it to be the Roman way by the gravel mixed with Roman brick-bats, and potsherds, and baked earth such as urns" (Aubrey, *MB*, 1:498). Wren's discovery was indeed of the major Roman street running east–west, in place apparently since the beginning of Roman settlement in the area. On the east it began at the western end of Fenchurch Street, ran along Lombard Street, and continued in a straight line that ended at the western end of Cheapside and Newgate Street. Peter Marsden, *Roman London* (London: Thames and Hudson, 1980), 9, 15, 18, 20. Ralph Merrifield, *London: City of the Romans* (London: Batsford, 1983), 42 and fig. 4.
10. The Via Appia was the wide, for the most part straight, military road from Rome to Capua. It was begun by Appius Claudius in 312 B.C. and extended farther south during the next century. See G. Lugli, *La tecnica edilizia romana con particulare riguardo a Roma e Lazio*, 2 vols. (Rome, 1957), 158ff. Christopher Jr.'s source is Bernard Montfaucon, *L'Antiquité expliquée et representée en figures*, 5 vols., 5-vol. supplement (Paris, 1719, 1724); English ed. *Antiquity explained, and represented in sculptures*, trans. D. Humphreys, 5 vols., 5-vol. supplement (London, 1721–5). The discussion of the Via Appia is in volume 5, part 2, book 1, chap. 1, paras. 2 and 3, pp. 113–14 (French ed.) or 178–9 (English ed.).
11. Remains of a second east–west road have been found along the western end of Eastcheap, continuing along Cannon Street to St. Swithin's Lane (Merrifield, *London*, 42–3). Recent archaeologists have not found sufficient evidence that it continued to the west along Watling Street, although remains of roads were discovered twice during the nineteenth century. See Royal Commission on Historical Monuments, *Roman London*, vol. 3 of *An Inventory of the Historical Monuments in London* (London: His Majesty's Stationery Office, 1928), 49, 145. Wren seems to have believed that Watling Street in the City of London was a segment of the great highway named Watling Street that ran through northern Kent. Beginning at the invasion port of Richborough, it ran south of the Thames and, evidence shows, bypassed London to make its crossing at Westminster (Marsden, 14–15; Merrifield, *London*, 28–32).
12. A river wall was built to make a complete circuit of fortifications around the city during the fourth century. It must have had gates to allow access to the river, but no evidence indicates the existence of one at Dowgate Hill. See Merrifield, *London*, 216–18.
13. St. Lawrence Jewry on Gresham Street near Aldermanbury. Construction occurred 1670–81. The bog that Wren came upon was probably part of the ancient streambed of Walbrook, which flowed into the river Thames. Ralph Merrifield, *The Roman City of London* (London: Ernest Benn, 1965), 228.
14. "Francerius": this personage is unknown. The mayor of London in 1414 was Thomas Fawconer. See Joseph Haydn, *The Book of Dignities*, 3d ed. (Baltimore: Genealogical Publishing, 1970), 489.
15. John Aubrey recorded in 1673 that London Stone was much reduced in height after burning in the Great Fire and was removed by Wren and Hooke with great difficulty due to its wide and deep (about ten feet) foundation of hard stone and mortar. Aubrey, *MB*, 1:508. The stone was located (inconveniently obstructing traffic) in the roadway of Cannon Street near Bush Lane until 1742, when its top was removed and placed in the south wall of St. Swithin's in Cannon Street. After the church was bombed during World War II, the stone was built into the wall of the bank that

replaced it. Made of Clipsham limestone, it had been regarded since at least the Middle Ages as a milestone equivalent to the Roman Milliarium Aureum, marking the heart of the city. Although its purpose is unknown, recent discoveries show, as Wren had conjectured, that it was an important monument within a complex of buildings located to the south. The stone stood on a direct axis with the palace, not with the forum that stood to the northeast, probably on center with a gateway fronting the Roman street. Marsden, 91–2; Merrifield, *London*, 75–7; and Fig. 11.

16. Augustus erected the Milliarium Aureum, a gilded bronze column, in Rome in 29 B.C. on the west side of the Forum. It recorded the distances between the gates of Rome and the postal stations located along the main roads radiating out from the capital. Rodolfo Lanciani, *The Ruins and Excavations of Ancient Rome* (New York: Benjamin Blom, 1967; orig. 1897), 280.
17. John Aubrey recorded these finds of mosaics of brick, marble, and flint, and, in the foundation, Roman mortar and bricks, based on information from Robert Hooke (Aubrey, *MB*, 1:500, 508; see also Aubrey, *MB*, 2:938). According to Aubrey, a piece was deposited at the Royal Society.
18. The Milion was a triumphal arch or domed tetrapylon that stood at the eastern end of the Mese in Constantinople, in front of Hagia Sophia on Augustaion square. It served as the initial milestone of the Byzantine Empire. (*The Oxford Dictionary of Byzantium* [New York: Oxford University Press], 1991.) See also Rodolphe Guilland, *Etudes de Topographie de Constantinople Byzantine*, 2 vols. (Berlin: Akademie, 1969), 2: 28–31; Wolfgang Müller-Wiener, *Bildlexikon zur Topographie Istanbuls* (Tübingen: Wasmuth, 1977), 216–18.

    The Milion is also described by various medieval writers, including:

    Georgius Cedrenus (after 1057), *Compendium historiarum*, in *Patrologia Graeca*, ed. J.-P. Migne (Paris, 1844–66), vol. 121, entry 564 (p. 614). "Supra miliarii fornicem duæ sunt statuæ, magni Constantini et matris ejus, et in harum medio crux. A tergo earum Trajanus eques, et juxta hunc Ælius Adrianus eques."

    "Suidas," that is, the lexicon entitled *Souda*, c. 1000. See *Suidae Lexicon*, ed. A. Adler, 5 vols. (Leipzig, 1928–38), under "μιλιον."
19. Wren is incorrect. The fort, built during the late first and early second centuries, was located farther north at Cripplegate. See Marsden, 83–7, and Merrifield, *London*, 77–83.
20. A Roman tombstone found on the site of St. Martin's Ludgate on 4 June 1669, according to John Aubrey. Aubrey sketched the monument, measured it (six feet high and two and a half feet wide), and transcribed the inscription of the dedication (see Aubrey, *MB*, 1:516). The stone remains at the Ashmolean Museum in Oxford, according to the editors of Aubrey, *MB*, 1:516. It has been dated as later than 197; see Merrifield, *London*, 176, and Julian Munby, "Art, Archaeology and Antiquaries," *Roman Life and Art in Britain*, pt. 2, ed. J. Munby and M. Henig, British Archaeological Report 41 (Oxford, 1977), 418. The monument is recorded in *Victoria History of London*, 27, 113–14; Royal Commission on Historical Monuments, *Roman London*, 173, fig. 76, pl. 60; R. G. Collingwood and R. P. Wright, *The Roman Inscriptions of Britain* (Oxford, 1965), 1:17.
21. As MS 313 reads "Marina."
22. William Camden, *Britannia*, ed. Edmund Gibson, 2d ed., 2 vols. (London: Churchill, 1722), 1:375.
23. "Dis Manibus Vivio Marciano [?] Legio Secunda Augusta. Ianvaria Martiana Coniunx

Pientissima Posuit Memoriam [To the spirits of the departed Vivius Marcianus (Centurion?) Second Legion Augusta. Januaria Martiana wife most devoted erected this memorial]." Translated in Aubrey, *MB*, 1:516.
24. The section in *Parentalia*, containing Wren's "Report on Westminster Abbey," which includes a discussion of whether a Temple of Diana was originally on the site of St. Paul's (81).
25. "in Vallo": within the fortification.
   "extra Portas in Pomærio": outside the gate in the pomerium (unbuilt space on either side of the city walls).
26. AS MS 313 and RS MS 249 read "therefore."
27. On the site of the new St. Paul's. Foundations begun in 1674.
28. According to William Camden (1551–1623) (*Britannia*, 1586, with subsequent enlarged editions in 1587, 1590, 1594, 1600, 1607, 1610, and 1695) ox heads were found on the site during the time of Edward I. Because oxen had been sacred to the goddess Diana, he conjectured that these skulls were the remains of the Taurobolia celebrated in her honor and thereby confirmed the tradition that a temple dedicated to this goddess had once stood on the site. Further evidence was provided by the church records calling the old buildings in this area the *Camera Dianae* and by the ceremony carried out in St. Paul's involving a stag's head fixed on the end of a spear. However, according to Plot, in his additions to the 1695 edition, only "teeth of *Boars* and of other beasts, a piece of *Buck*'s horn" were found there. Moreover, the *Camera Dianae* actually stood at some distance from the church (see Camden, *Britannia* [1695], 314, 330–1). Wren's "Of the taking down of the vast Ruins of the *Old Cathedral*" also states that no such remains were found in excavations for the new cathedral, see p. 32 and note 6, see also his "Report on Westminster Abbey," 81.
   The problem of a Temple of Diana on the site of St. Paul's continued to occupy antiquaries after Camden, including Stow (1598), Stillingfleet (1704), Bagford (1715), Woodward (1713), and Strype (1720). See Levine, *Dr. Woodward's Shield*.
29. One of the smaller of these pins was preserved by Ralph Thoresby (1658–1725), a Leeds merchant, in his museum. See Ralph Thoresby, *Ducatus Leodiensis, or the Topography of the Ancient and Populous Town and Parish of Leeds* (London, 1715), 563.
30. These burial remains at St. Paul's are confirmed by John Conyers, a London apothecary, in his manuscript dated 20 August 1675, BL MS Sloane 958, fols. 105–9. He describes these and numerous other discoveries that were made on the northeast side of the cathedral. Archaeologists believe there was a cemetery at this location dating from the late first century A.D. (Marsden, 24, 46).
31. John Conyers also reported the discovery of this red pottery. See n. 30.
32. The latter pottery lamp is recorded only in an illustration "reproduced from an old drawing" (of unknown origin or location) in *Victoria History of London*, 25, fig. 9.
33. "patera": "a broad, flat dish or saucer used by the Romans for drinking or for offering libations." Oskar Seyffert, *A Dictionary of Classical Antiquities* (London: George Allen, 1957).
34. Remains of burials had been discovered in Spitalfields since the time of John Stow, who recorded them in his *Survey of London* (1598). The so-called Spitalfields urn, actually discovered by John Conyers, was presented to the Royal Society by Wren on 22 August 1678. See Birch, 3:430, and 4:279, and Nehemiah Grew, *Museum Regalis Societatis* (London, 1681), 380. It was drawn by John Aubrey in his *Monumenta*

Britannica and described as "a white glass urn, of an oriental pearl colour. It is about the thickness of a half-crown: and not much thicker: it had only one ear, which was broken accidentally by the pickaxe. The height is eight inches: and the breadth is ten inches. It had in it ashes, which is now lost." See Aubrey, *MB*, 1:511, and 2: 668, 776.

Excerpt from "Of the taking down of the vast Ruins of the *old Cathedral*"

1. See "Of *London* in ancient Times."
2. John Aubrey recorded Wren's hypothesis that the banks of the Thames were built by the Romans. Aubrey, *MB*, 2:1028.
3. This is the only known reference to substantial repairs of the Thames embankment made by Wren.
4. These discoveries of pottery as well as a kiln were recorded by John Conyers in his manuscript dated 20 August 1675, BL MS Sloane 958, fols. 105–9. See discussion on p. 20.
5. See previous note.
6. The early editions, 1598, 1603, 1618, and 1633 of Stow, *Survey of London*, do not include this discussion. It appears only in the additions made by John Strype in the 1720 edition, vol. 1, book 2, chap. 8, p. 141. For Camden and related discussion, see above, "Of *London* in ancient Times," 27 and n. 28 and "Report on Westminster Abbey," 81.
7. Wren apparently made studies of London Bridge, built during the late twelfth century, that do not survive but were known to Nicholas Hawksmoor. In his *A Short Historical Account of London Bridge* (London: J. Wilcox, 1736), 8, he wrote that Wren believed "that every Pier was set upon Piles of Wood, which were drove as far as might be under low Water-mark, on which were laid Planks of Timber, and upon them the Foundation of the Stone Piers." Wren's hypothesis has been shown to be correct. See Gordon Home, *Old London Bridge* (London: John Lane, 1931), 34–6; see also Harris, *British Architectural Books*, 232.

CHAPTER 2. NOTES AND REPORTS ON GOTHIC CHURCHES

Introduction

1. "There is scarce any Gothick Cathedral, that I have seen at home or abroad . . . ," Wren, "Report on Salisbury Cathedral," p. 68. Wren's only trip abroad was to Paris in 1665–6.
2. *PAR*, 271–4. Not in BL MS Add. 25,071; in RS MS 249 and AS MS 313.
3. Kerry Downes, *The Architecture of Wren* (New York: Universe, 1982) 68.
4. See ibid., 6 and 48–9, on events concerning St. Paul's.
5. Jane Lang, *Rebuilding of St. Paul's after the Great Fire of London* (London: Oxford University Press, 1956), 6–10, and *WS*, 13:13.
6. See *WS*, 13:13–14 and 14–15.
7. *PAR*, part 2, sec. 3, 274–7; Christopher Wren–William Sancroft, 7 May 1666, Bodleian, Tanner 145, no. 115, reprinted in *WS*, 13:44; Downes, *Architecture*, 46.

8. Bodleian, Tanner 145, fols. 110–12, with reports by other commissioners; reprinted in *WS*, 13:15–17.
9. Christopher Wren–William Sancroft, 5 August 1666, Bodleian, Tanner 145, no. 117, reprinted in *WS*, 13:45. The drawings are AS II. 4, 6, 7.
10. Bodleian, Tanner 145, 112–13, reprinted in *WS* 13:18.
11. *The Diary of John Evelyn*, ed. E. S. De Beer, 6 vols. (Oxford: Clarendon, 1955), 3: 448–9, reprinted in *WS*, 13:19.
12. Bodleian, Tanner 145, fols. 129r–130v.
13. Salisbury Cathedral Library MS 192.
14. Francis Price, *A Series of particular and useful Observations, made with great Diligence and Care, upon that Admirable Structure, the Cathedral-Church of Salisbury* (London: Ackers, 1753).
15. See Tim Tatton-Brown, "Building the tower and spire of Salisbury Cathedral," *Antiquity* 65 (March 1991): 74–96; by the same author, "The Archaeology of the Spire of Salisbury Cathedral," in *Medieval Art and Architecture at Salisbury Cathedral*, ed. L. Keen and T. Cocke, *The British Archaeological Association Conference Transactions* 17 (1996): 59–67; and John Reeves, Gavin Simpson, and Peter Spencer, "Iron Reinforcement of the Tower and Spire of Salisbury Cathedral," *Archaeological Journal* 149 (1992): 380–406. See also Royal Commission on the Historical Monuments of England (with Thomas Cocke and Peter Kidson), *Salisbury Cathedral; Perspectives on the Architectural History* (London: The Stationery Office, 1993).
16. Hooke was Surveyor from 1691 to 1698, consulting on repairs of the choir as early as 1676, and in 1693 he investigated repairs to the exterior. See Hooke, *Diary 1672–80*, 18 July, 21 August, and 8–10 October 1676, cited in *DBA*.
17. This section was used by Christopher Jr. in pt. 2, sec. 8 of *Parentalia*, pp. 306–7. Despite his statement in this section that Wren's surveys of Gothic churches "induced the *Surveyor* to make some Enquiry into the rise and Progress of this Gothick Mode," the rest of the text (from the end of p. 306 up to the end of p. 307, where a reprint of Evelyn's "Account" begins) describing the organization of the freemasons, construction, and the elements of the style, are not specifically given as Wren's ideas, and are probably Christopher Jr.'s own opinions.
18. Downes, *Architecture*, 17. Wren's facade was replaced during the 1880s.
19. John Evelyn, "Account of Architects and Architecture," in Roland Fréart de Chambray, *A Parallel of the Antient Architecture with the Modern*, ed. John Evelyn, 2d ed. (London, 1707).
20. Alberti, *DRA*, 6, 1, 154: "Anyone who happens to build nowadays draws his inspiration from inept modern nonsense rather than proven and much recommended methods."
21. Bodleian MS Top. Gen. c. 25, fols. 150–79. See Howard M. Colvin, "Aubrey's *Chronologia Architectonica*," in *Concerning Architecture*, ed. J. Summerson (London: Allen Lane, 1968), 1–27.

Excerpt from "Of the ancient cathedral Churches of St. Paul"

1. Edward Stillingfleet, *Origines Britannicae, or, the Antiquities of the British Churches* (London: Flesher, 1685), chap. 1, "Of the first Planting a Christian Church in *Britain* by St. *Paul*," 1–48.
2. The legend of Saint Joseph of Arimathea, fabricated by the monks of Glastonbury

after 1184, told how he came to England in A.D. 63 and with his disciples converted the entire country. He also built the first church at Glastonbury and was later buried there. See T. D. Kendrick, *British Antiquity* (London: Methuen, 1950).
3. The next six paragraphs paraphrase the text of Paul de Rapin-Thoyras, *The History of England . . . Done into English with additional notes . . . by N. Tindal*, 2d ed., 5 vols. (London: Knapton, 1732), vol. 1, bk. 1, pp. 28–9 (1st ed., 15 vols., London, 1725–31).
4. Apostle Paul (died A.D. 67?).
5. Venantius Fortunatus (530/40?–early 600s), *Vita Sancti Martini*: "And he crossed the ocean, even where the island created a harbor, / And those lands which Britain holds and Thule furthest removed."
6. The Council of Nicaea of 325.
7. Restitutus, bishop of London, attended the Council of Arles in 314. Wren is mistaken about the date of the Council of Arles: the first was in 314, the second in 353. *The Catholic Encyclopedia*, 15 vols. (New York: Encyclopedia Press, 1914).
8. This reference to Louis Ellies-Dupin (1657–1719), *Nouvelle bibliothèque des auteurs ecclésiastiques*, 12 vols. (Paris, 1688–98), is made in Rapin's *History of England*. See the English edition, *A New History of Ecclesiastical Writers*, 10 vols. in 4 (London, 1692–3), 2:263.
9. The fort was not located near the site of St. Paul's. See "Of *London* in ancient Times," 26 and n. 19.
10. Diocletian, reigned 284–305.
11. Constantine, reigned 306–337.
12. Mellitus (d. 624), first bishop of London (from 604) and third archbishop of Canterbury. Ethelbert (552? – 616), king of Kent (*DNB*). According to Bede, the Saxon church was begun in 604. See Nikolaus Pevsner and Priscilla Metcalf, *The Cathedrals of England: Southern England* (Harmondsworth, Middlesex: Penguin, 1985), 126.
13. The fire took place in 1087. Pevsner and Metcalf, *Cathedrals: Southern England*, 126.
14. Mauritius, or Maurice, bishop of London from 1085 to 1108 (*Catholic Encyclopedia*).
15. William I, called William the Conquerer, reigned 1066–87.
16. This information on the "Palatine Tower" comes from William Dugdale, who writes that it was a "strong castle" that stood on the western end of the City by Fleet Ditch. After it was burned in the fire, its stones were used to rebuild St. Paul's and on its site was built the Dominican abbey of Blackfriars. William Dugdale (1605–86), *The History of St. Paul's Cathedral in London, from its Foundations until these Times* (London, 1658), 6 (2d enlarged ed. 1716).
17. That is, Early Christian churches.
18. Construction on this Norman fabric was slow, beginning in 1087 and continuing into the twelfth century. In 1136 a fire damaged the structure, and around 1175 funds were still being solicited for the building works. The church had a Latin-cross plan, with a nave of twelve bays and transepts of five bays, each with aisles. This portion of Old St. Paul's existed until the Great Fire, although it was recased by Inigo Jones from 1633. Hollar's engravings of it in Dugdale's *St. Paul's*, 1658, appear to be accurate (Pevsner and Metcalf, *Cathedrals: Southern England*, 126). The form of the choir, which was taken down for the first lengthening of the church in 1221, is unknown. Wren's hypothesis that it terminated in an apse is highly plausible. A. W. Clapham, *English Romanesque Architecture*, 2 vols. (Oxford: Clarendon, 1934), 2:32.
19. That is, pointed arches.

20. RS MS 249 and AS MS 313 read "Presbytery."
21. The cathedral was lengthened twice during the thirteenth century, the first time beginning around 1221, the second beginning in 1256 (Pevsner and Metcalf, *Cathedrals: Southern England*, 126). The text that follows indicates that Wren was aware of this. The form of the choir is recorded by Hollar, but his illustration is not completely accurate (see ibid., 128).
22. See "Of *London* in ancient Times," 23 and n. 11.
23. The passage "(then Watling Street) . . . and this Street" does not in AS MS 313.
24. RS MS 249 reads "Presbytery."
25. Wren's description provides the only existing evidence that the western end of the late eleventh-, early twelfth-century nave was a later addition (Clapham, *English Romanesque Architecture*, 2:32).
26. Dugdale, *St. Paul's* (1658), 6–7; (1716), 7.
27. AS MS 313 and RS MS 249 read "said."
28. Richard de Ely (Fitzneale), bishop of London from 1189 to 1198 (*Catholic Encyclopedia*). Wren is incorrect in his time frame for the first lengthening of the cathedral, which actually took place around 1221. The choir was consecrated in 1241. Pevsner and Metcalf, *Cathedrals: Southern England*, 126.
29. Richard the Lion-Hearted, son of Henry II, reigned 1189–99.
30. Henry II, reigned 1154–89.
31. This reference to Francis Godwin, *De Præsulibus Angliae Commentarius: omnium episcoporum, necnon et cardinalium eiusdem gentis, nomina, etc.*, 3 pts. (London, 1616; 2d ed. 1743), is taken from Dugdale's *St. Paul's* (1658), 6–7; (1716), 7.
32. See Dugdale, *St. Paul's* (1658), 10–11; (1716), 12.
33. Fifth year of the reign of Henry III, who reigned 1216–72.
34. Wren is incorrect. The second lengthening took place from 1256. The twelfth-century crossing tower was given a new spire from 1315. Pevsner and Metcalf, *Cathedrals: Southern England*, 126.
35. The Chapel of St. Faith was placed in the crypt of the church after the second lengthening of 1256 (ibid., 126).
36. Charles II, reigned 1660–85.
37. Inigo Jones (1573–1652) worked on the restoration of St. Paul's 1633–42. See John Summerson, *Inigo Jones* (Harmondsworth, Middlesex: Penguin, 1966), 97–106, and Vaughan Hart, "Inigo Jones's Site Organization at St. Paul's Cathedral: 'Ponderous Masses Beheld Hanging in the Air,'" *Journal of the Society of Architectural Historians* 53, no. 4 (December 1994): 414–27.
38. Seventh year of the reign of Charles I, reigned 1625–49.
39. The next in quotations is a loose paraphrasing of the material in the second edition of Dugdale's *St. Paul's* (1716), 146–8.
40. The passage "enlarging it . . . into the *Quire*" does not appear in AS MS 313.
41. A loose paraphrasing of material found in the second edition of Dugdale's *St. Paul's* (1716), 149.
42. See "Report on Old St. Paul's before the Fire."
43. Wren is discussing the Norman nave and chancel of the original fabric, built during the late eleventh and early twelfth century. See Pevsner and Metcalf, *Cathedrals: Southern England*, 126–8, who find Hollar's illustration of this part of the church to be accurate.
44. The new cloister and chapter house were added in the 1330s. Ibid., 126, 128–9.

45. The twelfth-century tower was given a new tall needle-spire in 1315. Ibid., 126.
46. John Stow (1525–1605), *Survey of London* (London, 1598), 264.
47. William Camden (1551–1623), *Britannia*, ed. Edmund Gibson (London, 1695), 314.
48. Dugdale, *St. Paul's* (1658), 16; (1716), 17. Dugdale makes the reference to the manuscript at Cambridge, now unknown, which records the inscription on the brass tablet that hung in the church. Plot, in his additions to Gibson's edition of Camden's *Britannia*, discusses the measures recorded on the tablet and mentions the manuscript, but his information appears to come from Dugdale.
49. William Camden, *Britannia*, ed. Edmund Gibson (London, 1695), 329; (2d ed., 1722), 378. Originally published by Camden in 1586, with subsequent enlarged editions in 1587, 1590, 1594, 1600, 1607, and 1610. Gibson's edition included additions to Middlesex made by Robert Plot. The comments by Plot (not Gibson) on the height of the spire occur on p. 329.
50. Followed by Wren's "Report on Old St. Paul's before the Fire."

Report on Old St. Paul's before the Fire

1. The members of the Commission for the Repairs of Old St. Paul's.
2. This condition is comparable to what Wren describes in "Report on Westminster Abbey," 87–8, and Fig. 27 and "Report on Salisbury Cathedral," 68.
3. The recasing of the exterior of the nave and transept was carried out by Inigo Jones from 1633 to 1642. See "Of the ancient cathedral Churches of St. Paul," 42 and n. 37.
4. On 4 June 1561. Dugdale, *St. Paul's* (1658), 133; (1716), 135.
5. These drawings were "with a great deal of paines finished" on 5 August 1666. Wren–Sancroft, 5 August 1666, Bodleian, Tanner 145, no. 117, reprinted in *WS*, 13:45.
6. A reference to Wren's 1665/6 trip to Paris. See Chap. 3.

Report on Old St. Paul's after the Fire

1. That is, 26 February 1667.
2. "Argo navis": the ship *Argo* that Jason sailed in search of the Golden Fleece. Martial, *Epigrams* 7. 19: "What you take for a paltry fragment, a useless piece of lumber, was the first keel to sail the unknown sea" (London: W. Heinemann, Loeb Classical Library, 1993).
3. Followed by "at first" deleted.
4. Wren's "Report on Old St. Paul's before the Fire."
5. Altered from "king."
6. Altered from "with."
7. The fire of 4 June 1561 during the reign of Elizabeth I (reigned 1558–1603).
8. Inigo Jones (1573–1652). See "Of the ancient cathedral Churches of St. Paul," 42 and n. 37.
9. Several words on fol. 129v are cut off by the edge of the page.
10. Possibly altered from "hathe."
11. Followed by "& then" deleted.
12. Possibly altered from "hath."
13. The Chapel of St. Faith was located in the crypt of the choir.
14. Followed by "& pillars" deleted.
15. Followed by an illegible deletion.

16. Followed by an illegible deletion.
17. Replacing "rowe" deleted.
18. Followed by "cheaper" deleted.
19. Followed by "&" deleted.
20. Altered from "century."
21. Replacing "a temporary" deleted.
22. 26 February 1667.
23. John Davenport was Master Carpenter at the Office of the Works from 21 July 1660 until his death in 1668, when he was succeeded by Richard Ryder (from 27 April 1668 to his death in 1683). Joshua Marshall and John Young were both master masons employed at the works at this time, Marshall becoming Master Mason on 2 October 1673 (until his death in April 1678). See *The History of the King's Works,* vol. 5, *1660–1782,* ed. H. M. Colvin (London: Her Majesty's Stationery Office, 1976).

Report on Salisbury Cathedral

1. William Dodsworth (1760–1826) was verger of the cathedral from 1777 to 1826. He wrote *A Guide to the Cathedral Church of Salisbury* (1792) and *An Historical Account of the Episcopal See and Cathedral of Sarum, or Salisbury* (1814). See S. Eward, "William Dodsworth," *Salisbury Cathedral Friends' Magazine (1984):* 17–22.
2. The only clerk who may possibly be "T. A." is a Mr. Atkinson who resigned in 1811. The numbers are a calculation of the years, 166, between the date Wren wrote his report and 1834.
3. Versions in *PAR, RS,* and *AS* start here.
4. Followed by illegible deletion.
5. For the complex chronology of building at Salisbury Cathedral, beginning in 1220, and the possible architects involved, see Pamela Z. Blum, "The Sequence of the Building Campaigns at Salisbury," *Art Bulletin* 73, no. 1 (March 1991): 6–38, who cites additional important sources.
6. Lower right-hand corner of fol. 3 is damaged.
7. Followed by "which" deleted.
8. Several words on fol. 3v are cut off by the edge of the page.
9. The lower edge of fol. 3v is damaged.
10. Followed by "bigger" deleted.
11. Followed by illegible deletion.
12. Followed by "and the fastning" deleted.
13. Followed by "much" deleted.
14. On the iron reinforcement at Salisbury from medieval times and as proposed by Wren later in this report, see John Reeves, Gavin Simpson, and Peter Spencer, "Iron Reinforcement of the Tower and Spire of Salisbury Cathedral," *Archaeological Journal* 149 (1992): 380–406.
15. Followed by illegible deletion.
16. The description that follows is comparable to Wren's discussion in "Report on Westminster Abbey," 87–8 and Fig. 27 and to his discussion in "Report on Old St. Paul's before the Fire," 49.
17. Replacing "of" deleted.
18. Wren traveled abroad only to Paris, in 1665/6. See Chap. 3.
19. Cut off by edge of page.

20. RS, AS, and *PAR* reprint end here.
21. Followed by "arising" deleted.
22. Followed by "decele" deleted.
23. "Chargeable": "Burdensome (as a tax or payment; costly, expensive)" (*OED*).
24. Followed by "crakes" deleted.
25. Followed by "together" deleted.
26. "Frushed": "liable to break; brittle, dry, fragile," or "to break, snap; to break or become broken under pressure; to become crushed" (*OED*); Inigo Jones, *The Most Notable Antiquity of Great Britain, Called Stone-Heng, ... Restored*, ed. John Webb (London, 1655): "Timber-Work ... to keep the Arras from frushing."
27. Followed by illegible deletion.
28. Abbreviated in Wren's original manuscript.
29. Followed by illegible deletion.
30. Replacing "must" deleted.
31. "Arace-wise," that is "arris-wise": "so as to present a sharp edge, diagonally, ridgewise" (*OED*). These flying buttresses, rising diagonally, do not appear in the drawings or descriptions of William Dugdale, *Monasticon Anglicanum* (1673), vol. 3, or of Francis Price, *A Series of particular and useful Observations ... upon that Admirable Structure, the Cathedral-Church of Salisbury* (London: Akers, 1753). The earliest visual record appears to be that of John Britton in his *The History and Antiquities of the Cathedral Church of Salisbury* (London, 1814), pl. 8 and 22.
32. Cut off by edge of page.
33. No asterisks are found in the manuscript.
34. "Yote": "To fasten in (a metal bar, a stone block, etc.) with lead; to 'lead in' " (*OED*).
35. "In his own hand."

Report on Westminster Abbey

1. Francis Atterbury (1662–1732), from 1713 bishop of Rochester and dean of Westminster.
2. See *DBA*.
3. The date given in *Parentalia*, in the heading: "Another eminent Work, in a different Style of Architecture, was the Reparation of the ancient Abbey-church of St. *Peter*, in *Westminster*, prosecuted by the *Surveyor*, to the Time of his Death, the Space of 25 Years ... A particular Account of which will be best understood from his own Words, in the following Memorial to the Bishop of *Rochester*, in the Year 1713."
4. In AS MS 313 "Collegiate" appears as "Ancient" with marginal note "Collegiate."
5. Antoninus Pius, reigned A.D. 138–61. William Camden, in his *Britannia*, 1586, was the first to record this information on the Temple of Apollo, attributing it to Fulcardus. See Camden, *Britannia* (1695), 317.
6. One of the northern indigenous tribes of Britain, the Picts occupied eastern Scotland, north of the isthmus. They are first mentioned in Roman sources in 297 and later attacked the Roman invaders numerous times during the fourth century. See Malcolm Todd, *Roman Britain (55 BC – AD 400)* (Sussex: Harvester Press, 1981), 217.
7. See "Of *London* in ancient Times," 27 and n. 28. "Of the taking down of the vast Ruins of the *old Cathedral*," 32 and n. 6.
8. The legendary King Lucius was buried in 156 A.D. in Gloucester Cathedral. He

reigned during the period when Britain was first converted to Christianity. See T. D. Kendrick, *British Antiquity* (London: Methuen, 1950), 8.

9. This sentence and those which follow, on Edward the Confessor, Henry III, Edward I, and their successors, appear to be derived from John Stow, *Survey of London* (London, 1598), 377–8. He, in turn, incorporates information from Camden's *Britannia* (1586); (1695), 317.
10. Sebert reigned A.D. 597–614.
11. Edgar reigned A.D. 959–75. No reliable record exists of the founding of an abbey on this site or its subsequent history until about 970. Pevsner and Metcalf, *Cathedrals: Southern England*, 160.
12. All of Wren's examples that follow are in fact Norman, dating after 1066.
13. Winchester Cathedral was begun in 1079 by Bishop Walkelin. The Norman work is preserved only in the transept arms. Pevsner and Metcalf, *Cathedrals: Southern England*, 324–30.
14. The Chapel of St. John in the White Tower, the great stone keep in the Tower of London, was built during the late eleventh century. See Geoffrey Webb, *Architecture in Britain: The Middle Ages* (Harmondsworth, Middlesex: Penguin, 1956), 66, 70. See also J. Charlton, ed., *The Tower of London: Its Building and Institutions* (London: Her Majesty's Stationery Office, 1978).
15. The chapel at the Hospital of St. Cross, Winchester, begun after 1151. The chancel aisles were completed first and are late Norman. Colin Platt, *The Architecture of Medieval Britain* (New Haven, CT: Yale University Press, 1990), 61–2.
16. The Cathedral Church of Christ at Oxford, located near the southeast corner of Tom Quad, the quadrangle of Christ Church College. The Augustinian abbey was established here in 1122, its church begun possibly in the 1170s. The Norman work remains in the choir, crossing, and transepts. Pevsner and Metcalf, *Cathedrals: Southern England*, 215–22.
17. William Rufus reigned 1087–1100. Wren is referring to the Norman nave and transepts of Old St. Paul's, dating from the late eleventh and early twelfth centuries. See "Of the ancient cathedral Churches of St. *Paul*," 40 and n. 18.
18. Edward the Confessor, reigned as king of England 1042–66.
19. The rebuilding of the church and monastic buildings under Edward the Confessor took place around 1050–60. The nave may have dated from around 1110–50. The only remains of this church lie underground. Pevsner and Metcalf, *Cathedrals: Southern England*, 160.
20. William Camden, *Reges, Reginae, Nobiles & alij in Ecclesia Collegiata B. Petri Westmonasterij sepulti* (1606), under section entitled "Fundatio Ecclesiae Beati Petri Westmonasterij." The same passage is found in Camden's *Britannia* (1695), 317.
21. Excavations show that the Norman church at Westminster Abbey was longer than any Norman churches remaining in Normandy. It had a nave of twelve bays with alternating supports, a western end with two towers, probably a transept with eastern apses and crossing tower, and a choir terminated by an apse. Pevsner and Metcalf, *Cathedrals: Southern England*, 160.
22. King Alfred of Wessex, reigned 871–99.
23. Henry III, reigned 1216–72.
24. The Lady Chapel was added, beginning in 1220, at the eastern end of the Norman choir. It was replaced during the first quarter of the sixteenth century by the Henry

VII chapel. Excavations show that it had a polygonal apse. Pevsner and Metcalf, *Cathedrals: Southern England*, 160.

25. A reference to the Crusades that took place from the late eleventh through the early thirteenth centuries (1096–9, 1147–9, 1202–4).
26. "Saracen": "Among the later Greeks and Romans, a name for the nomadic peoples of the Syro-Arabian desert which harassed the Syrian confines of the Empire; hence, an Arab; by extention, a Muslim, especially with reference to the Crusades" (*OED*). See also note 25 above on the Crusades; see another reference to "Saracen" on p. 85. For a full discussion, see "Tract II," 162 and n. 54.
27. Christopher Jr. adapted this text in a passage on page 306 of *Parentalia* (London, 1750), "The Life of Sir Christopher Wren, Knt.," pt. 2, sec. 8:

    These Surveys, and other occasional Inspections of the most noted cathedral Churches and Chapels in *England*, and foreign Parts; a Discernment of no contemptible Art, Ingenuity, and geometrical Skill in the Design and Execution of some few, and an Affectation of Height and Grandeur, tho' without Regularity and good Proportion, in most of them, induced the *Surveyor* to make some Enquiry into the Rise and Progress of this *Gothick* Mode, and to consider how the old *Greek* and *Roman* Style of building, with the several regular Proportions of Columns, Entablature, &c. came within a few Centuries to be so much altered, and almost universally difused.

    He was of Opinion (as has been mentioned in another Place) that what we now vulgarly call the *Gothick*, ought properly and truly to be named the *Saracenick Architecture refined by the Christians*; which first of all began in the East after the Fall of the *Greek* Empire by the prodigious Success of those People that adhered to *Mahomet*'s Doctrine, who out of Zeal to their Religion, built Mosques, Caravansaras, and Sepulchres, wherever they came.

    These they contrived of a round Form, because they would not imitate the christian Figure of a Cross; nor the old *Greek* Manner, which they thought to be idolatrous, and for that Reason all Sculpture became offensive to them.

    They then fell into a new Mode of their own Invention, tho' it might have been expected with better Sense, considering the *Arabians* wanted not Geometricians in that Age, nor the *Moors*, who translated many of the most useful old *Greek* Books. As they propagated their Religion with great Diligence, so they built Mosques in all their conquered Cities in Haste. The Quarries of great Marble, by which the vanquished Nations of *Syria, Egypt*, and all the East had been supplied; for Columns, Architraves, and great Stones, were now deserted; the *Saracens* therefore were necessitated to accommodate their Architecture to such Materials, whether Marble or Free-stone, as every Country readily afforded. They thought Columns, and heavy Cornices impertinent, and might be omitted; and affecting the round Form for Mosques, they elevated Cupolas in some Instances, with Grace enough. The Holy War gave the Christians, who had been there, an Idea of the *Saracen* Works, which were afterwards by them imitated in the West; and they refined upon it every Day, as they proceeded in building Churches. . . .

28. See note 26 above.
29. Henry III, reigned 1216–72.
30. The new abbey church was begun in 1245 by Henry III. Construction proceeded

rapidly. By 1255 the eastern end, transept, and first bay of the nave were complete. The nave was continued during the 1260s, with the westernmost bays, the tower bays, and the facade dating from the fourteenth through sixteenth centuries. Pevsner and Metcalf, *Cathedrals: Southern England*, 160.

31. Edward I, reigned 1272–1307. For more detailed discussions of the fabric and the chronology of its construction, see Pevsner and Metcalf, *Cathedrals: Southern England*, 163–74, and *The History of the King's Works*, vols. 1–2, *The Middle Ages*, ed. H. M. Colvin (London: Her Majesty's Stationery Office, 1963), 1:14–17, 130–57.
32. "Henry the Third is the founder of this church."
33. Begun under Henry III, probably around 1245–50. Pevsner and Metcalf, *Cathedrals: Southern England*, 201–2.
34. AS MS 313 reads "Art."
35. Edward I (reigned 1272–1307), Edward II (1307–27), Edward III (1327–77), Richard II (1377–99).
36. The ruling family of England, 1399–1461, holding the symbol of the white rose.
37. Wars of the Roses, 1455–71.
38. Henry VIII, reigned 1509–47, established the Church of England in 1533 and dissolved the monasteries from 1535 to 1539.
39. The chapter house was built under Henry III, begun soon after 1245 and substantially completed by 1250, or at the latest by 1253. Pevsner and Metcalf, *Cathedrals: Southern England*, 164, 202–4.
40. The House of Commons did indeed sit in the chapter house during the thirteenth and fourteenth centuries. Ibid., 162.
41. That is, flying buttresses.
42. Wren discusses similar problems at St. Paul's and how to gain control over the ground of these encroaching structures in his "Letter . . . for Building . . . Churches," 118.
43. AS MS 313 reads "ordered."
44. The condition discussed in the following passages is also described by Wren in "Report on Old St. Paul's before the Fire," 49 and "Report on Salisbury Cathedral," 68.
45. In AS MS 313 "as the Tower to" reads "to the Tower as."
46. "The Turn" does not appear in AS MS 313.
47. "Calceolus": "calceolaria" – " 'slipper-flower' or 'slipper-wort'; a genus of *scrophulariaceae*, the flower of which has some resemblance to a broad-toed slipper" (OED).
48. This drawing is unknown.
49. The following City churches are in the Gothic style: St. Mary Aldermary, 1679–82 (tower recased 1701–3); St. Dunstan-in-the-East, tower and spire 1695–8; St. Alban, Wood St., 1682–7 (tower finished 1697).

CHAPTER 3. LETTER FROM PARIS

Introduction

1. Edward Browne–Thomas Browne, September last 1665, *WS*, 18:180 (BL MS Sloane 1868).
2. "Letter . . . from Paris": "My Lord *Berkley* returns to *England* at *Christmas*, when I propose to take the Opportunity of his Company . . . ," 106.

3. *PAR*, 261.
4. *WS*, 13:40, note 3, suggests a Reverend Dr. Bateman, although it provides no evidence for this identification. Dr. Bateman was chaplain to the archbishop of Canterbury and a relation of Wren. He is mentioned in Christopher Wren, Jr.–James Hodgson, 3 June 1737, BL MS Add. 6209, fol. 203.
5. Robert Moray–Christiaan Huygens, 27 March 1665, Christiaan Huygens, *Oeuvres complètes*, 22 vols. (The Hague, 1888), 5:296: "On a donné a Monsieur Hook la province dont Monsieur Wren ne s'est pas pu descharger a cause d'un voyage qu'il va faire en France."
6. John Evelyn–Christopher Wren, 4 April 1665, *Diary and Correspondence of John Evelyn*, ed. H. B. Wheatley, 4 vols. (London, 1960), 3:305; also in *WS*, 13:40. "I am told by Sr Jo Denham that you looke towards France this somer; be assur'd I will charge you wth some addresses to friends of mine there, that shall exceedingly cherish you; and though you will stand in no neede of my recom'endations, yet I am confident you will not refuse the offer of those civilities which I shall bespeake you."
7. Christopher Wren–Ralph Bathurst, 22 June 1665, *WS*, 5:14.
8. Henry Oldenburg–Robert Boyle, 6 March 1666, *CHO*, 3:48: "Dr Wren is returned, and very kindly inquired after you."
9. See Harcourt Brown, *Scientific Organizations in Seventeenth Century France (1620–1680)* (Baltimore: Williams and Wilkins, 1934), 64–134.
10. Henri Justel–Henry Oldenburg, c. 14 January 1666, *CHO*, 3:11–12.
11. Le Gallois, *Entretien servant de Préface in Conversations de l'Académie de Monsieur l'Abbé Bourdelot* (Paris, 1672), quoted in Brown, *Scientific Organizations*, 164.
12. General discussion of Justel based on Brown, *Scientific Organizations*, 161–84; see also *DNB*. After moving to England, Justel became keeper of the king's library at St. James. He was elected F.R.S. on 7 December 1681.
13. See Brown, *Scientific Organizations*, 231–53.
14. Henry Oldenburg–Robert Boyle, 24 August 1665, *CHO*, 2:480–2.
15. Ibid.
16. Brown, *Scientific Organizations*, 144–7, and *DSB* on Thévenot.
17. Ibid., 135–7, and *DSB*.
18. *DSB*.
19. Brown, *Scientific Organizations*, 137–8, and *DSB*.
20. Brown, *Scientific Organizations*, 141.
21. For example, his name does not appear in Chantelou's *Diary*.
22. Adrien Auzout–Henry Oldenburg, 1 July 1665, *CHO*, 2:428–9.
23. J. A. Bennett, *The Mathematical Science of Christopher Wren* (Cambridge: Cambridge University Press, 1982), 91. On Auzout's scientific work, see *DSB*.
24. Adrien Auzout–Henry Oldenburg, 23 September 1665, *CHO*, 2:517–19; 2 February 1666, *CHO*, 3:36–8; 4 April 1666, *CHO*, 3:81–5.
25. Brown, *Scientific Organizations*, 139–40. The Observatoire was built according to the design of Claude Perrault from 1667 to 1669. Auzout's involvement remains unclear. A plan of the Observatoire was sent by Henri Justel to Oldenburg, as a present from Auzout (Justel–Oldenburg, c. 10 June 1668, *CHO*, 4:461–2), and according to Francis Vernon, "the first Modell & designe" of the observatory "it seems was Monsieur Auzouts" (Vernon–Oldenburg, 24 April 1669, *CHO*, 5:497–8). There is, however, no clear evidence for this attribution. For the history of the Observatoire project and Auzout's possible role, see Michael Petzet, "Claude Perrault als Architekt des Pariser

Observatoriums," *Zeitschrift für Kunstgeschichte*, 30, no. 1 (1967): 1–54, and Antoine Picon, *Claude Perrault, 1613–1688, ou la curiosité d'un classique* (Paris: Picard, 1988), 197–223.

26. Bibliothèque Nationale, Cabinet des Manuscrits, Fonds Français 23254, Lantiniana, quoted in Brown, *Scientific Organizations*, 139.
27. Martin Lister, *A Journey to Paris in the year 1698* (London, 1699), 30, 101–2; reprint, ed. R. P. Stearns (Urbana: University of Illinois Press, 1967). Auzout left the Académie des Sciences in July 1668 and went to live the rest of his life in Italy. According to Lister, Auzout visited England around 1684 and admired Jones's Banqueting House. Records of Auzout in Italy include Justel–Oldenburg, 18 November 1668, *CHO*, 5:180, and Henri Justel–Henry Oldenburg, 24 September 1673, *CHO*, 10: 257. In 1693 the Royal Society attempted to recover Auzout's manuscript notes on Vitruvius. 29 March and 3 May 1693, *JBO*, 8.
28. Adrien Auzout–Henry Oldenburg, 8 May 1666, *CHO*, 3:113–15. Henry Oldenburg–Robert Boyle, 6 March 1666, *CHO*, 3:48.
29. This discussion is based on Brown, *Scientific Organizations*, 208; Georges Dethan, *Gaston d'Orléans: Conspirateur et prince charmant* (Paris: Arthème Fayard, 1959), 318–25; David Murray, *Museums: their History and their Use*, 3 vols. (Glasgow: MacLehose, 1904), 1:92–3; and Arthur MacGregor, "Collectors and Collections of Rarities in the Sixteenth and Seventeenth Centuries," in *Tradescant's Rarities*, ed. A. MacGregor (Oxford: Clarendon, 1983), 82. The duke's cabinet is now part of the Bibliothèque Nationale, the Cabinet des Médailles, and the Musée d' Histoire Naturelle.
30. 1 April 1644, John Evelyn, *The Diary of John Evelyn*, ed. E. S. de Beer, 6 vols. (Oxford: Clarendon, 1955), 2:128.
31. Paul Fréart de Chantelou, *Diary of the Cavaliere Bernini's Visit to France*, ed. Anthony Blunt (Princeton, NJ: Princeton University Press, 1985), 103, 299.
32. Anthony Blunt, *Art and Architecture in France 1500–1700* (Harmondsworth, Middlesex: Penguin, 1981), 324.
33. Henry Oldenburg–Robert Boyle, 24 August 1665, *CHO*, 2:480–2. See also Henri Justel–Henry Oldenburg, c. 14 January 1666, *CHO*, 3:11–12, for reference to the king's bust. There is no record of this meeting in Chantelou, *Diary*.
34. The bust of the king was commissioned on 20 June. Bernini was working on a clay model from 24 June, which was shown to Colbert on 1 July. His assistants began sculpting the block of marble, placed at the Louvre, on 6 July, and Bernini took over from 14 to 18 July. The bust was moved to the Palais Mazarin on 11 August, and it was completed on 5 October. Cecil Gould, *Bernini in France: An Episode in Seventeenth-Century History* (Princeton, NJ: Princeton University Press, 1982), 42–51.
35. See ibid., 73–74.
36. Blunt, *Art and Architecture*, 256, 430 n. 97. Anthony Blunt, ed., *Baroque and Rococo: Architecture and Decoration* (New York: Harper and Row, 1978), 113–14.
37. After Mazarin's death, the property was divided, with the old Hôtel de Tubeuf going to the duc de la Meilleraye, husband of Mazarin's niece, Hortense Mancini, and the remaining buildings to Philippe Mancini, duc de Nevers. See Allan Braham and Peter Smith, *François Mansart*, 2 vols. (London: Zwemmer, 1973), 1:70–74, 223–6. See Roger-Armand Weigert, "Le Palais Mazarin: Architectes et décorateurs," *Art de France* 2 (1962): 146–69 and Pierre Gasnoult, ed., *La Bibliothèque mazarine: 1689, 1789, 1989* (Paris: Bibliothèque Mazarine), 1989.
38. Wren, "Report on Old St. Paul's before the Fire."

39. The Val-de-Grâce was begun by Mansart in 1645 and completed by Lemercier and others. Mansart's Visitation dates from 1632–3. Lemercier's Church of the Sorbonne was begun in 1626. His Oratoire was begun in 1621 and completed by others. See Blunt, *Art and Architecture*, 195–8, 201–13, and Maurice Dumolin and George Outardel, *Les Eglises de France: Paris et la Seine* (Paris: Letouzey, 1936).
40. The foundation stone was laid in November 1662, but construction ceased before 1669 and did not resume until 1714. See David Coffin, "Padre Guarino Guarini in Paris," *Journal of the Society of Architectural Historians* 15, no. 2 (1956): 3–11; H. A. Meek, *Guarino Guarini and His Architecture* (New Haven, CT: Yale University Press, 1988), 27–34.
41. Edward Browne–Thomas Browne, September last 1665, *WS*, 18:180.
42. Hilary Ballon, *The Paris of Henri IV: Architecture and Urbanism* (Cambridge, MA: MIT Press, 1991), 122, 125, 146.
43. René Pillorget, *Nouvelle Histoire de Paris: Paris sous les premiers Bourbons 1594–1661* (Paris: Hachette, 1988), 284–6, and Pierre Lavedan, *Nouvelle Histoire de Paris: Histoire de l'urbanisme à Paris* (Paris: Hachette, 1975), 228.
44. The quai des Grands Augustins was begun under Philippe Auguste and finished much later. The quai de la Mortellerie on the Right Bank, built in 1369 under Charles V, was probably replaced by the quai de la Mégisserie (de l'Ecole or la Ferraille), built 1530–9 under François I (Lavedan, *Histoire*, 111, 141). The sloping embankment of Charles V's fortified wall along the Seine was made into a quai by François I around 1536. (On the Louvre and Grande Gallerie, see Ballon, *Paris*, 15–16, 22.) The remarkable quai Pelletier, running eastward from the Pont Notre-Dame to the place de Grève, was constructed by Pierre Bullet and François Blondel in 1673–9. See Louis Hautecoeur, *Histoire de l'architecture classique en France*, 7 vols. (Paris: Picard, 1943–57), 2, pt. 1, 429–30.
45. Edward Browne–Thomas Browne, September last, 1665, *WS*, 18:180.
46. *DNB*.
47. On 14 March 1666, Wren and Hooke were asked to study the chariot. On 21 March 1666, it was reported that Wren had given Hooke a description of chariots in France (Birch, 2:66, 74).
48. "Report on Westminster Abbey," 85: "*France*; the Fashions of which Nation we affected to imitate in all Ages, even when we were at Enmity with it."
49. "Tract II," 159: "the *French* King, *Lewis* the fourteenth, proposed Rewards to such Artists as should find out a *Gallick Order*, ... neither will the Flower-de-luce of the French, nor the Palms of *Villalpandus*, ... come up to the Grace of the old Form of the *Corinthian* Capital." See also n. 44 on the same page.

Letter to a Friend from Paris

1. According to Christopher Wren, Jr., in *PAR*, 261, Wren begins his letter with passages "wherein he returns Thanks for his Recommendation of him to the Earl of St. *Albans*, who in the Journey, and ever since, had us'd him with all Kindness and Indulgence imaginable, and made good his Character of him, as one of the best Men in the World." See discussion on p. 93.
2. As Colbert wrote Bernini in a memorandum, two and a half of the four sides of the Cour Carrée were complete by 1665; that is, the south and west wings and the western half of the north wing. Since the death of Lemercier in 1654, Louis Le Vau

had been overseeing construction of the north wing and, during the early 1660s, designing the east wing. Some construction of his design had already taken place when in 1664 Colbert was appointed superintendent of royal buildings and called a halt to it. He submitted Le Vau's design to French architects for their criticism, then sent it to the leading Italian architects, who were eventually invited to make their own designs. Bernini was ultimately awarded the job, and he entered Paris on 2 June 1665. He had produced a second design while still in Rome, and then a third design upon his arrival in Paris. The foundation stone was laid 17 October 1665 by Louis XIV. Wren would have observed the construction of these foundations, but probably also the completion of the north wing. Moreover, the Petite Galerie (now Galerie d'Apollon), burnt in 1661, was being restored in 1665. See Gould, *Bernini*, 9–10, 106, and Chantelou, *Diary*, xvi, 336–7.

3. Collège des Quatre-Nations, now the Institut de France, was begun in 1662. Located across the Seine from the Louvre, it was designed to be on axis with the Cour Carrée by Louis Le Vau (1612–70), who also planned a connecting bridge. See Blunt, *Art and Architecture*, 326.

4. The Académie Royale de Peinture et de Sculpture, founded 1648, reorganized in 1663 by Colbert. It had held meetings at the Palais Brion since 1661, when its rooms at the Louvre were given over to the Royal Printing Press. The academy returned to the Louvre in 1692. See Blunt, *Art and Architecture*, 324; Chantelou, *Diary*, 165 note.

5. Jean-Baptiste Colbert (1619–83), finance minister and minister of the navy to Louis XIV, *surintendant des bâtiments du roi* from 1664.

6. "Abbé Charles": could be one of three possible persons: François or Francesco Butti (1604–92), a secular abbot who went to France in exile with his patrons, the Barberini; Monsignor Carlo Roberti de' Vittori, the papal nuncio at the court of Louis XIV; or the Carmelite Charles de l'Assomption, the former Charles de Bryas, an amateur scientist. Chantelou, *Diary*, 12 note; Gould, *Bernini*, 73–4; Brown, *Scientific Organizations*, 141.

7. Bénigne Bruneau or Breunot (1591–1666). Eduard Sekler, *Wren and His Place in European Architecture* (New York: Macmillan, 1956), 45; see M. Chabouillet, "Le Sieur Bruno," *Nouvelles archives de l'art français* 2 (Paris, 1873):282ff. It is unclear if this is the "Mons. Bruno" cited later. See note 30 below.

8. Gaston, duc d'Orléans (1608–60), brother of Louis XIII, a noted amateur of the sciences. See *Biographie universelle*, ed. M. Michaud, 45 vols. (Paris: Madame C. Desplaces, 1854–65).

9. Abbé Bourdelot (1610 or 1620–85), formerly Pierre Michon, a physician who spent most of his life serving the Prince of Condé. At the end of the reign of Louis XIII, he was briefly *médecin du roi*. For a short time from 1651 he was in the service of Queen Christina of Sweden. He was in Paris from 1659 and attended meetings of the Montmor Academy. The earliest mention of an academy held at his own home is in 1664. See Brown, *Scientific Organizations*, 231–53.

10. Fontainebleau: The medieval castle at Fountainebleau was altered for François I by Gilles Le Breton (d. 1553) from 1528 to 1540. Interior decoration was undertaken by Giovanni Battista Rosso and Francesco Primaticcio c. 1533–40. Sebastiano Serlio designed the Salle du Bal during 1541–7. Alterations were made by Philibert Delorme from 1548 to 1559. Further additions were carried out in the reign of Henri IV. (See Blunt, *Art and Architecture*, 54–7, 61–6, 75, 84.) Illustrated in J. A. Du Cerceau, *Les*

Plus Excellents Bastiments de France, ed. David Thomson (Paris: Sand and Conti, 1988, original two-volume edition 1576, 1579), 187–98.

11. St-Germain-en-Laye: the château built for François I by master mason Pierre Chambiges from 1539 to 1544, continued by Guillaume Guillain and Jean Langeois, finished 1549. It served as the primary country retreat for the French kings until 1682, when it was superseded by the extensive developments at the château at Versailles (Blunt, *Art and Architecture*, 50, 51, 53). The Château-Neuf at St. Germain was begun for Henri II from 1557 by Philibert Delorme. Terraced gardens were added for Henri IV (reigned 1589–1610) by Etienne Du Pérac (Blunt, *Art and Architecture*, 93, 159; illustrated in Du Cerceau, *Bastiments*, 95–102).

12. Versailles: The small château built for Louis XIII in 1624 was replaced in 1631–4 by a second château designed by Philibert Le Roy that was inherited by Louis XIV. It was a modest building of brick and white stone, arranged around a forecourt with corner pavilions and covered by a steep slate roof. Renovations during the 1660s included the addition of new outbuildings, redecoration of the rooms, redesign of the approach, and the beginning of additions of new gardens by Le Nôtre. The old brick château was later encased from 1668 by Louis Le Vau's Enveloppe, with its courtyard facade preserved in the area of the Marble Court. Guy Walton, *Louis XIV's Versailles* (Chicago: University of Chicago Press, 1986), 53–66.

13. Palais Mazarin: The first portion originally built for Duret de Chevry from 1635 by Jean Thiriot, it was enlarged in 1641 by Pierre Le Muet after being acquired by Jacques Tubeuf. From 1643 Cardinal Mazarin leased the property and hired François Mansart to make additions to house his large library and art collection, including the Galerie Mazarine, decorated 1646–7 by Giovanni Francesco Romanelli, a pupil of Pietro da Cortona. After Mazarin's death in 1661 the property was divided. It is now part of the Bibliothèque Nationale. Blunt, *Art and Architecture*, 167, 430 n. 95; Blunt, *Baroque and Rococo*, 110, 114; Braham and Smith 1: 70–4, 223–6. See Roger-Armand Weigert, "Le Palais Mazarin: Architectes et décorateurs," *Art de France* 2 (1962):146–69; also Madeleine Laurain-Portemer, "Le Palais Mazarin à Paris et l'offensive baroque de 1645–50," *Gazette des Beaux-Arts* 1 (1973): 151.

14. "Pierres de raport": "pierres de rapport," according to André Félibien, in his *Des Principes de l'architecture, de la sculpture, de la peinture et des autres arts qui en dépendent* (Paris, 1676), 436–9, was a form of mosaic work employed by modern craftsmen, where natural stones were used to represent figures in the manner of paintings.

15. The new summer apartment of the queen mother, Anne of Austria, located under the Petite Galerie of the Louvre. It was decorated 1655–7 by Giovanni Francesco Romanelli. Although the rooms have been altered, the frescoes survive. Blunt, *Art and Architecture*, 251, 430 n. 97; Blunt, *Baroque and Rococo*, 113–14; see also D. Bodart, "Une Description de 1657 des fresques de Giovanni Francesco Romanelli au Louvre," *Bulletin de la société de l'histoire de l'art français* (1974): 43–50.

16. Vaux-le-Vicomte: Built 1657–61 by Louis Le Vau. Blunt, *Art and Architecture*, 229–33.

17. Maisons: Château de Maisons was built 1642–6 by François Mansart.

18. Rueil: Owned by Cardinal Richelieu, the enlargement of the château and addition of gardens were carried out by Jacques Lemercier from 1633. Blunt, *Art and Architecture*, 199, and Rosalys Coope, "Lemercier, Jacques," *Macmillan Encyclopedia of Architects*, 4 vols. (New York: Free Press, 1982), 2:659.

Courances: Built c. 1624 for Claude Gallard. The architect is unknown. Illustrated in engravings by Israël Henriet. Margaret Whinney, "Sir Christopher Wren's Visit to Paris," *Gazette des Beaux-Arts*, 6th ser., 51 (April 1958): 238 n. 8; Blunt, *Art and Architecture*, 422 n. 17; Georges Poisson, *Promenades aux châteaux de l'Ile-de-France* (Paris: Balland, 1967), 268.

Chilly: The château de Chilly or Chilly-Mazarin was built for Richelieu by Clément Métezeau from 1629. Blunt, *Art and Architecture*, 426 n. 7; see also Edouard-Jacques Ciprut, "La Construction du château de Chilly-Mazarin," *Bulletin de la société de l'histoire de l'art français* (1961): 205–9.

"Essoane": probably the château at Ecouen, or "Escouan," as it is given by Du Cerceau. The original building was the work of Pierre Tacheron from around 1538. Jean Bullant made additions from around 1555 for the Constable Anne de Montmorency. Blunt, *Art and Architecture*, 135–6; illustrated in Du Cerceau, *Bastiments*, 269–80.

St. Maur: The château of St-Maur-les-Fossés built 1541–63 for Jean du Bellay by Philibert Delorme (Blunt, *Art and Architecture*, 87–8). It was enlarged by Jean Bullant 1573–9. See Anthony Blunt, *Philibert de l'Orme* (London: Zwemmer, 1958), 21–6, 89–91; Naomi Miller, "Delorme, Philibert," *Macmillan Encyclopedia*, 1:544; illustrated in Du Cerceau, *Bastiments*, 227–34.

Saint-Mandé: near Vincennes, owned by Nicolas Fouquet from 1654, decorated by Le Brun and Anguier. This château predated Fouquet's work at Vaux-le-Vicomte. Whinney, "Wren's Visit," 238 n. 8.

Issy: "Le Petit Olympe," the house owned by Marguerite de Valois, was replaced by a new château in 1681–6 designed by Pierre Bullet. See Runar Strandberg, "Le Château d'Issy: La construction de Pierre Bullet," *Gazette des Beaux-Arts* 96 (December 1980): 197–208, with n. 5 on p. 207 on the earlier house.

Meudon: The sixteenth-century château, with grotto c. 1555 designed by Francesco Primaticcio, was owned by Antoine Séguier, who sold it to Charles de Guise, cardinal de Lorraine in 1552. It was purchased in 1654 by Abel Servien, *surintendant des finances*, who had improvements made by Louis Le Vau from 1654 to c. 1657 (Blunt, *Art and Architecture*, 94, 427 n. 48; Chantelou, *Diary*, 98 n.). Later, at Meudon, J.-H. Mansart designed the Château-Neuf for the Grand Dauphin.

Raincy: Le Raincy was owned by Nicolas Bordier, *intendant des finances*, and designed by Le Vau during the early 1640s. Blunt, *Baroque and Rococo*, 119–20; illustrated by Jean Marot, Silvestre, and Pérelle; see Robert W. Berger, "Louis Le Vau's Château du Raincy," *Architectura* 6, no. 1 (1976): 36–46.

Chantilly: Alterations of the medieval castle were carried out by the master mason Pierre Chambiges 1528–31 for Constable Anne de Montmorency, the owner of Ecouen. For the same man the Petit Château was built at Chantilly c. 1560 by Jean Bullant. Blunt, *Art and Architecture*, 139; illustrated in Du Cerceau, *Bastiments*, 243–56.

Verneuil: The château of Verneuil-sur-Oise was begun by Philippe de Boulainvilliers, count of Dammartin and Courtenay, around 1560, possibly according to his own design. The duc de Nemours soon took over, substantially completing the building using a revised plan by Jacques Androuet du Cerceau the Elder. Salomon de Brosse finished the work 1600–16 after Henry IV presented the château to his mistress Henriette d'Entragues. Blunt, *Art and Architecture*, 143; illustrated in Du Cerceau, *Bastiments*, 119–40.

19. "taille-douce": copperplate engraving.
20. Gianlorenzo Bernini (1598–1680); François Mansart (1598–1666); Louis Le Vau (1612–70); Thomas Gobert (1630?–1703); and Antoine Le Pautre (1621–79). For Gobert, see Blunt, *Art and Architecture*, 344; Philippe Laurent, "Saint-Didier d'Asfeld," *Monuments historiques*, no. 145 (June/July 1986): 19–24; P. Moisy, "Sur une fantaisie architecturale de Thomas Gobert,"in *Urbanisme et architecture, études en l'honneur de P. Lavedan* (Paris: Laurens, 1954), 261–8; Françoise de La Moureyre, "Thomas Gobert (vers 1640–1708), Architecte des Bâtiments du Roi et de Monsieur, ingénieur, inventeur . . . et sculpteur," *Gazette des Beaux-Arts*, ser. 6, 116 (September 1990): 67–93.
21. The brothers François (1604–69) and Michel Anguier (1612 or 1614–86); see Blunt, *Art and Architecture*, 318; Chantelou, *Diary*, 112 n. Jacques Sarrazin (1588–1660), see Blunt, *Art and Architecture*, 316.
22. "Perrot": Jacques Perrot, established in Paris c. 1650, or Salomon Perrot (d. 1675), sculptor and painter. Whinney, "Wren's Visit," 238 n. 8.
23. Gerhard van Obstal or Opstal (c. 1597–1668). Of Flemish origin, he was a student of Jacques Sarrazin and a founding member of the Academy of Painting and Sculpture. See Blunt, *Art and Architecture*, 319; Chantelou, *Diary*, 301 n. "Arnoldin": Identity unknown.
24. Jean d'Armand, called Lorfelin (1600–69), *Graveur général de la Monnaie de Paris* in 1630. "de Tour": Identity unknown. Whinney, "Wren's Visit," 238 n. 8.
25. Charles Le Brun (1619–90); Sébastien Bourdon (1616–71); Nicolas Poussin (1593/4–1665). "Ruvine": Possibly Noel Jouvenet or Jean Jouvenet (1647–1717) or Jacques Rousseau (1630–93), painter of architecture and ruins; Whinney, "Wren's Visit," 238 n. 8. Philippe de Champaigne (1602–74); see Blunt, *Art and Architecture*, 251–8. Etienne Villequin (1619–88). Nicolas Pierre Loir or Loyr (1624–79); see ibid., 314. Noël Coypel (1628–1707); see ibid., 439 n. 74. Etienne Picard (1632–1721), engraver, or Jean Michel Picaut, (1600–83), painter of flowers, still lifes, and landscapes. See M. Faré, "Jean Michel Picaut (1600–1683), peintre de fleurs et marchand de tableaux," *Bulletin de la societé de l'histoire de l'art français* (1957): 91.
26. The brothers Pierre Mignard (1612–95) or Nicolas Mignard (1608–68); see Blunt, *Art and Architecture*, 314, 350–3; also *Mignard D'Avignon (1606–1668)*, exh. cat., Palais des Papes (Avignon, 1979).
27. Either of the cousins Charles Beaubrun (1604–92) or Henri Beaubrun (1603–77); see Blunt, *Art and Architecture*, 259.
28. Jean-Baptiste Monnoyer (1634–99); see Blunt, *Art and Architecture*, 439 n. 72. Nicolas Robert (1614–85); see *Biographie universelle*.
29. Identity unknown.
30. It is unclear whether this is Bénigne Bruneau, the "Abbé Bruno" cited earlier. See p. 103 and n. 7 above.
31. See p. 103 and n. 9 above.
32. Jean de la Quintinie (1626–88), author of *Instruction pour les jardins fruitiers et potagers, avec un traité des orangers* (Paris 1690); renamed, in the second edition, *Le Parfait Jardinier, ou instruction pour les jardins frutiers et potagers* (Paris, 1695). Trans. John Eve-

lyn, *The Compleat Gardiner; or Directions for Cultivating and Right Ordering of Fruit-Gardens and Kitchen-Gardens* (London, 1693).
33. John Berkeley, 1st Baron Berkeley of Stratton (d. 1678) (DNB).

CHAPTER 4. LETTER ON BUILDING CHURCHES

Introduction

1. *Statutes of the Realm*, 9:473 (9 Anne, Cap. 17); Statutes at Large, 4:487–9 (9 Anne, Cap. 22), quoted in H. M. Colvin, "Fifty New Churches," *Architectural Review* 107, no. 639 (March 1950): 189. The following discussion is based on Colvin, 189–90, and Kerry Downes, *Hawksmoor* (London: Zwemmer, 1959), 156–8.
2. Commons Journals (1708–1711), 495, quoted in Colvin, 189.
3. *The Examiner*, no. 42 (24 May 1711) (*The Prose Works of Jonathan Swift*, ed. H. Davis, 14 vols. [Oxford, 1939–68], 3:160), quoted in Colvin, 189.
4. See Kerry Downes, *The Architecture of Wren* (New York: Universe, 1982), 50–1; Thomas Sprat, *The History of the Royal Society* (London, 1667), 78, 112–13; John Evelyn, *A Character of England* (1659), *Fumifugium: or the Inconvenience of the Aer and Smoak of London Dissipated* (1661), and *Londinium Redivivum, or London restored not to its pristine, but to far greater beauty commodiousness and magnificence*, posthumously published as *London revived: considerations for its rebuilding in 1666*, ed. and intro. E. S. de Beer (Oxford: Clarendon Press, 1938); Kerry Downes, "John Evelyn and Architecture: A First Inquiry," in *Concerning Architecture*, ed. John Summerson (London: Allen Lane, 1968), 28–39; T. F. Reddaway, *The Rebuilding of London After the Great Fire* (London: Arnold, 1940).
5. For illustrations of the City churches, see John Clayton, *The Dimensions, Plans, Elevations, and Sections of the Parochial Churches of Sir Christopher Wren* (London, 1848–9), reprinted in *WS*, 9, which includes site plans for many examples. See also the discussion in Downes, *Architecture*, 56–64, and in Paul Jeffery, *The City Churches of Sir Christopher Wren* (London: Hambledon, 1996), which appeared as this work was going to press.
6. One church that does not have the east–west orientation is St. Edmund, Lombard Street.
7. On the City church towers, see Downes, *Architecture*, 117–18.
8. On Wren's City churches, including issues of liturgy, see Downes, *Architecture*, 60–2; G. W. O. Addleshaw and Frederick Etchells, *The Architectural Setting of Anglican Worship* (London: Faber and Faber, 1948), 52–8; and Horton Davies, *Worship and Theology in England: From Andrewes to Baxter and Fox, 1603–90* (Princeton, NJ: Princeton University Press, 1975), 41–56. On Anglican preaching, see Davies, 133–84.

On 18 June 1688, at the Royal Society, "A Discourse arising about the sence of Hearing, Sir John Hoskins said that Sir Christopher Wren had told him, that one use of Pillars in great Churches was to facilitate hearing, by breaking the sound and so preventing Echoes" (*JBO*, 7). On studies of acoustics by Robert Hooke and Wren's involvement, see Penelope Gouk, "The Role of Acoustics and Music Theory in the Scientific Work of Robert Hooke," *Annals of Science* 37 (1980): 573–605.
9. Addleshaw and Etchells, 52–3. Screens were used at St. Peter, Cornhill, and All

Hallows the Great, Thames Street (its screen was moved, after it was demolished in 1876, to St. Margaret Lothbury). Addleshaw and Etchells, 50.
10. "Proposals about Building ye New Churches," Bodleian MS Rawlinson. B. 376, fols. 351–2; reprinted in Kerry Downes, *Vanbrugh* (London: Zwemmer, 1977), 257–8.

Letter to a Friend on the Commission for Building Fifty New City Churches

1. St. James, Piccadilly, in London, 1676–84.
2. Wren must have heard preaching during his trip to Paris in 1665/6. Prior to the Restoration, many Englishmen exiled to France, including Charles II, heard and admired the preaching at the French court. See Davies, *Worship and Theology*, 177.
3. As MS 313 reads "Ailes."
4. See Wren's discussion of similar problems with encroaching structures at Westminster Abbey in his "Report on Westminster Abbey," 86.

CHAPTER 5. TRACTS ON ARCHITECTURE

Introduction

1. Suggested by Eduard Sekler, *Wren and His Place in European Architecture* (New York: Macmillan, 1956), 52.
2. Roger North, *The Lives of the Right Hon. Francis North, baron Guilford; the Hon. Sir Dudley North; and the Hon. and Rev. Dr. John North*, ed. A. Jessopp, 3 vols. (London: G. Bell, 1890; orig. ed. 1742, 1744), 2:238.
3. Roger North, *Of Building: Roger North's Writings on Architecture*, ed. Howard M. Colvin and John Newman (Oxford: Clarendon, 1981), 10. In another version in BL MS Add. 32540, fol. 11, he writes: "I had once some discourse with Sir Christopher Wren on this subject, who for argument sake, held that there was that distinction in Nature, of gracefull and ugly; and that it must be so to all creatures that had vision. . . . He alledged, that of triangules, an Equilater, was more agreable than a scalene, and some other such instances, as the stated dimensions of Columnes, which I shall consider anon." See also Howard M. Colvin, "Roger North and Sir Christopher Wren," *Architectural Review* 110, no. 658 (October 1951): 259.
4. Wren, "Tract I," 154: "Geometrical Figures are naturally more beautiful than other irregular; in this all consent as to a Law of Nature. . . ." "Oblique Positions are Discord to the Eye, unless answered in Pairs, as in the Sides of an equicrural Triangle."
5. Christopher Wren–William Brouncker, 30 July 1663, Birch, 1:289 (RS *Letter Book of the Royal Society*, 1: 97).
6. Hooke, *Diary 1672–80*, 234, 432.
7. The engraving was possibly from the popular topographic book by Giacomo Lauro, *Antiquae Urbis Splendor* (1612).
8. Hooke, *Diary 1672–80*, 317.
9. Ibid., 320–1.
10. Ibid., 321.

11. Ibid., 322.
12. Aubrey, *MB*, 2:670–1.
13. Ibid., 674–5.
14. Birch, 6:315. This discourse and drawing are not at the Royal Society. The sketch of Hooke's scheme is in Aubrey, *MB*, 2:676/7.
15. See p. 223. For dating of the Great Model, see Kerry Downes, *The Architecture of Wren* (New York: Universe, 1982), 68, 129.
16. *JBO*, 10. This edition of Josephus was probably *The Works of Flavius Josephus*, trans. Sir R. L'Estrange. To which are added two discourses [by Dr. Willes, with notes by J. Hudson] (London, 1702; 2 ed. 1709).
17. Finished 93–4 A.D., Josephus's *Antiquities* covers the beginnings of Jewish history to the Great War with Rome in 66 A.D. Josephus Flavius, *Works*, (Cambridge, MA: Harvard University Press, Loeb Classical Library, 1950–65).
18. Aubrey, *MB*, 2:670–1.
19. Mentioned by John Aubrey in *MB*, 2:672. Hooke's description and drawings are lost, but are cited in Royal Society minutes, 25 May 1692, *JBO*, 7, and 15 and 22 June 1692, *JBO*, 8. Discussed with some Royal Society fellows, 26 April 1693 (Hooke, *Diary 1688–93*, 234).
20. Hooke, *Diary 1672–80*, 179.
21. Constantine Huygens–Christopher Wren, 7 October 1674, in *De Briefwisseling van Constantijn Huygens (1608–1687)*, ed. J. A. Worp (The Hague: Martin Nijhoff, 1917), 6:356–7 (no. 6954).
22. For example, Francis Bacon (*The Works of Francis Bacon*, ed. James Spedding, R. L. Ellis, and D. D. Heath, 14 vols. [London: Longman, 1857–74], 4:81–2) declares that "men have been kept back as by a kind of enchantment from progress in the sciences by reverence for antiquity..." (*Novum Organum*, Aph. 84). See Richard Foster Jones, *Ancients and Moderns: A Study of the Rise of the Scientific Movement in Seventeenth-Century England* (St. Louis, MO: Washington University, 1962), 43–6.
23. See Wolfgang Herrmann, "Antoine Desgodets and the Académie Royal d'Architecture," *Art Bulletin* 40 (1958): 23–53.
24. Wren, "Tract II," 157.
25. Francis Bacon, *Works*, 4:254, states that natural history "is used either for the sake of the knowledge of the particular things which it contains, or as the primary material of philosophy and the stuff and subject-matter of true induction" (*Parasceve*, Aph. 2); see Jones, *Ancients*, 53–4. On the question of reliability, see Barbara J. Shapiro, *Probability and Certainty in Seventeenth-Century England* (Princeton, NJ: Princeton University Press, 1983), 15–27.
26. Hooke, *Diary 1672–80*, 328.
27. Robert Hooke–Pulleyn, 9 August 1680, and Robert Hooke–Henri Justel, 10 August 1680, in R. T. Gunther, ed., *Early Science in Oxford*, 15 vols. (London and Oxford, 1930–67), 7:561, 562; John Evelyn, *The Diary of John Evelyn*, ed. E. S. de Beer, 6 vols. (Oxford: Clarendon Press, 1955), 4:212–13 (30 August 1680). Christopher Wren–unknown person, 9 August 1681, Sotheby Sale, 25 January 1955, Lot 493, quoted in Kerry Downes, *Hawksmoor* (London: Zwemmer, 1959), 29; John Chardin, *Voyages de Monsieur le Chevalier Chardin en Perse et autres lieux de l'Orient*, 3 vols. (Amsterdam, 1711).
28. Hooke, *Diary 1672–80*, 328.
29. *PT* 13, no. 152 (20 October 1683): 335–46, and 14, no. 155 (20 January 1684): 431–

54. Originally published as *Epistolae de Moribus et Institutis Turcarum* (Oxford, 1674) and, in English, *Remarks upon the Manners, Religion and Government of the Turks* (London, 1678).
30. Wren, "Tract II," 163.
31. North, *Lives of the Norths*, 2:138.
32. Aubrey, *MB*, 2:678–9.
33. John Stukeley, *Stonehenge*, Cardiff Central Library, MS 253, first leaf. My thanks go to Michael Hunter for this reference.
34. E.g., huts in Bermuda, *PT* 2, no. 23 (11 March 1667): 420–1, and Stafford–Oldenburg, 16 July 1668, *CHO*, 4:550–3. Only one Renaissance writer seems to have taken notice of contemporary primitive huts: Daniele Barbaro, ed., *I dieci libri dell'architettura di M. Vitruvio* (Venice, 1567; orig. ed. 1556), bk. 2, chap. 1, 69, "si ha a di nostri essere nell'Isola Spagnola, & nelle parti del mondo scoperte da i moderni, che le stanze, & le habitationi sono fatte di alberi, tessuti di canne, coperti di paglie...."
35. Egyptian temples: e.g., "A Narrative of some Observations lately made by certain Missionaries in the *Upper Egypt*; communicated in a Letter written from *Cairo* the sixth of January 1670," *PT* 6, no. 71 (22 May 1671): 2151–3.

    Persepolis: e.g., drawing by Nicholas Witsen, *PT* 18, no. 210 (May 1694): 117–18.

    Palmyra: e.g., *PT* 19, no. 217 (October 1695): 83–110, and *PT* 19, no. 218 (November/December 1695): 129–60.

    Byzantine architecture in Constantinople: e.g., Guillaume-Joseph Grelot, *Relation nouvelle d'un voyage de Constantinople* (1680; English ed. 1683), with illustrations of Hagia Sophia.
36. Islamic architecture: e.g., Grelot, with drawings of mosques and the Grand Signior's palace; John Chardin, F.R.S., *Travels into Persia and the East-Indies, the first volume containing the Author's Voyage from Paris to Isphahan*, 2 vols. (London, 1686); George Wheler, F.R.S., *A Journey to Greece* (London, 1678).

    Chinese architecture: e.g., John Nieuhoff, *An Embassy from the East-India Company of the United Provinces to the Grand Tartar Cham, Emperor of China*, ed. John Ogilby (London, 1669; 2d ed. 1673), with descriptions and illustrations of important Chinese monuments and building types. The title refers to the first part, a translation of the 1665 Dutch account by Jan Nieuhoff. The appendix of Ogilby's edition includes translated excerpts from Athanasius Kircher's *China Monumentis Illustrata* (Amsterdam, 1667), another important book on the subject.
37. The debate on the origins of Stonehenge, begun in 1655 with the publication of Inigo Jones's *Stone-Heng Restored*, was continued by several Royal Society fellows, including Aubrey and Walter Charleton in his *Chorea Gigantum* (1663). These writers also had theories about Avebury. Discussions about this site took place at the Royal Society in July 1663. See Peter J. Ucko, Michael Hunter, Alan J. Clark, and Andrew David, *Avebury Reconsidered from the 1660s to the 1990s* (London: Unwin Hyman, 1991), 8–35. Michael Hunter, "The Royal Society and the Origin of British Archaeology," *Antiquity* 65 (1971): 113–21, 187–92.
38. Wren, "Tract I," 156.
39. For example, Robert Boyle states: "But as the two great books, of nature and of scripture, have the same author; so the study of the latter does not at all hinder an inquisitive man's delight in the study of the former," in *The Excellency of Theology*

(1665, published 1674), in Robert Boyle, *Works*, ed. Thomas Birch, 2d ed. (London, 1772), 3:429.
40. Wren, "Tract V," 188.
41. Wren, "Tract II," 158.
42. Vitruvius 2.1.1–3.
43. Vitruvius 4.1.1–8.
44. Vitruvius 5.1.3.
45. Wren, "Tract II," 158.
46. Vitruvius 2.1.3 and 5.1.3.

   Alberti, *DRA*, bk. 9, chap. 1, 293, describes the use of "columns, especially for garden porticoes, that resembled tree trunks, their knots removed and their branches tied into bundles, and the shaft scrolled and plaited with palms and carved with leaves, birds, and channels. . . ."

   Francesco di Giorgio Martini, in his *Trattati di architettura ingegneria e arte militare*, 2 vols. (Milan: Il Polifilo, 1967), 1:14v, 15 (pls. 24, 25) (Cordex 148 Saluzzo, Biblioteca Reale, Turin, c. 1475), illustrates one "colonna a tronchoni" as a smooth shaft entwined by a thick vine and another as a tree trunk with its branches cut off.

   Four stone tree-trunk columns were used by Bramante at the Canonica at S. Ambrogio, Milan, begun 1492. He may have used the device as a reference to the origins of the orders or because the tree was in the coat of arms of Ludovico il Moro. (See Arnaldo Bruschi, *Bramante* [London: Thames and Hudson, 1977], 62.) For Leonardo's interest in this issue, see Pietro C. Marani, "Leonardo e le colonne ad tronchonos; tracce di un programma iconologico per Ludovico il Moro," *Raccolta vinciana* 21 (1982): 103–20.

   The tree-trunk column was also known to sixteenth-century French architects. Philibert Delorme illustrates a tree-trunk column in *Le Premier tome de l'Architecture* (Paris, 1567), fol. 213v, as another possible order to be used in architecture. He states on fol. 217 that the ancients used "des piles & trons d'arbres, au lieu de colomnes" prior to the invention of the Doric, and describes how the column originated in the tree trunk (Anthony Blunt, *Philibert de l'Orme* [London: Zwemmer, 1958], 118). The tree-trunk column is also mentioned in the *Recepte Véritable* (1563) of Delorme's enemy, Bernard Palissy. Of related interest is Ernst Kris, "Der Stil 'rustique': Die Verwendung des Naturabgusses bei Wenzel Jamnitzer und Bernard Palissy," *Jahrbuch der Kunsthistorischen Sammlungen in Wien* 1 (1926): 137–208.

47. Wren, "Tract II," 158–9.
48. Vitruvius 4.2.6. See Vitruvius 4.1.9–10 and 4.2.2–6.
49. Wren, "Tract IV," 169.
50. Wren, "Tract I," 156.
51. 1 Kings 5–7 and 2 Chronicles 3–4.
52. See Helen Rosenau, *Vision of the Temple: The Image of the Temple of Jerusalem in Judaism and Christianity* (London: Oresko, 1979).
53. Juan Bautista Villalpando (1552–1608), *In Ezechielem Explanationes et Apparatus Urbis ac Templi Hierosolymitani*, 3 vols. (Rome, 1596, 1604), vol. 2 (1604) entitled "De Postrema Ezechielis Prophetae Visione." See René C. Taylor, "Hermeticism and Mystical Architecture in the Society of Jesus," in *Baroque Art: The Jesuit Contribution*, ed. R. Wittkower and I. B. Jaffe (New York: Fordham University Press, 1972), 66–76, and "Architecture and Magic: Considerations on the Idea of the Escorial," in *Essays in the History of Architecture presented to Rudolf Wittkower*, ed. D. Fraser et al.

(London: Phaidon, 1967), 90–1. Roland Fréart de Chambray, *Parallèle de l'architecture antique e de la moderne* (1650; English trans. by John Evelyn, 1664), 76.

On the spiral columns at St. Peter's, see J. B. Ward-Perkins, "The Shrine of St. Peter and Its Twelve Spiral Columns," *Journal of Roman Studies* 42 (1952): 21, 24, 32–3.

54. Wren, "Tract V," 191. Mark 13:1 and Josephus, *Antiquities of the Jews*, 15:413–14.
55. Wren, "Tract IV," 169.
56. See Karl H. Dannenfeldt, "The Renaissance and the Pre-Classical Civilizations," *Journal of the History of Ideas* 13, no. 4 (October 1952): 435–40.
57. For example, the description and drawings of two porphyry obelisks in Egypt, in *PT* 14, no. 161 (20 July 1684): 624–9, and *PT* 15, no. 178 (December 1685): 1252 and pl. 1. For Renaissance knowledge of Egyptian antiquities, see Leslie Greener, *The Discovery of Egypt* (New York: Viking, 1966).

    See also, for example, drawings of the ruins at Persepolis by Nicholas Witsen, *PT* 18, no. 210 (May 1694), 117–18, and by Chardin, *Voyages*, 3: 99–126.
58. Inigo Jones, *The Most Notable Antiquity of Great Britain, Called Stone-Heng, . . . Restored*, ed. John Webb (London, 1655); Aylett Sammes, *Britannia Antiqua Illlustrata: or the Antiquities of Ancient Britain, Derived from the Phoenicians* (London, 1676); Aubrey, *MB*, 1:24–7. See Stuart Piggott, *The Druids* (Harmondsworth, Middlesex: Penguin, 1981), and Ucko et al., *Avebury Reconsidered*.
59. Wren, "Tract IV," 169, 184.
60. Examples of sketchbooks are those of Francesco di Giorgio from the late 1450s and 1460s and of Giuliano da Sangallo from the late 1460s. Published examples are Sebastiano Serlio's book 3 on antiquities from 1540 and Palladio's book 4 from 1570. The first "archaeological" treatment of the Roman antiquities is by Antoine Desgodets, in his *Les edifices antiques de Rome* (Paris, 1682).
61. Alberti, *DRA*, bk. 6, chap. 1, 154, contrasts ancient buildings following "proven and much commended methods" with those inspired by "inept modern nonsense." In bk. 6, chap. 3, 157, he discusses how building "enjoyed her first gush of youth, as it were, in Asia, flowered in Greece, and later reached her glorious maturity in Italy." The Assyrians and Egyptians had wealth and created buildings as large and as splendid as possible. The Greeks had ingenuity and sought to draw the qualities of building from the "very bosom of Nature." In Italy, thrift prompted builders to design buildings by analogy to animals, joining grace of form with suitability for use. The Romans "probed so thoroughly into the art that there was nothing so recondite, concealed, or abstruse as not to have been explored, traced out, or brought to light."

    The "Raphael" letter was probably written by Raphael and Castiglione. It discusses four periods: the "good" antique; the decline after the domination of the Goths and barbarians until 100 years after; the German style until our own time, "wholly without grace"; and finally, our own age, which approaches very nearly the antique style, as in the work of Brunelleschi. "A Report to Pope Leo X on Ancient Rome," in *A Documentary History of Art*, vol. 1, "The Middle Ages and the Renaissance," ed. Elizabeth G. Holt (Garden City, NY: Doubleday, 1957; reprint Princeton, NJ: Princeton University Press, 1981), 289–96.

    Giorgio Vasari, *Le Vite de' più eccellenti pittori, scultori e architetti* (Florence, 1550; 2d ed. 1568). Vasari discusses five periods or styles: the ancient; the decline into the "barbarous" "German" style after Constantine; the period of improvement from Buschetto the Greek to Arnolfo di Cambio and Giotto; and the rebirth of the antique with Brunelleschi and Francesco di Giorgio, culminating in the state of perfection with Leonardo and Michelangelo. *The Lives of the Artists*, trans. George Bull (Harmondsworth, Middlesex: Penguin, 1978), 32–6, 84–7, 90–1, 253–4.

62. For freemasonic history, see Douglas Knoop and G. P. Jones, *The Genesis of Freemasonry* (Manchester: Manchester University Press, 1949), 73–7. The earliest published freemasonic history is *The Constitutions of the Free-Masons. Containing the History, Charges, Regulations &c. of that most Ancient and Right Worshipful Fraternity*, ed. James Anderson (London, 1723). See also James Stevens Curl, *The Art and Architecture of Freemasonry* (Woodstock, NY: Overlook Press, 1991).

   For universal history, see Frank E. Manual, *Isaac Newton: Historian* (Cambridge: Belknap, 1963), 37–41, 89–93; Adalbert Klempt, *Die Sakularisierung der universalhistorischen Auffassung* (Göttingen: Musterschmidt, 1960), 63–4, 69–90, 106–14; Donald J. Wilcox, *The Measure of Times Past: Pre-Newtonian Chronologies and the Rhetoric of Relative Time* (Chicago: University of Chicago Press, 1987), 187–90; and Paolo Rossi, *The Dark Abyss of Time: The History of the Earth and the History of Nations from Hooke to Vico* (Chicago: University of Chicago Press, 1984).

63. Wren, "Tract I," 154.
64. Alberti, *DRA*, bk. 6, chap. 3, 157.
65. Wren, "Tract I," 153.
66. Fischer may have met Wren in London in 1704 during a journey from Vienna. See Johann Bernhard Fischer von Erlach, *A Plan of Civil and Historical Architecture*, trans. Thomas Lediard (1730), "The Author's Preface"; see also Eileen Harris, *British Architecture Books and Writers 1556–1786* (Cambridge: Cambridge University Press, 1990), 194–6, 505, and Hans Aurenhammer, *J. B. Fischer von Erlach* (Cambridge, MA: Harvard University Press, 1973), 11, 30, 153–9.
67. Wren, "Tract I," 154. Cf. Vitruvius 1.3.2.
68. Wren, "Tract I," 154.
69. Alberti, *DRA*, bk. 6, chap. 2, 156.
70. Francis Bacon, *Works*, 4:26 (*Great Instauration*). See also Jones, *Ancients*, 50–1.
71. Wren, "Tract I," 154.
72. Important discussions of Wren's theory of beauty include the classic essay by John Summerson, "The Mind of Wren," in *Heavenly Mansions* (New York: Norton, 1963), 73–82, and the following more recent publications. By J. A. Bennett: "Christopher Wren: The Natural Causes of Beauty," *Architectural History* 15 (1972): 5–22; "Christopher Wren: Astronomy, Architecture, and the Mathematical Sciences," *Journal for History of Astronomy* 6, pt. 3 (1975): 174–5; and *The Mathematical Science of Christopher Wren* (Cambridge: Cambridge University Press, 1982), 118–24. By Kerry Downes: *The Architecture of Wren* (New York: Universe, 1982), 22–9, and *Hawksmoor* (London: Zwemmer, 1959), 16–32. See also Joseph Rykwert, *The First Moderns* (Cambridge, MA: MIT Press, 1980), 148–9.
73. Wren, "Tract I," 154.
74. Alberti, *DRA*, bk. 6, chap. 4, 159 and chap. 2, 156.
75. Ibid., bk. 9, chap. 5, 302. "The very same number that cause sounds to have that *concinnitas*, pleasing to the ears, can also fill the eyes and mind with wondrous delight" (305).
76. Ibid.
77. Ibid., bk. 7, chap. 3, 194. A little later, he states that the temple must be so beautiful that "anyone who entered it would start with awe for his admiration at all the noble

things, and could scarcely restrain himself from exclaiming that what he saw was a place undoubtedly worthy of God." Alberti's statements reflect the Christian tradition of beauty as a manifestation of God, beginning with Saint Augustine's idea of "divine illumination" – the recognition of beauty as the knowledge of the Creator. See Rudolf Wittkower, *Architectural Principles in the Age of Humanism* (New York: Norton, 1971), 7–16, 27, and Christine Smith, *Architecture in the Culture of Early Humanism* (Oxford: Oxford University Press, 1992), 83, 92.

On Augustine's ideas of beauty and their long influence, see Joseph A. Mazzeo, "The Augustinian Conception of Beauty and Dante's *Convivio*," *Journal of Aesthetics and Art Criticism* 15, no. 4 (June 1957), 435–48; Jan Bialostocki, "The Renaissance Concept of Nature and Antiquity," in *The Renaissance and Mannerism, Studies in Western Art II* (Princeton, NJ: Princeton University Press, 1963), 19–30; Erwin Panofsky, *Idea: A Concept in Art Theory* (New York: Harper and Row, 1968); and Emmanuel Chapman, *Saint Augustine's Philosophy of Beauty* (New York: Sheed and Ward, 1939).

78. There are numerous writings by scientists defending the New Science against accusations that it promoted atheism and asserting instead that it promoted Christian belief. The classic statement was made by John Ray in his *The Wisdom of God Manifested in the Works of Creation* (1691): "There is no greater, at least no more palpable and convincing Argument of the Existence of a Deity than the admirable Art and Wisdom that discovers itself in the make and constitution, the order and disposition, the ends and uses of all the parts and members of this stately fabrick of Heaven and Earth" (11–12). In describing stones, he writes "What variety? What beauty and elegancy? What constancy in their temper and consistency, in their Figures and Colours?" (67). See Michael Hunter, *Science and Society in Restoration England* (Cambridge: Cambridge University Press, 1981), 173–7.

Although he made no specific statements, Wren seems to have shared these sentiments. In his inaugural speech at Gresham College in 1657, he discussed the subject of astronomy – "the beauteous Heavens (infinite in Extention, pure and subtile, and sempiternal in Matter, glorious in their starry Ornaments, of which every one affords various Cause of Admiration, most rapid, yet most regular, most harmonious in their Motions, in every Thing, to a wise Considerer, dreadful and majestick) . . ." (*PAR*, 200).

79. See Hunter, *Science and Society*, 16.
80. *PAR*, 200–1.
81. The discussion that follows is based on Bennett, "Natural Causes," 12–15 and *Mathematical Science*, 118–22.
82. *PAR*, 204.
83. *PT* 4, no. 43 (11 January 1669): 867–8.
84. William Neile–Henry Oldenburg, 18 December 1668, *CHO*, 5: 263.
85. Ibid., January 1669, *CHO*, 5: 363.
86. Wren, "Tract I," 155–6.
87. Vitruvius 3.3.11–13; 3.4.5; 3.5.9; 6.2.1–5; and 6.3.11.
88. Wren, "Tract IV," 176–7, 181–2.
89. For modern treatments of these issues, see Branko Mitrović, "Objectively Speaking," *Journal of the Society of Architectural Historians* 52 (March 1993): 59–67; Karsten Harries, *The Meaning of Modern Art* (Evanston, IL: Northwestern University Press, 1968).
90. See Bennett, *Mathematical Science*, 32–4.

91. Wren, "Tract I," 154–5.
92. Alberti, *DRA*, bk. 6, chap. 2, 157.
93. Alberti, *DRA*, bk. 9, chap. 5, 302.
94. Bennett, "Natural Causes," 13; Francis Bacon, *Works*, 4:431 (*De augmentis scientiarum*, vol. 5 chap. 4) and *Works*, 4:54–5 (*Novum Organum*, vol. 1, Aph. 43).
95. Wren, "Tract II," 157 and "Tract V," 188.
96. Wren, "Letter from Paris," 104; "The Women ... sway also in Architecture; Works of Filgrand, and little Knacks are in great Vogue ... ;" Wren, "Report on Westminster Abbey," 85, where he complains of France, "the Fashions of which Nation we affected to imitate in all Ages, even when we were at Enmity with it."
97. Wren, "Tract II," 159.
98. Ibid., 157, 158.
99. Wren, "Tract I," 155.
100. Ibid., 154–5 and "Report on Westminster Abbey," 90.
101. Wren, "Tract IV," 169.
102. Wren, "Tract I," 153–4.
103. North, *Of Building*, 10.
104. Wren, "Tract II," 157.
105. Wren, "Tract I," 153–4.
106. Wren owned a copy of the 1684 edition of Perrault's *Vitruve* (Wren's Library, Lot 545) and the 1708 English edition of his *Ordonnance* (Lot 561, *A treatise of the Five Orders of Columns in Architecture*, trans. John James).
107. Guarino Guarini, *Architettura civile* (Milan: Il Polifilo, 1968), bk. 3, chap. 13, obs. 1, 207–9: "liberali, ma anche ingegnosi edificatori," "edificate con grande spesa, e non senza grand'arte," "però stupire gl'intelletti e rendono gli spettatori atterriti. . . ."
108. See Guarini, bk. 1, chap. 1, 9, chap. 3, obs. 6, 15, and obs. 1, 20; bk. 3, chap. 3, obs. 4, 135, and chap. 4, obs. 3, 138; Claude Perrault, *Ordonnance for the Five Kinds of Columns after the Method of the Ancients*, trans. I. K. McEwen (Santa Monica, CA: Getty Center, 1993), preface, 48.
109. Perrault, *Ordonnance*, preface, 48–9, 51–2.
110. For a general discussion of the methods of Bacon and Descartes, see the following: Herbert Butterfield, *The Origins of Modern Science 1300–1800*, rev. ed. (New York: Free Press, 1965), 108–28; A. Rupert Hall, *The Revolution in Science, 1500–1750*, 3d ed. (London: Longmans, 1983; 2d ed. entitled *The Scientific Renaissance 1500–1800* [1962]), 164–8, 177–85; A. Rupert Hall, *From Galileo to Newton 1630–1720* (New York: Harper and Row, 1963), 103–31; Ralph M. Blake, Curt J. Ducasse, and Edward H. Madden, *Theories of Scientific Method: The Renaissance through the Nineteenth Century* (Seattle: University of Washington Press, 1960), reprinted as vol. 2 of *Classics in the History and Philosophy of Science*, 7 vols. (New York: Gordon and Breach, 1989), chap. 3, "Francis Bacon's Philosophy of Science," 50–74, and chap. 4, "The Role of Experience in Descartes' Theory of Method," 75–103; Mary Hesse, "Francis Bacon's Philosophy of Science" (originally published 1964), in *Essential Articles for the Study of Francis Bacon*, ed. Brian Vickers (London, 1972), 114–39; R. F. Jones, *Ancients and Moderns: A Study of the Rise of the Scientific Movement in Seventeenth-Century England* (St. Louis, MO: Washington University, 1961), chap. 3, "The Bacon of the Seventeenth Century," 41–61; Evert van Leeuwen, "Method, Discourse, and the Art of Knowing," in *Essays on the Philosophy*

and Science of René Descartes, ed. Stephen Voss (Oxford: Oxford University Press, 1993), 224–41.
111. Guarini, bk. 1, chap. 2, 10: "E perché l'Architettura, come facoltà che in ogni sua operazione adopera le misure, dipende dalla Geometria, e vuol sapere almeno i primi suoi elementi...''; ibid., chap. 6, intro., 36: "Matematica, di cui l'Architettura si professa discepola."

On Guarini's theory, see: Rudolf Wittkower, "Guarini the Man," in *Studies in the Italian Baroque* (London: Thames and Hudson, 1975), 177–86; Nino Carboneri, introduction to Guarino Guarini, *Architettura civile* (Milan: Il Polifilo, 1968), and, in the same volume, Bianca Tavassi la Greca, "La posizione del Guarini in rapporto alla cultura filosofica del tempo," 439–59; P. di Paolo, "L'*Architettura civile* del Guarini e la trattatistica architettonica del XVII secolo," in R. Pisa, ed., *Scuola Normale Superiore. Annali. Classe di Lettere e Filosofia*, ser. 3, 2, no. 1 (1972): 311–50. In *Guarino Guarini e l'Internationalità del Barocco*, 2 vols. (Turin: Accademia delle Scienze, 1970): A. Cavalleri Murat, "Struttura e forma nel trattato architettonico del Guarini," 1:451–96, and Corrado Maltese, "Guarini e la prospettiva," 1:557–72. More recently, see Elwin C. Robison, "Optics and Mathematics in the Domed Churches of Guarino Guarini," *Journal of the Society of Architectural Historians* 50, no. 4 (December 1991): 384–401.

112. Guarini, bk. 1, chap. 3, intro., 10–11: "L'Architettura, sebbene dipenda dalla Matematica, nulla meno ella è un'arte adulatrice, che non vuole punto per la ragione disgustare il senso: onde sebbene molte regole sue sieguano i suoi dettami, quando però si tratta che le sue dimostrazioni osservate siano per offendere la vista, le cangia, le lascia, ed infine contradice alle medesime...."
113. Ibid., chap. 3, obs. 6, 15: "L'Architettura può correggere le regole antiche, e nuove inventare."
114. Ibid., bk. 3, chap. 22, obs. 6, 255–7: "La forza dell'immaginazione corregge le immagini e la spezie degli occhi in molte occasioni."
115. Ibid., chap. 3, obs. 4, and chaps. 21 and 22.
116. Ibid., bk. 1, chap. 3, obs. 7, 17: "Per serbare le dovute proporzioni in apparenza l'Architettura devesi partire dalle regole e dalle vere proporzioni."
117. Ibid., bk. 3, chap. 3, intro., 127: "è ben difficile sapere qual sia la radice di questo diletto, non meno difficile ella è la notizia della radice della bellezza d'un vago vestito..."; ibid., obs. 4, 134: "È difficile investigare in che propriamente consista la simmetria, e quella corrispondenza delle parti, per le quali un'ortografia ben disegnata tanto diletta l'occhio, e forsi non è men difficile che il sapere da che venga la discordanza de' suoni nella Musica, o la varietà de' colori nella Pittura; e pure l'Architettura...."
118. Ibid., intro., 127: "massime che talvolta veggiamo che gli uomini cangiano mode, e che quello che prima era ammirato per bello, vien poi abborrito per diforme...."
119. Ibid., obs. 1, 127–8.
120. Ibid., 128: "altri dal genio del proprio Paese portati abborriscono quello ch'è contro la loro consuetudine...." Ibid., intro., 127: "quello che piace a una nazione displace all'altra, e nello stesso nostro affare veggiamo che l'Architettura Romana prima spiacque ai Goti, e l'Architettura Gotica a noi stessi dispiace...."
121. Ibid., bk. 1, chap. 3, obs. 9, 19: "l'Architettura Gotica, la quale doveva pur piacere a que' tempi...."

122. Ibid.: "né altra ragione la governa, se non l'aggradimento di un ragionevole giudizio, e di un occhio giudizioso."
123. Ibid., bk. 3, chap. 3, obs. 1, 127: "L'occhio, al quale deve dilettare la simmetria degli ordini, deve essere giudizioso e libero da ogni propensione."
124. Claude Perrault, *Ordonnance for the Five Kinds of Columns after the Method of the Ancients*, trans. I. K. McEwen (Santa Monica, CA: Getty Center, 1993). For Perrault's theory, see two works by Wolfgang Herrmann, *The Theory of Claude Perrault* (London: Zwemmer, 1973), and "Unknown Designs for the 'Temple of Jerusalem' by Claude Perrault," in *Essays in the History of Architecture Presented to Rudolf Wittkower* (London: Phaidon, 1967), 143–58. See also the introduction by Alberto Pérez-Gómez to the recent English translation of Perrault's treatise, *Ordonnance*, 1–44.
125. Claude Perrault, *Les dix livres d'Architecture de Vitruve* (Paris, 1673), 204, note C, translated by Herrmann in *Theory*, 75.
126. Perrault, *Ordonnance*, pt. 2, chap. 7, 161, 158.
127. Ibid., preface, 50.
128. Ibid., 50–1.
129. Ibid., 49.
130. Ibid., 53.
131. Ibid.
132. Ibid., 54.
133. Ibid., 62.
134. Ibid., 61.
135. Ibid., 55.
136. Ibid., 60.
137. Ibid., 54, 55.
138. See Jean Marie Pérouse de Montclos, "Le Sixième Ordre d'Architecture, ou la Pratique des Ordres Suivant les Nations," *Journal of the Society of Architectural Historians* 36 (1977): 226, 231.
139. Perrault, *Vitruve*, 79, n. 16, quoted in Herrmann, *Theory*, 49.
140. Perrault, *Ordonnance*, pt. 2, chap. 8, 169.
141. See Perrault, *Ordonnance*, pt. 2, chap. 7, "Abuses in the Alteration of Proportions," 153–66.
142. For historical background on Louis XIV and Colbert in relationship to the arts, see Anthony Blunt, *Art and Architecture in France 1500–1700* (Harmondsworth, Middlesex: Penguin, 1981), 321–6.
143. Guarini, bk. 3, chap. 4, intro., 135–6: The architect "should go through various inventions outside of the secure path, in which, in the disposition of the orders, he has discovered the long experience of many centuries [vada per varie invenzioni fuora del sicuro sentiero, che nella disposizione degli ordini ha ritrovato la lunga experienza di molti secoli]." Also bk. 1, chap. 3, obs. 6, 15: "L'Architettura può correggere le regole antiche, e nuove inventare." For the new orders, see ibid., bk. 3, chaps. 5–10; chap. 18, obs. 1, 233: "In tal modo si potrà specular in ogni ordine, onde lo lascio all'ingegno ed industria de' virtuosi."
144. See Robison, "Optics."
145. Ibid., 400; H. A. Meek, *Guarino Guarini and his Architecture* (New Haven, CT: Yale University Press, 1988), 5–6. See also A. Boase, "Sant'Anna Reale," in *G. G. e l'Internazionalità del Barocco*, 1:345–58.
146. Wren, "Tract I," 153, 155.

147. Wren, "Tract I," 154 and "Tract II," 159.
148. See Edoardo Benvenuto, *An Introduction to the History of Structural Mechanics*, 2 pts. (New York: Springer-Verlag, 1991) 2:313–15; Rowland Mainstone, *Developments in Structural Form* (Cambridge, MA: MIT Press, 1975), 284; Howard Dorn, "The Art of Building and the Science of Mechanics: A Study of the Union of Theory and Practice in the Early History of Structural Analysis in England" (Ph.D. diss., Princeton University, 1970), 113–15.
149. Wren, "Tract II," 161–2.
150. Ibid., 162. Cf. Wren, "Report on Westminster Abbey," 84: "It is by due Consideration of the Statick Principles, and the right Poising of the Weights of the Butments to the Arches, that good Architecture depends; and the Butments ought to have equal Gravity on both Sides."
151. Wren, "Tract II," 163.
152. 8 December 1670, Birch, 2:461.
153. *Correspondence of Isaac Newton*, ed. H. W. Turnbull and J. F. Scott, 7 vols. (Cambridge: for the Royal Society at the University Press, 1959–77), 3:387, n. 1, gives evidence of "Wren. de onerand Arcu" ("Wren's problem of the loaded arch") in the marginalia of topics discussed in May 1694 with Newton or Fatio.
154. 7 December 1671; Birch, 2:498. *A Description of Helioscopes* (London, 1676 [1675]). The anagram, "Ut pendet continuum flexile, sic stabit contiguum rigidum inversum," was deciphered by Richard Waller in the introduction to Hooke's *Posthumous Works* (London, 1705). Benvenuto, *Structural Mechanics*, 2:328–9.
155. Hooke *Diary 1672–80*, 163. See Stanley B. Hamilton, "The Place of Sir Christopher Wren in the History of Structural Engineering," *Newcomen Society Transactions* 14 (1933/4): 37; Dorn, "Art of Building," 118–21.
156. Harold Dorn and Robert Mark, "The Architecture of Christopher Wren," *Scientific American*, n.s. 245 (July 1981): 160.
157. Rowland Mainstone, "Structural Theory and Design before 1742," *Architectural Review* 143, no. 854 (April 1968): 306–7.
158. There is no definitive work on stereotomy. The following discussion is based on Werner Müller, "The Authenticity of Guarini's Stereotomy in his *Architettura Civile*," *Journal of the Society of Architectural Historians* 27 (1968): 202–4, and his "Guarini e la stereotomia," in *G. G. e l'internazionalità del Barocco*, 1:531–40. See also Dora Wiebenson, "Building Technology in France (1685–1786)," *Journal of the Society of Architectural Historians* 39, no. 4 (December 1980); 314–15; Robin Middleton, "The Abbé de Cordemoy and the Graeco-Gothic Ideal," *Journal of the Warburg and Courtauld Institutes* 25 (1962): 291–4; and Alberto Pérez-Gómez, *Architecture and the Crisis of Modern Science* (Cambridge, MA: MIT Press, 1983), 227–32.
159. Philibert Delorme, *Le Premier tome de l'Architecture* (Paris, 1567). See also Anthony Blunt, *Philibert de l'Orme* (London: Zwemmer, 1958), 114–16.
160. Girard Desargues, *Brouillon project d'exemples d'une manière universelle . . . touchant la practique du trait à preuve pour la coupe des pierres en architecture* (Paris, 1640). Desargues's work was elaborated by his follower Abraham Bosse, *Pratique du trait à preuves de M. Desargues . . . pour la coupe des pierres en l'architecture* (Paris, 1643). Claude François Miliet Deschales, "De Lapidum Sectione," in *Cursus seu Mundus Mathematicus* (Lyon, 1674); Philippe de la Hire, *Traité de méchanique* (Paris, 1695), and "Sur la construction des voûtes dans les édifices," 27 February 1712, *Mémoires de l'Académie*

Royale des Sciences (1713), 69–77; see also Benvenuto, *Structural Mechanics*, 2:321–6, 331–6.

Another important writer on stereotomy is Mathurin Jousse, *Le secret d'architecture découvrant fidèlement les traits geométriques, couppes et dérobements necessaires dans le bastimens* (La Flèche, 1642).

161. Guarino Guarini, *Architettura civile* (Turin, 1737). This is the conclusion of Müller in "Guarini e la stereometria"; see also Robison, "Optics."

162. For a general discussion of geometrical methods up to the early eighteenth century, see Mainstone, "Structural Theory," 303–10. The classic discussion of the importance of geometrical methods in Gothic design is James Ackerman, "*'Ars sine scientia nihil est'*: Gothic Theory of Architecture at the Cathedral of Milan," *Art Bulletin* 30, no. 1 (1949): 89. For a recent analysis of the geometry used in the design of a Gothic church, see Linda E. Neagley, "Elegant Simplicity: The Late Gothic Plan Design of St.-Maclou in Rouen," *Art Bulletin* 74, no. 3 (September 1992): 395–422. For late Gothic treatises on geometrical methods, see Lon R. Shelby, *Gothic Design Techniques: The Fifteenth-Century Design Booklets of Mathes Roriczer and Hanns Schmuttermayer* (Carbondale: Southern Illinois University Press, 1977).

163. On Francesco di Giorgio and the use of his geometrical methods in Renaissance structural design, see Richard J. Betts, "Structural Innovation and Structural Design in Renaissance Architecture," *Journal of the Society of Architectural Historians* 52, no. 1 (March 1993): 5–25. On Rodrigo Gil's new, original methods, see Sergio L. Sanabria, "The Mechanization of Design in the 16th Century: The Structural Formulae of Rodrigo Gil de Hontañón," *Journal of the Society of Architectural Historians* 41, no. 4 (December 1982): 281–93. See also Delorme, *Le Premier tome*, fol. 235, whose method is based on Francesco's.

164. François Blondel, "Résolution des quatre principaux problèmes d'architecture," *Mémoires de l'Académie Royale des Sciences depuis 1666 jusqu'à 1699* 5 (1729): 355–530; Benvenuto, *Structural Mechanics*, 2:311. Carlo Fontana, *Templum Vaticanum, et ipsius origo, cum aedificiis maxime conspicuis antiquitus et recens ibidem constitutis* (Rome, 1694).

Tracts I through IV

1. This concept of architecture as a catalyst for national prosperity and pride echoes the prologue of Leon Battista Alberti's 1485 treatise *De re aedificatoria*, where he describes "the satisfaction, the delight, but even the honor that architecture has brought to citizens at home or abroad," and how one can build "to increase greatly not only your own honor and glory, but also that of your family, your descendants, and the whole city" (*DRA*, prologue, 4).

2. Empress Helena (c. A.D. 257–337?), mother of Emperor Constantine, took a pilgrimage to the Holy Land in 326–7. Among the buildings she subsequently sponsored were the basilica (begun 325/6) and the Anastasis Rotunda (337 or after) in Jerusalem, the latter containing the Sepulchre of Christ on Golgotha. See Richard Krautheimer, *Early Christian and Byzantine Architecture* (Harmondsworth, Middlesex: Penguin, 1986), 60–3.

3. "Capable": "able to be affected by; of a nature, or in a condition, to allow or admit of; admitting; susceptible" (*OED*).

4. Cf. Vitruvius 1.3.2: "Haec autem ita fieri debent, ut habeatur ratio firmitatis, utilitatis,

venustatis [Now these (various building types) should be so carried out that account is taken of strength, utility, grace]."

5. Cf. Alberti, *DRA*, bk. 6, chap. 2, 156, "Beauty is some inherent property, to be found suffused all through the body of that which may be called beautiful..."; "Beauty is that reasoned harmony of all the parts within a body, so that nothing may be added, taken away, or altered, but for the worse."

6. Cf. Alberti, *DRA*, bk. 6, chap. 2, 157: "Yet some would disagree who maintain that beauty, and indeed every aspect of building, is judged by relative and variable criteria, and that the forms of building should vary according to individual taste and must not be bound by any rules of art. A common fault, this, among the ignorant – to deny the existence of anything they do not understand." Cf. Alberti, *DRA*, bk. 9, chap. 5, 302: "When you make judgments on beauty, you do not follow mere fancy, but the workings of a reasoned faculty that is inborn in the mind.... What arouses and provokes such a sensation in the mind we shall not inquire in detail, but shall limit our consideration to whatever evidence presents itself that is relevant to our argument. For within the form and figure of a building there resides some natural excellence and perfection that excites the mind and is immediately recognized by it."

7. Cf. Alberti, *DRA*, bk. 7, chap. 4, 196: "It is obvious from all that is fashioned, produced, or created under her influence, that Nature delights primarily in the circle."

8. AS MS 313 reads "necessary."

9. "Equicrural triangle": "having legs of equal length; isosceles" (*OED*).

10. See note 6 above.

11. Cf. Alberti, *DRA*, bk. 9, chap. 10, 317: "But he [the architect] should forsake painting and mathematics no more than the poet should ignore time and meter.... But I can say this of myself: I have often conceived of projects in the mind that seemed quite commendable at the time, but when I translated them into drawings, I found several errors in the very parts that delighted me most, and quite serious ones; again, when I return to drawings, and measure the dimensions, I recognize and lament my carelessness; finally, when I pass from the drawings to the model, I sometimes notice further mistakes in the individual parts, even over the numbers."

12. Cf. Vitruvius 6.2.1–2: "When therefore account has been taken of the symmetries of the design and the dimensions have been worked out by calculation, it is then the business of his skill to have regard to the nature of the site.... For one kind of appearance is seen near at hand; another, in a lofty building; yet another in a confined site; a different one in an open site. And it is the business of a fine judgment to determine exactly what is to be done in these cases. For the eyes do not appear to bring accurate results, but the judgment is often deceived by it...."

13. See previous note.

14. "Visto": vista, view. "The form *visto* exhibits the common tendency to substitute -o for -a in adoptions of Romanic words" (*OED*).

15. "Tympan": tympanum.

16. For "Heighth;... as broad as high" AS MS 313 reads "Descent, and as ill to be above 3 times the Breadth as Heighth."

17. The commemorative marble column of Trajan, dedicated in 112, rises to the height of 125 feet in the Forum of Trajan in Rome and is carved with a continuous spiral

frieze depicting the Dacian Wars. J. B. Ward-Perkins, *Roman Imperial Architecture* (Harmondsworth, Middlesex: Penguin, 1981), 87.
18. This is an interesting conception of obelisks, pyramids, and columns as objects. It also suggests a reductive idea of the column as a basic element, complete in and of itself, from which compositions are made.
19. See Vitruvius 4.1 and 2.
20. "Artificial": "displaying special art or skill;" "skilfully made or contrived" (*OED*).
21. "Dotard": "A tree that has lost its top or branches, and of which the trunk alone remains, more or less in a state of decay" (*OED*).
22. "Bole": "The stem or trunk of a tree" (*OED*).
23. AS MS 313 reads "enjoyn'd."
24. Wren seems to be describing tie-beams or cross-beams, the ends of which, by resting on the beam or architrave, form the triglyphs of the frieze. See Vitruvius 4.2.
25. No illustration accompanies this text.
26. Augustus, reigned 27 B.C.–A.D. 14.
27. The facade of the Theater of Marcellus in Rome, dedicated 13–11 B.C., is comprised of two superimposed arcades, articulated by Doric half-columns below and Ionic above, supporting an attic story. See Ward-Perkins, *Roman Imperial Architecture*, 26–8. Wren's use of the theater as an example of the Doric follows the lead of earlier writers. Sebastiano Serlio, in book 4 on the orders (1537), in his *Tutte l'opere d'architettura et prospetiva* (Venice, 1619), cites "that most beautiful work, the Theatre of Marcellus in Rome, which from the middle down is Doric work, the columns of that theatre have no bases...." (*Sebastiano Serlio on Architecture*, trans. Vaughan Hart and Peter Hicks [New Haven, CT: Yale University Press, 1996], bk. 4, chap. 6, fol. 139). Giacomo Barozzi da Vignola, in his *Regola delli cinque ordini d'architettura* (Rome, 1562), took his Doric order from the theater, writing "l'ordine Dorico; ho considerato quel del Teatro di Marcello essere fra tutti gli altri da ogni huomo il più lodato" ("A i lettori"). Andrea Palladio, in *I quattro libri d'architettura* (1570; Eng. ed. by Isaac Ware, London, 1738), cited the theater as one of the three prime examples in Italy of the baseless Doric (Palladio [Ware], bk. 1, chap. 15). Although he recognized its use in other ancient monuments and by modern authors, Roland Fréart de Chambray, in his *Parallèlle de l'architecture antique et de la moderne* (Paris, 1650; Eng. ed. by John Evelyn, London, 1664), considered the theater's Doric the most authoritative, "as being the most regular of all the rest, by the universal suffrage of the Profession; and so conformable to what *Vitruvius* has written concerning the general Proportions of this *Order*, that some are of Opinion he was himself the *Architect* of this magnificent Work" (Fréart [Evelyn], 17).

Both Serlio and Palladio, who pointed out that the Doric order at the theater had no base, were aware that this was an anomaly in Roman architecture. In his discussions of the Doric order, Serlio gave it a base (bk. 4, chap. 6). Palladio illustrated the Doric with and without a base, concluding: "This order has no base peculiar to it, which is the reason that in a great many edifices the columns are to be seen without bases" (bk. 1, chap. 15). During the seventeenth century, the majority of theorists believed the Doric should be used with an Attic base in the most prevalent manner of the Romans. See Nikolaus Pevsner, "The Doric Revival," in *Studies in Art, Architecture, and Design* 1 (New York: Walker, 1968), 198–200.

In his discussion of the orders in Tracts II and III, Wren does not mention the base, completely focusing instead on the form and origin of the shaft and the entablature. He seems to cite the Theater of Marcellus only because it was a traditional example of the Doric used by modern writers before him.

28. The rectangular temple located in the Forum Boarium, dating from the second half of the second century B.C. Axel Boëthius, *Etruscan and Early Roman Architecture* (Harmondsworth, Middlesex: Penguin, 1978), 159–60. Although it is illustrated by both Serlio (bk. 3) and Palladio (bk. 4, chap. 13), neither comments on its Ionic order. Fréart, however, considered it "one of the most regular Examples of the whole *Ionick Order*, which is now extant of ancient *Architecture*," and "a *Master-piece* of supreme Perfection," using it as "the Model I shall follow, and which shall here serve for the *Rule* of this *Order*" (Fréart [Evelyn], 41, 42).

29. The Pantheon in Rome, c. 118–c. 128, was considered after the fifteenth century as one of the most beautiful, if not *the* most beautiful ancient building. In presenting the proportions of the Corinthian base, Serlio wrote, "I will choose one from the most beautiful building in Rome, the Pantheon, called la Ritonda, setting up its measurements as rules" (*Serlio on Architecture*, bk. 4, chap. 8, fol. 169). It is the first building he presents in his book on antiquities, writing, "the measurements of all the members are better observed than in any other building that I have seen and measured. In truth, this temple could be said to be an architectural exemplar" (bk. 3, chap. 3, fol. 50v). Vignola used the Pantheon as the model for the Corinthian order in his treatise: "Questa cornice Corintia è cavata da diversi luoghi di Roma, ma principalmente dalla rotonda, e dalle tre colonne che sono nel foro Romano" (pl. 26). The Pantheon also was an important model for Palladio: "In the design of a simple [Corinthian] colonnade the intercolumniations are of two diameters, as they are in the portico of *St. Maria la Rotunda* at *Rome*" (bk. 1, chap. 17, 21). He also presents ten plates of the building in book 4, chap. 20. Fréart de Chambray agreed with his predecessors: "having ever obtained the universal Approbation of knowing persons, as being the most regular *Corinthian* Work, and indeed the most famous among all the Remainders of *Antient Rome*, [the Pantheon] appears to me to be the very best *Model* which I could possibly make choice of" (Fréart [Evelyn], 67).

30. The Arch of Titus in Rome, located between the Forum Romanum and the Colosseum, was begun by Titus and finished after 81 by Domitian (see Ward-Perkins, *Roman Imperial Architecture*, 72–4). Not only did he illustrate the arch in his treatise (bk. 3), Serlio also recognized its order as an important example of the Composite, along with the second story of the Colosseum (bk. 4, chap. 9). Neither Vignola nor Palladio made any comment on this monument in their discussions of the Composite order. Fréart de Chambray, however, used the Arch of Titus and the Arco dei Leoni in Verona as the models for his Composite, the former for "the Richness of its Ornaments," leading him to conjecture that "the Inventor thereof might possibly accompany *Titus* at the *Expedition* and *Siege of Jerusalem*; and that it was *there* he had contemplated the divine *Architecture* of the *Temple of Solomon*," and imitated it in his work (Fréart [Evelyn], 108).

31. Pirro Ligorio (1513/4–83), famous for his design of the Casino of Pius IV (1558–65) and the Villa d'Este at Tivoli (1550–72), was also known as a painter and archaeologist. The provenance and present location of this alleged sketchbook is unknown, but there are references to similar material that was in the possession of Inigo Jones (1573–1652) and his pupil John Webb (1611–72). Jones cited drawings by Ligorio in his *Stone-Heng Restored*, published by Webb in 1655, in a discussion on round buildings with double colonnades: "Which double *Order of Columns Pyrrho Ligorio*, a

famous *Neapolitane* Architect, and great Discoverer of *Antiquities*, in his Description thereof, designs without a Roof also" (Inigo Jones, *The Most Notable Antiquity of Great Britain, Called Stone-Heng, . . . Restored* [London, 1655], 51). It is possible that after Jones's death these drawings came into the possession of Webb, whose "Book of Capitols" (*sic*) at the Royal Institute of British Architects reads "Pirrho 41/not taken" on the verso of one drawing. (See John Bold, "John Webb: Composite Capitals and the Chinese Language," *Oxford Art Journal* 4, no. 1 [July 1981]: 14–15, and idem, *John Webb* [Oxford: Clarendon, 1989], 32–4.) Therefore a sketchbook by Ligorio could well have existed, originally owned by Jones and available to Wren through Webb.

32. Inserted into the text after this passage is the following, with the source given as "*Hist. of Amphitheatres* by C. Maffei, *Edit.* Lond. 1730," probably Francesco Scipione Maffei, *A compleat history of the ancient amphitheatres . . . Made English from the Italian by A. Gordon* (1730):

> In further Proof of this, we have now a very remarkable Account of an eminent and learned Critick in Architecture, *viz.*
>
> "The first Story of the *Colisèo* at *Rome* is said to be *Dorick*, and yet the *Freeze* of it is not plain and smooth. The third Story is *Corinthian*, but without Carving or Ornaments, except in the Capitals. The fourth Story is *Composite*, but with *Corinthian* Capitals, and like those of the third Order; the Corbills in the Freeze shewing them of the *Composite* Order. The Pillars of the *four Orders*, one above the other, do not diminish in Dimension, according to Rule, but are all of a Thickness; and the Void of the Arches, the Parts, Ornaments, and Measures in the different Stories, have not that Diversity of Proportion, which is believed to be essential to different Orders. By the Example of this Amphitheatre, (the noblest Remain of ancient Magnificence) as well as by many others, it is evident, that in the Rules of the Proportions, and different Members, &c. of the Orders, there was no certain perpetual and universal Law, but the same Orders, Measures, and Manners differed, according to the various Kinds of Buildings, the Judgment of the Architect, and the different Circumstances of Things."

33. Seneca, *Epistulae Morales* 86.7 (Cambridge, MA: Harvard University Press, Loeb Classical Library, 1953): "Quantum statuarum, quantum columnarum est nihil sustinentium, sed in ornamentum positarum impensae causa! (What a vast number of statues, of columns that support nothing, but are built for decoration, merely in order to spend money!)"

34. Judith 3:7–8 (*The New Oxford Annotated Bible with the Apocrypha* [New York: Oxford University Press, 1973]): "And these people and all in the country round about welcomed him [Nebuchadnezzar] with garlands and dances and tambourines. And he demolished all their shrines and cut down their sacred groves; for it had been given to him to destroy all the gods of the land, so that all nations should worship Nebuchadnezzar only, and all their tongues and tribes should call upon him as god."

35. Virgil, *Aeneid* 1.441 (Cambridge, MA: Harvard University Press, Loeb Classical Library, 1978): "Amid the city was a grove, luxuriant in shade."

36. Cf. Wren's letter, probably to Barrow, describing his design of Trinity College Library, Cambridge, with a ground-floor colonnade: "I have chosen middle pillars and a double portico and lightes outward rather than a middle wall, as being the same expense, more graceful, and according to the manner of the ancients who made

double walks (with three rowes of pillars, or two rowes and a wall), about the forum" (*WS*, 5:32).
37. See Vitruvius 3.3.
38. AS MS 313 reads "Propositions."
39. RS MS 249 and AS MS 313 read "carrying."
40. Pheidias or Phidias (fifth century B.C.) supervised all the works on the Acropolis of Athens under Pericles. Among his famous works are the exterior sculpture of the Parthenon and the colossal statue of Athena located within it. See A. W. Lawrence, *Greek Architecture* (Harmondsworth, Middlesex: Penguin, 1983), 190–4.
41. According to Vitruvius, 7. preface. 13, one of the four Greek sculptors of the friezes and statues in the base of the Mausoleum of Halicarnassus (completed c. 349 B.C.).
42. AS MS 313 reads "begun to grow."
43. "Honor fosters the arts," Cicero, *Tusculan Disputations* 1.2 (Cambridge, MA: Harvard University Press, Loeb Classical Library, 1950).
44. A reference to the competition of 1671 to design a new order for the attic story of the Cour Carrée at the Louvre. Most of the entries proposed a Corinthian order with the acanthus replaced by fleurs-de-lis, the lily that was originally the coat of arms of the French monarchy. See Jean Marie Pérouse de Montclos, "Le Sixième Ordre d'Architecture, ou la Pratique des Orders Suivant les Nations," *Journal of the Society of Architectural Historians* 36 (1977): 223–40.
45. See Vitruvius 4.1.9–10.
46. "Flower-de-luce": fleur-de-lis. See note 44 above.
47. A Corinthian capital with palm leaves instead of acanthus, supporting a Doric entablature, was presented by Juan Bautista Villalpando (1552–1608) in his reconstruction of the Temple of Solomon found in volume 2 (1604) of *In Ezechielem Explanationes et Apparatus Urbis ac Templi Hierosolymitani*, 3 vols. (Rome, 1596, and 1604, written with Hieronymo Prado (1547–95).
48. Wren's demonstration that follows was first presented by François Derand in *L'Architecture des voûtes, ou l'art des traits et coupes des voûtes* (Paris, 1643), pt. 1, chap. 6, p. 10. It was later known as "Blondel's rule," having appeared in François Blondel's *Cours d'architecture*, 5 pts. (Paris, 1675, 1683; 2d ed. 1698), 419. From Derand's description it is apparent that this rule had been practiced for a long time, perhaps even during the Middle Ages. Viollet-le-Duc during the mid-nineteenth century found evidence of its usage in Gothic churches (*Dictionnaire raisonné de l'architecture française du XI° au XVI° siècle* [Paris, 1854–68]). Derand's rule was popular during the eighteenth century, although it was challenged by some writers. Edoardo Benvenuto, *An Introduction to the History of Structural Mechanics*, 2 pts. (New York: Springer-Verlag, 1991), 2:313–15.
49. Archimedes (287?–212 B.C.), Greek mathematician and inventor, who wrote a treatise entitled *On the Equilibrium of Planes or their Centers of Gravity*. Wren probably had in mind the work of John Wallis (1616–1703), F.R.S. In his *Mechanica, sive Tractatus de Motu* (London, 1670), Wallis claimed: "All the writers of mechanics assume that in every heavy body, there is a point called center of gravity, but I do not know whether any one of them has demonstrated its existence before me" (chap. 4, "De Centro Gravitatis"). See Benvenuto, *Structural Mechanics*, 1:43–55.
50. Wren would have known Donato Bramante's design for the dome of St. Peter's in Rome (1505–6) from the plan and section/elevation recorded in Serlio's book 3 on antiquities, first published in 1540. It consisted of a circular drum erected over pen-

dentives. The drum supported a hemispherical dome, the form of which, like that of the drum, was inspired by the Pantheon. Although it is unknown what materials and constructional techniques Bramante had envisioned for his design, it would have been a very weighty structure. Arnaldo Bruschi, "Plans for the Dome of St. Peter's from Bramante to Antonio da Sangallo the Younger," in *Domes from Antiquity to the Present*, Proceedings of IASS-MSU Symposium, Istanbul, 1988 (Istanbul: Mimar Sinan University, 1988), 234–5. See also Robert Mark, ed., *Architectural Technology up to the Scientific Revolution* (Cambridge, MA: MIT Press, 1993), 171.

Wren would have known about past criticisms of Bramante's design, particularly in relation to the four supporting piers and their crossing arches. In his book 3 of 1540, Serlio doubted that "such great height and weight" could be supported at such a height, observing that "the pillars already built with their arches, without any weight upon them, are already suffering and in some places are cracked" (bk. 3, fol. 66). These piers already had to be strengthened soon after Bramante's death. Wren's concern here is more with the form itself of Bramante's dome. His confidence in its stability may have been based on its similarity to the design of the Pantheon, with step-rings loading the extrados of the dome.

Wren possibly knew of the design and structure of St. Peter's as built through Carlo Fontana's *Templum Vaticanum, et ipsius origo, cum aedificiis maxime conspicuis antiquitus et recens ibidem constitutis* (Rome, 1694). The dome of St. Peter's was built by Giacomo della Porta in 1588–90 based on Michelangelo's design (1558–64), with modifications that had important structural implications. These included the pointing of the dome profile by adding 26.5 feet to its height, the reduction of the shell thickness, and the addition of two irons chains at the haunches.

See Wren's "Report on Salisbury Cathedral," 67, for a discussion of the use of iron in masonry structures. Wren does not seem to have been aware that he was correct in his caution about depending too greatly upon iron. Cracks were discovered in the dome of St. Peter's in 1631 and reported with concern in 1680. The damage had become so alarming by the 1740s that the pope asked Giovanni Poleni to make a study, which appeared as *Memorie istoriche della gran cupola del Tempio Vaticano* (Padua, 1748). When, according to Poleni's recommendations, five chains were added around the dome, it was discovered that the chains placed there by della Porta during construction had broken. The failure of these chains to endure could have been the initial cause of the cracks that had widened so alarmingly by the eighteenth century. See Elwin C. Robison, "St. Peter's Dome: The Michelangelo and della Porta Designs," in *Domes from Antiquity to the Present*, Proceedings of IASS-MSU Symposium, Istanbul, 1988, 254–9; see also Mark, *Architectural Technology*, 174–6. On Poleni and St. Peter's, see Benvenuto, *Structural Mechanics*, 2:351–71; also Roberto Di Stefano, *La Cupola di San Pietro*, 2d ed. (Naples: Edizioni Scientifiche Italiane, 1980).

51. See note 54 below.
52. Cf. Wren, "Report on Westminster Abbey," 85: "The *Romans* always concealed their Butments, whereas the *Normans* thought them ornamental." Wren's description of the "buttresses" of the Romans is a mystery, particularly given the fact that he probably knew the architecture of the examples that follow only through the illustrations of Serlio, book 3, 1540 (for both the Baths of Diocletian and the "Temple of Peace") and of Palladio, 1570 (for the "Temple of Peace"). Neither author illustrates the "buttress" detail Wren is describing.
53. The Baths of Diocletian in Rome were built c. 298–305/6 (see Ward-Perkins, *Roman*

Imperial Architecture, 418–21). The "Templum Pacis": the Basilica of Maxentius and Constantine in Rome, begun 307–12, completed after 312. It appears that confusion about the identity of the basilica began during the Middle Ages when it was called *templum Romuli supra templum Latonae* in chapter 24 of the guidebook entitled *Mirabilia urbis Romae*, dating from as early as the mid-twelfth century. During the Renaissance it was known as the *Templum Pacis*, confusing it with the Temple of Peace built by Vespasian from 71 and dedicated in A.D. 75. This designation can be found on a drawing of the basilica by Francesco di Giorgio dating from the 1470s and 1480s (fol. 76, Codex 148 Saluzzo), and in later treatises by Serlio, Palladio, and others. It was not until the early nineteenth century, with the excavations of Antonio Nibby, that its correct identity was established (see Antonio Nibby, *Del Tempio della Pace e della Basilica di Costantino* [Rome, 1819]). For the real *Templum Pacis* in the Forum of Vespasian, just to the north of the basilica, see Ward-Perkins, *Roman Imperial Architecture*, 71–9.

54. Wren uses three different terms – "moderns," "freemasons," and "Saracens" – to refer to Gothic architects. Though he uses the term "modern" in reference to things recent or contemporary, he also uses it as did fifteenth- and sixteenth-century writers on art and architecture. Alberti was the first to distinguish between the good "ancient" and the bad "modern," i.e., medieval, forms of architecture that continued to be used in his own time: "Examples of ancient temples and theaters have survived that may teach us as much as any professor, . . . And anyone who happens to build nowadays draws his inspiration from inept modern nonsense rather than proven and much commended methods" (Alberti, *DRA*, bk. 6, chap. 1, 154). John Evelyn, in his "Account of Architects and Architecture," described "a certain Fantastical and Licentious manner of Building, which we have since call'd *Modern* (or *Gothic* rather) Congestions of heavy, Dark, Melancholy and *Monkish Piles*, without any just Proportion, Use or Beauty, compar'd with the truly *Ancient*" (Evelyn, "Account," 9, in *A parallel of the ancient architecture with the modern . . . by Roland Fréart, Sieur de Chambray*, trans. John Evelyn, 2d ed. [London, 1707]).

During the seventeenth century the term "freemasons" had several meanings. Since the fourteenth century it had referred to operative masons who worked in freestone. During Wren's time, another meaning developed, with the term "free and accepted masons," referring to nonoperative members of freemasonic lodges, admitted for their architectural and antiquarian knowledge. By the end of the seventeenth century, societies of accepted freemasons had evolved that were completely nonoperative in nature, coming together only for social reasons. See Douglas Knoop and G. P. Jones, *The Genesis of Freemasonry* (Manchester: Manchester University Press, 1947), 12–15, 129–58; James Stevens Curl, *The Art and Architecture of Freemasonry* (Woodstock, NY: Overlook Press, 1991), 20–1. Wren's use of the term "freemason" in conjunction with "modern" is interesting in what appears to be a historical perspective, associating a particular form of architecture, the Gothic, with a particular craft. This may reflect his own experiences with masons, who during the second half of the seventeenth century perpetuated a Gothic survival through their traditional methods, but at the same time were also called upon by architects such as Wren to work in the Classical style. See Kenneth Clark, *The Gothic Revival* (New York: Harper and Row, 1962), 14–23.

Wren's use of the term "Saracen" is related to his theory that the Gothic style of architecture originated in the Levant with the Arabs and was brought to western

Europe, and particularly to France, by the returning Crusaders beginning during the late eleventh century. This architecture was characterized by the use of pointed arches. See Wren's "Report on Westminster Abbey," 83, 85.
55. That is, domes and half-domes.
56. That is, the barrel vault.
57. The Basilica of Maxentius and Constantine. See note 53 above.
58. That is, the pointed arch.
59. Wren is describing a Gothic fan vault.
60. Hagia Sophia in Constantinople, 532–7.
61. Wren probably had in mind the Ottoman mosques in Constantinople, typically covered by a large dome on pendentives and preceded by a forecourt surrounded by domed loggias. He would have known of these buildings through travel books. For example, Guillaume-Joseph Grelot, in his *Relation nouvelle d'un voyage de Constantinople* (1680; Eng. ed. 1683) discussed and illustrated three mosques of this form: the "New Mosque" (Mosque of Ahmed I, 1609–17), the "Solimany" (Süleymaniye Mosque, 1550–7), and the "Mosque of Validea" (Yeni Valide Complex, from 1597). These mosque complexes often had outbuildings that were organized around courtyards with domed passages. Among them was the *tabhane*, a hospice for travelers, in particular for the wandering dervishes – members of the Moslem orders. This may be the source for Wren's idea of the "Cloysters of the Dervises." On Ottoman architecture, see Godfrey Goodwin, *A History of Ottoman Architecture* (London: Thames and Hudson, 1971), and Sheila S. Blair and Jonathan M. Bloom, *The Art and Architecture of Islam 1250–1800* (New Haven, CT: Yale University Press, 1994).
62. Wren is describing a dome on pendentives.
63. Wren is not correct in his examples. The dome of Hagia Sophia does not rest on a drum but directly on the pendentives. The piers at St. Peter's are chamfered, so the pendentives, which support the drum and dome, are generated based on an octagonal plan, not the square described by Wren.
64. The Seraglio or Grand Signior's palace was the Topkapi Palace in Istanbul, the royal palace and seat of the Ottoman imperial administration. Replacing an olive grove and a few residences, it was built on the ancient acropolis of the city, from the second half of the fifteenth century, by Sultan Mehmed II. Expansions and modifications continued through the sixteenth century under Süleyman the Magnificent and his successors. A few spaces were accessible to ambassadors and dignitaries, some of which were covered by domes on pendentives. They include the Council Chamber or Hall of the Divan, the Chancery, and the archives; the last two were also called the Offices of the Divan. See Gülru Necipoglu, *Architecture, Ceremonial, and Power: The Topkapi Palace in the Fifteenth and Sixteenth Centuries* (Cambridge, MA: MIT Press, 1991), 3–4, 79–84.

Wren would have known of the Topkapi Palace through the limited information in travel books, for example, Grelot's *Relation nouvelle d'un voyage de Constantinople*, and from travelers, including his acquaintance Sir Dudley North. Brother of the architect Roger North, Dudley had spent twenty years in Smyrna and Constantinople, returning to England in 1680, and was known as a keen observer of Turkish buildings (see p. 125 and *WS*, 19: 116). Whatever his sources, Wren did not have complete or fully accurate information. He was incorrect in placing the palace of the bishop or patriarch, which had stood along the south side of Hagia Sophia, on this

site. See Rowland J. Mainstone, *Hagia Sophia* (New York: Thames and Hudson, 1988), 110.
65. The Great Palace of the Byzantine emperors was in fact located to the southwest of the Seraglio or Topkapi Palace. It was begun by Constantine after 324 and was in use until the sack of Constantinople by the Crusaders in 1204. It was in ruins by the time the city was conquered by the Ottomans in 1453. See Richard Krautheimer, *Three Christian Capitals: Topography and Politics* (Berkeley: University of California Press, 1983), 47–50, and idem, *Early Christian and Byzantine Architecture*, 70–2.
66. The earliest use of dome on pendentives in Wren's designs for St. Paul's appears in the Pre-Fire Design, finished 5 August 1666 (figs. 13, 15). The drawing of the section shows the nave and transept arms recased in the Classical style and covered by a series of domes on pendentives. This vaulting appears again in the aisles of the Greek Cross Design and the Great Model, and in the nave of the final design. See Kerry Downes, *The Architecture of Wren* (New York: Universe, 1982), fig. 10. Wren did not use this structural system at the crossing until the final design. In the Penultimate Design, begun sometime after the Warrant Design of 14 May 1675, the final dome began to take shape, where eight pendentives were used to make the transition from octagonal ground plan to circular drum to dome (John Summerson, "The Penultimate Design for St. Paul's Cathedral," [orig. publ. 1961], in *The Unromantic Castle and Other Essays* [London: Thames and Hudson, 1990], 74–5). Foundations were begun 18 June 1675, so this decision was made sometime in May or June 1675.
67. Wren is describing a cross vault based on a semicircular arch.
68. Wren is describing a vault of four pendentives generated from a square plan.
69. Wren is describing the Roman cross vault based on a semicircular arch.
70. Wren is describing a Gothic cross vault based on the pointed arch.
71. These passages recapitulate Figs. III and IV of Fig. 33.
72. Wren is describing the fill placed up to the haunches of the arch to provide resistance to the lateral thrust.
73. That is, the barrel vault.
74. This incomplete passage appears to be a review of the abutment of the arch found in Fig. II of Fig. 33, as described above on p. 162.
75. See Vitruvius 4.1.3.
76. For more recent theories on the origin of the Doric order, see William B. Dinsmoor, *The Architecture of Ancient Greece* (London: Batsford, 1950), 50–8, and additional bibliography on page 350; and J. J. Coulton, *Ancient Greek Architects at Work* (Ithaca, NY: Cornell University Press, 1977), 37–41.
77. See Vitruvius 4.2.1–2. "Sub tectis, si maiora spatia sunt, et transtra et capreoli [Under roofs, if the spans are considerable, both cross pieces and stays]."
78. Cornelius de Bruin or Le Brun, *Reizen van C. de Bruyn door de vermaardste deelen van Klein Asia, de eylanden Scio, Rhodus, Metelino, Stanchio, &c.* (Delft, 1698); translated as *Voyage au Levant* (Delft, 1700) and as *A Voyage to the Levant* (London, 1702).
79. These passages appear to be based on a variety of ancient descriptions of Alexandria, including: Vitruvius 2.preface.4; Diodorus Siculus 17.52.1–3; Pliny, *Natural History* 5.11.62–3; Strabo, *Geography* 17.1.6–8; Josephus, *Jewish War* 2.487–8; and Josephus, *Against Apion* 2.35.
80. Palmyra in present-day Syria. Wren is referring to the second-century colonnaded streets built there under the Romans.

81. Strabo, *Geography* 14.5.9 (Cambridge, MA: Harvard University Press, Loeb Classical Library, 1960–7): "Then, a little above the sea, to Anchiale, which, according to Aristobulus, was founded by Sardanapallus. Here, he says, is the Tomb of Sardanapallus, and a stone figure which represents the fingers of the right hand as snapping together, and the following inscription in Assyrian letters: 'Sardanapallus, the son of Anacyndaraxes, built Anchiale and Tarsus in one day. Eat, drink, be merry, because all things else are not worth this,' meaning the snapping of the fingers." Tarsus was a city on the southern coast of Asia Minor (Turkey) in Cilicea; "Anchiala," or Anchialos, a Greek colony on the western coast of the Black Sea in Thrace. See *Atlas of the Classical World*, ed. A. A. M. Van der Heyden and H. H. Scullard (London: Nelson, 1959).
82. Antoine Desgodets, *Les Edifices antiques de Rome* (Paris, 1682), chap. 1, 1–63, and pls. 1–23.
83. Wren's Monument to the Great Fire, located in London and dating from 1671 to 1676, is a colossal fluted Doric column 112.5 feet high, with a diameter of 15 feet, making a proportion of 1:7.5.
84. Pliny the Younger, *Letters* 9.39 (Cambridge, MA: Harvard University Press, Loeb Classical Library, 1975): "To Mustius: I am told by the soothsayers that I must rebuild the temple of Ceres which stands on my property; it needs enlarging and improving, for it is certainly very old and too small considering how crowded it is on its special anniversary, when great crowds gather there from the whole district on 13 September and many ceremonies are performed and vows made and discharged. But there is no shelter near by from rain or sun, so I think it will be an act of generosity and piety alike to build as fine a temple as I can and add porticoes – the temple for the goddess and the porticoes for the public. Will you then please buy me four marble columns, any kind you think suitable, and marble for improving the floor and walls. . . ."
85. The biblical Temple of Dagon described in Judges 16:25–30: "Then the lords of the Philistines gathered them together for to offer a great sacrifice unto Dagon their god, and to rejoice: for they said, Our god hath delivered Samson our enemy into our hand. . . . And they called for Samson out of the prison house; and he made them sport: and they set him between the pillars. . . . Now the house was full of men and women; and all the lords of the Philistines were there; and there were upon the roof about three thousand men and women, that beheld while Samson made sport. . . . And Samson took hold of the two middle pillars upon which the house stood, and on which it was borne up, of the one with his right hand, and of the other with his left. And Samson said, Let me die with the Philistines. And he bowed himself with all his might; and the house fell upon the lords, and upon all the people that were therein."
86. AS MS 313 reads "which."
87. RS MS 249 reads "walls and all" deleted.
88. Cf. "Tract V," 191, on the "Pillar of Absalom," which Wren presented "by the description given of it, and what I have learnt from Travellers who have seen it." The nomenclature of both "pillar" and "tomb" is due to the fact that two different monuments were associated with Absalom, son of David. According to 2 Samuel 18: 17–18, and Josephus, *Antiquities* 7.241–3 (Cambridge, MA: Harvard University Press, Loeb Classical Library, 1950–65), there was "a marble column" erected by Absalom to commemorate his own name after his death, as well as his actual tomb, a large

pit covered with a heap of stones. Although some pilgrims to Jerusalem during the late sixteenth and early seventeenth centuries, such as Christian van Adrichem (1590) and Thomas Fuller (1650), observed a pillar which they ascribed to Absalom, others, including Henry Timberlake (1603), William Biddulph (1609), and George Sandys (1615), saw a different monument, which they called alternately the "tomb" and "pillar" of Absalom. An illustration of this second structure was first presented by George Sandys, *A relation of a journey begun Anno domini 1610* (London, 1615, with editions up to 1672), who described a square structure surrounded by Doric half-columns and covered by a bell-shaped dome, all cut out of the living rock in the Valley of Jehosaphat or Kedron (147). This monument still exists today as Absalom's tomb, located in the Kidron Valley with other cave-tombs cut into the slope of the Mount of Olives facing the Temple Mount. It consists of a cubical monolith containing a single tomb and is ornamented by Ionic half-columns and corner pilasters supporting a Doric frieze. Above is an attic crowned by a trumpet-shaped roof of ashlar stone. Historically it was the funereal monument for the associated burial chambers, known as the Tomb of Jehosaphat, which as a group probably formed a funerary complex of a high-ranking or priestly family of the Herodian period, around 50 A.D. See Benjamin Mazar, *The Mountain of the Lord: Excavating in Jerusalem* (Garden City, NY: Doubleday, 1975), 224–5, and Dan Bahat, *Jerusalem: Selected Plans of Historical Sites and Monumental Buildings* (Jerusalem: Ariel, 1980), 105. Wren's description of a square or hexagonal monument with pillars and dome probably derives from Sandys, for an accurate depiction of the tomb did not exist until 1698, when Cornelius de Bruyn or Le Brun published his travels (French ed. 1700; Eng. ed. 1702).

89. 1 Kings 5:1–18. "And Hiram king of Tyre sent his servants unto Solomon; . . . And Solomon sent to Hiram, saying, . . . And, behold, I purpose to build an house unto the name of the Lord my God, . . . Now therefore command thou that they hew me cedar trees out of Lebanon; and my servants shall be with thy servants: and unto thee will I give hire for thy servants according to all that thou shalt appoint: for thou knowest that there is not among us any that can skill to hew timber like unto the Sidonians. . . . So Hiram gave Solomon cedar trees and fir trees according to all his desire. . . . And the king commanded, and they brought great stones, costly stones, and hewed stones, to lay the foundation of the house. And Solomon's builders and Hiram's builders did hew them, and the stonesquarers: so they prepared timber and stones to build the house."

90. RS MS 249 reads "and."
91. RS MS 249 and AS MS 313 read "manner."
92. 1 Kings 6:2–6. "And the house which king Solomon built for the Lord, the length thereof was threescore cubits, and the breadth thereof twenty cubits, and the height thereof thirty cubits. And the porch before the temple of the house, twenty cubits was the length thereof, according to the breadth of the house; and ten cubits was the breadth thereof before the house. . . . And against the wall of the house he built chambres round about, against the walls of the house round about, both of the temple and of the oracle: and he made chambers round about: The nethermost chamber was five cubits broad, and the middle was six cubits broad, and the third was seven cubits broad. . . ."

2 Chronicles 3:3–4. "The length by cubits after the first measure was threescore cubits, and the breadth twenty cubits. And the porch that was in the front of the

house, the length of it was according to the breadth of the house, twenty cubits, and the height was an hundred and twenty...."
93. See note 47 above.
94. According to Pliny, *Natural History* 36.179 (Cambridge, MA: Harvard University Press, Loeb Classical Library, 1956–66): "It was in the earlier temple of Diana at Ephesus that columns were for the first time mounted on moulded bases and crowned with capitals, and it was decided that the lower diameter of the columns should be one-eighth of their height, that the height of the moulded bases should be one-half of the lower diameter and that the lower diameter should exceed the upper diameter by a seventh."
95. According to Pliny, *Natural History* 36.95: "Of grandeur as conceived by the Greeks a real and remarkable example still survives, namely the Temple of Diana at Ephesus, the building of which occupied all Asia Minor for 120 years."
96. Pliny, *Natural History* 36.95–7: "The length of the temple overall is 425 feet, and its breadth 225 feet. There are 127 columns, each constructed by a different king and 60 feet in height. Of these, 36 were carved with reliefs, one of them by Scopas. The architect in charge of the work was Chersiphron."

There were two temples dedicated to Diana built on the same site in Ephesus. The first, dating c. 560 B.C., was built by King Croesus of Lydia and was indeed one of the earliest temples to use the Ionic order. Destroyed in a fire of 356, the temple was rebuilt by Paeonius of Ephesus, Demetrius, a slave of the temple, and possibly later by Deinocrates. This second temple, not the first, is the one described by Pliny (see Lawrence, *Greek Architecture*, 161–6, 254–6); A. Bammer, *Die Architektur des jüngeren Artemision von Ephesos* (Wiesbaden, 1972); A. Rügler, *Die Columnae Caclatae des jüngeren Artemisions von Ephesos* (Tübingen, 1988).
97. Coins depicting the Temple of Diana at Ephesus often showed the many-breasted figure of the goddess under the portico. They were recorded by Pirro Ligorio (see Maria Luisa Madonna, "*Septem Mundi Miracula* come Templi della Virtu: Pirro Ligorio e l'Interpretazione cinquecentesca delle Meraviglie del Mondo," *Psicon* 3, no. 7 [1976]: 51) and Fischer von Erlach (see *Entwurff einer historischen Architektur* [Vienna, 1721], 28, pl. 7). See also Bluma L. Trell, "The Temple of Artemis at Ephesus," *Numismatic Notes and Monographs 107* (New York: American Numismatic Society, 1945).
98. AS MS 313 reads "Architects."
99. Acts 19:24: "For a certain man named Demetrius, a silversmith, which made silver shrines for Diana, brought no small gain unto the craftsmen."
100. Wren probably knew of these models from travelers to the Near East. The text may be a reference to the model of the sepulchre deposited by Thomas Povey at the Royal Society on 29 March 1677, which Wren must have seen. The minutes state: "Mr. Povey produced a model of the Sepulchre of our Saviour at Jerusalem, said to have been made upon the place by the Maronites" (Birch, 3:337). Thomas Povey (born c. 1615), F.R.S., was an administrator and courtier, and a friend of Evelyn and Pepys (*DNB*). The model is listed in the two inventories made in the eighteenth century and described in the later one as "A Model of the holy sepulchre in wood, inlayed with Mother of pearl" (RS MS 417 [1765], item 34).
101. According to Pliny, *Natural History* 36: "The crowning marvel was his [Chersiphron's] success in lifting the architraves of this massive building into place.... But the greatest difficulty was encountered with the lintel itself when he was trying to

place it over the door; for this was the largest block, and it would not settle on its bed. The architect was in anguish as he debated whether suicide should be his final decision. The story goes that in the course of his reflections he became weary, and that while he slept at night he saw before him the goddess for whom the temple was being built: she was urging him to live because, as she said, she herself had laid the stone. And on the next day this was seen to be the case. The stone appeared to have been adjusted merely by dint of its own weight."

102. For example, Jacob Spon and George Wheler, who together observed the remains at Ephesus in 1675 and each of whom published his own account. Jacob Spon, *Voyage d'Italie, de Dalmatie, de Grece et du Levant, fait aux années 1675 & 1678* (Amsterdam, 1679; orig. ed. Lyon, 1678), 254; George Wheler, *A Journey into Greece* (London, 1682; orig. ed. London, 1678), 258.

103. See note 97 above.

104. The Basilica of Maxentius and Constantine in Rome (see n. 53 above). For contemporary scholarship on the monument, see Ward-Perkins, *Roman Imperial Architecture*, 426–8; A. Minoprio, "A Restoration of the Basilica of Constantine," *Papers of the British School at Rome* 12 (1932): 1–25.

105. The Great Hall of Richard II in the Palace of Westminster in London. Built 1394–1402 by Hugh Herland, carpenter, and Henry Yevele, mason, its wooden hammer-beam roof has a span of 67.5 feet. Geoffrey Webb, *Architecture in Britain* (Harmondsworth, Middlesex: Penguin, 1956), 188–91.

106. Wren was Surveyor of the Abbey from 1698 until his death (Downes, *Architecture*, 17). No mention of this condition in the aisles is made in his 1713 report on the abbey.

107. This passage indicates that Wren based his description on the reconstruction by Andrea Palladio, published in the *Quattro Libri dell'Architettura* of 1570, bk. 4, chap. 6, and pls. 1–3, but also available in Italian and French seventeenth-century editions. Palladio's reconstruction had the unique feature, matching the circular apse in the central chapel, of small rectangular rooms projecting from the flanking chapels. Based on Palladio's statement, "This temple was begun by the emperor CLAUDIUS, and finished by VESPASIAN after he returned victorious from *Judea*, in which he preserved all the vessels, and ornaments (which he carried in his triumph) of the temple of *Jerusalem*" (Palladio [Ware], bk. 4, chap. 6, 86), Wren presumed these rooms were used to store these spoils.

108. The entablature above the composite columns inside the Basilica of Maxentius and Constantine does indeed leave out the corona, the vertical-faced projection typically located between the uppermost molding, the cymatium or sima, and the bed-molding just above the under-surface of the soffit with its modillions. For example, compare fig. 39, Palladio's detail of the basilica (bk. 1, pl. 14), with his detail of the portico of the Pantheon, pl. 56. Wren appears to be the first writer to have noticed and given an explanation for the design of the cornice at the basilica.

109. Roger North recorded Wren's response to the problem of obtaining stones large enough to make giant-story columns and continuous entablatures in monumental buildings. In their discussions North was critical of the broken entablatures and superimposed orders at Jones's Banqueting House and at the new St. Paul's, but Wren explained why they were used: "For they could not have materialls to make good single Columnes, nor to project the entabletures so farr as to range strait over the heads of the columns, but were force't in the one to double the orders, and

in the other to double both columnes and the orders, and in both to break the entablements without, which shift Sir Christopher Wren informed me of when I observed to him the exility of his columns, with respect to the grandeur of his fabrick at Paulls" (BL MS Add. 32540, fols. 42v–43, reprinted in Roger North, *Of Building: Roger North's Writings on Architecture*, ed. Howard M. Colvin and John Newman [Oxford: Clarendon, 1981], 22, note). On the structural problems of St. Paul's facade, see Colvin, preface to ibid., xvii, n. 16.

110. This information, which is incorrect, has its source in Palladio's treatise. See notes 53, 104, and 107 above.

111. The so-called Temple of Vesta at Tivoli dates from the early first century B.C. (Boëthius, *Etruscan and Early Roman Architecture*, 163). Wren would have known of Palladio's drawings of the temple (bk. 4, chap. 16, and pls. 34–6); only a cornice, with no architrave or frieze, is shown around the interior of the circular portico.

112. In AS MS 313 "in the open Air . . . from the Weather" reads "whether."

113. For recent scholarship on the Temple of Mars Ultor, located in the Forum of Augustus and dedicated in 2 B.C., see Ward-Perkins, *Roman Imperial Architecture*, 29–33, and James C. Anderson, Jr., *The Historical Topography of the Imperial Fora* (Brussels: Latomus, Revue d'Etudes Latines, 1984), 65–100; also Paul Zanker, *Forum Augustum* (Tübingen: Wasmuth, 1972); Valentin Kockel, "Beobachtungen zum Tempel des Mars Ultor und zum Forum des Augustus," *Mitteilungen des Deutschen Archäologischen Instituts, Römische Abteilung* 90, no. 2 (1983): 421–48; Joachim Ganzert, "Der Mars-Ultor-Tempel auf dem Augustusforum in Rom," *Mitteilungen* 92 (1985): 201–19.

114. This passage is based on Palladio's text: "Near the tower of the *Conti's* the ruins are to be seen of the temple built formerly by AUGUSTUS to MARS the *Avenger* . . ." (Palladio [Ware], bk. 5, chap. 7, 87). The Plan shown in fig. 40 is also from Palladio, book 4, plate 4.

115. Ovid, *Fasti* 5.577 (Cambridge, MA: Harvard University Press, Loeb Classical Library, 1959): "Thou shalt receive a temple, and shalt be called Avenger, when victory is mine."

116. The Basilica of Maxentius and Constantine in Rome. See previous section.

117. AS MS 313 reads "Building."

118. Vitruvius 3.3.11. "Then, too, the columns at the corners should be made thicker than the others by a fiftieth of their own diameter, because they are sharply outlined by the unobstructed air round them, and seem to the beholder more slender than they are. Hence we must counteract the ocular deception by an adjustment of the proportions."

119. Ovid, *Fasti* 5.559–68: "The god of arms surveys the pinnacles of the lofty edifice, and approves that the highest places should be filled by the unconquered gods. He surveys on the doors weapons of diverse shapes, and arms of lands subdued by his soldiery. On this side he sees Aeneas laden with his dear burden, and many an ancestor of the noble Julian line. On the other side he sees Romulus carrying on his shoulders the arms of the conquered leader, and their famous deeds inscribed beneath the statues arranged in order. He beholds, too, the name of Augustus on the front of the temple; and the building seems to him still greater, when he reads the name of Caesar."

120. Ovid, *Fasti* 5.555: "The god is huge and so is the structure: no otherwise ought

Mars to dwell in his son's city. That shrine is worthy of trophies won from giants...."
121. Palladio, bk. 4, chap. 7, text and pls. 4–10.
122. Palladio (Ware), bk. 4, chap. 31, 109–10: "Opposite to the temple of MARS the Avenger, of which the designs have been already given, in the place that is called *in Pantano*, which is behind *Morforio*, was antiently the following temple, the foundations of which were discovered in digging to build a house; and there was also found a very great quantity of marbles, all of them most excellently wrought. It is not known by whom it was built, nor to what god it had been consecrated. But because in the fragments of the gola diritta of its cornice, one sees dolphins carved, and in some places between each dolphin there are tridents, I believe that it was dedicated to NEPTUNE."

The remains observed by Palladio were those of the Forum Iulium (Forum of Caesar) located to the southwest of the Forum Augustum, as rebuilt by Domitian from c. A.D. 95. There, intertwined dolphins were used as a decorative motif (Anderson, *Imperial Fora*, 56–7).
123. Marcus Tullius Cicero: the reference is unknown.
124. Wren seems to be describing the coffering used in the Temple of Mars Ultor, found in the soffit of the portico, alternating between sunken squares with rosettes and raised rectangles with a key pattern. They are depicted by Palladio in book 4, pl. 8. Earlier, Serlio had recognized the similarities between such patterns used for ornamented ceilings and garden designs. In bk. 4, chap. 7, 192v–99, he presented elaborate paneled ceilings alongside geometrically patterned parterres and mazes.
125. Palladio, bk. 4, chap. 7, pl. 22. "Which ornaments in the inside have been added by me, taken from some antient fragments found near this temple" (Palladio [Ware], bk. 4, chap. 7, 88). No further evidence is known for either these horse-head capitals or their original location.
126. Pliny, *Natural History* 36.24.102, refers to the true Templum Pacis of Vespasian (begun A.D. 71 and dedicated 75) abutting the Forum Transitorium, but does not name the Pantheon: "Even if we are not to include among our great achievements the Circus Maximus built by Julius Caesar, three furlongs in length and one in breadth, but with nearly three acres of buildings and seats for 250,000, should we not mention among our truly noble buildings the Basilica of Paulus, so remarkable for its columns from Phrygia, or the Forum of Augustus of Revered Memory or the Temple of Peace built by his Imperial Majesty the Emperor Vespasian, buildings the most beautiful the world has ever seen?"
127. For "the Ancients ... geometrical Figures," AS MS 313 reads "Geometrical Figures were used by the Ancients."
128. For recent scholarship on the Mausoleum of Halicarnassus, see K. Jeppesen et al., *The Maussolleion at Halikarnassos*, 3 vols. (Copenhagen: in commission at Gyldendalske Boghandel, Nordisk Forlag, 1981–91); Burkhardt Wesenberg, *Beiträge zur Rekonstruktion griechischer Architektur nach literarischen Quellen*, Mitteilungen des Deutschen Archäologischen Instituts, Athenische Abteilung, no. 9 (Berlin: Mann, 1983), 68ff.
129. Pliny, *Natural History*, 36.4.30–2: "The contemporaries and rivals of Scopas were Bryaxis, Timotheus and Leochares, whom we must discuss along with him because together with him they worked on the carvings of the Mausoleum. This is the tomb that was built by Artemisia for her husband Mausolus, the viceroy of Caria,

who died in the second year of the 107th Olympiad. These artists were chiefly responsible for making the structure one of the seven wonders of the world.... On the north and south sides it extends for 63 feet, but the length of the facades is less, the total length of the facades and sides being 440 feet. The building rises to a height of 25 cubits and is enclosed by 36 columns. The Greek word for the surrounding colonnade is 'pteron,' 'a wing.' The east side was carved by Scopas, the north by Bryaxis, the south by Timotheus and the west by Leochares; and before they completed their task, the queen died. However, they refused to abandon the work without finishing it, since they were already of the opinion that it would be a memorial to their own glory and that of their profession; and even to-day they are considered to rival each other in skill. With them was associated a fifth artist. For above the colonnade there is a pyramid as high again as the lower structure and tapering in 24 stages to the top of its peak. At the summit there is a four-horse chariot of marble, and this was made by Pythis. The addition of this chariot rounds off the whole work and brings it to a height of 140 feet."

The apparent contradictions in Pliny's measures of the building's sides and total circumference have been discussed by Kristian Jeppesen, *Paradeigmata: Three Mid-Fourth Century Main Works of Hellenic Architecture Reconsidered*, Jutland Archaeological Society Publications 4 (Aarus: Aarus University Press, 1958), 6–7.

130. Martial, *De Spectaculis* 1: "Mausolea poised on empty air" (trans. by Jeppesen, in *Paradeigmata*, 10).
131. "Aliter": "otherwise." RS MS 249 reads "Aliter 106°."
132. In fact, archaeological excavations have shown that the Mausoleum had 36 Ionic columns.
133. Pliny, *Natural History* 36.4.30–1: "pteron vocavere circumitum." ("The Greek word for the surrounding colonnade is 'pteron,' 'a wing' ").

The edition of Pliny by Jean Hardouin: *Caii Plinii Secundi Naturalis Historiae Libri XXXVII interpretatione et notis illustravit J. Harduinus*, 5 vols. (Paris: F. Muguet, 1685). I am using a later revised edition with Hardouin's notes, *Caii Plinii secundi Historiae Naturalis ex recensione I. Harduini et recentiorum adnotationibus*, 11 vols. (Augustae Taurinorum [Turin]: Iosephi Pomba, 1833).

134. The Latin "Alae" is the equivalent to the Greek "Ptera."
135. Vitruvius uses the term *pteroma*, meaning the colonnade that surrounds the temple (3.3.9): "Pteromatos enim ratio et columnarum circum aedem dispositio ideo est inventa, ut aspectus propter asperitatem intercolumniorum habeat auctoritatem, praeterea, si ex imbrium aquae vis occupaverit et intercluserit hominum multitudinem, ut habeat in aede circaque cellam cum laxamento liberam moram [For the columns round the temple were so devised that the view of them was impressive, because of the high relief given to the intercolumniations; moreover, if a number of people have been unexpectedly cut off by showers of rain, they have plenty of room to linger in the building space]." The word is also used in 4.4.1.
136. Hardouin's footnote to "Pteron vocavere" (36.4.18–19 [30–1 in modern editions]), in vol. 9 of his edition of Pliny's *Natural History*, states: "in re aedificatoria muri duo sunt in altitudinem consurgentes, alarum instar." This can be translated as "Pterai, in construction, are two walls rising together in height, like wings."
137. Wren's interpretation of *pteron* as an "Attick Order," that is, an attic story with columnar orders located between the colonnade of 36 columns and the stepped pyramid, appears to derive from Pliny's statement that above the pteron "there is

a pyramid as high again as the lower structure." Modern scholarship concurs, defining it as "the part of the monument below the pyramid," although it differs from Wren by equating the pteron with the colonnade of 36 columns and placing it on a tall substructure (Jeppesen, *Paradeigmata*, 7–8).
138. For "by this term, . . . now lost," AS MS 313 reads "in this Term, by *Greek* Authors of Architecture was lost."
139. Text ends here in AS MS 313.
140. See Vitruvius 3.3.1.
141. Pliny, *Natural History* 36.31: "tapering."
142. "Saile": "Amount of projection from a surface" (*OED*).

Tract V, "Discourse on Architecture"

1. Josephus, *Antiquities* 1.60–2: "He was the first to fix boundaries of land and to build a city, fortifying it with walls and constraining his clan to congregate in one place. This city he called Anocha after his eldest son Anoch."
2. Ibid. 69–71: "Moreover, to prevent their discoveries from being lost to mankind and perishing before they became known – Adam having predicted a destruction of the universe, at one time by a violent fire and at another by a mighty deluge of water – they erected two pillars, one of brick and the other of stone, and inscribed these discoveries on both; so that if the pillar of brick disappeared in the deluge, that of stone would remain to teach men what was graven thereon and to inform them that they had also erected one of brick. It exists to this day in the land of Seiris."
3. Genesis 6:14–16: "Make thee an ark of gopher wood; rooms shalt thou make in the ark, and shalt pitch it within and without with pitch. And this is the fashion which thou shalt make it of: the length of the ark shall be three hundred cubits, the breadth of it fifty cubits, and the height of it thirty cubits. A window shalt thou make to the ark, and in a cubit shalt thou finish it above; and the door of the ark shalt thou set in the side thereof; with lower, second and third stories shalt thou make it. . . . And take thou unto thee of all food that is eaten, and thou shalt gather it to thee; and it shall be for food for thee, and for them [the animals]."
4. "Trireme": "an ancient galley (originally Greek, afterwards also Roman) with three ranks of oars one above another, used chiefly as a ship of war" (*OED*).
5. Followed by "more" deleted.
6. Genesis 11:3–9: "And they said one to another, Go to, let us make brick, and burn them throughly. They had brick for stone, and slime had they for mortar. And they said, Go to, let us build us a city and a tower, whose top may reach unto heaven. . . . and the Lord came down to see the city and the tower, which the children of men builded."
7. Herodotus 1. 181 (Cambridge, MA: Harvard University Press, Loeb Classical Library, 1963), describes "the sacred enclosure of Zeus Belus": "In the centre of this enclosure a solid tower has been built, of one furlong's length and breadth; a second tower rises from this, and from it yet another, till at last there are eight. The way up to them mounts spirally outside all the towers; about halfway in the ascent is a halting place, with seats for repose, where those who ascend sit down and rest. In the last tower there is a great shrine; and in it a great and well-covered couch is laid, and a golden table set hard by."

8. Genesis 41:48: "And he gathered up all the food of the seven years, which were in the land of Egypt, and laid up the food in the cities...."
9. Amphion was the son of Zeus and Antiope who, by playing a lyre that charmed the stones into place, built a wall around Thebes. See Oskar Seyffert, *A Dictionary of Classical Antiquities* (London: George Allen, 1957).
10. See "Tract IV," 169 and n. 88.
11. See ibid. and n. 89.
12. See ibid. and n. 92.
13. See "Tract II," 159 and "Tract IV," 169.
14. The Court of the Gentiles; Josephus, *Antiquities* 15.413–15: "Now the columns (of the portico) stood in four rows, one opposite the other all along – the fourth row was attached to a wall built of stone, – and the thickness of each column was such that it would take three men with outstretched arms touching one another to envelop it; its height was twenty-seven feet, and there was a double moulding running round its base. The number of all the columns was a hundred and sixty-two, and their capitals were ornamented in the Corinthian style of carving, which caused amazement by the magnificence of its whole effect. Since there were four rows, they made three aisles among them, under the porticoes."
15. Mark 13:1: "And as he went out of the temple, one of his disciples saith unto him, Master, see what manner of stones and what buildings are here!"
16. 1 Kings 6:21–22. "So Solomon overlaid the house within with pure gold: and he made a partition by the chains of gold before the oracle; and he overlaid it with gold. And the whole house he overlaid with gold until he had finished all the house...."

2 Chronicles 3:5, 7: "And the greater house he cieled with fir tree, which he overlaid with fine gold, and set thereon palm trees and chains.... He overlaid also the house, the beams, the posts, and the walls thereof, and the doors thereof, with gold...."

Josephus, *Antiquities* 8.68–69: "And under the beams he laid a ceiling of the same material [cedar], which was all smoothly divided into panels and overlaid with gold. The walls he covered at intervals with cedar boards, which he embossed with gold, so that the whole temple gleamed and dazzled the eyes of those who entered by the radiance of the gold which met them on every side."
17. See 1 Kings 6:21 in previous note. Josephus, *Antiquities* 8.70: "He also overlaid the temple both inside and outside with cedar boards fastened together with thick chains, so as to serve as support and strength."
18. Altered from "What."
19. 1 Kings 5:1: "And the king commanded, and they brought great stones, costly stones, and hewed stones, to lay the foundation of the house."
20. "Spring-tree": "A bar or cross piece to which the ends of a horse's traces are attached" (*OED*).
21. In the margin are added the following numbers: 320, 160, 80, 40, 20, 10, to equal 630; with the addition of 10 to equal 640.
22. 1 Kings 5:15: "And Solomon had threescore and ten thousand that bare burdens, and fourscore thousand hewers in the mountains."

2 Chronicles 2:2: "And Solomon told out threescore and ten thousand men to bear burdens, and fourscore thousand to hew in the mountain, and three thousand and six hundred to oversee them."

23. Altered from illegible word.
24. Altered from "proceeded."
25. Herodotus 1.178–81: "It lies in a great plain, and is in shape a square, each side an hundred and twenty furlongs in length; thus four hundred and eight furlongs make the complete circuit of the city. Such is the size of the city of Babylon; and it was planned like no other city whereof we know. Round it runs first a fosse deep and wide and full of water, and then a wall of fifty royal cubits' thickness and two hundred cubits' height. The royal cubit is greater by three fingers' breadth than the common cubit. . . . As they dug the fosse, they made bricks of the earth which was carried out of the place they dug, and when they had moulded bricks enough they baked them in ovens; then using hot bitumen for cement and interposing layers of wattled reeds at every thirtieth course of bricks, they built first the border of the fosse, and then the wall itself in the same fashion. On the top, along the edges of the wall, they built houses of a single chamber, facing each other, with space enough between for the driving of a four-horse chariot. There are an hundred gates in the circle of the wall, all of bronze, with posts and lintels of the same. . . . These walls are the city's outer armour; within them there is another encircling wall, well-nigh as strong as the other, but narrower."
26. Followed by "metal" deleted.
27. Historically, Porsenna was an Etruscan king of the late sixth century B.C. His tomb in Clusium (Chiusi) is known only from Pliny's writings. For modern scholarship on the monument, see Boëthius, *Etruscan and Early Roman Architecture*, 99, 213, and Franz Messerschmidt, "Das Grabmal des Porsenna," in *Das neue Bild der Antike*, 2 vols. (Leipzig: Koehler and Amelang, 1942), 2:53–63.
28. Pliny, *Natural History* 36.91–3: "For it is appropriate to call 'Italian,' as well as 'Etruscan,' the labyrinth made by king Porsena of Etruria to serve as his tomb, with the result at the same time that even the vanity of foreign kings is surpassed by those of Italy. But since irresponsible story-telling here exceeds all bounds, I shall in describing the building make use of the very words of Marcus Varro himself: 'He is buried close to the city of Clusium, in a place where he has left a square monument built of squared blocks of stone, each side being 300 feet long and 50 feet high. Inside this square pedestal there is a tangled labyrinth, which no one must enter without a ball of thread if he is to find his way out. On this square pedestal stand five pyramids, four at the corners and one at the centre, each of them being 75 feet broad at the base and 150 feet high. They taper in such a manner that on top of the whole group there rests a single bronze disk together with a conical cupola, from which hang bells fastened with chains: when these are set in motion by the wind, their sound carries to a great distance, as was formerly the case at Dodona. On this disk stand four more pyramids, each 100 feet high, and above these, on a single platform, five more.' The height of these last pyramids was a detail that Varro was ashamed to add to his account; but the Etruscan stories relate that it was equal to that of the whole work up to their level, insane folly as it was to have courted fame by spending for the benefit of none and to have exhausted furthermore the resources of a kingdom; and the result, after all, was more honour for the designer than for the sponsor."

Pliny's source for the description of Porsenna's tomb, as he states, was Marcus Terentius Varro (116 B.C.–A.D. 27). A prolific Roman writer, only a fragment of his work survives. Pliny probably used his principal work of 41 books, *Antiquitates rerum humanarum et divinarum*, treating the political and religious life of the Romans from their early history to the present. Seyffert, *Dictionary*, 1957.

29. See previous note.
30. Followed by "measures" deleted.
31. Followed by "cont" deleted.
32. Pliny, *Natural History* 36.92: "Singula latera pedum trecenum": "each side being 300 feet long." Wren's emendation of Pliny's text corrects *tricenûm*, genitive plural of *triceni -ae, -a* "of thirty feet," to read *tricentinûm*, apparently a biform of the genitive plural of *trecenteni, -ae, -a*, "of 300 feet." My thanks go to James Girsch for this explanation.

CONCLUSION: WREN'S METHOD OF DESIGN

1. Francis Bacon, *De dignitate et augmentis scientiarum* (1623), in *The Works of Francis Bacon*, ed. James Spedding, R. L. Ellis, and D. D. Heath, 14 vols. (London: Longman, 1857–74), 4:296–7.
2. William Cunningham, *Cosmographical Glasse* (1559), 4–5, quoted by J. A. Bennett, *The Mathematical Science of Christopher Wren* (Cambridge: Cambridge University Press, 1982), 8. See J. A. Bennett, "Architecture and Mathematical Practice in England, 1550–1650," in *English Architecture Public and Private: Essays for Kerry Downes*, ed. John Bold and Edward Chaney (London: Hambledon, 1993), 23–9.
3. See Bennett, *Mathematical Science*.
4. Wren, "Report on Westminster Abbey," 84, "Tract II," 162.
5. Wren, "Letter . . . for Building . . . Churches," 116.
6. Wren, "Tract II," 163.
7. Wren, "Tract I," 154.
8. Wren, "Letter . . . for Building . . . Churches," 116.
9. Wren, "Tract IV," 176.
10. Roger North, *Of Building: Roger North's Writings on Architecture*, ed. Howard M. Colvin and John Newman (Oxford: Clarendon, 1981), 10.
11. Wren, "Tract II," 157.
12. This and the following discussion are based on Wren, "Tract I," 155–6.
13. Wren, "Report on Old St. Paul's before the Fire," 50.
14. Wren, "Report on Salisbury Cathedral," 62–3.
15. Wren, "Report on Old St. Paul's before the Fire," 53.
16. Wren, "Tract IV," 176.
17. This and the following discussion is based on Wren, "Tract I," 154–5.
18. Wren, "Report on Old St. Paul's before the Fire," 53–4.
19. Wren, "Letter . . . for Building . . . Churches," 113.
20. Wren, "Tract I," 156.
21. What Alberti called "lineaments," *DRA*, bk. 1, chap. 1, 7. See, for example, Eduard Sekler, *Wren and His Place in European Architecture* (New York: Macmillan, 1956), 131–6.
22. For plans and views of the City churches, see Kerry Downes, *The Architecture of Wren* (New York: Universe, 1982), 55–64, and Sekler, 71–108. See also Paul Jeffery, *The City Churches of Sir Christopher Wren* (London: Hambledon, 1996).
23. On Trinity College Library, see *WS*, 5:32–4, and Plates 15–26; Downes, *Architecture*,

72–6; and Howard Colvin, "The Building," in David McKitterick, ed., *The Making of the Wren Library, Trinity College, Cambridge* (Cambridge: Cambridge University Press, 1995), 28–49.
24. Colvin, "Building," 33–4, cites Palladio's drawing of an ancient Roman building in bk. 2, pl. 32.
25. *WS*, 5:33. The filling of the lunettes with a mezzanine level appears in the wings of Le Vau's College des Quatre-Nations, which Wren saw while in Paris. Sekler, 149.
26. Downes, *Architecture*, 99. The facades of the Fountain Court have ground-floor arcades with large pedimented windows above. The principal floor level was kept low in order to reduce the number of steps that King William, who suffered from asthma, would have to climb. The added depth of the recessed segments accommodates the lowered floor level and allows the window sills to be located at a normal height above the floor.
27. There are numerous examples of the divisions of the facade, suggesting an interior regularity or arrangement other than what actually exists, particularly among French townhouses, for example, François Mansart's Hôtel de la Vrillière, Paris, 1635–8. See Allan Braham and Peter Smith, *François Mansart*, 2 vols. (London: Zwemmer, 1973), 1:35–8. Also notable are English country houses like Robert Smythson's Wollaton Hall (1580–8) and Hardwick Hall (1590–7).

Beginning with Bramante's House of Raphael of c. 1510, it became common to insert a mezzanine level within the crowning entablature of a facade. This is the case at the Palazzo del Te in Mantua, begun 1525, and other houses by Giulio Romano, as well as in the works of Sansovino, including his Library of San Marco in Venice.

Another example of treating an arch illusionistically to accommodate the needs of the section is the third floor of the Palazzo Barbarini in Rome by Carlo Maderno, where the arched windows are given surrounds that create a false perspective that the windows are as large as those below. The surrounds were used in order to accommodate the depth of the vault within. See Rudolf Wittkower, *Art and Architecture in Italy 1600–1750* (Harmondsworth, Middlesex: Penguin, 1973), 114.
28. Wren, "Report on Old St. Paul's before the Fire," 48.
29. Wren, "Tract II," 163.
30. Ibid., 162.
31. Wren, "Report on Salisbury Cathedral," 67.
32. Wren, "Report on Westminster Abbey," 85. Also in Wren, "Tract II," 162: "The *Romans* never used Buttresses without, but rather within, though they cut off a part of the Arch, but not of the Vaulting that depended on the Arch."
33. Wren, "Tract IV," 173–6.
34. Wren, "Tract II," 162.
35. Wren, "Report on Salisbury Cathedral," 68. See also Wren, "Tract IV," 173: "in the *Gothick* Cathedrals, the Vault of the Ailes resting against the Middle of the Pillars of the Nave, bend them inward."
36. Wren, "Report on Salisbury Cathedral," 68. See also Wren, "Report on Westminster Abbey," 88: "This is the Reason why in all *Gothick* Fabricks of this Form, the Architects were wont to build Towers or Steeples in the Middle, not only for Ornament, but to confirm the middle Pillars against the Thrust of the several Rows of Arches, which force against them every Way."
37. Wren, "Tract I," 154, and "Report on Westminster Abbey," 85.

38. Kenneth Clark, *The Gothic Revival* (New York: Harper and Row, 1962), 21. Inigo Jones's Queen's Chapel, St. James's Palace (1623–7), has a barrel-vaulted ceiling of timber covered in plaster to resemble Palladio's reconstruction of the coffered masonry barrel vault of the Temple of Venus and Rome. John Summerson, *Inigo Jones* (Harmondsworth, Middlesex: Penguin, 1966), 64.
39. Wren's truss was greatly admired as a scientific achievement and displayed as a model at the Royal Society. According to Robert Mark, ed., *Architectural Technology up to the Scientific Revolution* (Cambridge, MA: MIT Press, 1993), 227, the truss is a tied arch where the upper members act in compression and the lower horizontal chord acts as a tension tie, reducing outward thrust to the exterior walls. Rowland Mainstone, *Developments in Structural Form* (Cambridge, MA: MIT Press, 1975), 153, believes that the heaviness of Wren's truss is due to conception of the horizontal tie member as a beam.
40. Wren, "Tract I," 153.
41. See, for example, John Evelyn, "An Account of Architects and Architecture" (1707), 10, in *A Parallel of the Antient Architecture with the Modern* (London, 1664).
42. See John Summerson, *Architecture in Britain* (New Haven, CT: Yale University Press, 1993), 142–72, and Clark, *Gothic Revival*, 19–23.
43. John Evelyn, *Fumifugium* (London, 1661), "To the Reader." (The reference is to Suetonius, *Augustus* 28.) Eileen Harris, *British Architectural Books and Writers 1556–1785* (Cambridge: Cambridge University Press, 1990), 196–7.
44. John Evelyn, *A Parallel of the Antient Architecture with the Modern* (London, 1664), dedication.
45. Thomas Sprat, *Observations on Monsieur de Sorbier's Voyage into England, written to Dr. Wren* (London, 1665), 283–95.
46. For a discussion of aspects of the scientific quarrel at the end of the seventeenth century, see Joseph M. Levine, *Dr. Woodward's Shield: History, Science, and Satire in Augustan England* (Berkeley: University of California Press, 1977). For a discussion of the literary quarrel, known as the Battle of the Books, see Joseph M. Levine, *The Battle of the Books: History and Literature in the Augustan Age* (Ithaca, NY: Cornell University Press, 1991).
47. This expression was frequently used by writers supporting scientific progress, including Francis Bacon. See Richard Foster Jones, *Ancients and Moderns: A Study of the Rise of the Scientific Movement in Seventeenth-Century England* (New York: Dover, 1982 [1961]), 37, 43–46, 238. Hans Baron, "The *Querelle* of the Ancients and the Moderns as a Problem for Renaissance Scholarship," *Journal of the History of Ideas* 20 (1959): 3–22.
48. Another popular simile used in the controversy of the ancients and the moderns. See Jones, *Ancients*, 27, 67, 280 n. 12; Richard Foster Jones, "The Background of *The Battle of the Books*," in *The Seventeenth Century* (Stanford, CA: Stanford University Press, 1951), 10–40.
49. Wren, "Report on Old St. Paul's before the Fire," 54.
50. Wren, "Tract I," 154.
51. Wren, "Report on Salisbury Cathedral," 63–4.
52. Wren, "Report on Old St. Paul's before the Fire," 50.
53. Wren, "Tract I," 153, 154, and "Tract II," 157.
54. Aubrey, *MB*, MS Top. Gen. c. 25, "Chronologia Architectonica," 1671, fols. 168–9.
55. Wren, "Tract V," 188.
56. Wren, "Report on Westminster Abbey," 92.

57. Wren, "Tract I," 154. See Howard M. Colvin, "The Church of St. Mary Aldermary and Its Rebuilding after the Great Fire of London," *Architectural History* 24 (1981): 24–31. This same problem was faced by Italian architects from the fifteenth century on who were completing medieval buildings. See Rudolf Wittkower, *Gothic vs. Classic: Architectural Projects in Seventeenth–Century Italy* (New York: Braziller, 1974).
58. Wren, "Report on Westminster Abbey," 90, 91.
59. For fifteenth- and sixteenth-century Italy, see Rudolf Wittkower, *Architectural Principles in the Age of Humanism* (New York: Norton, 1971).
60. See Kerry Downes, "Wren and Architectural Detail," in Kerry Downes and J. A. Bennett, *Sir Christopher Wren*, exh. cat., Whitechapel Art Gallery (London: Trefoil, 1982), 22–33.
61. Attempts have been made by Sekler, 131–7, and by Viktor Fürst, *The Architecture of Sir Christopher Wren* (London: Lund Humphries, 1956).
62. Sekler, 42–3; Downes, *Architecture*, 30–2. The model appears to have been the Temple at Tivoli in Sebastiano Serlio, *Tutte l'opere d'architettura* (Venice, 1619), bk. 3, 64, with triumphal arches on 99–112. Possibly also the amphiprostyle temple in Cesare Cesariano, *Di Lucio Vitruvio Pollione de architectura libri dece* (Como, 1521), bk. 3, liiv.
63. *PAR*, 335; Sekler, 39–42; Downes, *Architecture*, 32–7; Howard M. Colvin, *The Sheldonian Theatre and the Divinity School* (Oxford: Oxford University Press, 1981), no pagination; John Summerson, *The Sheldonian in Its Time* (Oxford: Oxford University Press, 1964), 6–8. The plan has been compared to the Roman theater depicted in Barbaro'a Vitruvius edition, *I dieci libri dell'architettura* (Venice, 1567), bk. 5, chap. 6, 154. The Theater of Marcellus is shown in plan in Serlio, bk. 3, 70r and in Etienne Du Perac's *I vestigi dell'antichità di Roma* (Rome, 1653), pl. 38.
64. *PAR*, 314; John Summerson, *Sir Christopher Wren* (Hamden, CT: Archon Books, 1953), 87; Downes, *Architecture*, 63.
65. Drawings of the design are AS 11. 24, 26, 28. Sekler, 119, and Downes, *Architecture*, 187. Wren's reconstruction and lantern design inspired Hawksmoor, who made four of his own reconstructions of the Mausoleum and designed the steeple of St. George Bloomsbury in 1716 after the same idea.
66. Wren also designed the funeral car or "chariot" to carry the body from Whitehall to the Abbey. The catafalque was made by the carpenter John Churchhill with carvings by Grinling Gibbons. Hawksmoor was paid £5 to copy Wren's designs. Public Record Office, Office of Works, 5/47, in *The History of the King's Works*, vol. 5, *1660–1782*, ed. H. M. Colvin (London: Her Majesty's Stationery Office, 1976), 455. The monument is listed among Wren's works in *PAR*, 327. Visual records of the catafalque include an undated print by J. Mynde among the Abbey Records, reprinted in *WS*, 5:13. A plan of the choir and a view are in an account of the funeral by Samuel Gruterus, *Funeralia Mariae II Britanniarum D. G. reginae Guilielmi III augustae conjugis, declamata, et decantata de Samuele Grutero* (Haarlem: Margaretae a Bancken, 1695), with fourteen etchings by Romain de Hooghe. Gruterus, called "Minister of Haarlem," was proposed as F.R.S. by R. Southwell on 4 December 1695. A copy of this book was given by him to Southwell, who presented it to the society (*JBO* 8). There is an image on the reverse of a medal of Mary reproduced in Rapin and Tindal, *History of England* (London: Knapton, 1744), vol. 3, "The Metallick History of the Reigns of King William III and Queen Mary, Queen Anne, and King George I" (1747), pl. 17, no. 10.
67. Wren, "Report on Westminster Abbey," 91.

68. Colvin, "St. Mary Aldermary," 29; Downes, *Architecture*, 90. Downes believes the tower was designed by Hawksmoor.
69. BL, King's Library, reprinted in *WS*, 10, pl. 3. An illustration of old St. Mary-le-Bow's steeple is in Sekler, pl. 10b. Other imperial crowns were used at St. Giles at Edinburgh (c. 1495) and King's College, Aberdeen (c. 1500). See Paul Johnson, *British Cathedrals* (New York: Morrow, 1980), 233, 244; Sekler, 76; Nicholas Pevsner, *Northumberland: The Buildings of England* (Harmondsworth, Middlesex: Penguin, 1957), 224–5; and Downes, *Architecture*, 90. Imperial crowns are also found at Cross Steeple, Glasgow, and formerly at Haddington and Linlithgow. Francis Bond, *Gothic Architecture in England* (London: Batsford, 1912), 625.
70. Christopher Wren–John Fell, 26 May 1681, *WS*, 5:17. See also W. Douglas Caroë, *Tom Tower* (Oxford: Clarendon, 1923).
71. John Summerson, "The Mind of Wren"(orig. publ. 1936), in *Heavenly Mansions* (New York: Norton, 1963), 74.
72. The story of St. Paul's has been best told by Kerry Downes in *The Architecture of Wren* (New York: Universe, 1982), 46–54, 64–72, 77–82, 111–17, and most recently in *Sir Christopher Wren: The Design of St. Paul's Cathedral* (London: Trefoil, 1987), 12–26, and "Wren and the Cathedral of London," in *Sir Christopher Wren and the Making of St. Paul's*, exh. cat., Royal Academy of Arts (London: Royal Academy of Arts, 1991), 6–24. Also of importance are Kerry Downes and J. A. Bennett, *Sir Christopher Wren*, exh. cat., Whitechapel Art Gallery (London: Trefoil, 1982); Vaughan Hart, *St. Paul's Cathedral: Sir Christopher Wren* (London: Phaidon, 1995); Jane Lang, *Rebuilding St. Paul's* (Oxford: Oxford University Press, 1956); Margaret Whinney, *Wren* (London: Thames and Hudson, 1971); and John Summerson, "The Penultimate Design for St. Paul's Cathedral" (orig. publ. 1961), in *The Unromantic Castle and Other Essays* (London: Thames and Hudson, 1990), 69–78. The most accurate measured drawings of the building as constructed are by Arthur Poley, *St. Paul's Cathedral London, Measured, Drawn, and Described* (London, 1927).
73. According to William Dugdale, *The History of St. Paul's Cathedral in London, from its Foundations until these Times* (London, 1716), "The Continuation of the History of Saint Paul's Cathedral," 148.
74. This and the following discussion are based on Wren, "Report on Old St. Paul's before the Fire," 48–53.
75. See Nikolaus Pevsner and Priscilla Metcalf, *The Cathedrals of England: Midland, Eastern, and Northern England* (Harmondsworth, Middlesex: Viking, 1985), 117–20.
76. Octagonal chapter houses are at Westminster Abbey and Salisbury Cathedral, where the diameter is almost 60 feet. There was one spanning about 30 feet without a central column at Old St. Paul's (see Fig. 6). See Nikolaus Pevsner and Priscilla Metcalf, *The Cathedrals of England: Southern England* (Harmondsworth, Middlesex: Viking, 1985), 20, and Wolfgang Braunfels, *Monasteries of Western Europe* (Princeton, NJ: Princeton University Press, 1972), 169–70.
77. Wren, "Report on Old St. Paul's before the Fire," 50, 53–4.
78. Wren, "Tract II," 163.
79. Wren, "Report on Old St. Paul's before the Fire," 55.
80. This and following discussion based on Downes, *Architecture*, 47–8, and Sekler, 111.
81. John Evelyn, *The Diary of John Evelyn*, ed. E. S. de Beer, 6 vols. (Oxford: Clarendon, 1955), 3:448–9 (27 August 1666); reprinted in WS, 13:19.
82. Wren, "Report on Old St. Paul's before the Fire," 54.

83. Wren's plan for London is AS. I, 7; Downes, *Architecture*, 50, and Downes and Bennett, *Sir Christopher Wren*, 63.
84. Downes, *Architecture*, 52–4. The auditory is recorded in the model at St. Paul's and a drawing (Worsley Collection, Hovingham, published in *Burlington Magazine* 97 [1955]: 40–4, and see Downes and Bennett, *Sir Christopher Wren*, 75). The vestibule is known only from Sir Roger Pratt's criticisms dated 12 July 1673 (reprinted in WS, 13:25–6).
85. *PAR*, 282.
86. Ibid.
87. For a general discussion of the designs for the new St. Peter's, see Ludwig H. Heydenreich and Wolfgang Lotz, *Architecture in Italy 1400 to 1600* (Harmondsworth, Middlesex: Penguin, 1974), 157–62, 164–6, 173–7, 198–200, 254–7. A new edition of the second half of this work has recently appeared: Wolfgang Lotz, *Architecture in Italy 1500–1600* (New Haven, CT: Yale University Press, 1995), 17–20, 23–5, 31–4, 54–6, 98–101.
88. Kerry Downes, "Sir Christopher Wren, Edward Woodroffe, J. H. Mansart, and Architectural History," *Architectural History* 37 (1994): 56. Braham and Smith, 1: 115–18; Sekler, 116.
89. See Summerson, "Mind of Wren," 76, and Downes, *Architecture*, 65–6, 68–72.
90. *PAR*, 282.
91. See Summerson, *Inigo Jones*, 98–106.
92. There are three drawings by Wren, AS II. 59, 61, 62, of a scheme copying Palladio's reconstructions of the facade and section of the Basilica of Maxentius and of the elevation and section of the dome of the Pantheon (reprinted in *WS*, 1: pl. 28).
93. Wren was critical of the dome of St. Peter's. In Tract II he wrote: "the Butment of the Cupola was not placed with Judgement: however, since it was hooped with Iron, it is safe at present, and, without an Earthquake, for Ages to come." At this point he evidently had not heard about the cracks discovered in 1631 in the dome of St. Peter's, but he may have learned of them later on, for in 1680 there were reports of the dome's worsening condition (see "Tract II," 162 and n. 50).
94. Wren, "Tract I," 154.
95. For the latest conclusions on the dating of the designs for St. Paul's, see Downes, "Wren, Woodroffe, Mansart," 38–40.
96. Downes, *Architecture*, 80.
97. Wren, "Tract I," 154.
98. Ibid.
99. See Harold Dorn and Robert Mark, "The Architecture of Christopher Wren," *Scientific American*, n.s. 245 (July 1981): 168.
100. See Downes, *Sir Christopher Wren*, nos. 88, 92, 95 (the Definitive Design), 97, 98, and 158 (the final design).
101. Hooke, *Diary 1672–80*, 5 June 1675.
102. Dorn and Mark, 171–2; Downes, *Architecture*, 115–17; Poley, 19–20.
103. According to *PAR*, 292, note (a). James Thornhill's false perspective painting depicting "The Life of St. Paul" was executed in 1715.
104. Wren, "Tract I," 154.
105. Wren, "Report on Old St. Paul's before the Fire," 54.
106. Wren, "Tract I," 153, 155.
107. Wren, "Tract V," 188.

Selected Bibliography

Bennett, J. A. "Christopher Wren: The Natural Causes of Beauty." *Architectural History* 15 (1972): 5–22.

———. "A Study of *Parentalia* with two unpublished letters of Sir Christopher Wren." *Annals of Science* 30, no. 2 (June 1973): 129–47.

———. *The Mathematical Science of Christopher Wren.* Cambridge: Cambridge University Press, 1982.

Blunt, Anthony. *Art and Architecture in France 1500–1700.* Harmondsworth, Middlesex: Penguin, 1981.

Clayton, John. *The dimensions, plans, elevations, and sections of the parochial churches of Sir Christopher Wren.* London, 1848–49.

Colvin, Howard M. "Fifty New Churches." *Architectural Review* 17, no. 639 (March 1950): 189–96.

———. Ed. *The History of the King's Works.* Vol. 5, *1660–1782.* London: Her Majesty's Stationery Office, 1976.

Curtis, Alexander D. "Sir Christopher Wren's City Churches: A Critical Reappraisal." Ph.D. diss., Princeton University, 1995.

Dorn, Harold, and Mark, Robert. "The Architecture of Christopher Wren," *Scientific American,* n.s. 245 (July 1981): 160–73.

Downes, Kerry. *Hawksmoor.* London: Zwemmer, 1959.

———. *The Architecture of Wren.* New York: Universe Books, 1982.

———. *Sir Christopher Wren: The Design of St. Paul's Cathedral.* London: Trefoil, 1987.

———. "Sir Christopher Wren, Edward Woodroffe, J. H. Mansart, and Architectural History." *Architectural History* 37 (1994): 37–67.

Downes, Kerry, and Bennett, J. A. *Sir Christopher Wren.* Exh. cat., Whitechapel Art Gallery. London: Trefoil Books, 1982.

Fürst, Viktor. *The Architecture of Sir Christopher Wren.* London: Lund Humphries, 1956.

Harris, Eileen. *British Architectural Books and Writers 1556–1785.* Cambridge: Cambridge University Press, 1990.

Hart, Vaughan. *St. Paul's Cathedral: Sir Christopher Wren.* London: Phaidon, 1995.

Hunter, Michael. "The Making of Christopher Wren." *London Journal* 16, no. 2 (1991): 101–16.

Jeffery, Paul. *The City Churches of Sir Christopher Wren.* London: Hambledon Press, 1996.

Lang, Jane. *The Rebuilding of St. Paul's after the Great Fire of London.* London: Oxford University Press, 1956.

Little, Bryan. *Sir Christopher Wren: A Historical Biography.* London: Robert Hale, 1975.

Pevsner, Nikolaus, and Priscilla Metcalf. *The Cathedrals of England: Midland, Eastern and Northern England.* Harmondsworth, Middlesex: Penguin, 1985.

———. *The Cathedrals of England: Southern England.* Harmondsworth, Middlesex: Penguin, 1985.

Poley, Arthur. *St. Paul's Cathedral London, Measured, Drawn and Described.* London, 1927.

Sekler, Eduard. *Wren and His Place in European Architecture.* New York: Macmillan, 1956.

Sir Christopher Wren and the Making of St. Paul's. Exh. cat. Royal Academy of Arts. London: Royal Academy of Arts, 1991.

Soo, Lydia M. "Reconstructing Antiquity: Wren and His Circle and the Study of Natural History, Antiquarianism, and Architecture at the Royal Society." Ph.D. diss., Princeton University, 1989.

Summerson, John. "The Mind of Wren." *Heavenly Mansions and Other Essays on Architecture*, 51–86. New York: Norton, 1963 (originally published 1936).

——— "Christopher Wren: Why Architecture?" *The Unromantic Castle and Other Essays*, 63–8. London: Thames and Hudson, 1990 (originally published 1960).

——— "The Penultimate Design for St. Paul's Cathedral." *The Unromantic Castle and Other Essays*, 69–78. London: Thames and Hudson, 1990 (originally published 1961).

——— *Architecture in Britain 1530–1830.* New Haven, CT: Yale University Press, 1993.

Weaver, Lawrence. "Notes on an Interleaved Heirloom Copy of Wren's *Parentalia*." *Proceedings of the Society of Antiquaries of London*, 2d ser., 22 (17 June 1909): 524–30.

Whinney, Margaret. "Sir Christopher Wren's Visit to Paris." *Gazette des Beaux-Arts*, 6th ser., 51 (April 1958): 229–42.

——— *Wren.* London: Thames and Hudson, 1971.

Wiebenson, Dora. *Architectural Theory and Practice from Alberti to Ledoux.* Architectural Publications, 1982.

Wren, Christopher, Jr. *Parentalia: or Memoirs of the Family of the Wrens.* London, 1750. Facsimile ed. Farnborough, Hants.: Gregg, 1965.

Wren Society. Ed. A. T. Bolton and H. D. Hendry. 20 vols. Oxford: for the Wren Society at Oxford University Press, 1924–43.

Index

People and Institutions

Académie Royale d'Architecture, 148
Académie Royale des Peinture et Sculpture, 98, 103
Académie Royale des Sciences, 95, 96, 152
Alberti, Leon Battista, 3, 4, 6, 37, 131, 132, 133–4, 135, 138, 142, 210, 213, 278n46
Alexander the Great, 167, 190
Alfred, King, 82
Amphion, 190
Anguier, François and Michel, 105
Archer, Thomas, 108, 110
Archimedes, 149, 161
Arnoldin, 105
Atterbury, Dean Francis, 36
Aubrey, John, 8, 12, 122, 123, 130, 215
    Chronologia Architectonica, 38
    Monumenta Britannica, 20, 21, 125
Augustine, St., 134
Augustus, 157, 179
Auzout, Adrien, 94, 95, 96–7

Bacon, Francis, 7, 133, 138, 139, 142
Bagford, John, 20–1
Baptist, 105
Barbaro, Daniele, 277n34
Beaubrun, 105
Belus, 189
Bennett, J. A., 9, 10, 136, 138
Berkeley, Lord, 93, 106
Bernini, Gianlorenzo, 94, 96, 98–9, 103, 105
Blondel, François, 148, 152, 291n48
Blum, Hans, 3
Bourdelot, Abbé, 94, 95, 103, 106
Bourdon, Sébastien, 105
Boyle, Robert, 277n39
Bramante, Donato, 162, 223, 278n46, 307n27
Briaxes, 184
Browne, Edward, 93, 99–101
Bruneau or Breunot, Bénigne, 98, 103
Brunelleschi, Filippo, 131
Bruno, 106
Butti, Francesco, 98

Cain, 188
Callimachus, 159

Camden, William, 32, 44, 82
Cedrenus, Georgius, 26
Champaigne, Philippe de, 105
Chantelou, Paul Fréart de, 98
Chardin, John, 6, 124, 277n36
Charles de l'Assomption, 96, 98
Charles II, 35, 120
    as emperor Augustus, 212–13
Charles, Abbé, 96, 98, 103
Charleton, Walter, 277n37
Cicero, Marcus Tullius, 182
Claudius, 178
Colbert, Jean-Baptiste, 96, 98, 99, 103, 148
Colvin, Howard M., 107
Commission for Building Fifty New City Churches, 107, 112
Commission for the Repairs of Old St. Paul's, 34, 43
Compagnie des Sciences et des Arts, 95, 96
Compton, Henry, 100
Comte de Pagan, 97
Constantine, 40
Conyers, John, 20
Coypel, Nöel, 105
Crusaders, 37

d'Orléans, Gaston, 97, 99, 103
Davenport, John, 60
de Bruyn, Cornelius, 6
de la Hire, Philippe, 151
de Tour, 105
della Bella, Stefano, 97
della Porta, Giacomo, 226
Delorme, Philibert, 149, 151, 278n46
Denham, John, 35, 212
Denham, Joseph, 93
Derand, François, 149, 151, 152, 291n48
Desargues, Girard, 149, 151
Descartes, René, 142
Deschales, Claude François Miliet, 149, 151
Desgodets, Antoine, 6, 124, 146
Dickinson, William, 108, 217
Dinocrates, 167
Diocletian, 40
Dodsworth, William, 61, 62
Downes, Kerry, 15, 107

Du Cerceau, Jacques Androuet, 6
Dugdale, William, 7, 44

Edgar, King, 81
Edward the Confessor, 82
Ethelbert, king of Kent, 40
Evelyn, John, 4, 6, 8, 35, 37, 94, 97, 108, 124, 212, 213, 222

Fischer von Erlach, Johann Bernhard, 132–3
Flitcroft, Henry, 14–15
Fontana, Carlo, 152, 292n50
Francerius, 23
Francesco di Giorgio, 149, 152, 200, 278n46
Fréart de Chambray, Roland, 6, 129, 288n27, 289n28, n29, n30
freemasons, 162

Gayfere, Thomas Sr. or Jr., 79
Gibbs, James, 110
Gibson, Edmund, 46
Gobert, Thomas, 105
Grelot, Guillaume-Joseph, 6, 277n35, n36, 294n61
Grew, Nehemiah, 19
Guarini, Guarino, 99, 141–4, 147–9, 151

Hardouin, Jean, 185
Harwood, John, 125
Hawksmoor, Nicholas, 16, 108, 110, 217
Hearne, Thomas, 20
Helena, Empress, 153
Henry III, 83
Henry VIII, 84, 87
Herod, King, 191, 192
Herodotus, 6, 119, 126, 189, 190, 193
Hiram, King, 169, 191
Hollar, Wenceslas, 34, 35, 36, 37, 217
Hontañón, Rodrigo Gil de, 152
Hooke, Robert, 6, 8, 20, 36, 96, 119, 121, 122, 123, 124, 125, 150, 151, 237
Huygens, Christiaan, 96
Huygens, Constantine, 123

314

Jermyn, Henry, earl of St. Albans, 93
Jones, Inigo, 5, 34, 42–3, 54, 130, 157, 206, 212, 214, 215, 220–1, 222, 225, 227
Joseph, 190
Joseph, of Arimathea, St., 39
Josephus, 6, 119, 123, 126, 129, 188–9, 191
Julius Caesar, 22
Justel, Henri, 94–5

Kircher, Athanasius, 123, 277n36

Le Brun, Charles, 105
Le Pautre, Antoine, 6, 105
Le Vau, Louis, 105
Leigh, Charles, 7
Leland, John, 20
Lemercier, Jacques, 99, 222
Leochares, 184
Leon, Jacob Jehudah, 123
Ligorio, Pirro, 157
Loggan, David, 16
Loir or Loyre, Nicolas, 105
Lomazzo, Giovanni Paolo, 3
Lorfelin, 105
Louis XIV, 148, 159
Lucan, 22
Lucius, King, 81

Mainstone, Rowland, 151
Mansart, François, 94, 98, 99, 105, 225, 307n27
Marshall, Edward, 35
Marshall, Josuah, 60
Martial, 184
Matthews, 106
Maundrell, Henry, 6
Mauritius, bishop of London, 40, 43
Mausolus, 184
May, Hugh, 35
Mazarin, Cardinal, 99
Mellitus, bishop of London, 40
Michelangelo, 223, 226
Mignard, 105
Montfaucon, Bernard, 23
Montmor Academy, 94, 95
Montmor, Henri Louis Habert de, 94
Moray, Robert, 93
Morison, Robert, 97
Mynde, J., 15

Neile, William, 136
Newton, Isaac, 150
Nieuhoff, John, 277n36
Noah, 189
North, Dudley, 125, 294n64
North, Roger, 119, 125, 199, 299n109

Oldenburg, Henry, 96
Ovid, 179

Palladio, Andrea, 3, 4, 6, 15, 181, 182, 183, 199, 206, 288n27, 289n29
Paul, St., 39
Perrault, Claude, 6, 97, 141–8, 149
Perrot, 105
Petit, Pierre, 95, 96
Phidias, 159
Phillimore, Lucy, 13, 16
Picard, 105
Piggott, Catherine, 13
Plato, 187
Pliny the Younger, 6, 119, 121, 126, 168, 169, 172, 184, 185, 187, 193, 194, 195
Plot, Robert, 7, 18–19, 20
Poleni, Giovanni, 292n50
Poussin, Nicolas, 105
Povey, Thomas, 298n100
Pratt, Roger, 35
Praxiteles, 159, 173, 184
Price, Francis, 34, 36
Pythagoras, 195
Pythis, 187

Quintinie, Jean de la, 106

Raphael, 105, 131
Ray, John, 281n78
Restitutus, bishop of London, 39
Richard, bishop of London, 42
Rider, Richard, 60
Robert, Nicolas, 97, 105
Romanelli, Giovanni Francesco, 99
Romano, Giulio, 307n27
Rooke, Laurence, 136
Royal Institute of British Architects, 8, 12, 13
Royal Society, 4–5, 7–8
  program for the history of nature and the mechanical arts (trades), 7–8, 95, 101, 125
  reports and publications, 125
  study of antiquities, 7, 19–21, 30, 121, 129
  study of architecture, 7, 119, 120–2, 125, 150
Ruvine, 105

Sammes, Aylett, 7, 130
Sampson, 168
Sancroft, Dean William, 35
Sandys, George, 6
Sangallo the Younger, Antonio da, 223
Sansovino, Jacopo, 206, 307n27
Saracens (Arabs), 37, 162, 215
Sarrazin, Jacques, 105
Scopas, 173, 184
Sebert, King of the East-Saxons, 81
Seneca, 158
Serlio, Sebastiano, 3, 4, 6, 123, 216, 288n27, 289n29, n30, 292n50
Seth, sons of, 188

Shute, John, 3
Smith, Thomas, 124–5
Smythson, Robert, 307n27
Society of Antiquaries, 21
Solomon, King, 169, 191, 192
Spon, Jacob, 6
Sprat, Thomas, 212–13
Stow, John, 20, 32, 44
Strype, John, 20
Stukeley, John, 125
Suidas (Souda), 26
Summerson, John, 220
Swift, Jonathan, 107

Tacitus, 22
Thévenot, Jean, 6
Thévenot, Melchisédec, 94, 95–6
Timotheus, 184
Titus, 192

Van Obstal or Opstal, Gerhard, 105
Vanbrugh, John, 108, 110
Vandergucht, Gerard, 15
Varro, Marcus Terentius, 121, 194, 195
Vasari, Giorgio, 131
Venutius Fortunatus, 39
Vespasian, 173, 178
Vignola, Giacomo Barozzi da, 3, 288n27, 289n29
Villalpando, Juan Bautista, 123, 129, 138, 159, 169, 191
Villequin, Etienne, 105
Vitruvius, 3, 4, 6, 97, 124, 126, 127, 128, 129, 137, 141, 142, 146, 156, 159, 167, 179, 185, 207, 212, 213
Vittori, Monsignor Carlo Roberti de', 98–9

Wallis, John, 149, 291n49
Ward, Seth, 36
Ware, Isaac, 15
Webb, John, 7, 35, 289–90n31
Wheler, George, 6
William I, 43
Wood, Anthony, 12
Woodward, John, 19, 21
Wotton, Henry, 3
Wren, Bishop Matthew, 8, 13
Wren, Christopher Jr., 1, 108
  as editor, 2, 8–14, 15, 16, 18, 34
  Parentalia, 1, 8, 10, 14
    "Heirloom" copy, 8, 12–13, 15–16
    Stephen Wren's copy, 13
Wren, Dean Christopher, 8, 13
Wren, Margaret, 13, 16
Wren, Sir Christopher, 4–7
  education in the humanities, 4, 213, 214
  education in science, 4–5

315

Index

Wren, Sir Christopher (*cont.*)
  family and upbringing, 4–5
  library and print collection, 3, 5–6, 105
  professor of astronomy, 5
  scientific work and interests, 5, 13, 97, 101, 105, 106, 110, 136, 137, 197, 281n78
  Surveyor General, 5, 120
  travel to Paris, 5, 35, 93–101, 103–6
    interaction with French artists, 98–9, 103, 105–6
    interaction with French scientists, 94–8
  Wren, Sir Christopher, study of architecture, 120–7
    buildings, 4, 5, 93, 120, 126
    Gothic, 34–8
    French, 99–102, 103–5
    local antiquities, 2, 4, 7, 18–21
    reconstructions of buildings, 119, 120, 121–3
    written sources, 3, 5–7, 18, 120
  Wren, Sir Christopher, writings on architecture, 1–2, 4, 8–14, 196, 210
    accuracy and authenticity, 8–14, 119
    dating, 119
    general content and background
    letter from Paris, 2, 4, 10, 93
    letter on building churches, 2, 4, 10, 107, 108, 110–11
    notes and reports on Gothic churches, 2, 4, 34, 37
    Old St. Paul's after the Fire, 2, 12, 36
    Old St. Paul's before the Fire, 2, 10, 35
    Salisbury Cathedral, 2, 12, 36
    Westminster Abbey, 2, 10, 11, 14, 36
    notes on antiquities of London, 2, 4, 12, 18, 19
    Tracts, 119–20
      I through IV, 10, 11–12, 13, 14
      V, 12–13, 14, 188
    illustrations, 12, 13, 14–17
Wren, Stephen, 8, 13, 16
Wyck, Thomas, 36

Young, John, 60

Buildings, Places, and Subjects

acoustics, 109, 115, 221
Alexandria, city of, 167
  Pompey's Pillar, 167
Anchiala, 168
antiquarianism, 7, 21, 123
arch
  pointed, 37, 38, 40, 44, 83, 163
  round, 37, 38, 40, 44, 81, 163
  see also structure
architect
  authority and taste of, 139, 146
  imagination (fancy, intuition, wit) of, 139, 141, 154, 155, 177
  judgment (mind, reason) of, 139, 140, 141, 147, 149, 154, 155, 177, 203
  knowledge and experience of, 112, 141, 147, 203
  role as designer, 140–1, 144, 148, 229
  see also viewer
architecture
  accordance with nature, 3, 126, 142, 220, 241
  as promoter of social and cultural values, 148, 153, 190, 211, 241
  as reflection of society, 37, 38, 140, 141, 197, 220, 239, 241
  for eternity, 104, 139, 140, 141, 153, 155, 197, 220, 239, 241
  standard of good taste in, 139, 146, 147, 188, 241
architecture, definition of, 1
  as mathematical science, 196
  as mechanical art, 7, 196
  Vitruvian, 133, 197
architecture, discontinuity in, 220, 230, 241
  between different views, 206
  between exterior and interior, 230–1
  between form and structure, 209, 231–5, 236, 238
architecture, principles of, 127, 133, 141, 149, 154, 158, 196, 197
  beauty, structure, function, 3, 133, 140, 197, 198, 210, 211, 220, 239
  conformity, 90, 91, 215–16
  invention, 92, 139, 140, 141, 146, 147, 148, 149, 155, 169, 191, 216, 217, 218, 220
  novelty, 138, 139, 140, 148, 155
  rules, 137, 143, 146, 149, 157, 198, 210
  unity between beauty and structure, 48, 207–8, 209
architecture, sources for, 124–6
  material, 4, 18, 19, 21
  studied at first hand, 18, 21, 38, 93
  visual, 101
  written, 4, 5, 18, 126, 127
architecture, sources for, types
  ancient texts, 121, 126
  antiquarian topography, 7
  biblical exegesis, 6, 123
  Royal Society reports and publications, 125
  travelers and travel books, 6, 125, 126, 173
  see also Bible; Renaissance, treatises: individual authors by name
architecture, study of, 3, 8, 120–7, 140, 196; *see also* individual buildings by place
  ancient Near Eastern, 6, 124, 125
  biblical, 6, 121, 122–3, 130
  Egyptian, 100, 122, 129, 130, 131, 190
  classical antiquities, 6, 7, 121, 122, 131, 141, 154
  Etruscan, 6
  Greek, 6, 121, 130
  Roman, 130
  contemporary, 6
  English Renaissance, 5
  French, 4, 5, 55, 93, 99–101, 106, 221, 222
  Gothic, 4, 7, 34–7, 68
  local antiquities, 4, 7, 18–21, 121
  classical, 18
  prehistoric stone circles, 7, 125, 130
  non-European, 121
  Byzantine, 124–5, 277n35
  Chinese, 7, 125
  in Near East, 7

Index

in New World, Africa, 7
Islamic, 7, 125, 163
primitive, 7, 125
Argo (ship), 56
Argos, Doric temple, 167
auditory, 53, 54, 108, 221, 223
design of, 109–10, 115
authority of the ancients, 7, 124, 141, 143, 147, 157
in architecture, 146, 213
in science, 213
Avebury, 125

Babylon, 122, 130, 193
Tower of Babel, 122, 123, 130, 189, 190
walls, 193
beauty, 62, 133–7, 154–6
and association, 145–6
as absolute, 133, 134, 135, 142
as divine, 135
basis in geometry and mathematics, 143, 154, 184
basis in nature and God, 126, 127, 133, 134, 135
basis in society and man, 127, 135
degrees of, 198
empirical and relativistic, 143
beauty as geometrical appearance, 133, 136–7, 148, 168, 184, 203, 204, 206, 207, 208, 231, 238, 241
beauty, causes of, 241
customary, 133, 137–9, 154, 215
natural or geometrical, 133–4, 135, 136, 137, 139, 154
beauty, definition of, 2, 8, 120, 133
empirical and relativistic, 4, 133, 142, 144, 147, 149, 154, 196, 220, 231, 241
Fischer von Erlach, 133
Guarini, 141–4, 147, 148–9
Perrault, 141–2, 144–8, 149
beauty, judgment by mind of, 134, 137, 145
influence of imagination, 137, 138
influence of personal inclination and custom, 139
beauty, kinds of, positive and arbitrary, 144–6
beauty, perception by visual sense of, 133, 134, 135, 136, 137, 143, 144, 154
beauty, principles of, 136, 145, 214, 219
geometry, 134, 135, 154, 155, 179, 199
position, 154
proportion, 134, 135, 154, 199
symmetry, 133, 134, 135, 145
uniformity, 135, 145, 154, 199, 201
variety, 154–5, 199, 202, 204
Bible, 6, 126, 127, 169, 191

Cambridge
Pembroke College Chapel, 94, 216
Trinity College Library, 204–6, 290–1n36
Chantilly, château, 100, 105
chapter houses, 221
Chilly, château, 105
churches, design of, 4, 107–11, 112–18, 135, 198, 199, 203–4
and burials, 112–13
and site, 112, 113, 118
and towers, 113–14, 202
cities, ancient, building of, 167–8
civilizations, ancient, 169, 191
biblical, 189
Egyptian, 190
Hebrew, 192
Clusium (Chiusi), Porsenna's Tomb, 121–2, 130, 193–5, 217
collections
Cabinet d'histoire naturelle, 98
Cabinet des Medailles du Roi, 97
private, 19, 20
in Paris, 97, 99, 103, 104, 105
Constantinople
Great Palace, 163
Hagia Sophia, 124, 132, 163
Milion, 26
Topkapi Palace (Seraglio or Grand Signior's Palace), 125, 163
construction and materials, 7, 55, 72–6, 85, 86, 103, 108, 114–5, 177
ancient, 190–1, 192
masonry, 149, 150, 151
Courances, château, 105

Dagon, Temple of, 122, 130, 168
design, 197–210
and form, 197, 198
and function, 197, 198, 199
and site, 198
and structure, 197, 198
guidelines for, 137, 220
articulation and ornamentation, 155, 156, 184, 202
composition, 155–6, 200–1
geometry and proportion, 116, 148, 152, 156, 181, 184, 187, 200, 201, 202–3
massing, 202
variety among parts, 202
use of historical style and precedent, 197, 210, 215–19, 220, 221–31, 241
and associated meanings, 222, 225
models
ancient, 216–17, 225, 226
medieval, 217–18, 231
design for geometrical appearance, 203–10, 241
and function and site, 203–6, 231
and structure, 207–10, 238

design method, 1, 196–7, 210, 220
design, compromises in, 141, 229–30
domes, design of, 152, 162, 163, 166, 222, 224–5, 235–8

Ecouen, château, 105
Ely, Cathedral, 221, 225
empiricism, empirical approach, 133, 142, 143, 147, 152, 220, 230, 231, 241
engineering, 196
England, Restoration
architecture in, 211–12
as successor to Rome of Augustus, 212–13
Enos, 122, 130, 188
Ephesus, Temple of Diana, 14, 121, 122, 130, 169–73, 184, 191

fashion (mode), 40, 82, 85, 104
in architecture, 79–80, 81, 104, 138–40, 141, 148, 153, 157
in clothing, 101, 144, 145
in French architecture, 101, 104
in music, 144, 145
in painting, 144
in speaking, 101, 104, 145
of different nations, 144, 145
Fontainebleau, château, 103
functions, 133, 154, 189, 196

geometry, 133–34, 195, 196
catenary curve, 150–1
conic sections, 152
geometrical forms, 154, 179, 181
practical application of, 197
projective, 143
use by ancient Romans of, 184
see also beauty; design; structure
Giza, pyramids, 100, 122, 130, 131, 190
Great Fire, 18
Greenwich
Royal Hospital, 101
St. Alphege, 107

Halicarnassus, Mausoleum of, 15, 16, 121, 122, 130, 184–7, 217
Hampton Court, Fountain Court, 206
history
freemasonic, 132
universal, 132
history of architecture, 2, 4, 8, 120, 123, 130–2, 140, 167–87, 188–95
history of nature and the mechanical arts (trades), 7, 19, 21, 95, 101, 105, 106, 124
history, ideas of
biological approach, 131
diffusion from single source, 130, 132

317

Index

history, ideas of (*cont.*)
  historical consciousness, 130, 131–2, 147, 210

Issy, château, 96, 100, 105

Jerusalem
  Holy Sepulchre, 153, 172, 286n2
  Sepulchre of Absalom, 122, 123, 130, 169, 191
  Temple of Solomon, 17, 122, 123, 128, 129, 130, 132, 135, 153, 159, 169, 191–2

Le Raincy, château, 100, 101, 105
Liancourt, château, 100, 105
liturgy, Anglican, 110, 111, 115, 221, 231
London, antiquities, 18–21, 22–33, 40–41
  found at St. Paul's, 26–8, 31–3, 40–1
    burying place, 27
    graves, 27, 31
    pins, 28
    pit, 32
    skulls, etc., 27, 81
    urns, etc., 28, 32
    vessel with Charon, 28
  found elsewhere in City, 22–6, 30, 40–41
    causeway, 23
    Dour-gate, 23
    forum, 26
    highway, 23
    London stone, 26
    Moorfields, 23, 26
    pavements, 23, 26
    Praetorian camp, 26, 40
    Praetorian way, 23, 40
    sepulchral monument, 26
    Spitalfields urn, 30
    Thames embankment, 32
    wells, 40
  geology and geography, 18, 31, 32, 33
  temple to Apollo at Westminster Abbey, 80–1
  temple to Diana at St. Paul's, 26, 32, 81
London, buildings
  catafalque for Queen Mary II, 217
  Chapel of Henry VII, Westminster Abbey, 38, 82, 86
  London Bridge, 32
  Monument to the Great Fire, 168
  Palatine Tower, 40, 41
  Royal College of Physicians, 206
  Westminster Hall, 173
  White Tower, Tower of London, 81
London, city
  of Charles II, 212, 215

Wren's plan for rebuilding, 100, 108
London, City churches, 92, 101, 107, 109, 110, 113, 198, 202, 203, 209
  Christ Church, Newgate Street, 203
  St. Alban's, Wood Street, 218
  St. Clement Danes, 203
  St. Dunstan's-in-the-East, 218
  St. James, Piccadilly, 110, 198, 203
  St. Lawrence Jewry, 23
  St. Mary Aldermary, 217
  St. Mary-le-Bow, 22–3, 216, 218
  St. Stephen Walbrook, 209
  towers, 109, 218
London, Fifty New Churches, 107–8, 110, 112, 116
London, Old St. Paul's, 5, 34–6, 38, 40–7, 48–55, 56–60, 81, 82, 201, 220, 222, 225, 227, 259n18
  Early Christian fabric, 34, 40
  existing conditions, 35, 36, 41, 43, 44, 49–51, 56–8
  proposed repairs, 35, 36, 42, 50, 54–5, 58–60
  Saxon fabric, 34, 40
  tower, 35, 43, 44–6, 50, 56, 58
  work by Jones, 42–3, 54, 57, 220, 222
London, St. Paul's, 163, 220–38
  Definitive Design, 229–30
  final design, 16, 230–35
    dome, 151, 198, 209–10, 235–8
    screen wall, 231, 234
    site preparation, excavations, foundations, construction, 32–3, 34, 118, 299n109
  First Model, 223
  first sketch, 223
  Greek Cross Design, 223–4
  Great Model, 122, 217, 223–5, 228–9, 230–1
  Penultimate Design, 295n66
  Pre-Fire Design, 35, 51, 53–4, 99, 101, 201, 202, 220, 221, 222–3, 225, 230, 235, 238, 295n66
  Warrant Design, 225–7, 228–9, 230–1, 236
London, Westminster Abbey, 36–7, 79–92
  existing conditions, 37, 83–4, 85, 88, 91, 173, 209
  history, 36, 79, 83
  proposed designs, 37, 87, 88, 90–1, 215–16, 217, 218
  repairs, 37, 85–7, 91

Maisons, château, 105
mathematical science, 188, 197
mechanical art, 169, 191
Meudon, château, 105
models of buildings, 123, 155, 172

nature, laws of, 126, 127, 128, 134, 135, 136, 139, 140, 142, 154, 213, 220
  see also architecture
Newcastle, St. Nicholas, 218
Noah's Ark, 122, 130, 189

optical adjustments, 137, 143, 144, 147, 148
optical illusions, 143, 144, 148
optics, 154, 155
  skill of ancients in, 176
orders
  coupled, 147
  Gallic, 101, 138, 140, 147, 148, 159
  Gothic, 142
  new, 147, 148
  Solomonic, 129, 138, 148, 159, 191
  Tyrian, 128, 130, 167, 169, 184, 191
  see also origin of orders; style
orders, Classical, 140, 143, 146, 147, 153–4, 214
  as structural metaphor, 207
  Composite or Italic, 157, 159
  continual use of, 158
  Corinthian, 157, 159, 169, 184, 191
  disagreement on forms and proportions of, 124, 142, 157, 168
  Doric, 128, 129, 130, 156, 157, 167, 169, 184, 191
  eternal validity of, 148
  inventive use of, 176, 178, 206–7, 231
  Ionic, 130, 157, 159, 169, 172
  ready made columns of ancients, 168
  rules for, 157, 159, 199–200
  Tuscan, 159, 169, 191
origin of architecture, 2, 4, 8, 123, 127–8, 156, 158–9
  forum, 128, 156, 158
  primitive dwelling, 127
  temple, 127, 158, 172
origin of orders, 2, 4, 120, 127–30, 139–40, 156–9, 167, 207
  and human body, 127, 128, 142, 156
  and imitation in stone, 128, 158–9, 167
  and timber roof, 128, 142, 156–7, 158, 159, 167
  and tree, 127–8, 142, 156, 158–9, 172
  development by ancient civilizations, 128, 129, 130, 132, 140, 154, 167, 169, 191, 215
  in God, 129, 132, 135, 147, 214
  in nature, 128, 129, 132, 135, 147, 214

318

Index

origin of orders, Corinthian capital, 128
origin of orders, intercolumniations, 158–9
origin of orders, proportions of columns, 159
Oxford
  Cathedral church of Christ, 82
  Magdalen College, 218
  Merton College Chapel, 218
  Sheldonian Theater, 7, 14, 94, 209, 216
  Tom Tower, Christ Church College, 218–19

Palmyra, 277n35
Paris
  Bourbon Chapel, St. Denis, 225
  Church of the Sorbonne, 99, 222
  Collège des Quatre-Nations, 99, 103
  Louvre, 101, 105, 147
  Observatoire, 97
  Oratoire, 99
  Palais Mazarin (Hôtel Chevry-Tubeuf), 98, 99, 104
  quays, 99–100
  Ste-Anne-la-Royale, 99
  Ste-Marie de la Visitation, 99
  Val-de-Grâce, 99
Paris, Louvre, 98, 99, 103
  Bernini's design, 105
  Cour Carrée, 138
  East Front, 141
  summer apartment of Anne of Austria, 99, 105
Persepolis, 124, 129
perspective, 50, 109, 137, 155, 156, 176, 182, 196, 231
  use by ancient Romans, 182
  see also viewer; views of building
proportion, 62
  in architecture, 142, 143, 145–6
  see also beauty; design
  in music, 134, 142

Quarrel of the Ancients and Moderns, 213–14

rationalism, 133, 147, 149
Renaissance
  architecture, 216
  attitude towards past, 123, 129, 131
  theory, 1, 3, 4, 8, 37, 119, 126, 128–9, 132, 133, 134, 141, 152, 159, 200
  treatises, 3, 6, 149, 157
Rome
  Arch of Titus, 157
  Baths of Dioclesian, 162
  Milliarium Aureum, 26
  New St. Peter's, 157, 163, 207, 223, 226
  Bramante's design, 162
  dome, 237, 292n50
  Old St. Peter's, 40, 129
  Pantheon, 157, 162, 168, 178, 184, 226
  Septizonium, 121
  Temple of Fortuna Virilis, 157
  Temple of Mars Ultor, 14, 15, 121, 130, 137, 179–84
  "Temple of Neptune," 182, 183
  "Temple of Peace" (Basilica of Maxentius and Constantine), 121, 130, 137, 162, 163, 173–8, 179, 184, 199, 201, 207–8, 216, 225
  Theater of Marcellus, 157, 216
  Trajan's Column, 156
  Via Appia, 23
Rome, city, 153, 215
  of Augustus, 212–13
Rueil, château, 105

Saint-Mandé, château, 105
Salisbury, Cathedral, 36, 38, 62–78, 201, 207, 214
  existing conditions, 36, 62–9, 72–8
  proposed repairs, 36, 69, 72–8
  tower, 36, 62, 68
science, seventeenth century, 1, 2, 7, 8, 21, 38, 124, 125–6, 133, 135, 138, 139, 141, 196, 213
  concept of idols or false appearances, 138, 139
  importance of mathematics and geometry, 135–6, 142
  importance of senses, 133, 136, 142
  instruments, 197
  relationship to architecture, 120, 123–6, 142, 147, 196
scientific academies, private, in Paris, 94–5, 103
sites of buildings, 108
  problem of encroachments, 86, 118
society
  custom in, 133, 140, 143, 146, 147, 211, 215, 223, 225, 241
  judgment of architecture, 223, 225, 228, 230
  taste of, 138, 188, 215, 223
  see also architecture; beauty
St-Germain-en-Laye, château, 103
St-Maur-le-Fossés, château, 105
stereotomy, 143, 149, 151
Stonehenge, 7, 125, 132
structure, 2, 7, 149–52, 159–67
  basis in geometry and mathematics, 55, 149
  concepts prior to Wren
  geometrical methods, 150, 152
  quadrature, 152
  in ancient Roman architecture, 85, 162, 166, 210, 214
  in Gothic architecture, 36, 68, 85, 88, 152, 162, 163, 166, 173, 208–9, 210, 214
structure, elements of
  buttresses, 152
  flying buttress, 37, 62, 68, 69, 76, 85, 152, 154, 176, 208–9, 234
  imperial crown, 218
  iron, 56, 67, 69, 73–4, 76, 77, 88, 162, 173, 207, 237, 292n50
  see also arch; vaults
structure, hidden, 209
structure, mathematical and statical principles of, 4, 84, 120, 150, 151–2, 154, 162
  abutment of arches, 84, 149–51, 159, 161–2, 173, 196
  abutment of vaults, 149, 150, 161–2, 166, 173, 196, 207, 208
  center of gravity, 149, 150, 161–2, 163, 166
  position, 149, 154
style, 210–16
  and associated meanings, 211–13, 214
  and impact of custom, 215–16
  as reflection of society, 211
  for Restoration England, 111, 210, 211–12, 215, 223, 228–9, 241
  national, 4, 102, 140, 148
  see also design; orders; origin of orders
style, Classical, 3, 50, 140, 141, 143, 146–7, 148, 210
  as eternal and universal, 140
  development over time, 215
  goodness and superiority of, 37, 68, 92, 141, 210, 212–14, 215, 228, 241
style, French Classical, 102, 138, 147–8, 155
style, Gothic (modern, German), 34, 40, 42, 44, 79–80, 82, 131, 144, 148, 188, 210, 293–4n54
  characteristics of, 37–8, 85, 141–2, 155
  defects and inferiority of, 37, 50, 138, 210, 214–15
  development over time, 37, 85, 215
  in France, 37, 85, 101
  periods of, 37–8
  Saracen origin of, 36, 37, 83, 293–4n54
style, pre-Gothic, 40, 81, 82

Tadmor, 167
Tangier, fortifications, 5
Tarsus, 168
technology, 196
temples, design of, 134
Thebes, walls of, 190
Tivoli, Temple of Vesta, 178
trireme, 189

Index

Tuscany, Temple of Ceres, 168
Two columns built by sons of Seth, 130, 188

vaults, 143, 151
  masonry, 207
  timber, 209
  see also structure
vaults, types of, 150, 162, 207
  barrel, 166–7
  cross vault (Gothic), 166
  cross vault (Roman), 162–3, 166
  dome, 162
  dome on pendentives, 150, 163, 166, 198, 207, 222
  fan, 163
  half-dome, 162
Vaux-le-Vicomte, château, 105

Venice, Library of San Marco, 206, 307n27
Verneuil-sur-Oise, château, 100, 101, 105
Versailles, château, 100, 104
viewer, 138
  eye or visual sense of, 63, 133, 134, 135, 136, 137, 142, 143, 144, 148, 154, 155, 156, 168, 179
  imagination of, 143
  judgment or mind of, 134, 135, 137–8, 144
  taste of, 90, 138, 143
  see also architect; perspective
viewer, influences on judgment of, 137, 138, 154, 157
  customs of society, 144, 145
  opinions of others, 145, 188

  personal prejudices, 143–4, 145, 188
views of building, 136, 137, 143, 155, 200, 203
  angle of, 155–6, 200–1
  distance of, 155, 202
  interior, 201
  related and unrelated, 154, 201–2, 206
  see also perspective
visual devices, 203, 204, 206

Winchester
  Cathedral, 81
  Chapel, Hospital of St. Cross, 82
  Palace, 101
    discovery of antiquities, 252n3
Wonders of the World, 140, 184